ADEN TO AFGHANISTAN

FIFTY YEARS OF THE ROYAL ANGLIAN REGIMENT

1964–2014

Steven Bowns

OSPREY
PUBLISHING

First published in Great Britain in 2014 by Osprey Publishing,
PO Box 883, Oxford, OX1 9PL, UK
PO Box 3985, New York, NY 10185-3985, USA

E-mail: info@ospreypublishing.com

Osprey Publishing is part of the Osprey Group.

A CIP catalogue record for this book is available from the British Library.

ISBN: 978 1 4728 0805 9

Editor: Ruth Sheppard
Design by Myriam Bell, UK
Index by Zoe Ross
Typeset in Din, Adobe Garamond Pro and Gill Sans
Originated by PDQ Digital Media Solutions, Suffolk
Printed in China through Worldprint Ltd

14 15 16 17 18 19 10 9 8 7 6 5 4 3 2 1

Osprey Publishing is supporting the Woodland Trust, the UK's leading woodland conservation charity, by funding the dedication of trees.

www.ospreypublishing.com

Front cover
Vikings boarding a Chinook helicopter on Operation *Herrick 16*.

Back cover
Top: 3rd Battalion soldiers patrol past graffiti on buildings in Aden.
Bottom: Poacher in riot gear, 1981. (Clive Farmer)

Title page
Colour Sergeant Morgan on the move. (*Castle*)

Page iv
The Regimental Memorial at Duxford.

Pages 1–2
Steelback Lance Corporal Edgar trying to blend in on Exercise Sobraon Flyer. (*Castle*)

The notes in the text appear as endnotes at the end of each chapter.

This book is dedicated to all those members of the Regiment who have given their lives in the service of their Queen and Country and whose names are inscribed on the Regimental Memorial.

Every September the Regiment gathers at the Memorial, which along with the Regimental Museum
is at the Imperial War Museums' site at Duxford, roughly in the centre of the regimental region.
This gathering is a physical manifestation of something intangible, the spirit of the Regiment which
lives in the wider regimental family.

FOREWORD

This book is a celebration of The Royal Anglian Regiment's Golden Jubilee. The Regiment's formation in 1964 was a direct result of the political decision to withdraw from 'East of Suez' and to abolish National Service, and the consequential reduction of the armed forces in general and the infantry in particular. Despite the numerous cuts and defence reviews that have taken place during the intervening 50 years, the Regiment has survived and thrived. This book tells the story of those 50 years.

During this period there were at times four regular and three volunteer battalions. To record all their activities would be a monumental task and would inevitably lead to a dry and uninteresting tome. Such a level of detail properly belongs in the archives of the Regimental Museum. The challenge was how to record the Regiment's exploits while at the same time producing an interesting and readable book. The answer has been to focus on the operations in which the Regiment has taken part while not forgetting the everyday aspects of regimental life. This focus on operations is thoroughly appropriate for a regiment which has professional excellence as its byword, is modest and self-effacing, is only impressed by military prowess and which has proved itself totally reliable on the battlefield.

The Colonel-in-Chief on a visit to 1st Battalion in Afghanistan in 2006.

The book starts with an explanation of what it means to be a Royal Anglian and the Regiment's place in today's society, and ends with an account of how it sees itself in the future. In between, following extensive research, Steven Bowns concentrates on eyewitness accounts of actions and deeds of bravery from Aden to Afghanistan. The selection of operations he describes covers the full range, from the intensive full-scale infantry battles of the early days in Afghanistan to the chess-like move and counter-move, almost shadow boxing type of operations in Northern Ireland. We also read of family life at home and abroad, garrison life in Berlin, Gibraltar and Cyprus, and what it was like in Cold War Germany. The result is a fascinating and readable book that will have a wider appeal than to just the regimental family.

Visits to the Regiment in different operational theatres have been a highlight of my time as Colonel-in-Chief. These have confirmed my view that The Royal Anglian Regiment is the very best of county regiments. It is entirely fitting that we focus on its achievements on the battlefield, and I thoroughly commend this book.

HRH The Duke of Gloucester, KG, GCVO
Colonel-in-Chief, The Royal Anglian Regiment

ACKNOWLEDGEMENTS

My particular thanks go to the three people who have contributed directly by writing sections of this book. They are Lieutenant General Phil Jones, CBE for the section *The Future of the Regiment*, Major General John Sutherell, CB, CBE, DL for the section *Heritage and Ethos*, and Major Peter Williamson, MBE for the appendices. Peter also has my enduring thanks for all his rigorous checking of many facts, back to the primary sources – sometimes with surprising results.

This book could not have been written without the unselfish telling of individual recollections and stories, the sharing of photographs and other assistance by very many serving and former serving members of the Regiment and the wider regimental family. There are so many in fact, more than 70 in total, that normal form would be to give only a collective mention. To me, however, that would seem ungrateful. I hope the following people, who deserve my special thanks for their contribution, will forgive my not using ranks and decorations here:

AFGHANISTAN

Bev Allen, Mick Aston, Dan Benstead, Dominic Biddick, Dave Broomfield, Simon Broomfield, Nick Charlwood, David Crosbie, Chris Davies, Nick Denning, Andrew Ferguson, Mark Garner, Graham Goodey, Tim Hearne, Ashley Hill, Gavin Hudson, Paul Kennedy, Robbie McCall, Daniel Monks, Greg Napier, Tim Newton, Stuart Smith, Alex Stearne, Matt Stringer, Sam Thomas, Dan Tomlinson, Joe Warren, George Waterfield, Adam Wolfe, and James Woodham.

NORTHERN IRELAND

Charles Barnes, Paul Boucher, Steve Brunt, Kim Clarke, Brian Davenport, Peter Dixon, John Fisk, Michael Goldschmidt, Dick Gould, Jonathan Hall-Tipping, Dick Harrold, Mick Henson, Roy Jackson, Les Lay, Allen Orton, Tony Powell, Andy Price, Wanda Saunders, Nigel Spinks, Kev Stollery, Trevor Veitch, Kerry Woodrow, and Alan Wylie.

IRAQ, BOSNIA, ADEN AND OTHERS

Simon Browne, Jenny and Stan Bullock, Andrew Dexter, Penny Dixon, Tony Downes, Robert Dyson, Jack Dye, Steven Gill, Brian Harrington-Spier, Jan and Bob Hawkins, Kevin Jordan, Richard Kemp, Rupert Lucas, Martin Miele, Des O'Driscoll, Simon Poulter, Andy Rainey, Eddie Thorne, Kate Woodrow and Patrick Woodrow.

My thanks go to Major General Patrick Stone, CB, CBE for providing encouragement and financial top-cover for the project, to Colonel Kerry Woodrow, who chaired the Regimental History Committee and provided such unflagging support and assistance, supported by Lieutenant Colonel Tony Slater, OBE and Captain Mark Adkin. My deep thanks also go out to the regimental secretaries who have responded so magnificently to my many strange and no doubt sometimes irritating requests for information and assistance: Lieutenant Colonel Kevin Hodgson, OBE in the early years of the project, then Lieutenant Colonel Robert

Goodin, OBE towards the end. Andy Murkin, curator of the Regimental Museum at Duxford, has been a constant source of support, help and assistance, responding swiftly and cheerfully to my repeated and sometimes vague requests – my very particular thanks go out to him.

Clive Farmer, our artist, has my deepest gratitude for producing such wonderful plates that, with their attention to detail and sheer charisma, hopefully bring the book to life in a way that photographs alone could not do. Thanks to Lieutenant Colonel Crispin Lockhart for his assistance with the MOD approvals process. My thanks go to Ruth Sheppard and Sarah Broadway at Osprey Publishing for editing my draft effort into shape and for managing the production process so fluently. I would also like to thank the very large number of people, too many to list, who provided help in small ways, with favours, information, contact details and the like.

All of these good people are in no way responsible for any errors or for the opinions expressed in my chapters, for which, of course, I take full responsibility.

Steven Bowns
Cambridgeshire
April 2014

CONTENTS

SECTION 1
THE REGIMENT

Recce Scimitar.

INTRODUCTION

D (Cambridgeshire) Company of the Vikings on parade in the grounds of Ely Cathedral after Operation *Herrick 11*.

Military history does not readily spring to mind as a form of celebration, often being seen as dry and frankly dull. In addition, covering the experiences and deployments of all the battalions of The Royal Anglian Regiment over five decades would have afforded only a very superficial narrative. Instead, this book explores the story of the Regiment thematically, focusing on the Regiment's operations. The latter are the purpose of the Regiment, so it is entirely fitting to place them centre stage. Other aspects of regimental life are covered in later chapters.

Balancing the coverage across all the different areas of the life of the Regiment is inevitably an impossible task. Operations and aspects of the Regiment's life have been chosen because they are representative or interesting, but the selection is inevitably a matter of opinion, and some will disagree with what has been included and excluded. To this, the only response is that the task of selection was a very difficult one. As a result of the focus on operations, the Territorial Army (TA) and Cadet units are under-represented, but they have been included when opportunities arose. Part of this balancing has also involved adopting a portfolio type of approach, focusing on different aspects of events in order to avoid simply repeating other previously published works.

Similarly, previously unpublished photographs have been preferred where possible, and although the attempt to match a description with a photograph of the right people on the right operation has been made, clearly this has not always been possible. Some photographs therefore are of the right people on different operations, or different people on the operation in question. Inevitably, many have been taken from the last 50 years of *Castle*, the journal of

The Royal Anglian Regiment. There are more photographs of recent events than earlier ones, an inescapable consequence of the greater availability of images in the digital age.

First-hand eyewitness accounts have been used wherever possible, preferred as they tell the better story and can be more accurate than some official accounts. However, they come of course with several limitations, so multiple eyewitnesses and confirmation from written sources have been used whenever available.

In order to make the book widely accessible to a non-military readership, it avoids using most of the rules of military staff duties; this in turn might slightly surprise some military readers. Abbreviations are kept to a necessary minimum and ranks are not abbreviated, unless in quotation. The rank and decorations of the person are given as at the time of the events being described. This might trip up some readers, but to do otherwise would risk potential confusion as we might have, at one time for example, a four-star general commanding a battalion. This in turn might have introduced some errors, especially in getting the decorations correct at the time of the events, for which we hope the individuals will be forgiving. Wherever they are known, first names have been used as it adds a more human touch, together with the occasional use of just some of the more enduring nicknames.

BATTALION ORGANISATION

A British infantry battalion usually consists of around 650 people. On operations this can grow to over 1,000 as other units are attached; the battalion is then usually called a 'battle group'. It is normal for an infantry battalion to be organised into three rifle companies of about 120 men, each comprising a headquarters element and three platoons of approximately 30 men. There is also a support company with heavier weapons and an administrative headquarters company. This officially sanctioned organisation is usually referred to as 'establishment'. Although this general organisation has persisted since before the Second World War, there have been many variations at different times and according to different roles. In addition, the establishment is often adapted for specific operations: such organisation for battle is known as 'Orbat'.

The rifle companies of The Royal Anglian Regiment have almost always been designated by letters A, B and C, while D Company is the support company. This is generally true of most of the British infantry. In addition, different companies have had nicknames for themselves at various times, but since 1996 all the companies of the Regiment have adopted county sub-titles, usually shown in brackets. So, for example, A Company of the 1st Battalion referred to itself as 'the big red A' from 1965, but is now called A (Norfolk) Company.

The rifle platoons in the 1st Battalion, the Vikings, and the old regular 3rd Battalion, the Pompadours, have always been numbered as 1, 2 and 3 in A Company; 5, 6 and 7 in B

Far left: Poachers training in Afghanistan.

Left: Vikings in Afghanistan: Lieutenant Napier, Corporal Gibbs and Corporal McIlroy.

Company; and 9, 10 and 11 in C Company. The 'missing' platoons – 4, 8 and 12 – are a historical relic dating back to before the Second World War when companies had four platoons each. Because they were then repeatedly reorganised with between three and four platoons per company, it was prudent not to use the 4, 8 and 12 numbers when there were three platoons per company, to save having to renumber most of the platoons every time there was a reorganisation. This became a useful tradition as the battalions continued to be reorganised in the post-war period. Confusingly, the 2nd Battalion also used 1, 2, 3 for A Company, but 4, 5, 6 for B Company and 7, 8, 9 for C Company. More recently some, but not all, platoons in the Regiment have occasionally adopted the names of particular battles, so 1 Platoon in the 1st Battalion called itself Alamanza Platoon in 2010. However, this practice is less persistent and lacks the official sanction given to company county titles.

Support Company has from time to time been called D Company or Fire Support Company depending on role, date, battalion and sometimes even on the commanding officer's preference. Between 1964 and 1968, the 3rd Battalion, the Pompadours, used C Company for Support Company so had D Company as a rifle company, with platoons numbered 13, 14 and 15.

Support Company comprises a headquarters element and a number of support weapon platoons, which have varied greatly, ranging from as few as two to as many as six platoons. They have usually included mortar and anti-tank platoons but also machine-gun, reconnaissance, sniper and assault pioneer platoons. More recently mixtures of weapons have been combined into fire support groups (FSG) of approximately 30–40 men, which are often deployed to rifle companies on operations. Each FSG might contain various combinations of anti-tank weapons, medium, heavy and grenade machine guns and vehicles. There are usually three such FSG, often designated A, B and C, but the mortar platoon was normally, but not always, kept separate. In counter-insurgency operations, particularly in Northern Ireland, Support or D Company has usually deployed organised

Battalion diagram.

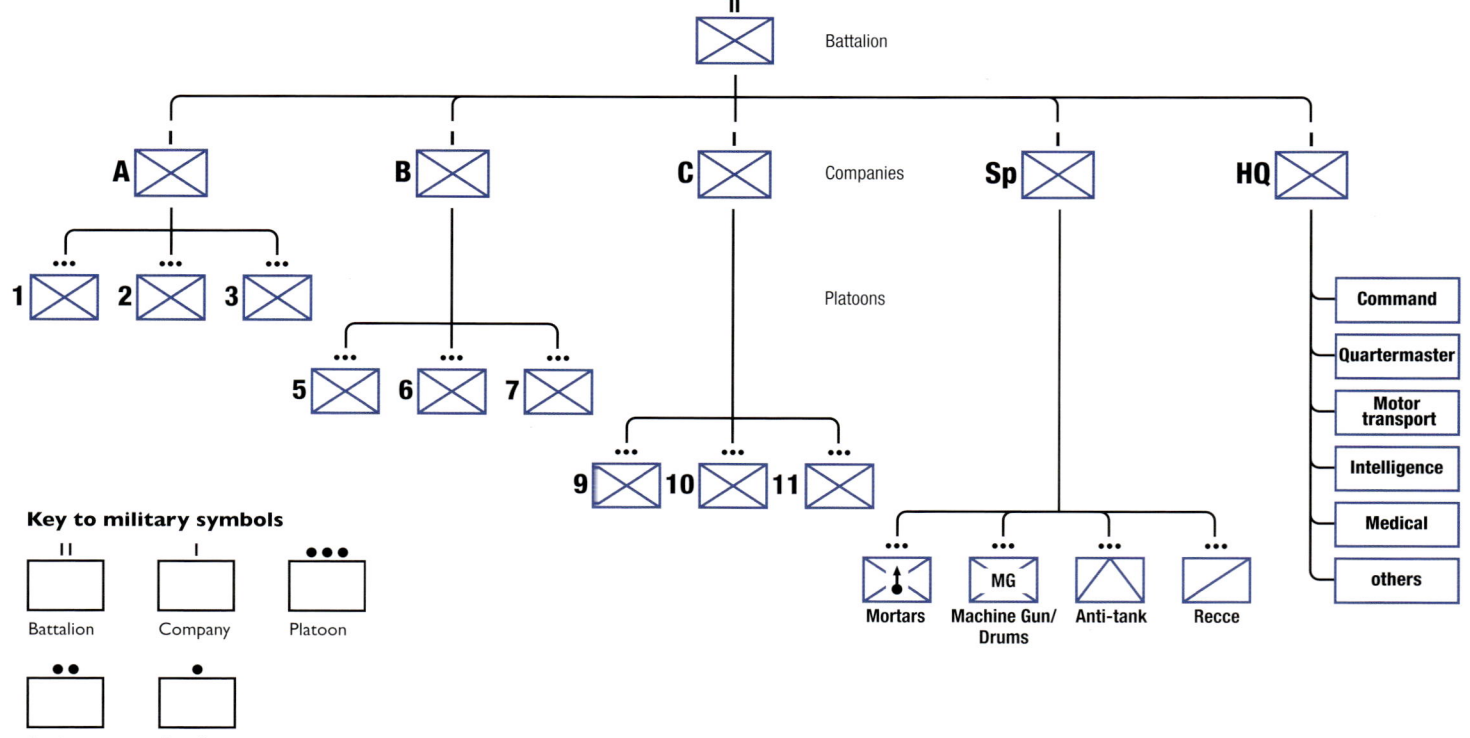

as a rifle company but with the platoons still called after their original role: mortar platoon, anti-tank platoon and so on. One further peculiarity is that sometimes the anti-tank platoons have taken the name of their main weapon – Wombat, Vigilant, Milan or Javelin Platoon for example. Finally, the drums platoon have often had a dual or even triple role within Support Company as they have often also formed a machine-gun platoon.

Headquarters (HQ) Company contains the remaining administrative and logistical elements that make up the battalion. It has also varied greatly, but usually contains battalion headquarters itself, with the commanding officer and other key personnel. In addition, it usually contains administration, intelligence, quartermaster, motor transport, medical,

BATTALION NICKNAMES

Most of the battalions of the Regiment have been known in common parlance by their nicknames for most of the 50 years, so they will be used extensively in the book.

VIKINGS – 1ST BATTALION

This nickname stems from late 1960 when the Commanding Officer of the 1st Battalion, The 1st East Anglian Regiment, Lieutenant Colonel A. F. Campbell, MC said it described the Nordic influence on the counties of Norfolk and Suffolk. The nickname stuck, was adopted by the 1st Battalion on formation, and is still widely used today.

POACHERS – 2ND BATTALION

Perhaps the most obvious of the Regiment's nicknames, this stems from the Regimental March, *The Lincolnshire Poacher*, of one of their predecessors, the Royal Lincolnshire Regiment.

POMPADOURS – 3RD BATTALION

In 1764 the 56th Regiment of Foot, later to become the 2nd Battalion of the Essex Regiment, received permission to change the colour of the facings of their uniforms to a shade of purple much favoured by Madame de Pompadour, mistress of the French King Louis XV, who had died early that year. The 56th very quickly became known as the Pompadours, and the nickname was handed down to the Essex Regiment, the 3rd East Anglian Regiment, and the 3rd Battalion of The Royal Anglian Regiment.

TIGERS – 4TH BATTALION AND 7TH (VOLUNTEER) BATTALION

In 1825 King George IV approved the 17th (Leicestershire) Regiment of Foot bearing on its Colours and appointments the figure of the 'Royal Tiger' in recognition of 19 years' exemplary service in India. The Leicesters were known as the Tigers from then on, retaining the nickname when they became the 4th Battalion of the Royal Anglian Regiment. Following that battalion's disbandment the 7th (Volunteer) Battalion, headquartered in Leicester, took up the nickname.

STEELBACKS – 5TH (VOLUNTEER) BATTALION AND 3RD BATTALION (TA)

This was the nickname of the 58th Regiment of Foot, later the 2nd Battalion of the Northamptonshire Regiment. It stems from Private Hovenden of the 58th being described as a 'Steelback' after a flogging in 1813. It was taken up by the 5th (Volunteer) Battalion, then later by the 3rd Battalion (TA).

BATTALION TOURS OF DUTY, 1964–2013

Year	1st Battalion		2nd Battalion	
1964	Aden		Felixstowe	
1965	Celle		Cyprus	
1966	Celle		Cyprus	Aden
1967	Celle		Felixstowe	
1968	Catterick		Felixstowe	
1969	Catterick		Colchester	Gibraltar
1970	Londonderry		Colchester	
1971	Londonderry		Münster	Belfast, Operation Banner
1972	Cyprus		Münster	Belfast, Operation Banner
1973	Cyprus		Münster	Londonderry, Operation Banner
1974	Tidworth	Armagh, Operation Banner	Münster	
1975	Tidworth		Münster	Belfast, Operation Banner
1976	Tidworth		Münster	Gibraltar
1977	Tidworth		Gillingham	Belfast, Operation Banner
1978	Tidworth		Gillingham	
1979	Celle	Belfast, Operation Banner	Berlin	
1980	Celle		Berlin	
1981	Celle	Fermanagh, Operation Banner	Londonderry	
1982	Cambridge		Londonderry	
1983	Cambridge	Belize	Londonderry	
1984	Cambridge		Colchester	Cyprus
1985	Londonderry		Colchester	
1986	Londonderry		Colchester	Fermanagh, Tyrone, Armagh, Operation Can... / South Armagh, Operation Banner
1987	Gibraltar		Celle	
1988	Gibraltar		Celle	
1989	Colchester	South Armagh, Operation Banner	Celle	Belfast, Operation Banner
1990	Colchester		Celle	
1991	Colchester	Fermanagh, Operation Banner	Celle	Kuwait, Operation Granby
1992	Colchester		Celle	
1993	Colchester		Celle	East Tyrone, Operation Banner
1994	Colchester	East Tyrone, Operation Banner	Celle	Bosnia, Operation Grapple 4
1995	Colchester	Croatia, Operation Grapple	Celle	
1996	Cambridge		Warminster	
1997	Cambridge	Belfast, Operation Banner	Warminster	
1998	Cambridge		Warminster	
1999	Londonderry		Cyprus	Falkland Islands
2000	Londonderry		Chepstow	Sierra Leone, Operation Basilica
2001	Londonderry		Chepstow	Belfast, Operation Faction
2002	Pirbright	Kabul, Operation Fingal	Chepstow	Belfast and Omagh, Operation Ban...
2003	Pirbright	East Tyrone, Operation Banner	Chepstow	Kabul, Operation Fingal 5
2004	Pirbright		Chepstow	
2005	Pirbright	Basra, Iraq, Operation Telic 6	Ballykelly	
2006	Pirbright		Tern Hill	Basra, Iraq, Operation Telic 8
2007	Pirbright	Helmand Province, Operation Herrick 6	Tern Hill	
2008	Pirbright		Celle	Basra, Iraq, Operation Telic 12
2009	Pirbright	Helmand Province, Operation Herrick 11	Celle	Falkland Islands
2010	Pirbright		Celle	
2011	Pirbright		Cyprus	
2012	Pirbright	Helmand Province, Operation Herrick 16	Cyprus	Falkland Islands
2013	Bulford		Cottesmore	Helmand Province, Operation Herric...
2014				

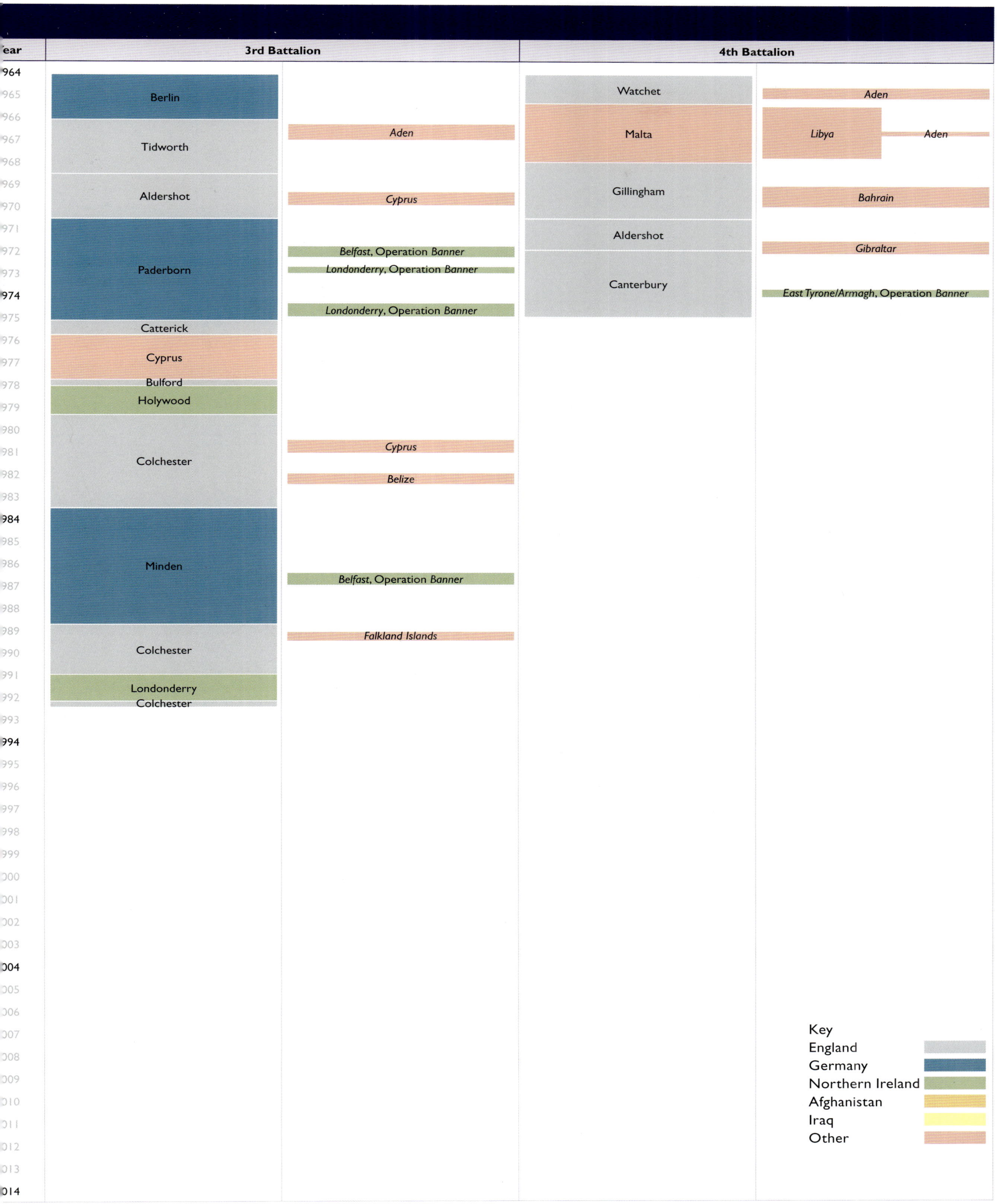

Year	3rd Battalion		4th Battalion	
1964				
1965	Berlin		Watchet	Aden
1966			Malta	
1967	Tidworth	Aden		Libya / Aden
1968				
1969	Aldershot		Gillingham	Bahrain
1970		Cyprus		
1971			Aldershot	
1972	Paderborn	Belfast, Operation Banner		Gibraltar
1973		Londonderry, Operation Banner	Canterbury	
1974				East Tyrone/Armagh, Operation Banner
1975	Catterick	Londonderry, Operation Banner		
1976	Cyprus			
1977				
1978	Bulford			
1979	Holywood			
1980	Colchester			
1981		Cyprus		
1982		Belize		
1983				
1984	Minden			
1985				
1986				
1987		Belfast, Operation Banner		
1988				
1989	Colchester	Falkland Islands		
1990				
1991	Londonderry			
1992	Colchester			
1993				
1994				
1995				
1996				
1997				
1998				
1999				
2000				
2001				
2002				
2003				
2004				
2005				
2006				
2007				
2008				
2009				
2010				
2011				
2012				
2013				
2014				

Key
England
Germany
Northern Ireland
Afghanistan
Iraq
Other

catering, paymaster, families, gymnasium, training and Regimental Police or provost elements, usually called departments rather than platoons. In addition, Headquarters Company might contain a Command and Information System platoon and the drums and reconnaissance platoons if they are not grouped in Support Company. Reconnaissance platoons in Northern Ireland were often grouped in HQ Company and re-named Close Observation Platoon (COP).

HERITAGE AND ETHOS

Almost 50 years from its formation on 1 September 1964, The Royal Anglian Regiment can be judged a success. Consistently, over five decades, it has delivered well-manned, fully trained and well-motivated Regular and Territorial battalions to the British Army's order of battle. It has provided commanders in a wide variety of theatres with reliable, professional and focused support. Its units have achieved operational success in a variety of environments and scenarios. It has become recognised as the local infantry regiment in the ten English counties from which it recruits, and has earned the support of the communities in those counties. However, when the Regiment was formed and in the early years, this success was by no means assured, and before reading about the highlights of those 50 years it is worth considering how and why the Regiment has become the success it is, and what it means to those who serve in its ranks and are part of its regimental family. Such reflection is also timely, since the fiftieth anniversary will coincide with the second five-yearly Defence and Security Review, which will again scrutinise the size, shape and organisation of the British armed forces and the British Infantry.

These 50 years have been characterised by periodic change and development in the British Army, and part of the reason for the Regiment's success is that it has been able to adapt to that change and evolve. Historically, British governments have struggled to sustain a volunteer army of a size and organisation sufficient to provide security to the homeland but also to meet overseas commitments at a cost acceptable to the taxpayer. Between 1870 and 1881, in an attempt to resolve this problem, two successive Secretaries of State for War, Edward Cardwell and Hugh Childers, completely re-structured the 'line' infantry, which

Men of the 5th Battalion, The Northamptonshire Regiment pick their way through the ruins of Argenta, Italy, 18 April 1945.

was at that time the bulk of the British Army. Among other changes their reforms created a system of regiments with two regular battalions, a depot, and volunteer reserve units, based in and specifically linked to UK counties. The seven forebear regiments of The Royal Anglian Regiment were all part of this system. Over the subsequent 140 years the 'Cardwell-Childers system' underpinned how the British Infantry was recruited and organised. It has, however, been changed and adapted extensively in response to circumstances.

The two world wars saw regiments recruit additional battalions, but halfway through each war, in the face of heavy casualties and with the introduction of conscription, individuals were sent where they were needed, irrespective of place of origin or regimental cap badge. In 1948 all 'line' infantry regiments lost their second battalions, but – in order to enable the transfer of manpower between regiments – they were grouped into brigade groups for organisational purposes, and a good deal of cross-posting between regiments took place to meet the needs of operations. This arrangement was seen as being increasingly unsatisfactory, and in 1956 a War Office Committee, chaired by the deputy Chief of the Imperial General Staff, Sir Richard Hull, suggested that the only way to maintain regimental *esprit de corps* while allowing flexible manning, was to create large regiments of three regular battalions with a regimental depot.

Troops of the 8th Battalion, The Lincolnshire Regiment, advancing along a country lane during anti-invasion exercises in Norfolk in 1941.

However, this proposal was overtaken by major political decisions to end conscription, cut spending on conventional defence and reduce the size of the Army. The 1957 Sandys White Paper on Defence reduced the number of infantry battalions by 17 to 60 and the Chief of the Imperial General Staff, Sir Gerald Templer, considered that the grief caused by

Private F. Slater (left) and Lance Corporal R. Hearn of the 1st Battalion, The Royal Norfolk Regiment, 3rd Division, aim their weapons in the ruins of Kervenheim, Germany, 3 March 1945.

these reductions and amalgamations would be exacerbated by moving to a large regiment structure. This decision, 76 years after the Cardwell-Childers reforms, had the effect of delaying the full implementation of a large regiment system for another 48 years. For those regiments that would eventually become The Royal Anglian Regiment, it meant an interim step, with the amalgamation of three pairs of regiments between 1958 and 1960 into 1st (Royal Norfolk and Suffolk), 2nd (Royal Lincolnshire and Northamptonshire) and 3rd (Bedfordshire & Hertfordshire and Essex) East Anglian regiments, with The Royal Leicestershire Regiment joining the East Anglian Brigade under its own name in May 1963.

In many ways the auguries were not promising. While the three regiments had the advantage of geographical proximity, there were many differences between them. In time some of these differences have contributed positively to the character of the Regiment today, but the time and effort it took to achieve this should not be underestimated.

For a start, while five of the amalgamating regiments made up the East Anglian Brigade, the sixth, The Royal Lincolnshire Regiment, was drawn in from the Midland Brigade, which also contained the Royal Warwicks, Royal Leicesters and the Sherwood Foresters. Then the histories of the component regiments were different; five regiments (Norfolks – 9th Foot; Lincolns – 10th Foot; Suffolks – 12th Foot; Bedfords – 16th Foot; and Leicesters – 17th Foot) were among those that had had two battalions prior to the Cardwell reforms and were historically 'senior' to those that were the product of amalgamations in 1881 (Northamptons – 48th/58th; Essex – 44th/56th). The memories of these previous amalgamations were still alive 77 years later when The 3rd East Anglian Regiment retained 16th/44th Foot in its title, while officers in the Poachers still toast 'the 48th' on Talavera Day.

There were also significant differences in where and how the soldiers for these regiments were recruited. Up until 1914 the typical infantry recruit was a young, unskilled, poorly educated urban labourer; on average across the infantry only 43% were born within their regimental districts. The Lincolns (32%), Northamptons (35.8%) and Leicesters (37.7%) were below this average, but the East Anglian Regiments were much more locally recruited, with the Suffolks (71.3%) being one of the three most 'local' in the line infantry, and the Norfolks (66.2%), Essex (50.3%), and Bedfords (48.8%) above the average, even though at least the first two had primarily rural populations.[1] Professor David French observes, 'Regiments would become reflections of their parent communities. But only a minority of regiments struck such deep roots in their local communities that they could recruit the majority of their men from their own districts.'[2] The contrast is striking in this respect between the 'East Anglian' and 'East Midland' regiments. One explanation of the difference may be the contrasting economic opportunities in these regions between 1880 and 1914, when agriculture was in depression. Young men in the East Midlands had the opportunity of finding work in nearby towns and cities, those in East Anglia less so since – with the exception of Essex on the fringes of London – there were no large industrial urban centres.[3]

The perceived social standing of the regiments also differed. This historical factor, which most directly affected officers and their recruitment, may also have influenced the profile

THE ROYAL ANGLIAN REGIMENT'S FAMILY TREE

Col. Henry Cornwall's Regiment 1685	ALMANZA 1707	9th Foot 1751		9th East Norfolk Regiment 1782		Norfolk Regiment 1881	The Royal Norfolk Regiment 1935
Henry Duke of Norfolk's Regiment 1685	12th Foot 1713	MINDEN 1759	GIBRALTAR 1779–83	12th East Suffolk Regiment 1782		The Suffolk Regiment 1881	*Cambridgeshire Regiment (TA) 1908*
Earl of Bath's Regiment 1685		10th Foot 1751		10th North Lincolnshire Regiment 1782	EGYPT 1801 SOBRAON 1846	The Lincolnshire Regiment 1881	
59th Foot 1741		48th Foot 1748		48th Northamptonshire Regiment 1782	TALAVERA 1809	The Northamptonshire Regiment 1881	
60th Foot 1755		58th Foot 1757	GIBRALTAR 1779–83	58th Rutlandshire Regiment 1782	EGYPT 1801		
Col. Archibald Douglas' Regiment 1688	BLENHEIM 1704 16th Foot 1713			16th Buckinghamshire Regiment 1782	16th Bedfordshire Regiment 1810	The Bedfordshire Regiment 1881	*The Hertfordshire Regiment (TA) 1908*
Col. James Long's Regiment 1741		55th Foot 1747 44th Foot 1751		44th East Essex Regiment 1782	EGYPT 1801 SALAMANCA 1812	The Essex Regiment 1881	
58th Foot 1755		56th Foot 1757	GIBRALTAR 1779–83	56th West Essex Regiment 1782			
Col. Solomon Richard's Regiment 1688	17th Foot 1713		PRINCETOWN 1777	17th Leicestershire Regiment 1782	INDIA 1804–23	The Leicestershire Regiment 1881	

and style of the new regiment. Comparative analysis of this factor across the British Army shows only one forebear regiment (Norfolks) in the top 34% of infantry regiments by perceived social standing (Guards, Rifles and line), none in the top 20% and only two others in the top 59% (Norfolks and Northamptons). The Suffolks, Lincolns, and Leicesters were in the bottom 27% and the Bedfords & Herts and Essex in the bottom 48%.[4] The Royal Anglian Regiment did not have a 'smart' pedigree.

On top of these factors, the operational experience of the forebear regiments, in both the Second World War and subsequently, was also very varied. For some there was shared experience, such as for the Norfolks, Suffolks and Lincolns in 3rd Division (but in different brigades), and the Leicesters, Essex, Northamptons, and Bedfords & Herts in other divisions from Normandy to VE Day. The eight territorial battalions from the Norfolks, Suffolks, Cambridgeshires, and Bedfords & Herts in 18th Division, and 1st Leicesters in 11th Indian Division were all involved in the disaster in Malaya in 1942 and the cruel years of imprisonment that followed. Other battalions served individually in the Middle East, Italy and Burma, with a variety of exposure and effect. The years subsequent to 1945 were even

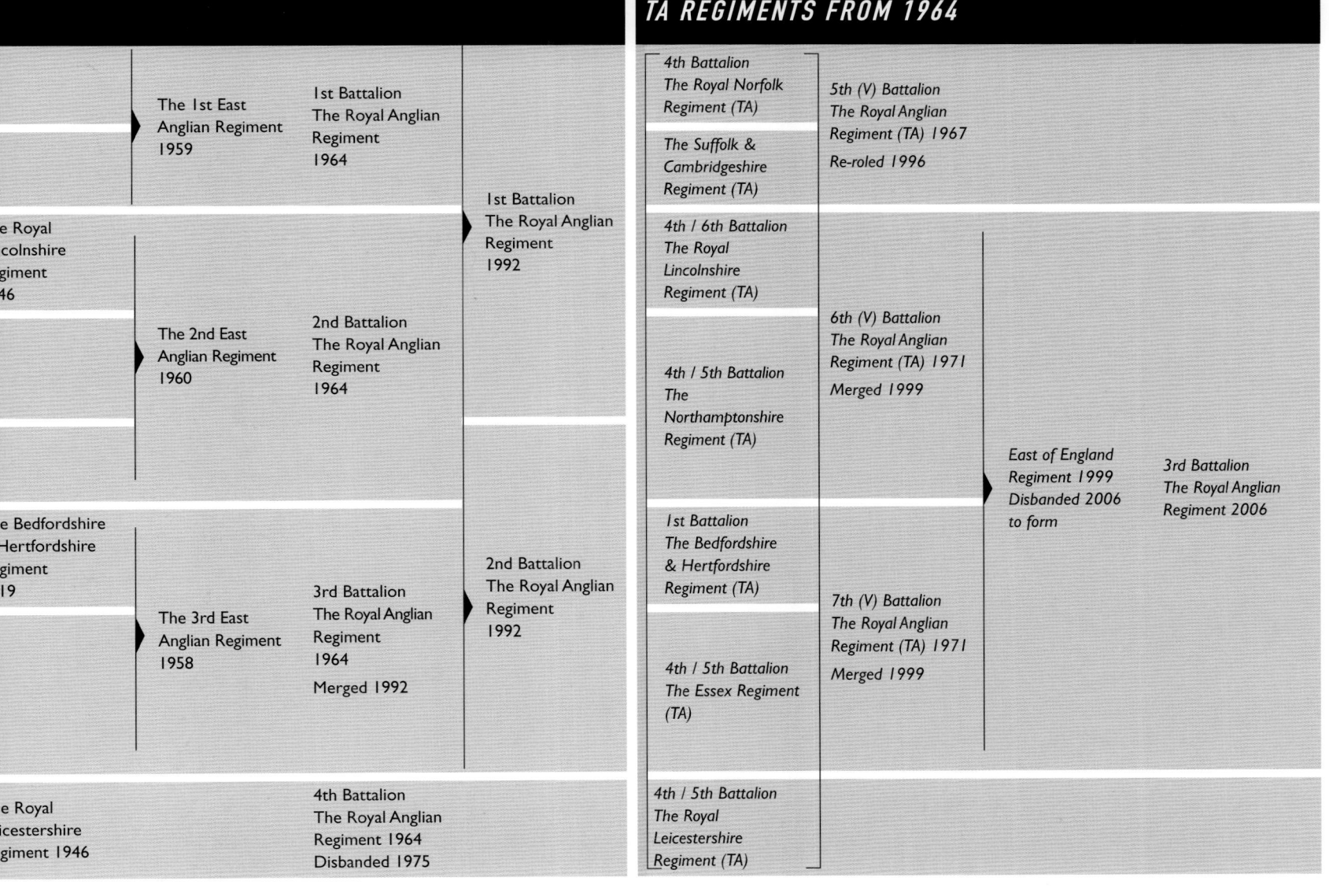

more varied. For instance, on amalgamation in 1959 the Suffolks – the most successful infantry battalion in the 12-year counter-insurgency campaign in the jungles of Malaya, not only in terms of Communist terrorists killed, but in the way they had conducted operations – joined the Royal Norfolks, whose post-war experience comprised the grim grind of positional defence in Korea and internal security in Cyprus. The Royal Lincolns, another successful jungle regiment, joined the Northamptons, whose post-war service had taken them to Austria, Germany, post-war Korea, Hong Kong and Aden.

Given this range of differences, it is scarcely surprising that there were tensions during and following the formation of the three East Anglian regiments in 1958, 1959 and 1960. Moreover, this key change had barely been accomplished when the report of the Army Committee, chaired by Lieutenant General Sir Roger Bower, triggered the further changes leading to the formation of The Royal Anglian Regiment, incorporating The Royal Leicestershire Regiment, with its strong pedigree from the 17th Foot, as the fourth regular battalion. When it formed in 1964, The Royal Anglian Regiment was the first 'large' line infantry regiment, preceding the evolution of the Green Jackets Brigade into The Royal Green Jackets by 18 months. *Crater to the Creggan*[5] explains the detail of the process that was followed and where the individual battalions served in the ten years following formation. However, Michael Barthorp also hints at some of the factors that not only made these developments a success but also have been a constant thread in the subsequent 40 years.

Firstly, the Regiment was blessed by a number of senior officers – until recently all 'inherited' from the forebear regiments – who were not only operationally experienced, understood the wider army, and knew what 'good' looked like when it came to building and leading infantry units, but were also both forward-looking and pragmatic. It was a bold decision to be the first 'large' regiment to form when there was considerable and sustained scepticism in other parts of the infantry. This strong leadership was generally matched at unit level by commanding officers who combined operational experience – in some cases from the Second World War and in others from Korea, Malaya, Cyprus, Kenya and Borneo – with the broader understanding derived from formal staff training and appointments. Several of these commanding officers were inspirational trainers of their officers and their units, and made a major investment in the future with an effect well beyond their tenure in command.

Secondly, there has generally been a closer working relationship between the different ranks than is found in some units. This aspect has developed over time, but has been a theme

Lieutenant General Sir Richard E. Goodwin, KCB, CBE, DSO lunching with Regimental Sergeant Major Martin Franks of the 2nd Battalion in 1966.

throughout. This may have something to do with the Regiment's outlook, something to do with the nature of the communities from which the Regiment recruits, and something to do with the practical effect of shared operational experience. There is a certain steady, understated quality about many of the Regiment's soldiers. There have been relatively few disciplinary issues in Royal Anglian battalions. There is a reasonably relaxed, informal but effective relationship between officers and soldiers, who have been prepared and had the confidence to bring issues to the attention of those in command. One reflection of this is that those commissioned from within the Regiment have transitioned naturally to become full and respected members of the Officers' Mess and have generally felt welcomed and accepted. This absence of barriers has enabled these 'Late Entry' officers (who, with a high proportion of the Regiment's Warrant Officers, have generally been intensely professional and forward-looking) to make a crucial contribution in capturing and passing on experience, setting the 'tone', and conditioning attitudes among junior officers, NCOs and soldiers. Their role has been as important, if not in some ways more important, as that of more senior officers in shaping the way the Regiment has developed, but there has usually been a judicious balance. The Regiment has not suffered from an excess of 'sergeant power' – a term coined by John Keegan to describe the situation in some regiments which were dominated by the sergeants and warrant officers, rather than the commissioned officers.

Private Tony Powell in 1966, driving his FV432, with Sergeant Brian Biggs and Lance Corporal Brian Hornigold.

Thirdly, while enjoying the sporting and social aspects of soldiering, the primary focus for the Regiment was and remains professional competence and operational effectiveness. The Regiment takes soldiering seriously. Perhaps because of the heritage, the Regiment is unpretentious, understated and quietly 'gets on with it'. Arrogance, and knowing better than everyone else, while not unknown, has not been a common characteristic among Royal Anglian officers or senior ranks. In approaching tasks members of the Regiment tend to be keen to learn from others, and from their own mistakes, as well as developing their own ideas. But there is also the confidence – after having thought problems through – to take a firm, independent line and accept appropriate risks. This tendency to focus on the professional and the operational has been progressively honed by the deployments covered in this book, as well as the developing professionalism of the British Army as a whole.

An interesting 'way point' on the Regiment's journey from formation to the present day was the publication of *Soldier, Soldier* in 1985.[6] This book consists of a series of edited interviews with officers, soldiers and their families from all three regular battalions of the Regiment. The interviews were recorded between 1982 and 1984, variously in Germany, Belize, Cyprus, Northern Ireland and England by Tony Parker, a professional author and lifelong pacifist. It is an unvarnished record, arguably edited to emphasise the more dramatic 'sound bites' and attitudes, and does not make for entirely comfortable reading. Twenty years from the Regiment's formation it reflects a range of attitudes, some naïve, some unenlightened to today's soldier, others thoughtful and forward-looking. It is a reminder that the 'learning curve' of the Regiment's development has not been smooth and continuous and there have been 'sticky' periods in all battalions as well as periods of excellence. However, it is notable for the courage and self-confidence required in the senior echelons of the Regiment at the time to engage in the project and for the openness of those interviewed. There was a resonance 23 years later in Lieutenant Colonel Stuart Carver's decision to give access to a film team on the 1st Battalion's 2007 Helmand tour (see photo overleaf).

Lieutenant Colonel Tony Powell, MBE, some 40 years later laying a wreath at the Menin Gate in 2006.

The book is also interesting in that there appears no obvious contrast between those serving with the three battalions, except in relation to location. There are many varied attitudes represented, but it is difficult to distinguish between units. In the early years of the Regiment, each battalion perceived itself to be distinct; there was no great feeling of regimental identity and a degree of suspicion of other battalions existed within the Regiment. Cross-posting was limited, tended to be restricted to officers at the rank of major and senior warrant officers and was not particularly popular prior to the event among those invited to move. There were, and

Ross Kemp recording with the 1st Battalion, in Helmand province, Afghanistan in 2007.

remain, strong battalion loyalties. The common jibe among officers of the other regiments in the Queen's Division was that The Royal Anglian Regiment was less a regiment than 'a loose confederation of warring tribes'. And yet handovers between battalions of the Regiment, which happened in Northern Ireland and also in Belize, worked well, and cross-postings when they did happen tended to be successful. It is possible that the differences were more in the perception of insiders than in the reality or in the views of outsiders.

This was reflected in the implementation of what was arguably the most fundamental event in the development of the Regiment. In 1992, following the 'Options for Change' Defence Review at the end of the Cold War, the Regiment was required to reduce from three regular battalions to two. The way this was conducted, by merging all three battalions into two, rather than simply disbanding the 3rd Battalion, showed considerable wisdom and foresight. Hard though it was for the Pompadours, whose operational tour of duty in Londonderry was cut short, the method retained the loyalty of the members of that battalion, many of whom went on to key appointments in the two new battalions and have made a formidable contribution to the development of the Regiment. In the years since that merger, eight of the 17 commanding officers of the two regular battalions and 22% (six out of 27) of regimental sergeant majors started their service in the Pompadours. In addition, nine out of 19 of the TA regimental sergeant majors originated in the Pompadours. Initially, battalion nicknames and certain embellishments on uniform in the two new battalions were dropped as being potentially divisive, but, significantly, were restored after two years on the initiative of Pompadours in the Warrant Officers' and Sergeants' messes.

The reduction to two regular battalions had other long-term effects. Once the merger was completed and manning adjusted, there was a much greater focus given to recruiting to keep the units up to strength. Demographics were in the Regiment's favour: recruiting for two regular battalions from ten counties with a population that is half as big again as that of Scotland, which still attempts to man five 'line' battalions as well as the Scots Guards. However, this large population to draw on would not in itself have kept battalions up to strength. Commanding officers took the issue of recruiting much more personally than before the merger, generally choosing quality individuals for recruiting appointments and then monitoring and rewarding performance. Recruiting for two rather than three regular battalions from the same demographic area meant that it was possible, with focused effort and a high priority, and notwithstanding the vagaries of army recruiting policy, to achieve full manning in both battalions, with all that meant for operational effectiveness and quality of life for those serving in the units. It also made it possible for the Regiment to be more selective in those officers and soldiers it recruited, retained and promoted. These were important factors in the Regiment's development as it became progressively engaged in a different and, in many ways, more demanding operational environment.

The priority given to recruiting also led to a renewed focus on the counties from which the Regiment recruited. The idea of designating battalion companies to counties originated in 1996 under Lieutenant Colonel Dick Harrold, then commanding 1st Battalion in Oakington. It had a powerful effect that extended beyond recruiting, giving a responsibility within the battalion to nurture the county link, and giving those living in the county and veterans from forebear regiments a clear focus for their commitment. Up to that point,

Vikings from D (Cambridgeshire) Company, Cambridgeshire Regiment veterans and members of Cambridgeshire Army Cadet Force share a ceremony of remembrance on a battlefield tour of the Schwaben Redoubt.

although The Royal Anglian Regiment had claimed to be a county regiment and conducted periodic events in the area, the links with the counties had attenuated compared to the intimate association enjoyed by the forebear regiments. Unless personally involved with The Royal Anglian Regiment, most people in the ten counties, including the civic hierarchy, tended to think of the forebear regiment as 'their' county regiment, while veterans, understandably focused on their experiences, were reluctant to identify with the 'new' regiment. Progressively over the subsequent decade – and extended to the 2nd Battalion – 'county companies' gradually helped to rebuild the links to the counties and with the gradually evolving regimental associations within those counties. The benefits have become fully apparent in the last ten years.

A vital role in the relationship between the Regiment and its counties has been and continues to be played by the Regiment's reserve army volunteer component. Traditionally the TA provided the regimental presence and representation when, as has usually been the case, the regular battalions have been based outside the regimental area. The TA has, in many ways, endured more change than the regular component, from a maximum strength of three battalions, with important Cold War roles, to a low point of four companies within the conglomerate 'East of England' Regiment from 1999 to the re-establishment of the 3rd Battalion of The Royal Anglian Regiment in 2006. The relationship between the regular and volunteer reserve components has also developed considerably over time, with individual TA officers and soldiers joining regular battalions for operational tours from the 1970s through to the deployment of 3 Royal Anglian on Operation *Tosca* in Cyprus in 2010–11. An important element that underpins both regular and reserve battalions is the Army and

The Steelbacks on their UN medal parade at the end of Operation *Tosca* in 2011.

Support from the Old
Comrades and people in
Luton.

Combined Cadet Forces in the ten counties. Many cadets wear the Regiment's cap badge and more than a few benefit from instructors who have served with the Regiment. They are an important link to the Regiment's county base as well as a source of committed recruits.

As the Regiment moved into the 21st century and its fifth decade, evolution accelerated. Northern Ireland had played a very significant part in the way the Regiment had developed, with all battalions benefitting from the operational imperative and edge provided by successive and frequent roulement and residential tours. However, while that experience varied over time and by area within the Province, it was, essentially, operationally one-dimensional. With the exception of individuals, the Regiment played no part in the Falklands War or the Gulf War of 1990–91, although the Poachers spent time in a garrison role in Kuwait. However, operational exposure was broadened by deployments into the very different environments of Bosnia in 1994 and 1995, Sierra Leone in 2000 and Kabul in 2002.

Technology also had an impact; in 2004–5 the 1st Battalion was selected as the infantry trials unit for the Bowman communications and management information system and was widely recognised to have fulfilled this demanding, unpopular but important task with great professionalism and thoroughness. In varying ways and degrees all these commitments stretched the experience and tested the capabilities of the units and the individuals involved.

The Regiment had always had a reputation for being reliable and 'steady'; the emphasis increasingly now moved to being flexible, adaptable and agile. Concurrently with this experience, and building on the positive relationships between the ranks, commanders placed even more emphasis on the development of individuals at all levels, creating the environment of mutual trust and a lightness of touch that was necessary for successful 'mission command'. Lieutenant Colonels Richard Kemp with the 1st Battalion and Roland Ladley with the 2nd paid particular attention to this issue. Subsequent commanders benefitted from their initiatives, and it has become a distinguishing characteristic of the Regiment.

In 2003, following a good deal of preliminary work, a group of soldiers and officers representing a cross-section of all ranks from private soldier to colonel and drawn from both

Poachers training in Cyprus, led by Sergeant Cousin.

regular battalions met for a day in Pirbright to reflect on these developments, attempt to capture the distinctive nature of The Royal Anglian Regiment and articulate how they felt they were different from other infantry regiments. The product was a simple statement of ethos to which all contributed and which all agreed:

> We are a county based Regiment, bound together by a closely-knit family spirit. Our approach is classless, based on mutual respect and trust, where developing and believing in our soldiers is paramount. We are a forward looking, self-starting and welcoming team for whom the mission remains key. By living this Ethos, we the Royal Anglian Regiment aspire to constantly deliver excellence. We make it happen.

At the time this seemed to capture what the Regiment had become and explained what it meant to be a 'Royal Anglian'. The next years brought the severest operational trials the Regiment has faced, in Iraq in 2006 for the 2nd Battalion, in the Helmand province of

The regimental ethos was produced as a business card.

Afghanistan in 2007 for the 1st Battalion and subsequent tours for both. The raw danger, complexity and sophistication of these very demanding operations put the Regiment to the test. In meeting the challenges, those involved brought all the strands of its development together, building on the past but embracing current thinking, equipment, tactics and human potential. This period represented a 'coming of age' for the organisation as well as for the individuals concerned, and provided confirmation of the Regiment's effectiveness and mettle.

This experience has certainly strengthened the links to the counties; during the deployments to Iraq and Afghanistan, people identified with 'their' boys, grieved for the casualties suffered and expressed their gratitude

Regimental Ethos of The Royal Anglian Regiment

We are a county based Regiment, bound together by a closely-knit family spirit. Our approach is classless, based on mutual respect and trust, where developing and believing in our soldiers is paramount. We are a forward looking, self-starting and welcoming team for whom the mission remains key. By living this Ethos, we the Royal Anglian Regiment aspire to constantly deliver excellence. We make it happen.

and admiration on their return. Veterans of the Second World War, Korea, and other post-war campaigns now find they can relate to the current generation of soldiers because of their comparable operational experience, and this has made a real difference in the county regimental associations. The 'close-knit family spirit' has been tested in adversity. It is not just that there are now numerous examples of successive generations of families who have served in the Regiment; or that there is a family feeling about the units, which is noted by those from other organisations that serve with it and are made welcome. The support of the families for those serving has been conspicuous and sustained, and the courage and generosity of spirit shown towards the Regiment by bereaved and suffering relatives has been humbling.

Moreover, it is the quality of the individuals who make up the battalions, and the way they are trained and developed and relate to each other, which remains at the heart of the Regiment's approach to its tasks. While many now have the self-confidence that stems from the successful conduct of operations, there also remains a hunger to learn from experience, do things better and respond to the next set of challenges in a positive, grounded yet flexible and imaginative way. That confidence and aspiration to excellence is tempered by a professional modesty that discourages complacency; it feeds a desire to learn more and hone capability and translates into sustained effectiveness.

To some extent the journey taken by The Royal Anglian Regiment over 50 years is a reflection of that taken by the Army as a whole. Many of the factors that have made for success are shared elsewhere in that army; but the particular mix and balance of factors, the way they have worked in combination and mutually reinforced each other has not only worked well, but is identifiably different. Those factors (which are at the heart of the Regiment), the close and positive relationship between the Regiment and the communities from which the vast majority of the Regiment's soldiers come, and the Regiment's capacity to evolve, together give significant value to both defence and the community in a time of uncertainty and change.

The Vikings' homecoming parade in Bury St Edmunds in 2007, after their demanding Operation *Herrick 6* tour.

MAJOR GENERAL PATRICK STONE'S VIEW OF THE REGIMENT'S SUCCESS

Major General Patrick Stone, CB, CBE was Colonel of the Regiment from 1991 to 1997 and as such he oversaw a period of considerable change. He believes that three key factors played a fundamental part in the successful creation of the Regiment and its subsequent reputation and professionalism:

> I am certain that the geographic closeness of the counties and the consequent homogeneity of the region from which our founder regiments had drawn their recruits for centuries, was of primary importance in the subsequent creation and success of our 'large regiment'. It was also vital in both maintaining and growing our links to the counties, towns and people of our area over the ensuing years.
>
> I also believe that by casting our officer recruitment net wider than the traditional public school, and by comfortably encompassing the graduate officer, together with our professionalism and experience, allowed us to recruit and develop a steady stream of excellent young officers over the years. Many have gone on to become outstanding commanding officers, who in their turn have contributed to the development and reputation of the Regiment. We have also been blessed by the large number of influential senior officers who have their roots in the regiment. Not many regiments can boast a roll call of Denning, Goodwin, Freeland, Creasey, Akehurst, Walker, McColl and Jones in its first half-century.
>
> Lastly, people should not forget that the larger and more painful mergers and amalgamations took place during the 1960s and 1970s, a period of wide social change, which saw the rigid social divisions of the great days of Empire, gradually eroded. This caused tensions and divisions in some of the more, how shall I put it, 'traditional' regiments, and remained a corrosive and divisive factor in their merger for some years. I am sure that our broader social mix and preparedness to move with the times, whilst maintaining the standards and traditions that matter, allowed us to avoid most of this and concentrate instead on developing our reputation and success.

NOTES

1. David French, *Military Identities – The Regimental System, the British Army and the British People c. 1870–2000* (Oxford University Press, 2005), p.46 and tables on pp. 59–60.

2. Ibid, p.58.

3. We owe this point to Professor David French.

4. Ibid, pp.166–67.

5. Michael Barthorp, *Crater to the Creggan: The History of the Royal Anglian Regiment 1964–1974* (Leo Cooper, 1976).

6. Tony Parker, *Soldier, Soldier* (Heinemann, 1985).

SECTION 2
OPERATIONS

Chinook debus in Afghanistan.

INTRODUCTION

General Purpose Machine Gun (GPMG) team, A Company, 1st Battalion, during Operation *Herrick 6*.

The primary focus of the Regiment has been and remains professional competence and operational effectiveness; it is therefore entirely logical that operations are at the core of this book. However, it is also true, as the Colonel of the Regiment concludes at the end of this history, that 'we are only as good as our next fight'. In thinking ahead to that 'next fight', as with the individual submitting a curriculum vitae for their next job, it is important to provide the most recent evidence of capability and effectiveness. This section is therefore presented counter-chronologically, presenting the evidence of the Regiment's most recent campaigns, Afghanistan and Iraq, first, and in the most detail. Moreover, for all serving readers, and those recently retired who are members of what the Army refers to as the 'warrior generation', it is the years of these campaigns that have dominated and shaped their professional and personal lives and will influence most directly their approach to the next decades.

However, it is important to understand how and why the Regiment has evolved into the current position, to appreciate those things that have changed but also where there are continuities, and where experience from the past may have relevance for the future. For these reasons, as well as completeness, this section also examines earlier operations, and revisits Aden and the early years in Northern Ireland, even though these were covered in some detail by Michael Barthorp in *Crater to the Creggan*.

In addressing the difficult task of selecting the particular examples of operations, the aim has been not only to highlight the representative and interesting, but also to show the variety of operations within each campaign, the tactical dynamics, and, by implication, the importance of the Regiment's flexibility and adaptability in addressing new challenges. Campaigns present those involved, and their enemies, with a 'learning curve'; success goes to those who understand what is going on, out-think the opposition and adapt accordingly. 'The enemy has a vote too', and slow learners pay a price in blood and, ultimately, failure.

Ideally there should also be an institutional 'learning curve', so that, with time, experience and training units become more effective. However, given the turnover of those serving in battalions, one of the real challenges for a regiment (and armies) is to collectively absorb the lessons of experience gained in previous campaigns and apply them intelligently to new circumstances, notwithstanding the change in personalities. One of the lessons to absorb is that of operating in adverse circumstances. The history of the British Army is replete with examples of ill-judged, badly planned and poorly conducted campaigns. Frequently, it has been the performance of well-trained, well-led and motivated battalions which has achieved a successful outcome or at worst mitigated setbacks. Regimental operational competence and effectiveness is crucial to the overall effort, but this cannot be assumed and requires continual striving and effort from successive generations of regimental soldiers.

Private Tower of the Vikings calling for ammunition on Operation *Herrick 6*.

AFGHANISTAN

View of Kabul taken during Operation *Fingal*.

The British Army has been in Afghanistan before – during the First (1839–42), Second (1878–80) and Third (1919) Afghan Wars – and has never had a comfortable experience there. The British are not the only country to have regretted entering Afghanistan; the Russian invasion of 1979–89 did not end well either.

Deployment to Afghanistan started in 2001, following the US-led campaign against the Taliban in response to their hosting al-Qaeda and the terrorist attack on the United States on 11 September 2001. This was a novel type of war, conducted by superpower intelligence agencies and Special Forces, and supported extensively by high-technology air power, all of which persuaded willing factions of Afghan warlords to topple the unpopular Taliban regime. Members of The Royal Anglian Regiment did fight in this campaign as part of the Special Forces, but the first full deployments were fairly peaceful, encountering relatively few hostile acts. These deployments were called Operation *Fingal,* based in Kabul, and the first was by the 1st Battalion, under command of Lieutenant Colonel Phil Jones, MBE, from March to June 2002. The 2nd Battalion, under command of Lieutenant Colonel Roland Ladley, MBE, conducted a similar tour from March to October 2003. These tours provided reassurance to the Afghan people by guarding elements of the capital and showing the flag. They passed off with little incident – although, sadly, Lance Corporal Darren George was killed in an accident on 9 April 2002.

The 1st Battalion then conducted three tours called Operation *Herrick*: *Herrick 6,* March–October 2007; *Herrick 11*, October 2009–April 2010; and *Herrick 16*, March–October 2012. The first and last of these saw the battalion deployed together as a battle group, whereas on *Herrick 11* it was deployed in company groups under command of others, although battalion headquarters also deployed as a training asset. At the time of writing, the 2nd Battalion has deployed on Operation *Herrick 19* in October 2013.

By 2004 the Taliban had recovered from the shock of being ousted from power and were significantly increasing their insurgency in the country, especially in the south. Attacks on the 3rd Battalion The Parachute Regiment increased alarmingly in the southern province of Helmand and this trend continued as they were rotated and replaced by 42 Commando, Royal Marines. At this stage it might be fair to say that the International Security Assistance Force (ISAF) higher command was not sure what to do next. The level of insurrection in Helmand had risen markedly over the year, and although 42 Commando held its own, it seemed probable that the level of violence would continue to increase. Indeed, the Taliban announced that a 2007 'spring offensive' would drive the infidel out of the country.

There was an additional dilemma: it was clear to most commanders that there were insufficient troops deployed to halt such a widespread insurgency, but the Labour government of 2007 was steadfastly opposed to greater commitment of force. In the face of the unpopularity of the war in Iraq at that time, they would agree to any additional deployment only very grudgingly.

Into this situation the 1st Battalion deployed as part of Operation *Herrick 6*. Ably led, and exceptionally well trained, they were determined to stamp their mark on an extremely difficult situation.

It is worth examining some of the overarching tactical difficulties that have made fighting in Afghanistan so arduous and complex. The first tactical conundrum was the difficulty of pinning down the highly mobile Taliban so that they could be engaged and destroyed. This was especially tricky when there was low force density, brought about by insufficient troops trying to control too large an area. With their detailed local knowledge, their superbly concealed escape routes, their ability to stash weapons and blend quickly into the population, and above all the lightness of their equipment and their tactical initiative, the Taliban could be a formidable opponent. They could undertake highly effective shootings, often involving simultaneous crossfire from several different firing points, usually within compounds. They could inflict casualties, quickly leave the area using their numerous 'rat runs' in drainage ditches or tunnels then reassemble in another set of compounds, ready to start the whole process again. The terrain of the Green Zone, which extends some 5–10km either side of the Helmand river, with its maze of drainage ditches, high crops and almost impregnable compounds, was ideal for this type of tactics. Dressed in the loose clothing of a 'dish-dash' and flip-flops, and

Major Alan Wylie of the 1st Battalion talks to children on Operation *Fingal*.

carrying only an AK-47 with a few magazines, fit and capable Taliban fighters had the will, knowledge and skill to move around the complex local terrain, appearing and disappearing almost at will, coordinating their action via mobile phones and small commercial radios. They were brave, sometimes to the point of being suicidal, which, when coupled with cunning and initiative, made for a highly challenging opponent.

A classic heavy infantry versus light infantry situation developed in Helmand. Against this highly mobile and deadly opponent the Royal Anglian soldier was deployed on foot carrying at least 40kg of equipment and usually much more – sometimes up to around

THE AK-47

The iconic 'Kalashnikov' AK-47 assault rifle is the Taliban fighter's personal weapon of choice. It is seen in many forms and with minor variations, such as the modified AKM, and the Chinese copy called Type 56.

The AK-47 has many plus points. It is readily available, with some estimates showing that between 70 and 100 million weapons have been produced, making it by far the world's most prolific assault rifle. It is consequently one of the world's cheapest, by some margin. Many were left behind in Afghanistan after the Soviet invasion, but many more have found their way into the country since then, in an array of variants. Ammunition resupply is relatively straightforward; it fires the former Soviet 7.62mm x 39 round at 600 rounds per minute, which is widely and easily available at a low price from Russian, Chinese, Pakistani and other sources.

It is simple both to train on and to maintain, but most importantly, it is reliable and durable.

It rarely has stoppages and will keep firing in wet, muddy or dusty conditions, even when it has not been maintained well.

These are powerful advantages, but it is far from the perfect weapon. It suffers from several drawbacks, especially a lack of accuracy. If fired in fully automatic mode, it has an alarming tendency to climb to the right, which can make accurate automatic fire very difficult. This is often compounded by the fact that older weapons may have suffered from excessive barrel wear, which can cause the rounds fired to disperse over a wide area. These issues are especially prevalent in the versions manufactured from stampings rather than milled, and in some copies and derivatives which are made from cheaper materials, often to lower manufacturing tolerances. This lack of accuracy can sometimes explain the remarkable, even miraculous, close shaves and escapes of ISAF soldiers who have been fired at, even from very close range.

AK-47.

70kg. This comprised the essential 'Osprey' body armour and helmet, weapon, ammunition and some water. Although the Royal Anglian soldiers were in peak physical form, they could never move as fast on foot as the lightly equipped and dressed Taliban fighters.

BvS10 in the Afghan desert.

Conversely, the Royal Anglian soldier could call upon significantly greater firepower: his own, from the air, artillery, mortars and the Regiment's own fire-support groups. In this situation the importance of vehicles increased, as they allowed faster movement, albeit at increased risk. Even the lightly protected but heavily armed vehicles with Weapons Mounted Installation Kits (WMIKs) played a significant role, and the fully armoured BvS10s were at times tactically vital. (The nickname for members of 1st Battalion, 'Vikings', is the same as the nickname of the BvS10 armoured vehicle. To avoid confusion, the nickname will be used only for the men, and the vehicle referred to simply as BvS10.) In later tours much more heavily armoured vehicles were used, like the formidable Mastiff 2 and Wolfhound. By using vehicles as weapons platforms and also to redeploy heavy infantry rapidly, it was possible to outflank and cut off, or at least threaten, Taliban escape routes. Through clever use of supporting fire, flanking and vehicles, it also proved possible on occasion to negate the Taliban mobility advantage.

The traditional advantage provided to Western troops by massive air mobility was never really available in Afghanistan. Helicopter lift was in short supply, especially in the early tours, mainly as a result of a combination of political intervention and organisational issues with the RAF. There was always sufficient lift for casualty evacuation, and this improved further as larger numbers of Chinooks and Merlin helicopters were deployed on later tours. Also, the use of supporting Apache attack helicopters was highly effective throughout the campaign. However, there was never a surfeit of helicopter lift available to the infantry.

As the Taliban always had the option to stash their weapons and pretend to be innocent locals, and the Royal Anglian soldier always had to try to minimise the possibility of civilian casualties, the rules of engagement were constantly difficult, and became even more rigorous in later tours.

In these later tours, essentially because the Taliban had found themselves losing far more casualties in fire-fights than they could sustain, they switched tactics and the Improvised Explosive Device (IED) became their new weapon of choice. From around mid-2008, IEDs were made in ever-greater numbers and deployed in ever more sophisticated and cunning arrays, so that on some occasions the ISAF troops felt as though they were effectively fighting in a minefield. Gradually, the adoption of better tactics and deployment of improved detectors and heavily armoured vehicles – together with some increases in air mobility – slightly reduced the impact of IEDs. However, by the later tours the threat had evolved into a highly complex mixture of attacks – including lures and deliberate attempts to cause civilian casualties – in ever more fiendish combinations as the metal content of the devices was reduced, making them harder or even impossible to detect.

LOCAL AFGHAN FORCES

The British Army in Afghanistan uses a sometimes confusing array of acronyms for the local Afghan forces:

ANA Afghan National Army, the main forces, organised into *Tolays* (companies) several of which make a *Kandak* (battalion), several of which make a brigade.

ANP Afghan National Police, a generic term for all types of police.

AUP Afghan Uniformed Police, the main police force.

ANCOP Afghan National Civil Order Police, something akin to a gendarmerie. These are paramilitary police, well trained and well armed.

ALP Afghan Local Police, a much more mixed group of local people, recently recruited into the police force. They are often poorly trained and equipped, but usually possess excellent local knowledge.

The Commanding Officer and Regimental Sergeant Major on *Herrick 6*.

OPERATION *HERRICK 6*, MARCH–OCTOBER 2007

Operation *Herrick 6* was the defining tour of The Royal Anglian Regiment's involvement in the war in Afghanistan. It was the first time that 'line' infantry had been deployed in Afghanistan, and the 1st Battalion impressed everyone with a superb fighting performance. This tour was also highly 'kinetic' – featuring an extremely high tempo of very intense operations; indeed, some said that this was indistinguishable from infantry combat in a full-scale war. *Herrick 6* has been extensively covered in print: *Attack State Red* by Colonel Richard Kemp and Chris Hughes is the definitive account, and James Cartwright has published his

HELMAND PROVINCE

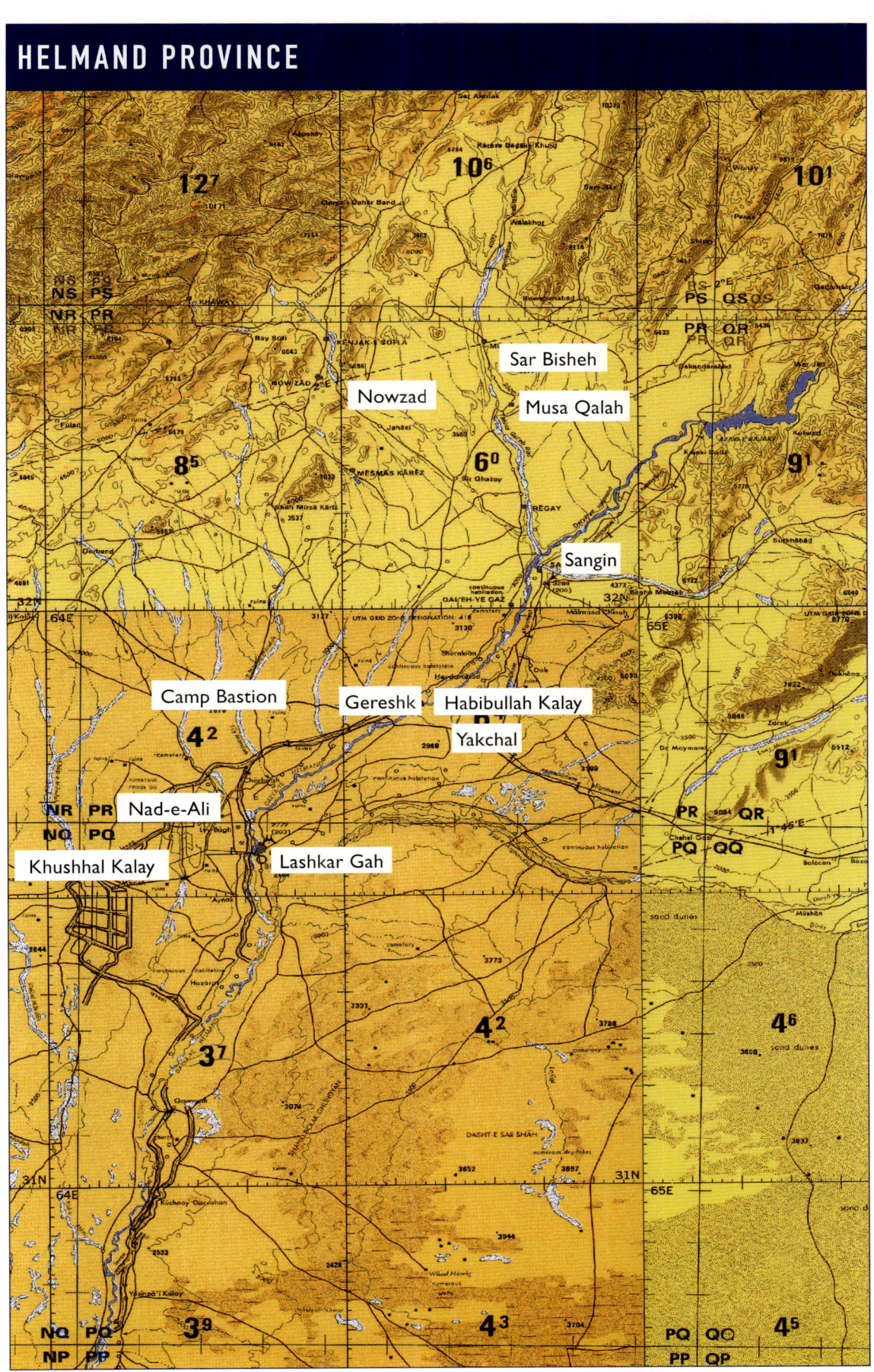

Sar Bisheh

Nowzad

Musa Qalah

Sangin

Camp Bastion

Gereshk

Habibullah Kalay

Yakchal

Nad-e-Ali

Khushhal Kalay

Lashkar Gah

own personal account in *Helmand Sniper*.[1] In addition, the TV actor Ross Kemp – who has a personal connection to the Regiment as his father served in the Royal Norfolk Regiment – accompanied the 1st Battalion for some of their time on *Herrick 6* and filmed an excellent documentary called *Ross Kemp in Afghanistan*. Rather than try to repeat or paraphrase all this outstanding coverage, we will look here instead at the details of two major operations from *Herrick 6* – *Silicon* and *Gharste Ghar*.

For *Herrick 6* the 1st Battalion deployed to Helmand province as the 1st Battalion Royal Anglian Battle Group with an attached Estonian armoured infantry company and a Danish reconnaissance squadron, bringing the battle group to over 1,500 personnel. After a year's warning and excellent pre-deployment training, the battalion was ready for an intense tour. During this time in Afghanistan it conducted four major battle group operations and over 100 company-level operations. There were more than 350 separate engagements and over 1,000 confirmed casualties were inflicted on the Taliban.

OPERATION *SILICON*, 27–28 APRIL 2007: THE EARLY MARKER

Although there were some earlier operations on the *Herrick 6* tour, Operation *Silicon* set the style and pace for the rest, and it showed the world and, importantly, the higher command in Afghanistan what good line infantry could do. It was the first occasion on which two companies of the 1st Battalion deployed, brought the Taliban to battle, and defeated them.

Operation *Silicon* was a battle group operation designed to push the Taliban further away from the important town of Gereshk by clearing an area to the north-east, leading to the securing of a village called Habibullah Kalay. For months the Taliban had been firing its longer-ranged indirect-fire weapons – at this stage ex-Soviet 82mm mortars and the occasional B-11 107mm recoilless rifle with a range of around 3–5km – into Gereshk and its congested approach roads. The 12 Brigade plan was to push the enemy further away so that a Taliban-free 'security bubble' could be established and then, most importantly, expanded so that Gereshk was no longer in range of Taliban rockets. The 12 Brigade commander, Brigadier John Lorimer, described the aim of the mission:

Below: Ex-Soviet 82mm mortar.

Below right: Ex-Soviet B-11 107mm recoilless rifle.

I want a Task Force operation to clear the Taliban out of their strongholds in the Green Zone to the north-east of Gereshk, to put a stop to the indirect fire. I want to secure the entire area on a permanent basis. So once the enemy is cleared out we will need to set up patrol bases as quickly as possible. I intend that the Afghan National Army supported initially by the

Worcestershire and Sherwood Forester Regiment will occupy the patrol bases when they are built.

This was the largest operation in Afghanistan to date and the first time a British unit had entered the Green Zone. Under commanding officer Lieutenant Colonel Stuart Carver, A (Norfolk) and B (Suffolk) companies of the 1st Battalion, with their Fire Support Groups (FSG) and Reconnaissance Platoon (Recce), were the main force, supported on their right by the Afghan National Army (ANA) together with their attached Operational Mentor and Liaison Team (OMLT) from the Queen's Company, the Grenadier Guards.[2]

FIRE SUPPORT GROUPS

For all the Afghanistan tours, the 1st Battalion formed Fire Support Groups (FSG). These were based on the support weapons specialists in the anti-tank and machine-gun platoons of D (Cambridgeshire) Company, but on operations were deployed one to each rifle company for the whole tour. They were named FSG-A, B and C, denoting the company to which they were attached, and a fourth, FSG-D, was sometimes formed. On some occasions they were regrouped for particular operations. Although they were normally kept together or grouped with the Reconnaissance Platoon, snipers were also often attached to FSGs, especially in the later tours.

An FSG was normally commanded by a captain or senior NCO, usually a colour sergeant or warrant officer, and was often divided into three or four teams, each commanded by a corporal. A typical FSG might have up to 20 men in total. Their equipment varied, with mixtures of support weapons, but normally it would include General Purpose Machine Gun Sustained Fire (GPMG (SF)), Heavy Machine Gun (HMG), Grenade Machine Gun (GMG) and Javelin missiles, mounted in various vehicles. These were initially the unarmoured Land Rover Weapons Mounted Installation Kit (WMIK) and then the Revised WMIK, replaced on later tours by Jackal and Mastiff protected patrol vehicles. The FSG would normally deploy in its vehicles but could on occasion deploy dismounted. Carrying equipment and supplies on a foot deployment – especially in the difficult Afghan terrain – was challenging, but the Vikings were trained for this. The main disadvantage of dismounted deployment was that far less ammunition could be carried. Some FSGs, especially on *Herrick 6*, fired prodigious quantities of ammunition – in excess of 10,000 rounds in one engagement.

One FSG commander from *Herrick 6* described how the weapon mix could work, each weapon fulfilling a complementary role:

> Generally the GPMG (SF) was good for suppressing the Taliban, to pin them in one place and discourage their movement with nearly continuous fire, but it would rarely kill, as they would be too well dug in. The GMG would be better at killing or wounding, especially if they were in ditches or treelines, but it had less continuous fire, so was less good at suppression. The HMG was halfway between the two, good for penetration and knocking bits off compounds but less accurate than the GPMG (SF). Some guys loved the HMG and it was good for our morale to hear it firing and it kicked up a lot of strike.
>
> Most Afghan compounds were bulletproof; the HMG might not penetrate the compound wall. You needed the 30mm Rarden cannon of the Scimitar vehicle or Javelin missile to get through if the Taliban were inside.

Fire Support Group B on Operation Silicon.

Battle group orders for Operation *Silicon* were delivered in Camp Bastion on 25 April 2007.[3] Although there was little hard information available on the numbers, disposition and weaponry of the Taliban in the area, they were known to be in occupation and their activity had been increasing of late, so tough resistance was expected. The Taliban needed the poppy harvest to go well so that they could afford to re-equip prior to attacking again towards Sangin via Gereshk. Although there were thought to be up to 1,000 Taliban in the Gereshk area, it was expected that 20–40 highly mobile insurgents were in Habibullah Kalay village, with more – possibly up to 120 – active in the surrounding area. In the main these fighters were armed with 7.62mm AK-47 assault rifles and PKM 7.62mm belt-fed machine guns, coupled with rocket-propelled grenades (RPG) of the RPG-7 type with some heavy weapon support. They also had access to IEDs and suicide bombers. Civilians of mixed sympathies

ROCKET-PROPELLED GRENADE (RPG-7)

This weapon has been in widespread use by the Taliban in a number of roles, such as anti-personnel, anti-tank, building-breaching and even against helicopters. Developed in the Soviet Union after the Second World War, it was the largest of a suite of shoulder-launched 'Panzerfaust-type' grenade launchers to see service with Warsaw Pact troops from 1961.

The RPG-7 fires an 83mm-diameter simple-shaped charge warhead of the high-explosive anti-tank or HEAT type. Range varies depending on the sight used, but also with the skill of the firer; its battle range is often quoted as 200m, but it can be fired further. Although a large number of different rounds are available for the RPG-7, such as improved tandem anti-armour HEAT, thermobaric and fragmentation types, these have rarely been encountered in Afghanistan, unlike in Iraq. In the main the Taliban seem to use the standard 83mm HEAT round, which is cheaply manufactured in huge quantities in China and Pakistan. There are also many later types of RPG available, such as the RPG-29 Vampir, but again these have not been seen much in Taliban hands.

The Taliban have become skilled in the use of the RPG-7 in a more general-purpose support role rather than in the anti-tank role for which it was originally designed. The main problem is that, because of the low velocity of the round and a general lack of optical sights, it tends to be inaccurate, often flying too high except in the hands of an especially skilled operator. There are many stories of troops watching RPG rounds fly over their heads. It has the ability to penetrate some compound walls, but it is not especially good at this, often producing a small, deep hole with little energy left to make an effect on the far side. The warhead is not especially lethal, being of a rather dated design focused on penetrating armour, but nevertheless it is still a potent weapon.

The Taliban use of the RPG-7 against helicopters is interesting because, although the weapon is rather short-ranged and not especially accurate, once fired it is not subject to the helicopter's counter-measures – such as decoy flares and chaff – which can defeat more specialised anti-aircraft weapons. Consequently, most of the NATO helicopters destroyed by the Taliban seem to have been hit by standard rounds fired by RPG-7s.

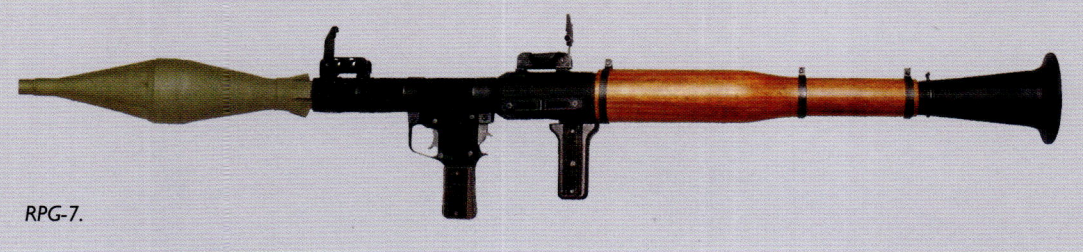

RPG-7.

were also in the area, so many compounds were expected to be occupied by Taliban fighters or hostiles.

The initial plan was that B Company would clear inside the Green Zone through a linear collection of compounds called Deh Adan Khan towards a line parallel to Habibullah Kalay. Once complete, A Company would take Habibullah Kalay, supported by both their FSGs and Recce from the high open ground on their left flank.

A Company deployed at 02.30 for their initial task of securing the start line for B Company's assault. The rocky terrain was difficult to traverse in the dark and en route two Vector vehicles rolled onto their sides. The vehicles were righted and the start line secured, but not before a brisk contact had broken out on the left with a party of six Taliban who opened fire, only to be cut down by A Company's 1 Platoon under the command of Lieutenant Nick Denning. Concurrently, B Company had been led into the forming-up point by Corporal Ashley Hill of Recce in Scimitar vehicles. Their BvS10 vehicles, however, had to go on a long detour to cross the river. They were under the command of Captain Will Goodman of the Royal Marines and B Company Sergeant Major Tim Newton. After several adventures involving thrown tracks and repeated small-arms contacts, these vehicles eventually arrived on the right of the start line.

The day dawned hot, with temperatures expected to exceed 30°C. B Company crossed their start line at 05.30, deployed with 5 Platoon on the left under command of Second Lieutenant Ben Howes; 7 Platoon on the right under the command of Lieutenant George Seal-Coon; and 6 Platoon in reserve under the command of Lieutenant Dave Broomfield. Each of the lead platoons occupied a frontage of around 300m, but this would widen as the clearance progressed; they would have to clear through more than 3km of Green Zone to reach level with Habibullah Kalay on the first day.

81MM MORTAR

The L16A2 81mm mortar has been in service with the British Army since the early 1960s. Although an older system, it is a reliable, accurate and useful mortar with a range of 5,650m. Normally deployed as a battle group asset with the mortar platoon, it can be deployed on foot when broken down into three main loads of barrel, base plate, and bipod with sights. In addition to the normal high-explosive bombs, this mortar was widely used throughout its life to provide night-time illumination using parachute flares.

It weighs 35kg and each mortar bomb weighs around 4kg, so it was normally deployed with vehicles for any sustained period of fire. However, unlike other support weapons, it is not normally fired from a vehicle; instead being fired from the ground, often from within an emplacement and sometimes using a 'Raschen Bag', a special bag of ballast placed under the base plate providing greater accuracy by giving a more consistent recoil effect, especially on soft ground.

A section of the Viking Mortar Platoon in action during Operation Silicon.

OPERATION *SILICON*, DAY 1 MORNING

Opposite top: Lieutenant George Seal-Coon directs fire to mark an enemy position.

By 09.30 B Company was making good progress; they had cleared several compounds and had not yet encountered any Taliban. At this point the BvS10 vehicles, which were moving along the southern boundary track, were hit by machine-gun fire and RPGs flew overhead. As Major Mick Aston commanding B Company swung 7 Platoon into support and called up air support from Apache gunships, Sergeant Major Snow, in command of the B Company FSG, reported that he was under mortar fire. FSG-B was deployed on high ground up to the north, in a prominent feature called the Red Fort. Unable to locate the mortar firing point the FSG used various observation devices to scan the area in detail. By 10.00 Lance Corporal Teddy Ruecker spotted armed men scurrying into Habibullah Kalay 600m away. Just as he was giving a fire order, the Taliban fired on his position with machine guns and RPGs, albeit rather inaccurately. As the return fire from the FSG mounted, the Taliban in Habibullah Kalay were first suppressed by the GPMG, HMG and GMG fire and eventually silenced by Private Brian Turner firing an AT-4 anti-tank rocket at the offending compound. Even though it was well beyond the supposed range of the weapon, Turner got a hit by aiming deliberately far too high.

Back at B Company, Sergeant Nieves of 7 Platoon had identified the tree line from which the Taliban fire was emanating and they were returning fire, but this was having little effect on the Taliban's prepared position. This had been given to an Apache attack helicopter overhead, but, despite the clear indication from 7 Platoon, they would not open fire until they had personally identified the target. This was highly frustrating for B Company; not only was it holding them up, but because of air safety, additional weapons such as other

SA80A2 RIFLE WITH UNDERSLUNG GRENADE LAUNCHER

The SA80, also called the L85, started life with a mixed reputation as a series of modifications were needed following its introduction into service from 1985. By the time the improved A2 variant was in service in 2001 – when it was also often equipped with a 40mm underslung grenade launcher (UGL) – the SA80 was a trusted, reliable and reasonably well-liked weapon. Its 'bullpup' configuration, with the magazine behind the pistol grip, means it is short and very handy, especially useful in close-combat situations. Although not especially light, weighing in at around 5kg, the ammunition is about half the weight of the equivalent 7.62mm, so many more rounds can be carried, in 30-round magazines. It can fire in single-shot or automatic mode out to ranges of around 400m.

The weapon can be equipped with an evolving range of day and night sights, but the standard sight for infantry is the Sight Unit Small Arms Trilux (SUSAT), which is a x4 magnification optical sight. This is being replaced by the x6 magnification Advanced Combat Optical Gunsight (ACOG). The Common Weapon Sight (CWS) is the standard image-intensification night sight, but on *Herrick 16* the Vikings used the thermal-imaging VIPIR-2.

Private Shepherd with his SA80A2 – B Company, Herrick 6.

Large explosion from an air-dropped 1000-lb Paveway bomb.

aircraft, mortars or artillery could not be used while the Apache was in the air over the target.

By 11.00 Major Aston had had enough, so he instructed the Apache to leave the area, planning to try alternative methods and to get the company moving again. As soon as it had gone, Corporal Mark Wilshire, his mortar fire controller, had 81mm mortar bombs landing on the area and the joint tactical air controller (JTAC) called up a Harrier GR7 with a 500-lb bomb that was aimed at the tree line. Amazingly, this bomb failed to explode, although the impact threw up clods of earth. The only additional bombs the Harrier was carrying were 1,000-lb Paveway IIs. Because they had a much larger danger area, there was a debate about the threat to friendly troops, but given the incoming small-arms and RPG fire, the Harrier was instructed to drop one anyway. There was a massive explosion, right in the centre of the enemy position, and a huge smoke cloud, and the Taliban firing from the tree line stopped. B Company could now press on with their clearance.

BRITISH MACHINE GUNS IN AFGHANISTAN

GENERAL PURPOSE MACHINE GUN (GPMG)

This 1950s-designed 7.62mm belt-fed machine gun is a long-standing favourite with those who use it. It packs a significant punch and reaches ranges out to 800m and beyond on its bipod. When used on a tripod in the sustained-fire role, called GPMG (SF), it can achieve ranges out to 1,800m with ease; this is the range at which normal tracer rounds burn out. Longer shoots out to 2,400m or even further are possible when the fall of shot is visible. When used in conjunction with the C2 sight, it can record targets and on occasion it can be used for indirect fire by especially skilled crew. The Vikings' main use for GPMG (SF) was as part of the Fire Support Groups.

The GPMG, usually pronounced 'Jimpy', was supposed to have been replaced, first by the Light Support Weapon (LSW), then by the Light Machine Gun (LMG), but its popularity has kept it in service. Indeed, as the campaign in Afghanistan progressed, the GPMG was used more and more, due to its range and its greater 7.62mm hitting power.

Private Roberts with his GPMG.

It is not a perfect weapon, however, with the weight of the gun (11.8kg) and ammunition a major drawback. It is large and so not especially handy in close-combat situations, and also quite difficult to clean, especially the gas plug, but if well maintained it is reasonably reliable. When asked, 'If you could choose any machine gun for a particular operation, which would it be?' one group of Viking Afghanistan veterans all said without hesitation, 'Jimpy!'

A firm favourite of the British infantry, the GPMG is likely to stay in service long into the 21st century.

LIGHT MACHINE GUN (LMG)

Private Burgess, A Company with his LMG.

The LMG, also called the Minimi in other armies, is effectively a scaled-down GPMG, modified to fire the standard NATO 5.56mm round in belts. It was first used on Operation *Telic*, and became popular. It is handier than the GPMG and as a result is more useful at closer rages, especially in built-up areas. At between 7kg and 8kg it is also much lighter than the GPMG, and the 5.56mm belt weighs about half the equivalent 7.62mm belt for the same number of rounds.

The major limitation with the LMG in Afghanistan was range: it is effective up to 500 or occasionally 600m, but this left a range gap which the Taliban exploited. Nevertheless, the LMG remained a reasonably popular weapon. The 12-man Viking multiples usually carried two or three each.

LIGHT SUPPORT WEAPON

This 5.56mm-calibre weapon, also called the L86, was introduced in conjunction with the SA80 but crucially is magazine-fed. Before and during Operation *Telic* several misgivings emerged about the use of magazine-fed Light Support Weapons (LSWs) and it was effectively replaced by the belt-fed LMG. It does have some advantages – when used with its bipod it is very accurate so can be used in a sniper-rifle-type role, especially when avoiding collateral damage is important, but only out to ranges of around 600m due to the limitations of the round. However, it was never a popular weapon as it cannot deliver sufficient firepower at team or squad level due to its magazine feed.

Generally, it was shunned by the Vikings on *Herrick 6* and earlier as they preferred the belt-fed LMG and GPMG – although it did make the occasional appearance, perhaps as a single weapon in some multiples.

L86A2 light support weapon.

Almost immediately, fire was received from the north as 5 Platoon approached Deh Adan Khan. As this platoon returned fire, 7 Platoon prepared to assault the next compound on their right, covered by fire from the BvS10s. They were forced to halt, coming under fire from a small compound to their left, but eventually this was silenced when Lance Corporal Michael Auckland, from the anti-tank platoon attached to B Company, aimed a Javelin anti-tank missile into the compound firing point, scoring a direct hit. Corporal Stuart Parker's section of 7 Platoon then assaulted into their target compound in 'Attack State Red' (attacking with small-arms fire and grenades). A bar mine was used to blow the entry hole,

Company Sergeant Major
Tim Newton.

followed by grenades, then the leading soldiers entered, firing on automatic; but the compound was empty. A message received from higher formation at the same time indicated that a new pair of shadowing Apaches had cut down the Taliban as they withdrew from the compound.

Meanwhile, 5 Platoon were in a large fire-fight just to the north, taking machine-gun and RPG fire and suffering minor casualties, with Private Allan Shepherd catching a lump of shrapnel in the eye. They were returning fire with all platoon weapons when Company Sergeant Major Tim Newton appeared and shouted for Second Lieutenant Howes. A famous wind-up now took place: the sergeant major got Howes to crawl over to him under fire, only to ask if he had any cigarettes. Newton was only joking about cigarettes – Ben Howes was needed for a face-to-face orders group with the company commander, but it took him a few moments to realise what was going on.

The orders group was necessary because 6 Platoon had pressed on well forward into another compound known as Objective 8, but had become almost surrounded. Typical of the aggressive Taliban, they had taken advantage of the distraction of 5 and 7 Platoons to infiltrate back around and past 6 Platoon, threatening to surround them. Major Aston issued quick battle orders for 5 Platoon to disengage and move through 7 Platoon into the compound beyond them. 7 Platoon were then to leapfrog through on to the next compound and so on until they reached the beleaguered 6 Platoon. Meanwhile 6 Platoon were still almost surrounded in their compound; they were out of water and suffering casualties from heat exhaustion, among them, Private Josh Hill, who was deteriorating fast. However, following a radio conversation with a doctor about appropriate treatment, he eventually started to stabilise and two hours later was back in action.

As 5 and 7 Platoons of B Company continued their efforts to reach 6 Platoon, Lieutenant Colonel Stuart Carver – well aware that the Taliban tended to withdraw when they were outflanked and their escape routes threatened – was keen to try to unlock the B Company position. Major Dominic Biddick, commanding A Company, suggested a daring idea: take Habibullah Kalay in the next few hours rather than the following day as planned, in the hope that a daring thrust a day early might panic the Taliban who were fighting B Company into withdrawing. Biddick suggested a further twist: FSGs and Recce could then move past Habibullah Kalay to a position still on the high ground, which would give them an excellent view of the area through which any retreating Taliban would have to escape. Carver liked this idea, although it was somewhat risky; if A Company became stuck in a fight in Habibullah Kalay while B Company was still fighting around Deh Adan Khan, he could become bogged down. Nevertheless, he gave the order for A Company to move and H-hour was confirmed as 15.40.

After swift battle orders from Biddick, A Company stepped off. When within 400m of Habibullah Kalay they dismounted from their BvS10s for the final assault. They were

Major Biddick, commander of A Company, gives quick battle orders.

2 Platoon commander, Lieutenant Graham Goodey, in the heat of action.

deployed with 2 Platoon, led by Lieutenant Graham Goodey, as the assault platoon; and 1 Platoon, under Lieutenant Nick Denning, deployed to their right as flank guard and to keep an eye on the Green Zone. In reserve with the vehicles was 3 Platoon, under Lieutenant Bjorn Rose.

Corporal Niphit Sawasdee's section led 2 Platoon's assault. Their engineer blew a hole in the village perimeter wall with half a bar mine. As the assault went in, a large volume of fire came into the platoon from their right in the Green Zone. This had been anticipated by Major Biddick, however, as he was with the FSG deployed on the high ground to the west forward of the Red Fort. Biddick himself identified the Taliban firing point and opened fire, followed by the full weight of the FSG, which suppressed the opposition. Meanwhile, 2 Platoon were assaulting through the village, compound by compound in State Red, but found it deserted. Biddick then ordered 2 Platoon to switch to State Green, which meant 'dry' assaults without firing or throwing grenades unless enemy were identified. Concurrently, Biddick sent off half of the Recce Platoon under Colour Sergeant Al Thurston with four Scimitars to skirt past Habibullah Kalay to their over-watch position beyond; they were joined by the WMIKs of FSG-A. They reached an excellent position that enabled them to observe and fire into the Green Zone behind the Taliban then fighting B Company in Deh Adan Khan.

GRENADE MACHINE GUN

GMG of D Company on Herrick 11.

The British Army was rather late in introducing an automatic grenade launcher – called the Grenade Machine Gun (GMG) in British service. It was brought into service in 2006, to supplement and partially replace the unsuccessful 51mm and later 60mm light mortars. Of 40mm calibre and made by Heckler & Koch, the GMG has a range of up to 1,500m for point targets, and further – possibly out to 2,000m – for area targets. It is belt-fed from a 32-round box magazine, but it is heavy, weighing 30kg. It is just about possible for one man to carry it, but this is demanding in the difficult terrain of Afghanistan. Carrying sufficient ammunition for sustained firing is also a challenge, so it is usually fired from a vehicle. The theoretical rate of fire is 340 rounds per minute, but up to 60 rounds per minute has proved a practical maximum.

The GMG remains a popular weapon because of the fragmentation effect of its high-explosive warhead, which has tended to offset the drawback of weight.

By 17.30 A Company had secured Habibullah Kalay and the Taliban down in the Green Zone were in a difficult position, though they may not have known it. They were fighting frontally with B Company and losing to the west, the north was blocked by A Company and the FSGs on the high ground, while the south was blocked by the canal and open ground covered by BvS10s and Apaches, so their only escape route was to the north-east. It is likely that at this stage the Taliban were unaware of all of the hazards they might face by trying to escape through the killing zone. They had had enough of fighting B Company, so they started to withdraw.

Lance Corporal Kisby on Operation *Silicon*, bayonet fixed.

HEAVY MACHINE GUN

Vikings test-firing an HMG on Herrick 11.

In British Army service the updated version of the venerable US M2 .50-calibre machine gun is called the L1A1 12.7mm Heavy Machine Gun (HMG). This popular weapon was deployed as part of the FSGs in all the *Herrick* operations and gave a good account of itself. The one drawback of this reliable, hard-hitting and popular machine gun was its weight and the weight of its ammunition. Like other support weapons, it was just feasible for a man to carry the HMG in Afghan terrain, but only for a short distance and with a limited supply of ammunition, so it was usually fired from a vehicle such as the WMIK. With a range of 1,500–2,000m and a rate of fire of over 400 rounds per minute, it was a very useful weapon, which combined well with the others deployed by a Fire Support Group. In British service it has a new 'soft mount' that limits the recoil and improves accuracy, and it has a quick-change barrel so that fire can be maintained over extended periods.

A Recce Scimitar on high ground.

There was a particularly wide gap in the trees, like a firebreak, which the Taliban now started to cross at speed, still carrying their weapons. The Recce Platoon was some 2km away, which the Taliban may have considered too long a range, but in fact was ideal for the Scimitar's 30mm Rarden cannon, linked to the excellent Battle Group Thermal Imager sight. Recce opened Rarden fire as the Taliban crossed the gap from right to left; the WMIKs of the FSG joined in too with their heavy machine guns. Colour Sergeant Thurston gave clipped fire-control orders to ensure the fire was distributed to best effect, and the Taliban died in droves – at least 30 over the next 45 minutes.

Viewed from high ground, past Habibullah Kalay, this is the area through which the Taliban had to retreat.

Meanwhile, back with B Company, 5 and 7 Platoons continued to press forward from 15.30 to 17.30. Major Aston heard what was happening on the battle group radio net, so he was determined to pin down as many Taliban as possible, but many of them were starting to flee to the northeast. He therefore ordered all his platoons to go firm in the compounds they were currently in and to mark their positions with smoke. He then brought in Apaches via his JTAC to target all sign of Taliban up close to the platoons. This was an effective tactic, as the Apaches had a good view and devastating weapons, and after this 5 and 7 Platoons were able to spring forward against greatly reduced resistance. 6 Platoon was reached by around 17.30 and resupplied with ammunition and water.

At battalion headquarters near the Red Fort, the brigade commander visited the commanding officer and confirmed

A Viking soldier in a poppy field on Operation *Silicon*.

that a battalion of US 82nd Airborne would be landed to the north that night to prevent any Taliban infiltrating back into the Habibullah Kalay area. Impressed with the speed of the Vikings' advance, the brigadier confirmed that the construction of a patrol base in Habibullah Kalay would start promptly the next day. Carver had a decision to make: he could either ask B Company to move forward again to the exploitation 'Line Purple' – literally a purple line marked on a map to indicate the limit of movement for tactical groupings on the ground – or he could pull back A Company and the ANA to conform to

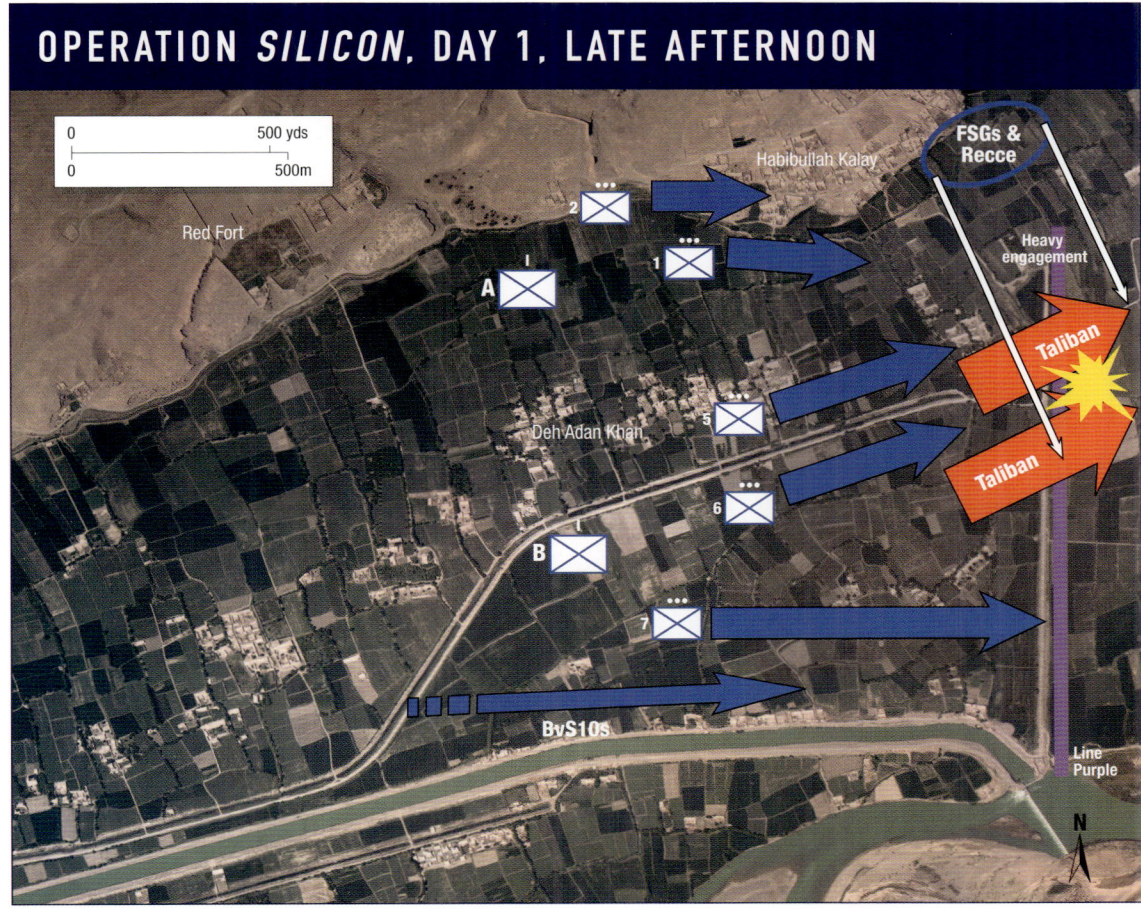

OPERATION *SILICON*, DAY 1, LATE AFTERNOON

A Company advancing in
BvS10s.

B Company's current location. Fully aware of how hard they had fought, Carver decided
that one last push was needed, and so he gave the order and B Company pressed on to Line
Purple before last light, across the killing zone littered with Taliban bodies.

The next day, after a short reconnaissance, the men from 8th Regiment (Armoured),
Royal Engineers started to build the Habibullah Kalay patrol base. During the morning of
Day 2, Major Biddick held a *shura* (meeting) with the locals in the village, to explain clearly
to them what was going on. That same, busy day, A Company was tasked with clearing out
the compounds that formed the village of Barak zai Kalay some 1.5km to the north-east,
both to keep the enemy on the back foot and to defend in more depth. There was intelligence
that the Taliban was planning something here. Assembling the whole of A Company Group
in BvS10s with Recce and FSG support, Biddick organised what could be described as an
intelligence-led mechanised advance to contact during the afternoon.

Dismounting near the compounds of Barak zai Kalay, with Recce and FSG to their left
on the higher ground, the plan was for A Company to provoke a Taliban response then take
it on with heavy fire support. No Taliban were encountered, so Biddick ordered 2 Platoon
to set off a bar mine – but even this very loud explosion did not provoke a response.
Eventually, just as dusk was falling, the Taliban opened fire on A Company with small arms,
82mm mortars and even B-11 107mm rockets. Most of their firing points were seen by the
thermal imagers of the FSG. There then followed 'a bit of a turkey shoot' which destroyed
many tens of Taliban and, importantly, their longer-ranged weapons.

Major Biddick holding a *shura* (or meeting).

By nightfall this phase of the operation was wound up, the patrol base in Habibullah Kalay was completed and occupied, and the Viking battle group recovered back to Camp Bastion.

Operation *Silicon* had been an unqualified success, with all its objectives achieved and at least 95 Taliban killed on the first day alone, but probably many more. In total, the Taliban may have taken more than 150 casualties. The Vikings suffered no fatalities on this operation, just a handful of minor injuries. The worst of these was Private Shepherd's shrapnel injury, but he was able to carry on fighting after being patched up. An early and critical test for the battle group had been passed with flying colours. The whole battle group felt that it had been exposed to intense combat, tested, but not found wanting. They had achieved the desired military effect and won their brigade commander's confidence.

As the first major operation of the tour, the success of *Silicon* was important. Had things gone wrong, *Herrick 6* might have been very different. The momentum established by this operation carried the 1st Battalion forward and several lessons were learned: principally, that a backstop or blocking force was as important as, or even more important than, the assaulting sweepers. However, the difficulty of positively identifying the Taliban who were so adept at blending into the local population at a moment's notice meant that the relative importance of sweeper and backstop would remain a complex equation.

Operation *Silicon* probably displaced and disrupted the Taliban badly. They needed time to reorganise, but the appearance of the new patrol base in Habibullah Kalay further complicated their position.

3 Section of 7 Platoon, B Company a month after Operation *Silicon*.

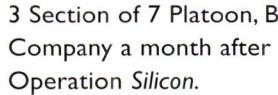

OPERATION *GHARSTE GHAR*, 28 JUNE–4 JULY 2007

With Gereshk now more secure due to Operation *Silicon,* the brigade commander next wanted to extend the area of security north-east to the area around Sangin, an important market town and a notable centre of Taliban activity. The first operation in late May, called *Lastay Kulang,* involved A Company operating in conjunction with Task Force 1 Fury of the US 82nd Airborne. By 7 June, this successful operation allowed 1 Platoon, led by Lieutenant Nick Denning, to move into Sangin town centre to occupy the base called Sangin DC, to be followed by the rest of the company by 11 June.

Throughout June, large numbers of Taliban were infiltrating back into Sangin, many from the Musa Qalah area but also numbers of foreign fighters. It was important to destabilise the Taliban by pushing troops into areas that they had previously seen as safe havens.

To counter this build-up of Taliban strength, Lieutenant Colonel Stuart Carver framed a battle-group operation to catch the Taliban between two pincers against a backstop feint. Faced with a conventional operation in the area, the Taliban would just skip away and escape to the west. To avoid this outcome, B (Suffolk) Company was to press south-west from Forward Operating Base Fox while A (Norfolk) Company pushed north-east from Sangin. In the centre a force of Estonian mechanised infantry and ANA would form the blocking force by conducting feints, while A and B Companies would press in as pincers behind the opponent. This would counter the recent Taliban practice of escaping across the Helmand river using a variety of improvised means. It was close to impossible for the Vikings to cross the river tactically – under Taliban fire it would be an almost suicidal move. At this stage there was insufficient helicopter lift available and the battalion had no boats. Although the BvS10 vehicles were supposed to be amphibious, it would be asking for trouble to use them to try to cross the difficult, fast-flowing Helmand river, especially if they came under fire. To complicate matters further, the RAF would not land in the Green Zone at this time, as a Chinook had been shot down a few days earlier, so casualty evacuation could be problematic. The only way to cut off the Taliban was to infiltrate on foot, but this too was full of dangers. It was difficult to balance these risks against the need to hurt the Taliban, but the commanding officer decided to go ahead with the operation, called *Gharste Ghar*.

A (NORFOLK) COMPANY

In the south, A Company prepared to make their thrust north-east from Sangin. Major Biddick was concerned that in order to trap the Taliban and prevent them escaping over the river, he needed to get his company behind them without them realising, which was potentially a tall order. The objective, named 'Caroline', was in the area of the village of Jusyalay in the middle of the Green Zone. At this stage in the conflict the IED threat was relatively minor; the main threat came from Taliban small arms. However, it was difficult for the ISAF forces to surprise the fleet-footed Taliban because they were becoming somewhat tied to their vehicles, reliant on them for both mobility and fire support. Wanting to break this reluctance to operate dismounted, Biddick devised a daring covert foot infiltration by night. The risk was greater, but so was the potential pay-off.

Their main opponents were known to be Mullah Kaduz's Taliban group, which was the last remaining group operating in the Jusyalay area. Once they were defeated, the intention was to switch to locally agreed building tasks, including laying the groundwork for an important Jusyalay irrigation project.

A Company planning and briefing.

The bulk of A Company would conduct their 12-km covert night infiltration on foot from Sangin on a narrow front between the main road and the river, while the vehicles simultaneously moved along the road, covered by Recce. At 20.30 on 28 June the company stepped off. Carrying enough equipment for three days' fighting, they were reasonably heavily loaded at around 40kg per man, but in day sack order, carrying their smaller packs. They expected to be in their lying-up point by 03.15 the following morning. The vehicles departed Sangin at 23.00. At 04.59 the following morning, the ANA and Estonian feint would begin.

A Company soldiers pause during their night insertion.

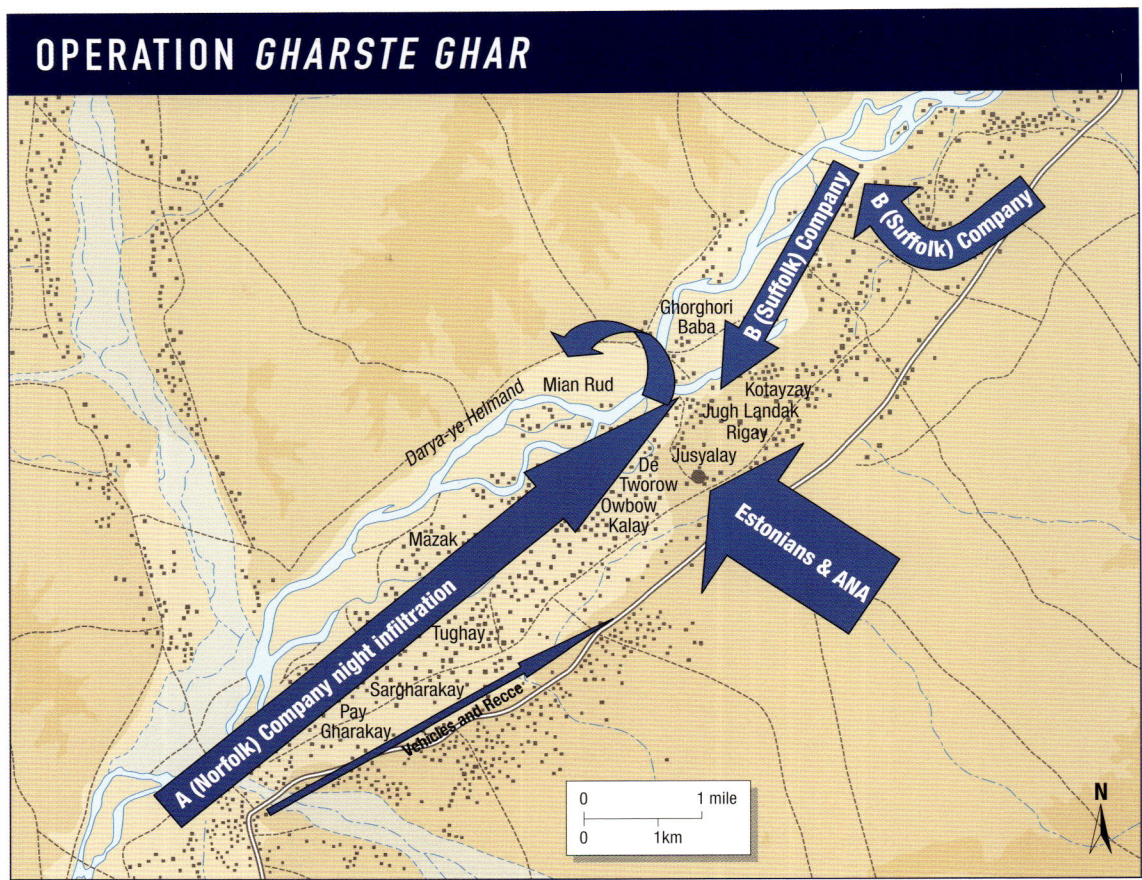

OPERATION *GHARSTE GHAR*

Somewhat against the odds, the covert move succeeded and the company arrived undetected. It is worth pausing briefly to look at the situation at first light from the Taliban's point of view. They would have been aware of the B Company approach from the north, and they would have seen the Estonians and ANA deploy into the centre and A Company's vehicles approaching along the road. However, the Taliban were unaware that the Estonians and ANA's deployment was a feint, nor did they realise that their rear escape routes to the river were blocked by A Company's dismounted infiltration.

Having got into the Taliban's backyard and achieved tactical surprise, A Company then embarked upon a long advance to contact; indeed, many involved described it as 'the longest day' of their tour. By this stage A Company was experienced, and the dismounted infantry were able to cooperate very effectively with their supporting weapons. The Taliban, almost impossible to see, even at less than 100-m range, were

A Company soldiers in the Green Zone on Operation *Gharste Ghar*.

SCREECH

Screech is a powder added to water to reduce the bad taste caused by sterilising it, usually with a tablet known as a 'steri tab'. Available in orange or lemon flavours, Screech has a very acidic taste, causing the drinker to pull a face as though about to scream or screech – hence the nickname.

effectively driven by the infantry 'beaters' into the fire of attack helicopters, mortars and other weapons. The advance became a string of company quick assaults, one after the other, each with the Taliban withdrawing as the Vikings closed in, only to be caught by supporting fires.

During this strenuous day, A Company had to live off the land to some extent, using local wells and the river for water. Their filtration and sterilisation equipment worked well, however, if occasionally supplemented by 'Screech'.

During the whole of this day, A Company had the initiative. All three platoons were in contact all day, driving the Taliban back and eventually linking up with the ANA. Private Charlesworth was injured and evacuated and there were several ANA casualties during these engagements. By late afternoon a Taliban counter-attack developed, but this was eventually defeated. Many Taliban started to leave the area, heading for the river as the light faded, but they were observed by the A Company Fire Support Group and destroyed by a barrage of 105mm light gun artillery fire. As dusk fell, the exhausted company went into all-round defence, occupying compounds and replenishing their food and water from local supplies.

Vikings advance on Operation *Gharste Ghar*.

A Company during
Operation *Gharste Ghar*.

On the following days the company concentrated on influencing operations, helping the locals, conducting *shura*s, providing cover for some of the work on irrigation ditches and consolidating their position in compounds. Most of the Taliban had departed the area by this stage, but there were some indications that they had gathered in Ghorghori Baba across the river. A rapid helicopter assault was organised and the company ran off the Chinook ramps, expecting to go straight into contact. However, there was no sign of the Taliban. They had clearly departed the area, so A Company moved on to the higher ground, where they could over-watch the river. This 'influence' stage of the operation lasted some eight days, with the company finally recovered to Sangin by vehicles on 2 July.

Another A Company *shura*
under way.

B (SUFFOLK) COMPANY

B (Suffolk) Company's part in the operation started on 28 June with 5 Platoon, under Lieutenant Ben Howes, and 6 Platoon, under Lieutenant Dave Broomfield, supported by their FSG, led by Captain Ollie Ormiston, and B Company Tactical Headquarters, as they deployed to Forward Operating Base Fox by Chinook. They set off at 15.00 into the Green Zone on what promised to be an extremely physically demanding operation. 7 Platoon remained in Nowzad.

Soon after setting off, 5 Platoon came under fire from a compound ahead. After silencing the Taliban with return fire, Major Aston ordered the platoon to go left flanking fast to catch the retreating Taliban as 6 Platoon gave covering fire. At this point 6 Platoon also came under fire, but with a swift manoeuvre Corporals Murphy and Adlington were able to kill two of the eight escaping Taliban as they headed away along a wall. Killing six more Taliban as they pressed forward, 6 Platoon cleared several compounds in Attack State Red and found a range of weaponry and Taliban equipment in the compounds.

By early evening the company was approaching the village of Kshatah Malazi, which they took swiftly, killing two armed Taliban in the process. They then pressed on to the bank of the Helmand river. Moving silently in the encroaching gloom, the company established over-watch locations on the riverbank, where they were pestered by insects all night. During the early evening, they received orders to press on to Jusyalay the next day. Following the proven sweep and backstop tactics, the commanding officer was seeking to use B Company to drive the Taliban south into A Company. Major Aston received permission to swing south via Kotayzay village, where he suspected a group of Taliban were based.

Vikings in the pre-dawn.

In the dark, moonless pre-dawn of 29 June, 5 Platoon led the company towards Kotayzay. By 05.00 they were halted 1,000m north of the village. Redeploying using the concealment of drainage ditches, the company shook out so that 5 Platoon was on the right (to the west), with Company Tactical Headquarters, 'Tac', in the centre and 6 Platoon to the left (east). Starting the assault just at first light, 5 Platoon got into Kotayzay unscathed, but 6 Platoon came under automatic fire during which Private Luke Watson was hit in the arm and ribs. Returning fire, 6 Platoon managed to silence some of the compounds, with Lance Corporal Ashby using an AT-4 anti-tank missile successfully against one.

AT-4

Although designed for anti-tank work, the Swedish-made AT-4 rocket launcher was employed on *Herrick 6* as a general-purpose weapon against enemy in compounds and dug-in positions. It has an 84mm warhead, fired from a single disposable launcher with a considerable back-blast due to the recoilless design and with a range of about 400m. The Vikings used the AT-4 with some success, but sometimes the effectiveness of the warhead against the thick walls of Afghan compounds was disappointing.

AT-4 rocket launcher.

With 5 Platoon almost flanking the Taliban-held compounds, mortar fire from the Vikings' own mortar platoon was soon also falling on the edge of the village, shortly followed by an airstrike from Harrier GR9s dropping a 500-lb bomb. The suppressive effect of this fire meant that the wounded Private Watson could be pulled back into cover. After some discussion with Lieutenant Broomfield, the company commander decided that, in the absence of a helicopter casualty evacuation, the whole company would have to turn around and patrol back 1,500m to cover the extraction of the casualty by BvS10 from Route 611, the main road.

Corporals Thorne and Mason regroup with Lieutenant Howes of 5 Platoon.

Emboldened by such an apparent retreat, the Taliban followed B Company and brought them repeatedly under automatic small-arms and RPG fire. Taking cover in canal ditches and compounds, the company sought to make the most of their considerable air power in order to turn the tables on the Taliban. Most members of the company will always remember the 'dash of death' they made over open ground to get into a compound, with covering fire being provided by US Apaches firing flechette rounds and even a B-1B Lancer strategic bomber. By 11.00 the company was secure in compounds near the main road, but they were exhausted and, reluctantly accepting the need for rest, Major Aston ordered an hour's break for the soldiers to replenish their water from a well and eat some food.

BvS10s were used for casualty evacuation (casevac).

Stepping off at midday with 5 Platoon in the lead, the company was in contact again within half an hour. 6 Platoon took a heat-exhaustion casualty as Corporal Adlington collapsed and Lance Corporal Tony Warwick in Company Tac was hit badly in the legs by shrapnel fragments from an RPG-7 burst. After an intense effort to fight and carry their three casualties out of the Green Zone, the company emerged at the rendezvous point on the main road to evacuate their wounded, who were driven back to Forward Operating Base Fox in BvS10s and taken on by Chinook to Camp Bastion.

By 16.00 the company had deployed back to the riverbank and established over-watch positions again, this time supported by snipers and Javelin missiles, but at midnight, after a brief rest, they were on the move once more. The next day, 30 June, was to be busy and difficult. Supported by snipers, 6 Platoon was deployed in a compound on the outskirts of Kotayzay to provide fire support; the snipers conducted an effective 600-m shoot to kill three armed Taliban. 5 Platoon pushed into the village, covered by 6 Platoon, but soon ran into trouble. Deploying a section on a compound roof for covering fire, Second Lieutenant Ben Howes led 5 Platoon round the side of the compound, but the Taliban had flanked him. After several more flanking movements, 5 Platoon was in danger of being entirely cut off and surrounded. It was by now 08.30 and Major Aston brought up 6 Platoon to destroy the offending Taliban. 5 Platoon were reasonably safe on their compound roof returning fire, but they could not manoeuvre.

Corporal Owen's section of 6 Platoon was deployed on one flank while Corporal Murphy's section led the way down a ditch. As they were making their way along, a brave Taliban fighter was able to close and fire an RPG-7 into the section at very close range. The rocket bounced off Private Thompson's body armour, exploding in the bank between him and Private Perry. In the confines of the ditch the RPG had a considerable blast effect, with fragments and shrapnel severely wounding four Vikings and a Royal Engineer. Thompson

A Chinook conducting casevac.

and Perry were lucky to survive such a near blast, and Corporal Murphy, Private Green and the Royal Engineer were badly wounded.

Taliban fighters concealed in a tree line continued to pour fire into Corporal Murphy's section. While Sergeant Browning set about that most difficult of a platoon sergeant's tasks – the evacuation of wounded under enemy fire – Lieutenant Broomfield eventually got enough fire organised and the platoon was able to extract all five wounded men safely without further casualties. Major Aston arrived at the safe area, where Sergeant Browning had lined up the casualties along a wall to make it easier for the medics to treat them.

Casualty evacuation was the priority. The air commander changed the rules, allowing a Chinook to come into the Green Zone to conduct the evacuation. After carrying the casualties on stretchers with all their equipment a gruelling 1,500m, the company arrived safely at the helicopter landing site and all five casualties were extracted within half an hour. During this phase the air assets were again effective, dropping 500-lb bombs and undertaking strafing attacks. The Taliban in the tree line were destroyed – the Apaches reported some 12 bodies, killed by a combination of B Company and the air assets.

The already under-strength 6 Platoon was now no longer able to carry on pressing the fight in Kotayzay. After a discussion with the commanding officer, it was agreed that

B Company would be reinforced by an additional platoon from 3 Company of the Grenadier Guards. Over the following five days, until 5 July, B Company continued to press the Taliban back by hard patrolling and fighting. They covered some 70km during this time, but suffered eight casualties. Perhaps the most important effect of this operation was that the Taliban could no longer consider this area a safe haven.

The combination of a sound plan, a surprise night infiltration on foot and some very intense fighting by A and B Companies made Operation *Gharste Ghar* a notable success. The Taliban were driven out of one of their key areas, which allowed the commencement of effective influence operations. Later an important irrigation project could begin in Jusyalay, which was seen as a considerable success.

Vikings crossing a ditch during *Gharste Ghar*.

STEELBACKS IN AFGHANISTAN

Throughout the Afghanistan campaign the territorial soldiers of the 3rd Battalion, the Steelbacks, have made a significant contribution. The challenges of operational deployment for a Territorial soldier are considerable. Not only does he have to integrate with his host unit, prove himself on operations and perform to the same high standard as a regular soldier, but he also has to re-integrate back into his civilian job on return. This last process can be quite difficult, but most Steelbacks would probably assert that the benefits of the life experience gained from an operational tour far outweigh any problems.

Some 30 members of the battalion deployed on *Herrick 5* in support of 42 Commando Royal Marines in 2006. Around 13 Steelbacks then deployed on *Herrick 6* with the Vikings, about 31 on *Herrick 11* and a further 25 deployed to support 66 Squadron in Afghanistan. During *Herrick 12* a total of 21 Steelbacks deployed in support of the 1st Battalion, The Mercian Regiment, and by *Herrick 16* some 29 Steelbacks deployed with the Vikings. In addition, two formed platoons of Steelbacks have been deployed as described later.

Overall, this has given the 3rd Battalion a vast leavening of recent operational experience. Precise figures are difficult, as many Steelbacks have served on more than one tour while others have left; however, it is likely that at any one time more than 100 members of the battalion have completed an operational tour. This probably makes the 3rd Battalion the most operationally experienced infantry battalion in the Territorial Army – a considerable source of pride for them and the Regiment as a whole.

Steelbacks on patrol in Kabul.

HERRICK 6: VIKING WITH SNIPER RIFLE AND LADDER

L96A1 SNIPER RIFLE

The L96A1 sniper rifle was introduced into service in 1986 and quickly proved to be dependable and accurate; it is still an effective weapon in well-trained hands. Although it fired the old standard NATO 7.62 x 51mm rounds, these were usually more carefully manufactured and so more consistent, accurate and expensive 'sniper ammunition'. The L96A1 was a single-shot, bolt-action rifle with a 10-round box magazine. It was normally used with a Schmidt and Bender 6 x 42 telescopic sight and was fitted, but not always used, with a small bipod for improved stability. There were also special variants adapted for Arctic warfare.

The L96A1 was used by the Viking sniper platoon on *Herrick 6* but was largely replaced by the L115A3 on later tours. However, some L96A1s continued in use in multiples of the rifle platoons on the later tours.

C Company snipers using the L96A1 on Herrick 6.

OPERATION *HERRICK 11,*
OCTOBER 2009–APRIL 2010

The next tour of Afghanistan for the 1st Battalion was very different. The build-up to *Herrick 11* was a stop-go process as the political machinations of Gordon Brown's Labour government strove to minimise the number of troops committed, while senior military officers argued a clear need for more troops on the ground. This went on throughout the summer of 2009 with the 1st Battalion repeatedly receiving orders to prepare for deployment, only to be stood down. Despite this, the battalion was well trained as it had just completed a session on a standby task called Spearhead and the commanding officer, now Lieutenant Colonel James Woodham, MC, was determined that the men would be as well prepared as possible during a seven-week spell of intensive pre-deployment training.

When the call finally came, the battalion was required to deploy 400 men as two rifle company groups to other battle groups, a support company and battalion headquarters on separate tasks. This led to a somewhat unusual but entirely logical grouping. A (Norfolk) and C (Essex) rifle companies deployed, each brought up to strength by a platoon from B (Suffolk) Company. 7 Platoon went to A Company, who deployed to the Household Cavalry Battle Group in Musa Qalah. 6 Platoon went to C Company, who deployed to the 1st Battalion Grenadier Guards Battle Group based in Nad-e-Ali. The support D (Cambridgeshire) Company deployed to a Danish battle group in Gereshk. Finally, battalion headquarters deployed to Lashkar Gah to take command of the Afghan National Police mentoring effort.

The situation in Afghanistan had also changed greatly, as a US troop surge had taken place, allowing some reductions in the UK area of responsibility. The overall ISAF command in Afghanistan had also undergone something of a transformation, as US General Stanley A. McChrystal – with his doctrine of 'Courageous Restraint' – had moved the focus to rebuilding trust and away from simple 'kinetic' operations. This represented a major switch in emphasis away from simply killing Taliban fighters, and towards a much more 'hearts and minds' approach. Concurrently, however, there had been a very effective but controversial US campaign against the Taliban and al-Qaeda leadership using precision weapons delivered by unmanned aerial vehicles. The importance of cooperating with the ANA and ANP also increased during this period; indeed, the forthcoming tour would see truly joint patrols.

The Taliban themselves had also changed and adapted – possibly forced upon them in part by heavy casualties. The main Taliban weapon of choice had become the IED, which could wound and kill ISAF personnel without the risk of heavy casualties that was associated with shooting incidents. The Taliban remained eminently capable of recruiting foreign fighters as well as a new generation of local insurgents. Their supply lines were also intact, and able to deliver large quantities of IED-making materials into Helmand province. They were still perfectly capable of mounting shooting attacks, but they had become ever more cunning in their combination of lures, multiple IEDs and, often, shootings. As time went on, they devised ever more clever ways of initiating IEDs, and reduced the metal content of their IEDs making them increasingly hard to detect. It was into this more complex and challenging situation that the well-trained Vikings deployed.

ISAF RANGE GAP

Ever observant of the battlefield behaviour of their enemies, during the period around 2008–2009 the Taliban increasingly noticed that the effectiveness of British return fire tended to fall away at ranges over 600m. This was due to a number of factors, but chiefly because the ballistic properties of the smaller NATO 5.56mm x 45 round meant that accuracy and hitting power fell away markedly at longer ranges. This applied regardless of whether the round was fired from an SA80, LSW or LMG. In addition, sights were normally calibrated only out to 600m and the then-current doctrine was not to train or to use section weapons beyond that range. Consequently, the Taliban started to open the range of shooting contacts, typically out to 800–900m, at which distance the PKM machine gun (see p.80) was still reasonably effective but would also be relatively immune from accurate return fire. In addition, more 7.62mm Dragunov sniper rifles with telescopic sights started to appear, although with this weapon accurate shooting at ranges of 800m was more a matter of the skill and training of the sniper. Combined, these factors put British troops at a temporary disadvantage in shooting contacts at long range. The response was swift and effective. In

the first instance, British troops began carrying more and more 7.62mm GPMGs per multiple; in some cases two or even three men were carrying this venerable but excellent and hard-hitting machine gun. The GPMG in the light role – that is, fired from its bipod – is easily effective out to 800–900m, and some good shots will even achieve hits out to 1,000m or more. Sniper rifles with telescopic sights were also issued more widely, although there was a slightly longer training delay, as more men needed to be trained in long-range shooting techniques. Initially these were the L96A1 sniper rifles, but from 2010 a new, even more accurate sniper rifle was issued: the L115, with an effective range of over 1,100m. Also, between 2008 and 2010 the new 7.62mm L129A1 sharpshooter rifle was purchased under an Urgent Operational Requirement process and issued. With the heavier 7.62mm round and an excellent sight, these weapons combined effectively to close the range gap. Ever adaptive in their tactics, the Taliban increasingly abandoned long-range shooting contacts after 2010 in favour of more IED attacks.

The 7.62mm Dragunov sniper rifle.

VIKING ON *HERRICK 11* WITH GPMG

C (ESSEX) COMPANY ON OPERATION *HERRICK 11*

C (Essex) Company Group was placed under operational command of the 1st Battalion Grenadier Guards Battle Group and employed as a ground-holding company in the southern part of the Nad-e-Ali district of Helmand province. The company was divided between three locations: Company Headquarters, 9 Platoon and Fire Support Group Charlie were based in the north-west in Patrol Base Silab; 6 Platoon, attached from B Company, was based to the south in Checkpoint Paraang; and 10 Platoon was based to the east in Checkpoint Haji-Alem. A large number of UK and US attachments were split between the three locations.

DATE	ORGANISATION	NAME	SUMMARY
October 2009	C Company	Start of tour	Company HQ, 9 Platoon and FSG Charlie deployed to Patrol Base Silab, 6 Platoon to Checkpoint Paraang and 10 Platoon to Checkpoint Haji-Alem.
7–19 November 2009	C Company	Operation *Tor Barratalal*	Some 22 compounds west of Silab were cleared for reoccupation by civilians. Taliban defeated in several engagements. Operation end marked with an outreach *shura*.
28–30 November 2009	C Company	Operation *Tor Wasal Kawal*	Large, eventful company resupply operation to Checkpoint Paraang in Khushhal Kalay (described in detail below).
5–10 December 2009	Battle Group	Operation *Tor Saakhtan*	Support to large aid convoy, highly kinetic with over 15 contacts and half the vehicle convoy either destroyed or damaged. Aid arriving at Khushhal Kalay had a very positive effect.
7 December 2009	6 Platoon		Lance Corporal Adam Drane killed while on duty in Paraang.
11 December 2009	C Company		Occupation of temporary Checkpoint Blue 37 until full checkpoint built.
13 December 2009	1 Royal Anglian Recce Platoon	Ambush	Moving into covert ambush position south of Noor Mohammed Khan Kalay, Recce Platoon springs a very successful ambush. Seven Taliban killed.
3 January 2010	6 Platoon		Private Robert Hayes killed while on patrol near Paraang.
29 January–5 February 2010	C Company	pre-Operation *Moshtarak*	Company shaping operations as a preliminary to Operation *Moshtarak* led to 30 Taliban killed and 14 wounded.
3 February 2010	C Company and D Company Royal Welsh	Operation *Moshtarak*	Khushhal Kalay village cleared.
11 February 2010	C Company HQ	Relocated	C Company HQ moved to Patrol Base Samsor north of Khushhal Kalay, next to 'Charing Cross' road junction.
24 February 2010	C Company	Khushhal Kalay rebuild	Central mosque refurbishment and new school building started in Khushhal Kalay; over 1,000 pairs of shoes distributed to village children.
3–8 March 2010	C Company	Learning to Learn initiative	Initiative to distribute over 3,000 exercise books and pens to children in area to stimulate desire to learn prior to completion of school building.
9–30 March 2010	C Company	Operation *Tor Chakush*	Sweep 2km south of Noor Mohammed Khan Kalay leads to arrest of 14 suspected Taliban; no shots fired.
2 April 2010	C Company	Handover	Handover to Corunna Company, 1st Battalion The Duke of Lancaster's Regiment.

Due to the intensity of insurgent activity, much of which emanated from Marjah, a Taliban-controlled district to the south, the first four months of the company's tour were characterised by intensive combat operations, with the result that attempts to interact with the local population proved very difficult. In spite of this, and thanks to the professionalism of the company group, a variety of initiatives were introduced in the early part of 2010 to encourage the local population to consider the Afghanistan government in a more favourable light. For this to happen the locals had to know that their basic security conditions had been met; this was achieved convincingly through Operation *Moshtarak*, which means 'together' in Dari, the official language of Afghanistan. This large ISAF offensive into Marjah in February 2010 was designed to defeat the last major Taliban stronghold in central Helmand. It was the largest joint operation in Afghanistan to date, consisting of approximately 15,000 British, American and Afghan forces. The associated benefits from the success of this large operation within C Company's area were vast, and included:

- Additional manpower, including partnering with an ANA and an ANCOP company.
- The creation of seven additional checkpoints in order to dominate the area.
- Increased freedom of movement for security forces and the local population.
- Increased interaction and support from expectant local tribal leaders.

Operation *Moshtarak* created the conditions for C Company Group, alongside its newly acquainted Afghan partners and Afghan government departments, to transform a once violent nest of insurgency into an area orientated towards reconstruction and enduring development. In order to place these events in more context, an overview of the key C Company events across the whole tour is shown in the above table.

Before the local cooperation and reconstruction that marked the end of the tour could begin, however, the first months of *Herrick 11* saw some darker days.

KHUSHHAL KALAY

Between 28 and 30 November 2009 a company group operation named *Tor Wasal Kawal*, which translates approximately as 'Black Link-Up', was conducted to enable the delivery of vital stores by road convoy between Patrol Base Silab and Checkpoint Paraang. Checkpoint Paraang was situated at the southern end of the 'gridded', square village of Khushhal Kalay, which by this stage of the tour had already lived up to its historical reputation as an exceptionally hostile environment. Insurgents were able to exploit the complicated and

A typical building in Khushhal Kalay.

challenging terrain, intimidate the local population and launch relentless attacks against C Company personnel – mainly 6 Platoon, as the village was situated within their platoon area. The atmosphere in the village always seemed sinister and cold, with a sense of imminent danger. Every man remained on full alert, sure that something would happen, but unsure what, when or where.

In outline, the operation was planned as follows: 6 Platoon, based inside Khushhal Kalay and having deployed by foot, and 9 Platoon, to the north of Khushhal Kalay and having inserted by helicopter with the company's Tactical Headquarters (Tac HQ), would dominate the route prior to a clearance operation by

C Company Tac and 9 Platoon at Camp Bastion prior to Operation *Tor Wasal Kawal*.

Royal Engineer search teams checking for IEDs. Once this was complete, a convoy of vehicles, escorted by Fire Support Group Charlie, would depart Patrol Base Silab and travel to Checkpoint Paraang to deliver the vital stores.

The drivable road route from Silab to Khushhal Kalay runs almost due east for 1.5km, then turns 90° at a road junction called 'Charing Cross' and continues almost due south for 500m before entering the village, then a further kilometre due south through the denser terrain of Khushhal Kalay before arriving at Paraang.

Throughout the operation, 10 Platoon would provide flank protection to the north and east of Khushhal Kalay, a variety of assets would provide over-watch from the flanks and above, and every member of the company would seek to engage with the local population in order to achieve influence and gain a better understanding of the environment. Once the stores were delivered and the vehicles had returned to Patrol Base Silab, the various cordons would be collapsed and all personnel would extract to their relevant bases. This was a simple plan, but one which would be tested to its limits, revealing both the ferocity and ingenuity of insurgents operating within the area and the courage and leadership of C Company Group.

SERGEANT HILL IN KHUSHHAL KALAY

The next part of Operation *Tor Wasal Kawal* is told mainly from the perspective of Sergeant Ashley Hill from Essex. His part in the operation began with the arrival at Camp Bastion of his multiple, along with the rest of 9 Platoon and the company commander's small Tac HQ, in order to conduct detailed planning and to liaise with the aircrew. A multiple – that is, a small group, usually of between eight and 12 men – was to be inserted into Khushhal Kalay at night by Chinook. While briefing the pilot Sergeant Hill was especially clear that he needed to avoid a particular small field near the landing site. Only about 100 metres square, the field had been irrigated a few days before and was now knee-deep mud.

Meanwhile, the rest of the ten-man multiple, call-sign 52 Bravo (52B), checked their weapons: two GPMG; two light machine guns (LMG); six SA80 A2 rifles, two with underslung grenade launchers (UGL). They carried Vipir thermal-imaging night sights, effective out to 600m, and the image intensifier Common Weapon Sight effective out to about 300m. In addition, they had a cut-down 2-m lightweight 'Barma' ladder and two LASM rocket-launchers. They also took three shovels. Every man had a Personal Role Radio (PRR) with a range of a few hundred metres in the open, less in built-up areas, and Sergeant Hill and his second-in-command Lance Corporal Gibbs had Bowman secure radios with a range of many kilometres.

SERGEANT HILL'S MULTIPLE, 52B ORGANISATIONAL DIAGRAM

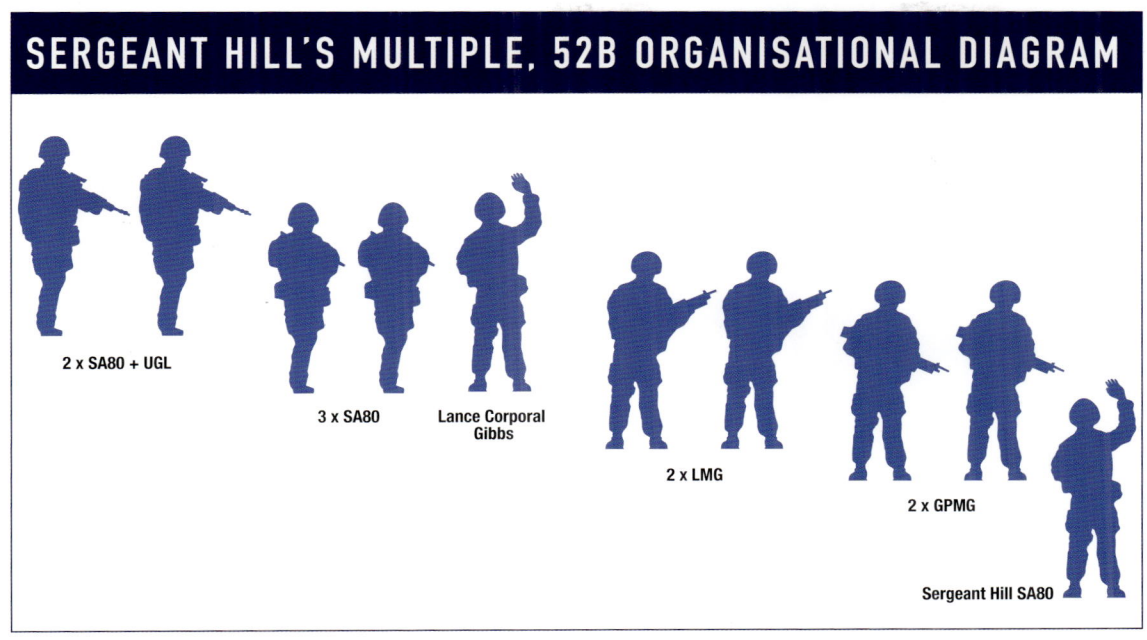

2 x SA80 + UGL

3 x SA80

Lance Corporal Gibbs

2 x LMG

2 x GPMG

Sergeant Hill SA80

LASM

LASM being carried by a US soldier in Afghanistan.

The Light Anti-Structures Missile (LASM) rocket launcher was purchased as an urgent operational requirement. It is a disposable system: a single rocket is fired from a telescopic launcher that is then discarded. It looks like the old M72 or 66mm rocket launcher that would be familiar to those who served more than 30 years ago; indeed, it is an anti-structures development of this venerable old anti-tank rocket. It has the significant advantages of being handy and reasonably lightweight, but because of its relatively small warhead it could not always deliver the impact required for targets hidden behind thick Afghan compound walls. Although sighted out to 500m, it was usually used at much closer ranges. It weighed 4.3kg per launcher and took only a few seconds to prepare for firing.

The 52B multiple was inserted into Khushhal Kalay in the early hours of 28 November 2009. It was a clear, cold night – without cloud cover night-time temperatures in this area in November regularly drop to -10°. True to form, the Chinook landed them in the only irrigated field for miles around, leaving them in knee-deep mud in the dark.

KHUSHHAL KALAY: SERGEANT HILL AND 52B, DAYS 1 & 2: 28–29 NOVEMBER

The multiple was on 'hard routine' – that is, with minimum equipment. The majority of the 50kg that each man carried was ammunition. They carried little spare clothing and very little food, as they were expecting the operation to last just one, possibly two days.

Struggling through the mud, the men of 52B made their way north out of the field into the next one, then dug three 1m-deep trenches before dawn broke at 05.00. Unfortunately Private Vaisy suffered a severe attack of diarrhoea and vomiting, leaving Sergeant Hill no option but to evacuate him as soon as it was light. His evacuation reduced the multiple to nine.

At the same time, 6 Platoon were moving north from Paraang along the main road through Khushhal Kalay with the aim of clearing and securing the main north–south road through the centre of the village. The main route clearance started at first light from Silab and they made steady progress along the road, reaching 'Charing Cross' junction by around 14.00. The right turn was uneventful, but as the Royal Engineer route-clearing search team, called Brimstone, approached the northern edge of Khushhal Kalay, they discovered an IED with a command wire, which took many hours to clear. As the light began to fail the company commander, Major Chris Davies, realised that it would not be possible to complete the resupply mission before nightfall, so he decided to halt the operation at that location and recommence the clearance at first light the next day. The decision was also influenced by the difficulties 6 Platoon had encountered as they cleared north through the village (described in the next section). As they had taken casualties, their ability to provide cover inside the village was reduced.

At this point it was decided that Sergeant Hill's multiple, which had spent the day on over-watch, would move into the north-west corner of the village at first light. They therefore spent an uneventful night in their trenches, 'staging on' with one man alert while two got some rest – although with temperatures of around -10° and having eaten very little food, sleep was not easy to come by for the nine men of 52B.

By 05.00 on 29 November, first light, the multiple rendezvoused with call-signs Mongoose 54A and 54B with their armed Mastiff vehicles, led by Captain James Perrin and Sergeant Roberts, at the 'Northern Gate' – where the main road enters Khushhal Kalay from the north. Sergeant Hill's multiple took the opportunity to strip down their equipment to the minimum so that were as agile as

Vikings on the outskirts of Khushhal Kalay.

possible to climb up ladders, over roofs and over walls inside the village. They kept all their ammunition, water, the ladder and their Vallon mine detector, but left many other items of equipment with the Mastiffs. Sergeant Hill admits that this was 'a bit of a risky call but I wanted to be as light as I could when moving within the village'. At this time, the Bowman radio belonging to Lance Corporal Gibbs – the multiple second-in-command – malfunctioned, 'dropping its fill'. The 'fill' was the cryptographic code that enabled the Bowman to operate securely, so the multiple was down to a single long-range radio. Although each man retained his PRR, the range would be considerably reduced in the close confines of the village, making communications a cause for concern.

The multiple made its way into the north of the village, then moved in single file down the first lane, which was bounded by 5m-high walls. The only breaks in the walls were into compounds or at intersections. Some 200m along the lane, using his remaining Bowman radio, Sergeant Hill had a conversation with Sergeant Vickery of 6 Platoon, who knew the complex urban terrain of the village very well and suggested that 52B get on top of Compounds 11 and 4. Once one fire team – call-sign 52C with five men – was on top of Compound 11, Sergeant Hill moved with the remaining team, four men in total, onto the roof of Compound 4. The time was around 09.00 and at this point, with the outer protection, which also included 6 Platoon, in place, the vehicle convoy started to move south down the main road through Khushhal Kalay.

The heavily protected
Mastiff 2 vehicle, call-sign
Mongoose 54.

The convoy was led by Mastiffs 54A and B, then a medium-wheeled tractor, followed by an 8-ton Man SV truck carrying supplies, then four Demountable Rack Offload and Pickup System (DROPS) vehicles carrying large International Standards Organisation (ISO) containers. The first Mastiff passed Compound 23, then 11, so the bulk of the convoy was between there and Compound 1 when there was a massive explosion on the road. Over time, the Taliban had probably placed IEDs in a matrix throughout the village; some of the devices would have been very old but there were also more recent ones, including undetectable non-metal devices. The explosion was caused by the detonation of one of these – a very large IED. It was most probably detonated by a recently attached command wire; as other vehicles had already gone past the location, it could not have been detonated by a pressure plate.

The bulk of the explosion hit the fourth vehicle in the convoy, the 8-ton Man SV truck. It was carrying a large quantity of grenade and machine-gun ammunition, but fortunately none of this was detonated, which speaks well of the packaging – or it might have had more to do with luck. However, the two men in the SV, Captain Bernie Broad of the Grenadier Guards and Private Gurung of the Queen's Own Gurkha Logistics Regiment, were severely injured. The Taliban were clever to have targeted this vehicle – which was probably the most vulnerable but was carrying a valuable cargo – or they may just have been lucky. The blast generated a significant shock wave over a radius of 300–400m and one of the SV wheels flew off, nearly hitting the team on Compound 11. The road was effectively blocked by the truck wreckage.

As the IED detonated, small-arms fire intensified all around the village, with both of Sergeant Hill's teams engaged from all sides. The fire was mainly automatic and probably 7.62mm calibre, and there were many firing points. Sergeant Hill recalls that he 'stopped counting after six'. Wherever enemy firing points could be located, 52B returned fire. Over the PRR radio came the dreaded call: 'Man down'. Initially Sergeant Hill was not sure whether this related to the men in the SV truck or perhaps to the wheel that had narrowly missed his other team, or it could have been an injury from the small-arms fire. 'At this point the net [Bowman radio traffic] was going wild, so I got Private Roberts to find out on his

PRR what was going on and we established that we had two casualties, gunshot wounds, one to the chest and one to the leg, on Compound 11.'

A Viking under fire on a compound roof.

Sergeant Hill jumped off Compound 4, shouting to his team to follow, and they made their way back to Compound 11 as fast as they could. By the time they arrived, the team there had jumped off the roof with the casualties. Lance Corporal Gibbs had received a bullet hit, probably 7.62mm, just below the top of the upper chest plate of his Osprey body armour. Although the body armour had prevented the bullet penetrating, he had received a significant golf-ball-sized bruise from the impact. Despite having buckled with the force, Sergeant Hill noted that 'Lance Corporal Gibbs was a good lad so he was soon back on his feet'. Private Sean Holroyd had a gunshot wound to the leg, probably from a 7.62mm bullet. It had passed 'through and through' his thigh, leaving obvious entry and exit wounds, but had not hit the bone. As yet there was little bleeding and in fact Private Holroyd was experiencing a bit of an adrenalin rush. Although very cold to the touch, he was laughing and saying, 'Come on, Sarge, we need a bit of a photo.' The photo duly taken, the medic continued to patch his wound with a first field dressing, and then the casualties were ready to move.

Sergeant Hill ordered the LASM rocket-launcher to be fired at a wall with the intention of making a hole through which to evacuate the casualties. Unfortunately, the wall was LASM-proof and only a small hole resulted. Sergeant Hill had to get Sean Holroyd to climb over two walls with his leg wound. He was able to walk without morphine and managed the climb, even jumping down from both walls. 'Strong man, like an ox,' commented Sergeant Hill later.

When they arrived at the main road from where the Mastiffs were to evacuate the two wounded, Sergeant Hill saw the two casualties in the SV truck. Captain Bernie Broad, the brigade liaison officer, was hanging out of the gunner's position on top of the cab and Private Gurung, the driver, was on the ground having been blown out of the cab. Both were very seriously injured. As he got Private Holroyd into the back of the Mastiff, Sergeant Hill was ordered to evacuate Lance Corporal Gibbs as well. This was very much against Gibbs's wishes and Hill queried the order, but it had to be followed because there was a rule that, due to the risk of internal injuries and internal bleeding, all casualties after a bullet impact on body armour had to be evacuated. Gibbs later made a full recovery. Meanwhile, casualty evacuation helicopters were en route – a pair of American UH-60 Black Hawks.

American UH-60 Black
Hawk, call-sign 'Pedro'.

Sergeant Hill then led his multiple swiftly to the casualties at the SV truck, with the two Mastiffs providing some cover. Hill 'got a grip' of the chaotic scene confronting him. Once the injured men were clear of the wreckage, Hill used one of the Mastiffs to push the wreckage clear so that the road could be used. After receiving immediate care from the medic from the Mastiffs, these two casualties were taken 100m north and put into the back of the Mastiffs, under sporadic small-arms fire. At this point only three casualties were evacuated, as Lance Corporal Gibbs had decided that, regardless of orders, he was not leaving, and he got out of the Mastiff. After 'a bit of a telling off from the company second in command', a second Mastiff came back to collect a slightly chastened Gibbs. All four casualties were eventually extracted by Black Hawk helicopters, called Pedro from their call-sign.

During the afternoon, Apache attack helicopters were deployed and provided some top cover to the operations on the ground, occasionally involving very low over-flights at almost rooftop level. The Mastiffs were able to escort the ISO container vehicles into Paraang at the south of Khushhal Kalay, and empty DROPS vehicles returned north to Silab. It was during this time that Sergeant Roberts in Mongoose 54B encountered another large pre-positioned and undetected 100kg IED. Although it destroyed his Mastiff, removing most of the front third of the vehicle, it left Roberts and the driver with only minor injuries. Roberts later said, 'Apparently I was talking gibberish on the company net for a minute or so but settled down after a Lucky Strike cigarette'. Also during this afternoon, an unguided rocket, probably a Chinese-made 107mm, was fired at the Northern Gate. It did not hit any troops, although it did damage a shop.

For 52B, however, the task was not yet complete. There was a large amount of ammunition and other stores mixed in with the wreckage of the SV truck and, after the options had been considered, it was decided that this had to be recovered to Paraang. The decision was complex, as it might have been possible to destroy some of the stores in situ, but the risk of ammunition and the cryptography in the communications equipment falling into the wrong hands was significant.

Sergeant Hill's multiple, now down to six men as the medic had gone with the casualties, was deployed along the road and ordered to carry the stores from the wreckage by hand to Paraang, about 400m away – almost 8 tons of stores with six men! Two additional men from the Fire Support Group were soon added. Faced with this difficult task, Sergeant Hill commandeered the medium wheeled tractor (MWT) that was doing some base-improvement work in Paraang and 'persuaded' the driver to help: 'To this day I can still remember his face when I said he had to do this. He asked how many runs it would take and I said 4 or 5, but it took 12 or so in the end.'

A medium wheeled tractor (MWT).

It was dark by this time, around 19.00. Shifting the stores developed into a bit of a comedy turn, as the MWT had an orange flashing light and a distinctive reversing siren that made a beep-beep-beep noise – all rather incongruous as it did shuttle runs up and down the road with the bucket full of ammunition and stores. As Sergeant Hill had eaten no food for quite some time, it is easy to imagine the temptation when a box of apples and a quantity of frankfurter sausages were removed from the wreckage. Perhaps the best thing to say is that 6 Platoon in Paraang probably did not receive their full allocation of fresh rations that night.

This effective example of improvisation was complete by around 04.00 of Day 3. Concurrently, a wrecker vehicle was tasked to recover the remaining wreckage of the SV truck, escorted by Mastiffs; this recovery was completed overnight.

The remaining six men of multiple 52B then patrolled back north to Patrol Base Silab, joining the other multiple of the platoon, 52A, led by Lieutenant Greg Napier, and arriving at dawn, around 05.00. Lieutenant Napier's multiple had spent the operation to the north and east of the village, providing flank protection. This was a complex and eventful operation, but quite typical of the sort experienced on *Herrick 11*. For his outstanding conduct and especially his brave and calm management of the difficult situation around the first explosion, Sergeant Ashley Hill was later awarded the Military Cross.

L129A1 SHARPSHOOTER RIFLE

This larger-calibre 7.62mm rifle was issued to British troops in Afghanistan in 2009–10 as an urgent operational requirement to offset the emerging range gap. It is an accurate, hard-hitting automatic rifle with a 20-round magazine, and with a comfortable range out to 600–700m and beyond, especially when fitted with the Advance Combat Optical Gunsight (ACOG) with x6 magnification. It can also be fitted with the older Schmidt and Bender telescopic sight and Common Weapon Sight (CWS) or VIPIR-2 night sights.

Corporal Joe Warren with L129A1 sharpshooter rifle.

There were no sharpshooter rifles on *Herrick 6*, but they were issued roughly on a scale of one per 12-man multiple on *Herrick 11*. More were used on *Herrick 16*, when this popular weapon could be found on a scale of two or sometimes even three per multiple. Most of the platoons in B Company, for example, had three per platoon. The users said they loved it, confident of hitting individual targets at 700m, even when fired in a standing position, providing the weapon was rested on a platform. They did not mind the extra weight of this weapon and ammunition, considering the added accuracy, range and hitting power to be a good offset. There is a variant of the L129A1 called the sniper support weapon, which has additional flash suppression and other minor modifications.

6 Platoon in their base at
Checkpoint Paraang.

6 PLATOON IN KHUSHHAL KALAY

6 Platoon was normally part of B (Suffolk) Company, but was attached to C (Essex) Company due to the complexities of the task organisation of the battalion's deployment on Operation *Herrick 11*. Calling themselves 'The Mighty VI', they were deployed to the small base called Checkpoint Paraang on the southern edge of the village of Khushhal Kalay. Essentially this was the most south-westerly deployment of British troops in the region, and from this position they were to experience an especially intense tour.

Their tour was rather more 'kinetic' than that of other platoons in the company, as they encountered almost daily engagements and suffered many more casualties. Most of the contacts were from the south, the village itself being quieter for some of the time, although it was still very hostile. The platoon was relatively light on the ground – at one point they were reduced to just 17 men. The dense terrain surrounding the base could absorb many more troops. Much of the time they were therefore operating in what in earlier times might have been called 'section-level fighting patrols'. Two members of the platoon were killed in action during the tour: Lance Corporal Adam Drane on 7 December 2009, and Private Robert Hayes on 3 January 2010. A further four members of the platoon were seriously injured, and many suffered a host of minor injuries.

Inside the base at Paraang.

Lieutenant Dan Benstead
briefs 6 Platoon in Paraang.

As mentioned in the previous section, 6 Platoon's role in Operation *Tor Wasal Kawal* was to secure the main supply route running north–south through Khushhal Kalay by dominating the northern part and flanks of the village, thereby providing cover for the rest of C Company as they moved in from the north.

At 07.00 on 28 November the platoon commander, Lieutenant Dan Benstead, led his multiple, call-sign 51 Alpha (51A), north out of Paraang, together with Fire Teams 51 Charlie (51C), commanded by Corporal Alex Stearne from Wisbech, also multiple second in command, and 51 Delta (51D), led by Lance Corporal Adam Drane from Bury St Edmunds – a total of 12 men. The multiple was armed with one GPMG and two LMG machine guns, while the rest of the patrol had SA80A2s, with two UGLs. They were also carrying a 2m combat ladder and electronic counter-measure equipment. They each had a PRR, but only one Bowman radio was working in the multiple as the other had 'dropped its fill'. The men wore either Kestrel or Osprey body armour and either a Mark 6A or Mark 7 helmet – the platoon had a mixture at this time. With ammunition and water, the total load was around 41kg per man.

Sergeant Vickery, the platoon sergeant, led the second multiple, call-sign 51 Bravo (51B), together with Fire Teams 51 Echo (51E), led by Corporal Joseph Warren, also multiple second in command, and 51 Foxtrot (51F), led by Lance Corporal Monks. They had roughly the same weapon and equipment mix as the Alpha multiple, except they also had a sharpshooter rifle. Sergeant Vickery's Bravo multiple was to the east and to the rear of the Alpha multiple as they moved north into the centre of Khushhal Kalay. Lieutenant Benstead's Alpha multiple had reached the mosque in the centre of the village by around 07.30. At the same time, Sergeant Vickery moved to the north on Alpha's right, arriving at some waste ground by the crossroads at the centre of the village at 07.30. Under cover from the Alpha multiple around the mosque, Bravo moved up to Compound 12. So far the operation had been uneventful, as no Taliban radio traffic had been heard and there was no obvious 'dicking' in the village. 'Dicking' is a term used to describe suspicious terrorist activity – the watching, monitoring and following of patrols, usually while posing as civilians; sadly, it is a task often carried out by youths or children.

6 PLATOON IN KHUSHHAL KALAY

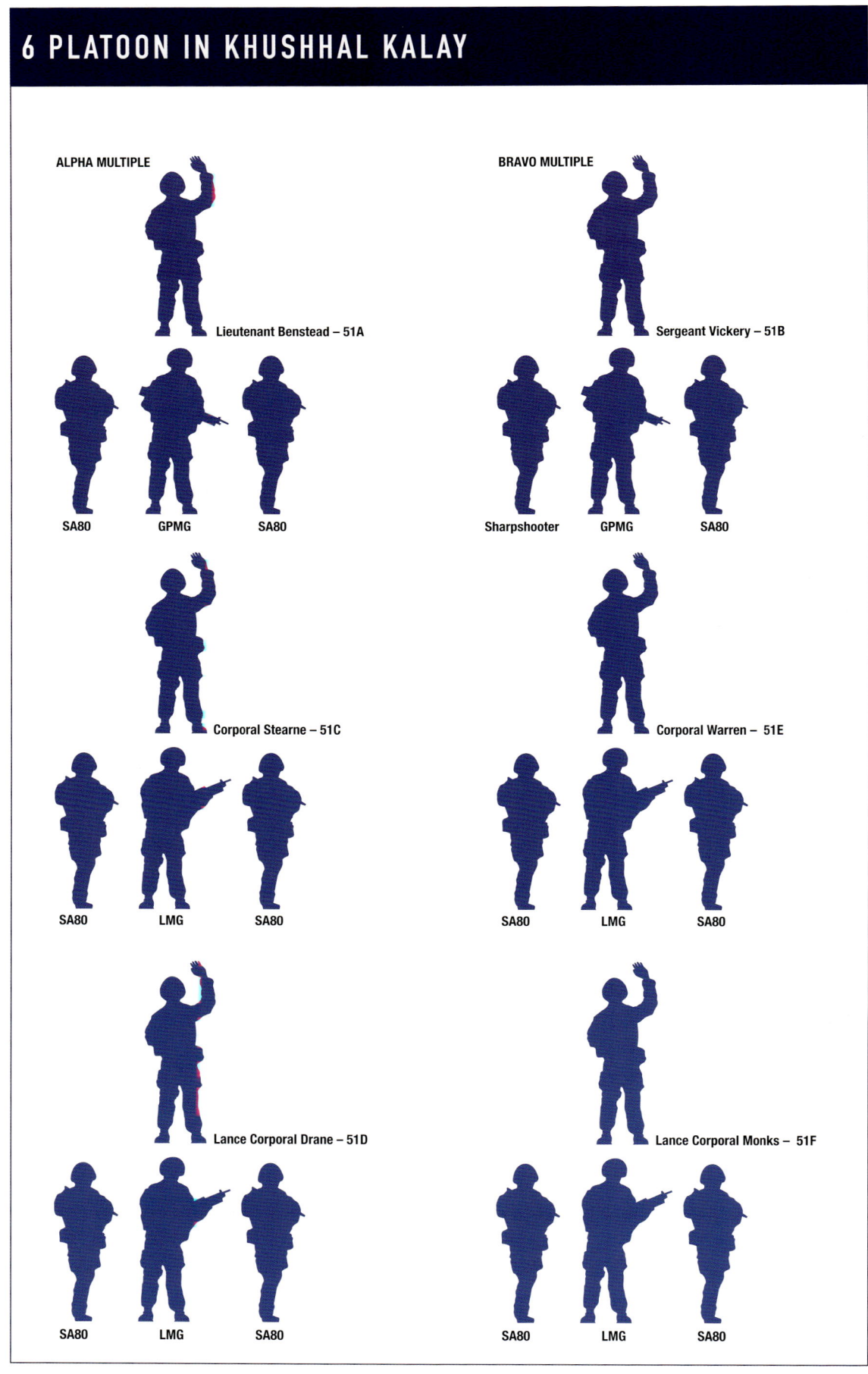

ALPHA MULTIPLE

Lieutenant Benstead – 51A

SA80   GPMG   SA80

Corporal Stearne – 51C

SA80   LMG   SA80

Lance Corporal Drane – 51D

SA80   LMG   SA80

BRAVO MULTIPLE

Sergeant Vickery – 51B

Sharpshooter   GPMG   SA80

Corporal Warren – 51E

SA80   LMG   SA80

Lance Corporal Monks – 51F

SA80   LMG   SA80

Both multiples then continued north. The Alpha multiple then split into two six-man teams, with the platoon commander and 51C arriving in Compound 23 by 08.30, leaving 51D, under Lance Corporal Drane, on the roof of Compound 1 as over-watch. As they moved, the Bravo multiple did the same: 51B and 51E went to Compound 21, leaving six men of 51F on the roof of Compound 12.

At this point Lieutenant Benstead reported into company headquarters by radio with his dispositions. He and Corporal Stearne were talking to four locals in the compound, but events then moved very quickly. Other members of the team found a Coca-Cola bottle converted into an IED initiation device, several car batteries, a vehicle under a tarpaulin and several motorbikes, all tending to confirm that the compound had been used for the preparation of IEDs. The local crowd quickly swelled to about 20 men, leaving the six men of 51C, who were spread widely

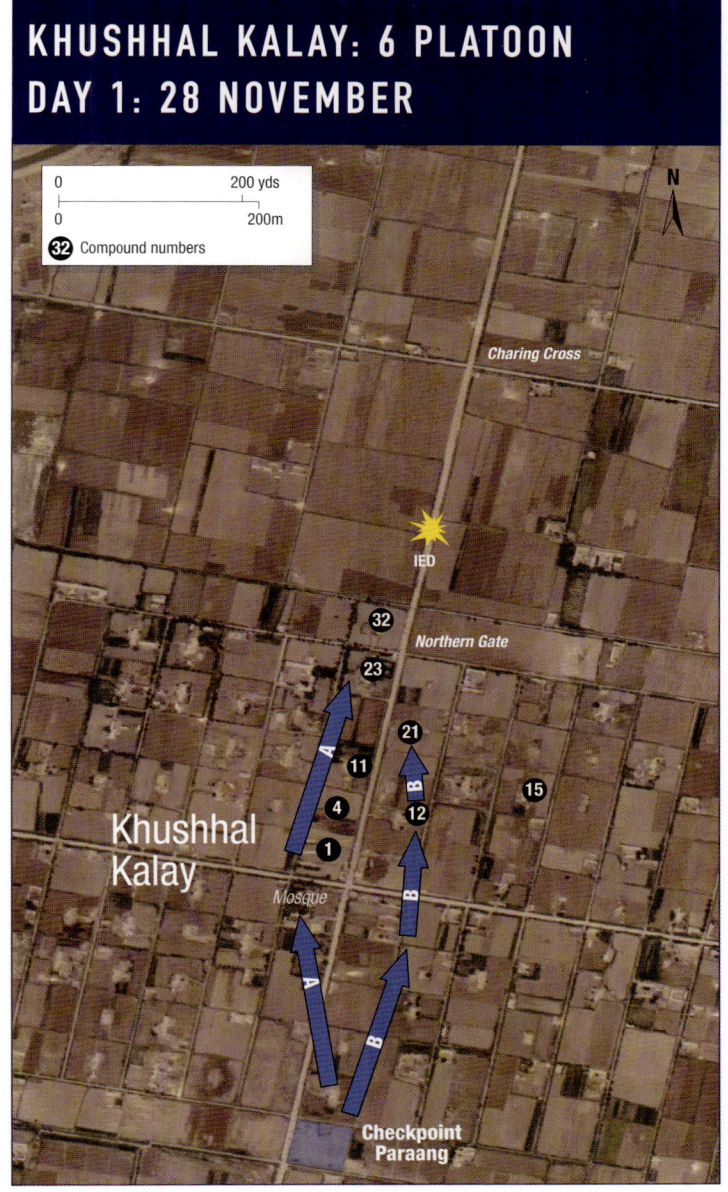

around the compound, feeling exposed. Privates Freddie Stanley and Zikhumbuzo Mkize, on the roof with their machine guns in over-watch, added much-needed security to this situation.

At this time, around 14.30, the route-clearing party, 'Brimstone', of the 28th Regiment Royal Engineers reported on the radio that they had found an IED on the main road north of the village, around 300m north of the crossroads. The Engineers traced a command wire back from the IED location to Compound 32. Locals were moving around all across the area, which prompted the Royal Engineers to ask Lieutenant Benstead to keep them back out of the way. However, there was by then a crowd of more than 30 people, in what was becoming an escalating public-order situation, and there were simply not enough troops to contain them. An Apache attack helicopter overhead at this time bizarrely reported seeing 'a fat man throw an apple core over a wall'. Corporal Stearne and Private Matthew Arrowsmith moved on to the crossroads to attempt to move the locals away. Meanwhile, at the north-western corner of Compound 23, Private Gareth Wells was up a ladder shouting over the wall at the locals to try to get them to move off.

Page 79:
Top right: 6 Platoon, Private Gareth Wells is front row, second from the left.

Top left: Mastiff and Chinook casevac from Khushhal Kalay.

Corporal Stearne of 51C, 6 Platoon.

Compound 23 and surroundings. Private Wells was injured by a grenade in the top left corner of the compound. He was evacuated north along the main road to the right of the compound.

A controlled explosion to dispose of the IED on the road was promptly followed by another loud explosion inside Compound 23. It was a hand grenade, probably an old Russian military grenade, thrown by one of the crowd of locals just outside the compound. It bounced off Private Gareth Wells' helmet and exploded on the ground below him, peppering his legs. It was a large, dangerous explosion, and luckily the magazines he was wearing on the front of his body took much of the shrapnel from the blast. Had it not been for them, the explosion would probably have ripped off his face as the blast travelled upwards. The locals scattered, and Private Mkize, still on the roof in over-watch, shouted 'Man down', but unfortunately he could not see who had thrown the grenade. Lieutenant Benstead and Private Jakes, the multiple's medic, raced over to Wells, who was trying to crawl out of the corner. The blast had torn off his electronic counter-measures (ECM) equipment and caused him to drop his rifle into the irrigation ditch; both had to be recovered, but the priority was to get him safely evacuated. Lieutenant Benstead and Private Jakes dragged Wells by his webbing straps across the field to the safety of the buildings to the east of Compound 23, started first aid and called for a casualty evacuation helicopter.

Wary of further grenade attacks, Lieutenant Benstead went back to recover the ECM equipment and weapon from the ditch while Private Jakes tended to Wells' injuries. Initially his leg looked the worst, but later the full extent of his arm injuries became clearer and he was found to be bleeding badly from a severed artery in one arm. Everyone thought he had lost his toes because the front of one boot had been blown off, but strangely his toes were intact inside the rest of his boot.

Fortunately, Captain James Perrin was on the main road with a heavily armoured Mastiff 2 vehicle, call-sign Mongoose 54A. Lieutenant Benstead called them on the radio and requested that four men use Vallon mine detectors to clear a route from the Mastiff to Compound 23. As they were placing the patched-up Wells into the Mastiff, they heard on the radio that the evacuation helicopter was just two minutes out, so they were able to drive Wells almost straight on to the Chinook as it landed to the north of the village. Some 19 hectic minutes had elapsed between the grenade explosion and Wells being taken onto the Chinook at around 15.00. Gareth Wells survived his injuries, although he nearly lost an arm. Shrapnel was stuck in an artery for some time and he was severely scarred. Although medically downgraded, he eventually went back to the battalion to work in the stores.

At this point, Major Chris Davies, the company commander, called a halt to the route-clearance as dusk was approaching and the Brimstone route-clearers could not operate in the dark. Since the Alpha multiple had been in Compound 23 for a long time and had taken casualties, Lieutenant Benstead wanted to get out and move back to Compound 1 to reunite the multiple with Fire Team 51D.

At the same time as the grenade attack, 51D had been under fire from a mixture of 7.62mm rounds, both single shots and automatic fire from several weapons. This was escalating in intensity, including the use of a machine gun – probably a PKM – but nobody was hit.

As they started to move, the Alpha multiple noticed that two 12-year-old boys in bright white dish-dash robes were moving parallel to the multiple along the next alleyway. They were probably acting as markers, their vivid white clothes showing potential ambushers the

Private Tony Bethell of 6 Platoon shows off a Soviet-made PKM 7.62mm belt-fed machine gun.

troops' location. As the now united multiple was about to cross a wall of Compound 1 next to the crossroads, they heard the 'plink' of an initiator, then saw a grenade fly over the wall, land and explode in the middle of the multiple. Private White received a small fragment in the arm, but fortunately nobody else was injured by this blast. The multiple moved swiftly back north, then went firm in Compound 4 to consolidate. Another grenade was thrown, but nobody was hurt by this third explosion. These looked like Second World War-vintage Russian grenades – 'pineapple types', possibly the F1, which could produce large, dangerous fragments with a blast radius of more than 15m, but their effectiveness depended on many factors.

The multiple still had to cross the main road near the crossroads. As they did so, they came under more automatic fire from down the axis of the road from the west. Although from a range of only about 40m, they could not see where it was coming from as the shooters were taking great care to conceal their line of fire. The multiple would have become stuck here, as their interpreter dived for cover and would not cross, had it not been for an act of prodigious bravery by Lance Corporal Adam Drane, who ran into the middle of the road, with bullets actually passing between his legs, and shouted at the interpreter to move. Probably somewhat surprised, the interpreter dashed over the road and the multiple was moving again. They eventually got past the mosque just as the call for prayers was going out.

TALIBAN MACHINE GUNS

The Taliban use two main types of machine gun, variants of what are usually called the RPK and the PKM. The RPK is a light machine gun, a relatively simple development of the AK-47 with a heavier barrel, bipod and larger magazine. It fires the same widely available 7.62mm x 39 round as the AK-47, often from 30- or 40-round curved or 75-round drum magazines. Although reliable, its barrel overheats quickly and this makes it difficult to sustain a high rate of fire over longer periods, since the barrel must be changed and left to cool. Despite the bipod, it still tends to move around too much during automatic fire for the average machine-gunner to deal with, which makes it less accurate. This movement also means that it is unpleasant to fire, and it is often described as lacking balance.

These drawbacks mean that over time the RPK has generally been replaced in Taliban use by the more reliable, better balanced and belt-fed PKM which is usually described as a general-purpose or universal machine gun. It appears in many different variants, such as the PKMS or Chinese copy called the Type 67, and it can be fired using a bipod and also mounted on a tripod, although the latter is rarely seen in use by the Taliban. Developed in the Soviet Union in the 1960s, the PKM fires a different round – the longer 7.62mm x 54R – which was derived from an old Russian rifle round. These are linked together in standard belts of 100, 200 or 250 rounds, often carried in metal boxes. Belt-feed means that additional belts can be joined on by an assistant, which allows for a more continuous rate of fire. Sustained firing is also supported by the fact that the heavy, easily detachable and finned barrel of the PKM also heats up more slowly than that of the RPK. It is a well-balanced machine gun, relatively easy to fire, reliable, accurate and appreciated by those who use it. These advantages outweigh the slightly increased difficulty in obtaining the belted ammunition at a higher price.

As the campaign in Afghanistan progressed, fewer and fewer RPKs and more and more PKM machine guns were encountered in the hands of the Taliban.

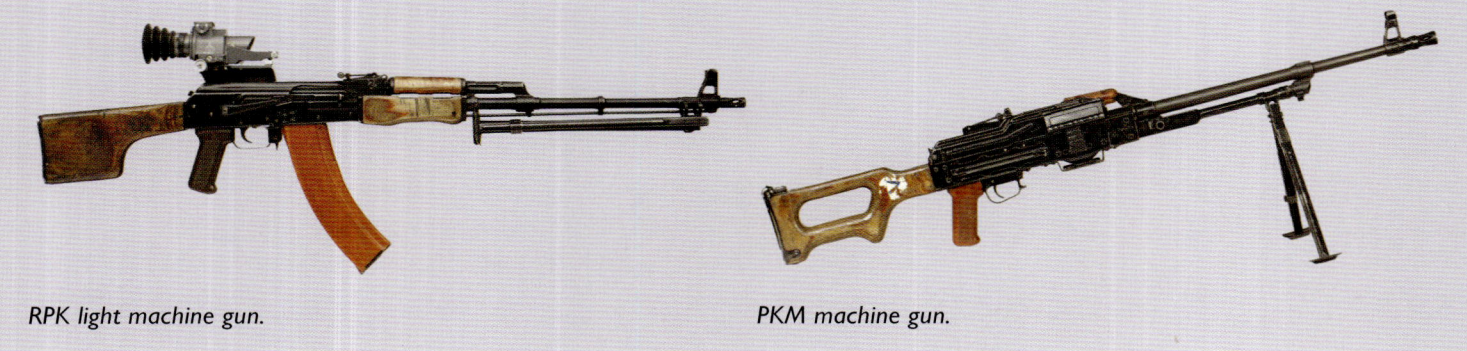

RPK light machine gun.   PKM machine gun.

Russian-made F1 hand grenade.

Meanwhile, the Bravo multiple had been under fire from the area of Compound 15, but they inflicted a probable kill on the Taliban machine-gunner responsible. As a result the fire then slackened. They were able to manoeuvre south to cover the eastern arc as the Alpha multiple came south. Both multiples then 'hard-targeted' at speed back to the Paraang base. The Bravo multiple was under fire for most of this phase, but got back unscathed. The time was around 17.00 – another busy day for 6 Platoon.

At the evening conference at 20.00, Lieutenant Benstead was able to talk through the day's tactics with his company commander and it was agreed that 6 Platoon would need to operate in a different area the next day. There was still much to do with too few soldiers. Consequently, an additional multiple from 10 Platoon, call-sign 53A, led by Second Lieutenant Phil Lenthall, was tasked to support 6 Platoon the following day.

Securing the route overnight, C Company resumed clearance at first light on 29 November. Both the 6 Platoon Alpha and Bravo multiples departed Paraang at 04.50, before first light, armed and equipped as on the previous day. The Alpha multiple moved north and deployed call-sign 51C into Compound 13 and call-sign 51D into Compound 14. The Bravo multiple, this time containing call-signs 51B and 51 Golf (51G), led by Corporal Smith, rotating the section left guarding the base, also moved north. Sergeant Vickery deployed call-sign 51G

MURDER HOLES

This slang term describes small gaps, usually in compound walls, through which the Taliban fired at ISAF soldiers. These have been a persistent feature of the fighting in Afghanistan for many years, and many compounds feature historical murder holes at opportune angles. They may be arranged so that the firer shoots through a series of two, or even more murder holes. These holes might be only a few tens of centimetres across, and be arranged along a very narrow line of fire, sometimes only a degree or so wide. In these cases, an assistant is often used to indicate to the firer when a target is about to pass across his line of fire, since the exposure can be very fleeting due to the narrow angle.

The presence of murder holes in compounds and 'dickers' broadcasting soldier movement were usually considered high threat indicators. The Taliban had become incredibly devious and cunning in the arrangement of these multiple murder-hole shootings, exploiting to the full their local knowledge of the terrain and of troop behaviour. The holes were almost impossible to see if two or more walls were intersected; even the muzzle flash at close ranges might not be seen by the target due to the narrowness of the arc. This explains how troops have been shot at from very close range, sometimes less than 40m away, without ever seeing the firing point, let alone being able to return fire.

Diagram showing how murder holes work.

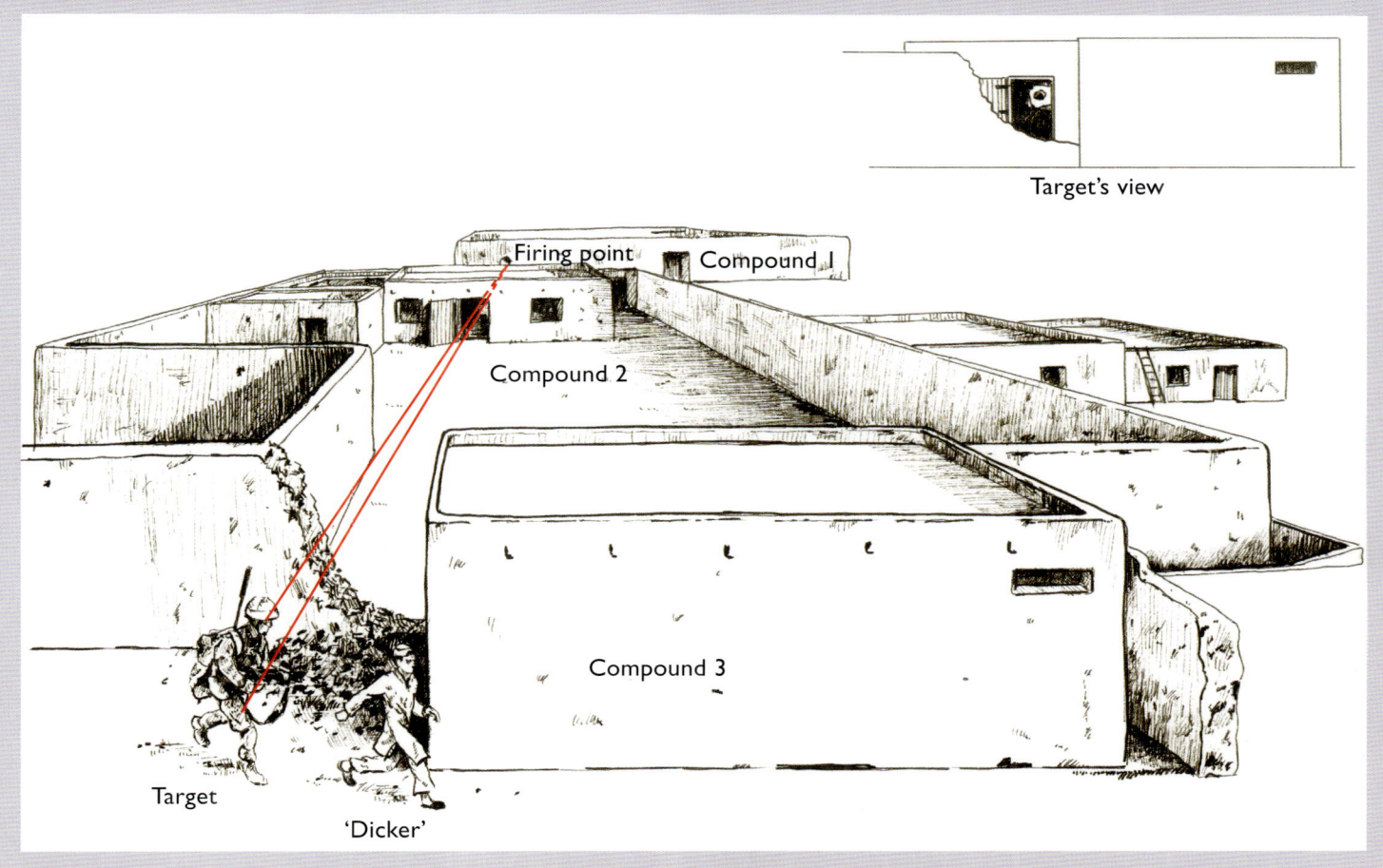

into Compound 21 and himself, 51B, into Compound 12. The platoon was in position by 05.30.

Concurrently, 9 Platoon of C Company, with one multiple under Lieutenant Greg Napier, call-sign 52A, was deployed north and east of the village as flank protection and Sergeant Hill, with call-signs 52B and 52C, moved into the north-west of Khushhal Kalay as described earlier. At this time Second Lieutenant Lenthall also led his 53A multiple into the south-

KHUSHHAL KALAY: 6 PLATOON
DAY 2: 29 NOVEMBER

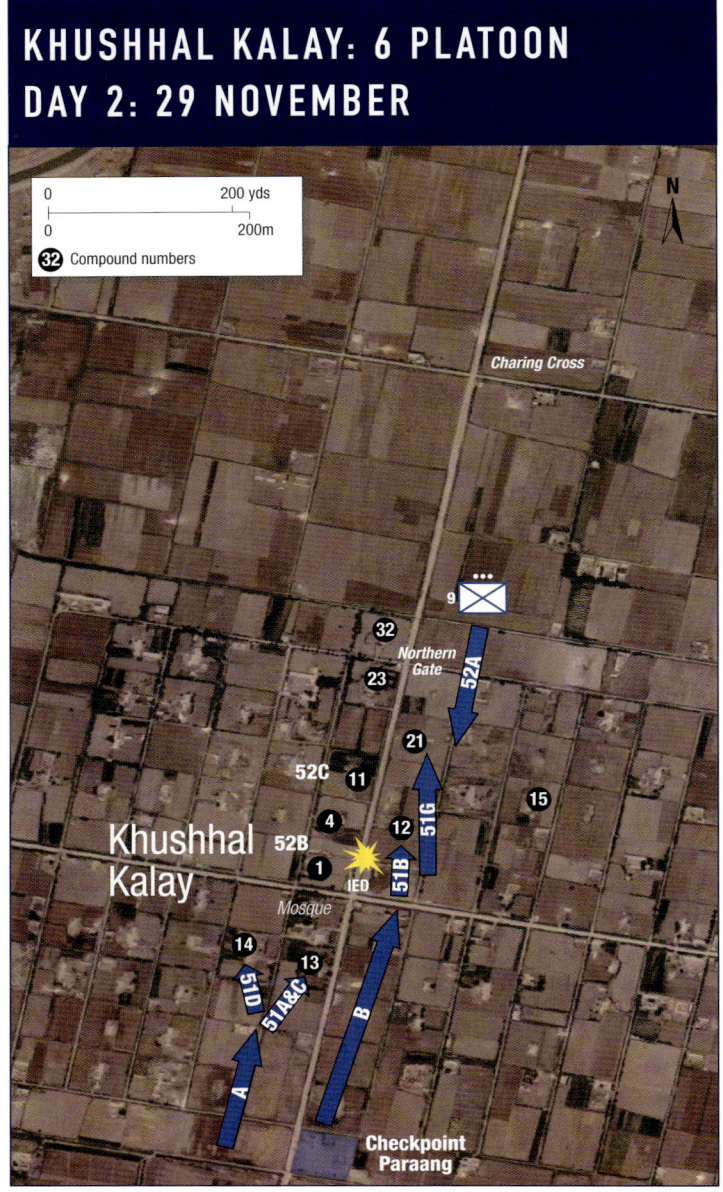

eastern part of the village, behind Sergeant Vickery, providing support and flank protection.

During the day, 6 Platoon's Alpha multiple had a few very fleeting glimpses of a two-man Taliban RPG team. On one occasion, a certain private asked whether he should open fire. When Corporal Stearne said yes, the private replied, 'Oh – they have gone now', the source of considerable mickey-taking later. The day was thus relatively uneventful until around 14.00, when the massive explosion which destroyed the SV truck occurred. Call-sign 51B was close and certainly felt the full effect of the blast, but fortunately suffered no injuries.

6 Platoon spent the rest of the day helping out with a number of tasks and securing the vital area while the scene of the IED was cleared and the remaining stores shuttled down to Paraang by the MWT. Its flashing light and the beep-beep noise of its reversing siren were a source of considerable amusement.

Meanwhile, back at the patrol base, the corner watchtowers, called sangars, reported seeing a man digging on a road some 400m due south of the base during the early evening. They were suspicious because it looked as though he might be placing an IED. Corporal Warren discussed the situation by radio with Lieutenant Benstead and they established that there was sufficient evidence to warrant opening fire under their strict rules of engagement. Private Gary Lowe in Sangar 2 and Private John Goggins in Sangar 1 both opened fire. They hit the suspect who crawled off behind a wall out of sight. His body was retrieved some days later and it was confirmed he was a Taliban bomber.

Eventually, by around 04.00 on 30 November, the majority of the tasks were complete and both multiples of 6 Platoon returned to Paraang to sort out their resupplied stores and

Above: 6 Platoon on the move with Vallon mine detector in the lead.

Left: Sunset over the base at Paraang.

Opposite far left: Lance Corporal Adam Drane in Paraang.

Opposite: View from a sangar in Paraang.

equipment. 6 Platoon had performed well in very trying and tiring circumstances. They nicknamed their part in this long and complex operation 'Black Hawk Down'.

A (NORFOLK) COMPANY ON OPERATION *HERRICK 11*

The following chart summarises A Company's tour as they were deployed under command of the Household Cavalry Battle Group:

DATE	ORGANISATION	NAME	SUMMARY
November–December 2009	A Company	Start of tour	During the first part of the tour, A (Norfolk) Company Group was based in Patrol Base Woqab and the Roshan Tower.
7 November 2009	A Company	Operation *Mar Brus 1*	Support to elections. Company operation as a series of vehicle checkpoints to provide a 'ring of steel' around Musa Qalah district centre. Multiple contacts on ground troops and patrol base. A potential IED factory identified and seven Taliban killed.
14 November 2009	A Company	Operation *Mar Brus 2*	Intelligence-led company operation with ANA searches. Non-kinetic due to deception, depth and domination of the area. Resulted in finds of IED components such as ammonium nitrate.
22 November 2009	2 Platoon	Operation *Mar Brus 3*	2 Platoon counter-IED ambush operation; people were seen in the killing area but not positively identified as Taliban bombers, so not engaged.
1, 3 & 5 December 2009	All platoons	Operation *Mar Brus 4*	Platoon-sized airborne 'Eagle' vehicle checkpoint operation using Chinooks as part of a deception plan in conjunction with US clearance of Nowzad.
11 December 2009	A Company	Operation *Mar Brus 5*	Company clearance operation of known Taliban firing points, working with the ANA. Multiple engagements requiring the use of Exactor (precision-guided munitions), Javelin missiles and the Dragon Gun (the name for a 105mm Light Gun based on the Roshan Tower). Six Taliban killed.
January–April 2010	A Company		During the second part of the tour, A Company deployed to Patrol Base Habib, fully embedded with local ANA.
6–14 January 2010	A Company	Operation *Mar Barcha 7*	Company-led joint ANA operation to establish partnered patrol base on 'Roundtop Hill' at Habib, 2km north of Woqab. Some 20 IEDs cleared during build, ATO Captain Daniel Read killed.
4 February–7 March 2010	Brigade	Operation *Moshtarak*	
21 February 2010	A Company Tac	IED strike	IED detonated on Company Tac. Captain Martin Driver seriously injured and died of wounds on 15 March in Selly Oak Hospital.
15–16 March 2010	A Company	Operation *Mar Sar 2*	Described in detail in the following section.
25 March 2010	A Company	Handover	Habib base handed over to US Marine Corps.

OPERATION *MAR SAR 2*: 15–16 MARCH 2010

Operation *Mar Sar 2* is a good example of how the nature of operations in Afghanistan had changed substantially since the early days of *Herrick 6*. It took place towards the later part of the tour. A (Norfolk) Company Group had been extending a 'security bubble' north from the town of Musa Qalah. Initially this was from a patrol base called Woqab, later from 2.5km further north, where a patrol base called Habib was established jointly with the ANA.

From January 2010 Habib was built up with additional troops, but it was in a high-threat area. As the Royal Engineers built the base, the company conducted a series of joint ANA–ANP patrols to dominate the area. An AGS-17 grenade launcher was destroyed to prevent an attack on the base. Some 20 IEDs were cleared as it was built, 14 of them by Captain Daniel Read, the Ammunition Technical Officer (ATO) personally. There were contacts every day and Captain Read was killed, along with an ANA warrior (term for an ANA soldier). Private Mark Allen and Trooper Mapp, Household Cavalry Regiment suffered life-changing injuries, and Private Kuria suffered a gunshot wound to the leg. At least 25 Taliban were killed.

By mid-March A Company Group was well established in Habib. It comprised 7 Platoon (from B Company), 2 Platoon and 3 Platoon, plus 3 Troop of C Squadron, the Household Cavalry, with their Scimitar reconnaissance vehicles, and an ANA company. By this point the Woqab base to the south had been closed, since the area was by then completely secure as the company pushed further north, displacing the Taliban. The next town on the list was Karamanda, a further 2km north. The company had patrolled into it and conducted several engagements with the Taliban, who were a mix of locals and out-of-area fighters armed with the usual assortment of AK-47 and PKM small arms and RPGs. They had, however, even used an automatic grenade-launcher, a Russian AGS-17, in the initial establishment of Habib, but it was located and destroyed with the assistance of an Apache attack helicopter.

Fire Support Group A on handover.

A Company's view from the Roshan Tower.

AGS-17

The Soviet-designed AGS-17 is a 30mm-calibre automatic grenade launcher, which entered service with Warsaw Pact troops around 1972. It was widely used during the Soviet invasion of Afghanistan in 1979 and, with a maximum range of 1,700m in direct fire and a theoretical rate of fire of 400 rounds per minute, it was seen as an effective weapon. Although its slightly smaller grenade means it is not quite as hard hitting as the NATO 40mm grenade launchers, the AGS-17 can nevertheless be used to deliver high-explosive fragmentation effects in both direct- and indirect-fire modes. In the latter, however, although it was used at ranges up to 2,500m in Afghanistan, it was difficult to be accurate using the sight on the weapon, so only experienced crews were consistently able to hit targets at longer ranges with indirect fire.

Ex-Soviet AGS-17 automatic grenade launcher.

The Taliban occasionally used AGS-17s, often in the indirect-fire mode, to deliver semi-random harassing-type fire on and around civilian targets, where the reach of the weapon was more important than its accuracy.

The main threat at this time was the IED in a wide range of types, used with various initiation methods. To begin with IEDs were 'heavy metal content' and so could be detected with the Vallon mine detector, but as the tour progressed, the threat switched to low metal content IEDs. Devices ranged in size from 5kg up to about 25kg of high-explosive content, giving a blast radius of up to 50m. By March even 'no metal content' IEDs were being encountered. Almost impossible to detect, the troops often had to rely on their ground-sign awareness and the Taliban were highly adaptive, ever more cunning in how they deployed IEDs, often responding to the behaviour of the troops. Secondary and tertiary devices – so-called 'come on' tactics – were also employed: an initial device was used to lure troops into an area where another device, or even a series of other devices, had been positioned. The Taliban were even known to be trying to capture some 'infidel flesh' after IED strikes, which meant after IED detonations, the location was carefully scoured by the troops after any casualties had been evacuated.

These almost daily engagements around Habib and Karamanda in February and early March had shown that the Taliban meant business, but at least 80 identified fighters had been killed in clashes with A Company – a considerable achievement. The company commander, Major Stuart Smith, decided that the time was right to press beyond Karamanda and further displace the Taliban by getting behind them, even further to the north. Consequently Operation *Mar Sar 2* was aimed at the village of Sar Bisheh, some 10km further north. It was hoped that this would further disrupt the already waning influence of the Taliban in the area, shaking them up completely and thus greatly extending the security bubble. A major effort was also being made to keep the local people informed about what was happening and to show them that the front line was moving north. Those locals behind the forward line of enemy troops had difficulties, however. As the Taliban moved into an area to fight, the locals would leave their fields and hunker down in the relative safety of their compounds until the fighting was over, emerging only when the Taliban had been repelled. Considerable diplomatic skills were required to explain why the fight was moving into their area, and in this the ANA had a key role to play. In the event, A Company and the

ANA handled this side of the operation so well that no civilian casualties were attributed to them – another impressive achievement and a practical demonstration of the 'courageous restraint' principle.

The main force for Operation *Mar Sar 2* was provided by 3 Platoon, consisting of 35 men led by Lieutenant Simon Broomfield, but the group was commanded by the tactical company headquarters led by Major Stuart Smith and also included a combat medical team; a Joint Tactical Air Controller (JTAC); a Fire Support Group comprising GPMG (SF) snipers and Javelin commanded by 2 Platoon's Sergeant Johnson; an artillery Fire Support Team; 2 ANP and 15 ANA, including their company commander. A quad bike and

1 Platoon, A Company pose with an Apache.

trailer was also included for transporting stores. On Monday 15 March 2010, three Chinook lifts landed this group to the north of Sar Bisheh at 09.30, and they then patrolled down into the village. By 11.30 the group had taken over a large, two-storey compound as its temporary base, soon to be christened 'Norfolk House'. Foot patrols were scheduled to coincide with the windows when the Apache attack helicopter support was available from 15.00. These patrols were partially covered by Javelin, snipers and GPMG (SF) on over-watch in Norfolk House. Light gun support was also available, although Sar Bisheh was at the extreme range of the guns.

At 14.50, Norfolk House came under small-arms fire from a nearby compound and bunker complex, soon to be nicknamed 'Javelin Compound' because Private Mason returned fire with a Javelin missile, together with Private Shea on the GPMG (SF) and the sniper. The JTAC, Sergeant Johnson of the Royal Tank Regiment, also coordinated a strafing attack by a US A-10 Thunderbolt II aircraft using its 30mm cannon. This combination of weapons both pinned the Taliban in position and ensured they would be suppressed. Because Javelin

The roof of Norfolk House, Sar Bisheh.

JAVELIN MISSILE

Javelin is a US-made anti-tank missile system that was introduced into British service in 2005 to replace the earlier but popular MILAN system. Javelin proved to be highly effective in Afghanistan and immensely popular with its crews. It is a fire-and-forget system, which means that once launched, the missile flies to the target even if the target moves, so the operator is free to select another target, move or take cover – all advantages over the earlier MILAN. In addition to the missile tube, there is a detachable, re-usable Command Launch Unit (CLU) – usually pronounced 'clue' by the crew. This is a highly effective surveillance device in its own right, as it has two fields of view – the wide field at x4 magnification for general surveillance, then a narrow field at x12 magnification, which allows a detailed examination of a target. The seeker, which has a x9 thermal image view, is then activated before launching the missile – a process that sounds tricky but is quite similar to using the zoom function on a modern camera. The large warhead has a tandem HEAT (high-explosive anti-tank) warhead which can work in top-attack mode against armoured vehicles or can be used in direct mode against buildings, bunkers and the like.

Although designed for destroying moving armoured vehicles out to a range of 2,500m, Javelin proved itself highly effective in Afghanistan as its range, accuracy and large, effective warhead could be used to destroy even the best-protected targets.

The main, indeed possibly the only, drawback to Javelin is its weight, as each missile is around 12kg and the CLU weighs 6.4kg, meaning that it was difficult to carry over the harsh terrain of Afghanistan. The Javelin was more often used by the Viking FSGs in conjunction with vehicles.

Javelin in over-watch next to a Scimitar.

Compound was somewhat isolated from the rest of the village, it was safe to use the heavier weapons without risk of collateral damage or civilian casualties.

Once the Taliban fighters were silenced, 3 Platoon went out to clear Javelin Compound, organised as three sections and platoon headquarters. The first section, call-sign Maverick 31, led by Lance Corporal Slater, swung out to the west on the right flank. The platoon commander, Lieutenant Broomfield as call-sign 30 Alpha (30A), and the second section, call-sign 32, led by Lance Corporal Scott Hardy, swung round to the east on the left flank before all headed south. Lance Corporal Garner, acting as call-sign 30 Bravo (30B), and the third section, call-sign 33, led by Lance Corporal Taylor, then took the direct southern route towards Javelin Compound. Major Smith, with the company tactical headquarters as call-sign 0 Alpha (0A), followed them, with the ANA just behind.

The Taliban in Javelin Compound opened fire with small arms at 3 Section, the ANA and Tac. Private Roland and the company commander ended up against the compound wall, facing each other, in preparation for throwing grenades over the wall. Because Major Smith had his right shoulder to the wall, he had to throw his grenade left-handed, which concerned him as he thought it might make him throw like a girl! A decision then had to be made as to whether to send in 3 Section to clear the compound in Attack State Red – the compound might be booby-trapped with IEDs – or whether to pull back and use helicopter firepower – which risked allowing some of the Taliban to escape. Much to the chagrin of 3 Section, Major Smith decided to pull back and use Hellfire missiles from the Apaches – but this was the right decision.

They pulled back around 100m and called in a Hellfire missile, but then as they went back towards the compound they were fired on again. So they again pulled back, this time around 70m, and called in a second Hellfire, at which point the Taliban went quiet. 3 Section went in and cleared the compound but in State Green, not throwing grenades or firing unless Taliban were definitely identified. A very careful check for IEDs was made with the mine-detector. One uninjured suspected local Taliban commander was captured and one dead insurgent was dug out from the rubble where the Hellfires had hit. A motorcycle, an AK-47 with three magazines, belted machine-gun ammunition and two mobile phones with a radio

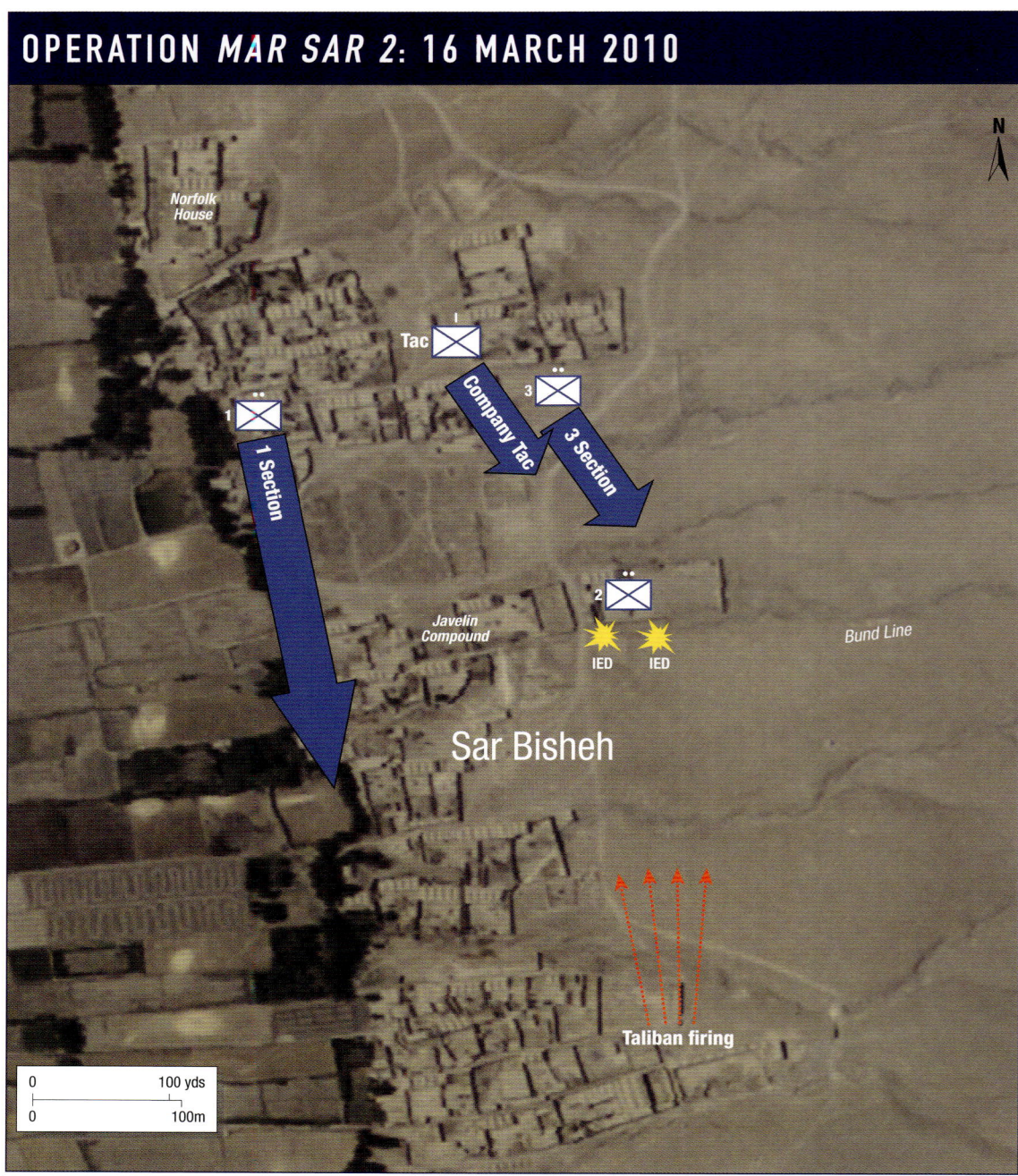

FLEXIBLE ORGANISATIONS

Unlike the multiple organisation described in earlier operations on *Herrick 11*, 3 Platoon has a more traditional organisation here. They were formed as a platoon headquarters of three to five men and three sections, each with between six and eight men. However, when 3 Platoon went to clear Javelin Compound on 15 March 2010, their organisation was far from the standard rank structure for a rifle platoon. The platoon's sergeant (Sergeant Daniel, attached from The Yorkshire Regiment) had been shot in the face so was recovering; 1 Section's corporal had gone back to the UK to do a career course at Brecon; 2 Section's corporal had moved to 2 Platoon; and 3 Section's commander (Lance Corporal Garner) had stepped up to cover the platoon sergeant role.

were also recovered from this rubble. A third insurgent was later discovered to have bled to death further south and two others were thought to have escaped using a cleverly concealed route. The prisoner was handed over to the ANP. It was an important capture, but it was decided not to call a helicopter to extract him immediately, as he could be taken back with the company when they extracted the next day. The A Company Group then returned to Norfolk House, much buoyed by their success.

Unbeknown to the company, Captain Martin Driver, A Company's popular second-in-command, died that night in Selly Oak Hospital after a three-week struggle to survive injuries from an IED blast. He had been acting as company commander at the time of the blast, covering for Major Smith who was on rest and recuperation. The commanding officer of the Household Cavalry rightly decided not to inform any of the company of his death until the end of this operation because their focus was on the Taliban. Unfortunately the news was transmitted on local British Forces Broadcasting Service, so the members of A Company back in Habib heard the news in this less than ideal way, though those in Norfolk House remained unaware.

Captain Martin Driver on patrol in October 2009.

The next patrol was organised to coincide with the first available attack helicopter window, 06.30–08.30 the following day, Tuesday 16 March. In order to maximise the familiarity with the ground, this patrol followed the same organisation as the earlier one: 1 Section to the west, 2 Section to the east and 3 Section in the centre patrolling towards Javelin Compound. This time the platoon commander and company Tac went with 1 Section on the westerly route into the Green Zone area. Finding some locals, it proved possible with the assistance of the ANA and ANP to organise an impromptu *shura* meeting, which lasted around 40 minutes. As Pashto speakers, the ANA and ANP commanders were extremely influential and persuasive. This was an almost model event; these locals had very little former knowledge of the ISAF or the ANA, so the *shura* was very successful. Otherwise the patrol was uneventful, and the company was back in Norfolk House by 08.30.

In order to extend their influence further to the south of the village, the next patrol was timed to coincide with the attack helicopter window at 13.30. In a similar formation, to maximise their ground-sign awareness, the patrol moved south. Again Lieutenant Broomfield moved with 2 Section on the eastern left flank, and company Tac and the ANA moved on the right flank. 3 Section went firm just beyond Javelin Compound.

The over-watching Apache helicopter reported two unidentified males acting suspiciously, and at 14.19 another was seen to be unravelling what could have been a command wire. The rules of engagement had to be interpreted carefully, because they were complicated by an earlier incident at Habib when a man had been seen unravelling a wire by a mosque. On that occasion, permission to shoot was refused by the company commander because it was not possible positively to identify the activity as a threat. This later proved to be the correct

Major Smith conducting a *shura*.

decision, as the man was an innocent builder using a plumb line, but such experiences greatly complicated decisions to open fire.

In this case, however, the Apache crewman was fairly confident in his identification and was planning to open fire once the three-man IED team came together. The Apache was about to engage when, at 14.28, there was an immense explosion on the eastern left flank and Lance Corporal Scott Hardy of 2 Section reported on the radio 'Contact IED wait' – but then there was a second large explosion and nobody in 2 Section could be raised on the radio net. Company Tac ordered 1 Section to stay on over-watch on the right and 3 Section to move in towards the incident. Concurrently, Company Tac moved the 200m to the site of the explosion. Company Tac included Lance Corporal McAdam of the Royal Army Medical Corps, while the other medic, Private Mellor, was with 3 Section. Both explosions had been on a bund line – a line of mounded earth around 70cm tall that ran perpendicular to the eastern edge of the village.

At 14.30 Lance Corporal Illsley, second in command of 2 Section, came on the radio net using Lieutenant Broomfield's radio and initially reported two casualties, Lance Corporal Hardy and Private James Grigg, and that the section was under automatic fire from a series of firing points to the south. They had been able to pull back Private Grigg into some cover and were providing covering fire that allowed the section medics to start working on the injuries while the rest of 2 Section returned fire. At this point 3 Section pressed on to the bund line, returning fire and assisting, allowing 2 Section to pull back Lance Corporal Hardy. The two medics with Company Tac, McAdam and Mellor, arrived and took over the treatment. It was at this point that they realised that Lance Corporal Scott Hardy was already dead. Private James Grigg was in a very bad way, slipping in and out of consciousness, and it was also realised that Lieutenant Simon Broomfield had been seriously injured.

A Company now undertook a great flurry of activity as casualty reports were sent to company headquarters in Habib, which tasked a casualty evacuation helicopter – a Chinook with a medical emergency response team on board, the highest possible level of support. A suitable landing site was located to the north and cleared with Vallon mine detectors, while constant suppressing fire was maintained on the Taliban to the south.

At 14.56 Private Grigg stopped breathing and the two medics began cardiopulmonary resuscitation. The Chinook landed at 15.04, under some fire from the Taliban, although they were suppressed by increased overhead fire, including another Javelin missile, sniper and GPMG (SF) fire from Norfolk House. The three casualties were loaded swiftly onto the Chinook and were quickly away. It transpired later that Lieutenant Broomfield had been badly hit in the right thigh and calf, and also in his arms by shrapnel from the second IED.

Concurrently, a second Apache arrived and both engaged the Taliban with Hellfire missiles and 30mm cannon, killing at least two. The battle then began to die down as the remaining Taliban headed away, still under fire from 3 Section once the Chinook had gone. Later it was estimated that in total between six and eight Taliban were killed in this engagement.

This phase was especially difficult for 1 Section because, acting as the blocking and fixing force, they had to stay put to cover the right flank of the company. The psychological impact of the IED attack on the ANA and ANP was considerable, and they subsequently had to be coaxed into action.

The incident was not yet over, however, as a large sanitisation clearance of the whole area had to be conducted because of the Taliban's known desire to capture 'infidel flesh'. Major Smith was determined to ensure that nothing was left behind, and the quad bike with trailer was called in to help, driven by Lance Corporal Sullivan and carrying 2 Platoon's Sergeant Johnson, who had been commanding Norfolk House. During the clearance, the bund line, which had been the site of the IEDs, was examined and it was assessed that the IEDs had probably been placed there the previous night. It was impossible, however, to extract much

Quad bike.

information from the seat of the detonation and it was too unsafe to request an ammunition technical officer team. Overall, it looked as though there was very little 2 Section could have done. They had simply been unlucky.

At 16.15 Major Smith heard from the commanding officer over the radio that Private James Grigg had died from his injuries at the hospital in Camp Bastion. Following the

L115A3 LONG-RANGE SNIPER RIFLE

This remarkable modern sniper rifle was introduced into service in 2008 and quickly became highly respected. It is also called the long-range rifle or sometimes the .338 after its calibre. Any sniper weapon is only as good as the sniper using it, but the accuracy and range of the L115A3 was so pronounced an improvement that it rapidly impressed and became very popular with Viking snipers. It fires a heavy 8.59mm round with a muzzle velocity of 936 metres per second, which has remarkably stable ballistic properties that impart much accuracy to the system. It was designed to achieve a high probability of a first-round hit at 600m range but proved able to hit out to 1,100m and more in service. It has a five-round box magazine and can be used with a range of new telescopic and night sights that

are part of a sniper improvement programme. It was deployed with considerable effect by the Viking sniper platoon on *Herrick 11* and *16*.

A Viking sniper with an L115A3.

A Company snipers on over-watch.

clearance, the company recovered back to Norfolk House, somewhat shocked by their experience.

Later that afternoon, the sniper in Norfolk House positively identified a member of the Taliban carrying a weapon and using a radio in the Green Zone on the far side of the wadi to the west of the village. This probable Taliban commander was killed with an impressive third shot at 1,100m range by the A Company Sniper using his L115A3 sniper rifle.

Following the news that two Chinooks would arrive at 17.30 for extraction, the company rapidly packed everything in their Norfolk House compound and cleared the landing site. In addition, Captain Matt Loosemore of the Royal Horse Artillery, Fire Support Team commander, organised a barrage of new 'base bleed' 105mm smoke rounds to cover the landing. Landing only 200m away, the smoke rounds caused some consternation.

On arriving back at Habib, members of the operation received official news of Captain Martin Driver's death in Selly Oak the previous evening. Later that night the whole of A Company held a short service, including the reading of the poem 'Death of a Comrade' by Martin Carter and a two-minute silence to honour their three dead. Major Smith then had the sad duty of writing their eulogies and letters to their next-of-kin.

Operation *Mar Sar 2* had been a success, with later indications showing that some 11 Taliban in total had been killed, but at the sad cost of two dead. All the young Vikings of A Company had performed magnificently under the most stressful of battlefield conditions

A Company remembers fallen comrades.

PRIVATE MATT STRINGER'S STORY

Private Matt Stringer was on patrol with 2 Section of 3 Platoon when they were caught up in the explosion on the second day of Operation *Mar Sar 2* on 16 March 2010.

On the day of the IEDs I was attached to the platoon commander, Lieutenant Broomfield, and we were on the bund line with Lance Corporal Hardy's section. From what I remember I saw the first IED go off and saw there were guys injured, so I went to go towards them and then the second IED went off and it knocked me back. I had massive ringing in my ears and singeing all over my face, neck and arm. At the time I didn't really feel any pain and was more worried about my mates and the boss. So I picked myself up and helped extract Lieutenant Broomfield a few metres back to safety where I began to help patch up his leg and arm. I then saw the other guys were having trouble with Private Grigg, so I went to help. When the other sections arrived they sent men forward to extract the injured guys. I thought to myself I am no way near as bad as the casualties, so I stayed on the bund line with the other guys and helped shooting and pointing out where to watch. It wasn't until we all were pulling back to Norfolk House that the Company Commander and medic told me to get on the back of the quad bike with the other injured guys' kit and get back to get my face washed. We were all back in Norfolk House when the Company Commander told us that Private Grigg and Lance Corporal Hardy had died. I didn't get a Medivac until a few hours later because I didn't think it was that bad, until my eye started hurting and I could see a black spot. The medic told me to go back to Camp Bastion and get it looked at. It was only when back in Camp Bastion that I found out I had a perforated right ear drum and a shattered left ear drum. All in all I had 21 pieces of dirt and shrapnel in my face, neck and arm.

Private Stringer eventually had to leave the Army in spring 2013 as a result of these injuries.

Private Matt Stringer on Norfolk House roof; his red face is due to the blast injuries.

11 PLATOON OF THE STEELBACKS, DEPLOYED TO KABUL

11 Platoon of the Steelbacks deployed to Kabul as a formed platoon commanded by Lieutenant R. Little and under command of Headquarters ISAF. They assumed command in Kabul on 18 August 2009. Although Kabul had previously been quiet, the Steelbacks were greeted by a series of IEDs, coinciding with local elections. The rest of their tour was a mix of quiet periods, punctuated by incidents, and very hectic times.

A large and complex incident around Kabul's Serena Hotel on 18 January 2010 involved not only an IED but also 20–30 Taliban firing on the ANA and ANP. Such operations were always difficult because there were so many different units operating in Kabul, usually not in communication with each other. 11 Platoon deployed as the Quick Reaction Force, but not before the Sky and Al Jazeera television networks had broadcast live footage of the incident from the hotel, further complicating matters. Lieutenant Little later wrote in *Castle*: 'The Afghan Police had become a little jumpy and decided that no one was allowed to move around the city and so, 200m from our holding area, we were stopped by a roadblock. After six hours the situation was under control and things moved back to normal.'

This was 11 Platoon's last major incident before they handed over at the end of January that year, having suffered no casualties.

11 Platoon of the Steelbacks, in Kabul.

RECONNAISSANCE PLATOON ON OPERATION *HERRICK 11*

Due to the complexities in the task organisation as the battalion prepared to deploy, the Reconnaissance Platoon (usually abbreviated to Recce) deployed initially as a dismounted platoon with D (Cambridgeshire) Company into Forward Operating Base Keenan in the Danish area of operations. They had an extremely busy tour and their platoon commander, Captain Graham Goodey, wrote this excellent summary for *Castle*:

Recce on patrol combining CVR(T) and foot.

Started the tour with D Company as a dismounted platoon for three weeks; became an Airborne Reserve Force for a Task Force Op for two weeks; took over and trained on a fleet of CVRT and Jackal in 4 days; filled in as the Danish Battle Group armoured platoon for two weeks; worked dismounted with C Company in southern Nad-e-Ali for two weeks; Operation *Tor Shap'ah* clearance of Nad-e-Ali north with the Grenadier Guards Battle Group, made a Patrol Base at 'Yellow 10' and held the northern forward line of enemy troops following Operation *Tor Shap'ah* for three weeks; Operation *Moshtarak* shaping operations for three weeks; Operation *Moshtarak* clearance of Abdul Wahid Kalay; back to C Company in southern Nad-e-Ali for one week; worked with the Household Cavalry in the Bolan Desert for one week; handed back vehicles in three days before returning to D Company for the final three weeks.[4]

Recce Scimitar during Operation *Moshtarak*.

This was clearly an intense tour, with many changes of organisation. By way of example, the 24 men of the platoon reorganised at Camp Bastion and in four days took over a suite of vehicles that included five Scimitar (also called Combat Vehicle Reconnaissance Tracked, or CVRT), three Jackal, a Spartan and a Samaritan Ambulance. Private Peter Webster from Diss in Norfolk, nicknamed 'Grub', was crucial to this phase as he showed considerable resourcefulness in 'obtaining' the equipment that the platoon required then and throughout the tour. As a result of his efforts, they were, for instance, able to improvise the addition of pipe fascines to improve the mobility of their vehicles.

Their organisation was highly flexible too, but they sometimes worked as two multiples, one under Captain Goodey and one under the second-in-command, Company Sergeant Major Goodman. Each multiple had a Scimitar section, and a dismounting section in Jackals, supported by either the Samaritan or Spartan. At other times, depending on the task, the dismounted section, led by Corporal Paul Kennedy from Cambridge, would operate separately. They were thus deployed in a variety of areas in a variety of roles for the rest of the tour, achieving considerable success and building quite a reputation.

It would be impossible, of course, to follow every operation that Recce undertook in detail here, but a successful ambush in the upper Gereshk valley area at the end of March 2010 provides a good example of the kind of action they saw. The terrain here was not as organised for farming as much of the Green Zone – it was less regular, a more jumbled mixture of compounds, fields and irrigation ditches alongside the Helmand river. The area was peppered with IEDs at this time – one tree line, for instance, was found to have an IED

Corporal Kennedy in novel headgear.

Satellite image of the upper Gereshk valley, showing the location of the Recce ambush at Bahadur.

about every 10m. They varied greatly, but a typical IED contained 10–15kg of explosive. Many had been pre-positioned for months or even years, but not connected to any form of initiation device. Many had at least some metal content, so there was a chance of detecting them with the Vallon mine detector. However, as the tour progressed the metal content declined as the Taliban responded to the ISAF mine-detecting capability. There had been a series of previous IED detonations in the area.

Recce's Alpha multiple, under Captain Goodey, moved into Patrol Base Bahadur one morning in late March. At around 13.00 on their second day their interpreter heard on the radio intercept a message: 'Come to the onion field so we can do the work'. It was obvious which field this was, as there was only one onion field in the area, which incidentally had a very powerful and distinctive smell. A remote reconnaissance asset informed the Recce Platoon that they could see two men at work laying out a piece of string along a wall. They were not visible to Recce in Bahadur, but were visible to the remote asset. This behaviour was especially suspicious given that a recent attack had been initiated by a simple 2m pull-string device.

The six-man dismounted team, call-sign Wildcat 21 Alpha, who were to hand, led by Captain Graham Goodey with Corporal Paul Kennedy, followed by Private Joe Roley from Southend (known as Jo-Jo), then Private Ricky Holland from Essex (known inevitably as Dutch), then Lance Corporal William Cooper from Southend and finally Private Keown. They headed out towards the onion field as fast as they could. Because there was only one entrance to the patrol base and it faced in the

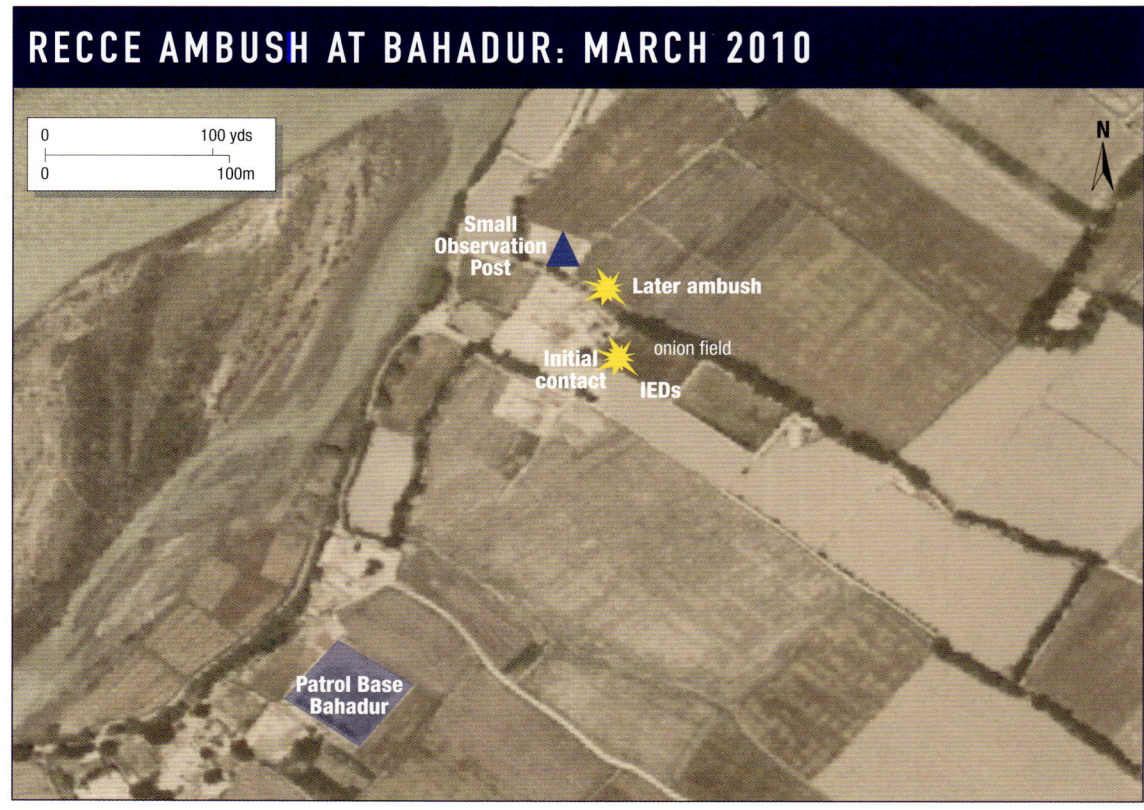

RECCE AMBUSH AT BAHADUR: MARCH 2010

The onion field and compound.

direction of the onion field, there was little chance of sneaking out of the base unseen, so they chose speed instead, moving on foot quickly across the fields. On arrival, rounding the corner of a wall, Corporal Kennedy saw the bomber and fired four rounds at about 60m range, but missed. Almost at the same time, a Taliban cover team, well over to the right and so unseen by Corporal Kennedy, opened fire at him with long bursts of automatic fire, causing him to duck back around the corner into cover. Kennedy recalled, 'It was all pretty chaotic, we did not really know where the fire was coming from and I was annoyed I had missed the bomber'. Both sides were surprised, and the IED team headed off one way and the cover team the other. In the space of a few seconds the firing had stopped.

Although pretty frustrated, Captain Goodey decided not to pursue because of the risk of leading his small team into an IED field or another ambush. They consolidated their position and noticed that the IED bomber had left behind his shoes and his dish-dash robe with some remnants of the IED wire. Reasoning that this bomber must be rather brazen to lay an IED in daylight so close to Bahadur base, Captain Goodey concluded there was a reasonable chance the man might return to collect his kit. The team talked to locals who had seen the recent action, and examined the terrain. Once no civilians were around, they carefully entered a compound that would give them a view of where the bomber's equipment had been left, and set up a small observation post. They had called up another team from Bahadur on the radio, call-sign Wildcat 21 Delta (21D), under Lance Corporal Graham Theobald from Suffolk, and they established a classic quick ambush. By swapping the men around, Recce were able to deceive the locals into losing count of the troops, so that when the troops returned to Bahadur, the locals were unaware that the ambush had been set. The time was then around 13.30.

Private Adam Sloan, from King's Lynn, with his SA80 and Private Luke Nadriva, a Fijian, were positioned inside the compound. Sloan was observing the location of the bomber's kit through a tiny aperture. The aperture was too small to fire through, but the idea was that, on seeing the bomber, two of the team would step out and either arrest or engage him, as he would be only 20m away. Lance Corporal Theobold wondered aloud, 'How stupid do you have to be to come back for your flip-flops?' As he whispered this, somebody walked past the aperture. Theobold with his SA80 and Private Roley with his LMG stepped out and shouted

View of the ambush site.

a challenge at the suspected bomber, who was at that moment tinkering with an IED only 20m away.

Completely surprised by the challenge, the bomber pivoted around, shouting as he did so. At this point an unseen cover team of Taliban opened fire with their AK-47s. Returning fire, Private Roley saw that the bomber was hit repeatedly but managed to dive through a gap in a wall and into a ditch. Theobald and Roley followed up and threw an L109 grenade, which landed and then exploded in the crook of the bomber's arm, taking his head off. In this confused situation, the Taliban cover team was still firing; later it transpired that one of them was hit in the leg. Unsupported, with only four men to hand and unsure how big the enemy cover team was, Lance Corporal Theobald decided to pull back slightly. Meanwhile, the rest of the multiple were rushing to their aid as fast as they could, covering the 300m from Bahadur in record time.

By the time they arrived, the Taliban cover team had gone, so the ambush site was reoccupied and the multiple conducted what they called 'site specific exploitation', taking photographs and collecting samples in evidence bags. The bomber's body was in place but headless. About an hour later, as he talked to the locals, Captain Goodey was approached by a group of 20–30 men saying they wanted to take the body away. They were not locals, and although they were unarmed they may have been Taliban. Captain Goodey was concerned

Viking Recce Platoon on
Herrick 11.

that they understood that a grenade had caused the damage so that they did not think the troops had mutilated the body. It later emerged from the evidence that the bomber was called Tufaan and had a long track record of laying IEDs, including several that had seriously injured ISAF soldiers. The incident was all over by around 14.30.

Herrick 11 had been a difficult and arduous tour for the Vikings, but they had acquitted themselves well, impressing the units under whose command they had served. The complexity of the IED threat when combined with the mission requirement had tested them in new ways, but again they proved how much could be achieved by courage, intelligence and determination.

12 PLATOON OF THE STEELBACKS DEPLOYED TO HELMAND

In October 2009 12 Platoon of the Steelbacks also deployed as a formed platoon, commanded by Lieutenant I. J. Ginns to Musa Qalah in Helmand province and under command of the Household Cavalry Battle Group. They had a busy tour, fulfilling many roles including as police mentoring team, escort platoon, security platoon and battle group reserve. They were especially proud of the impact they had on their Afghan National Police colleagues, living with their unpredictability but staying with them in many difficult situations, to the point where many were seen as friends.

Half of 12 Platoon deployed to guard Checkpoint Zulu for some 26 days during a large battle group operation called *Mar Barcha III*. They were relieved by a much larger force, one officer commenting, 'Well, I'm glad you didn't get overrun.' Lieutenant Ginns later wrote in *Castle*:

We were also incredibly fortunate not to take any casualties. We patrolled daily, often staying overnight in various locations; we narrowly missed a suicide bomber; we had a car drive through our call-sign at high speed, we had Colour Sergeant Shaw and Lance Corporal Catchpole assaulted and we had small-arms shoots. But all we suffered were minor battle injuries with bad backs, ankles and shoulders.

VIKING BY A COMPOUND, JACKAL IN THE BACKGROUND

OPERATION *HERRICK 16,*
MARCH TO OCTOBER 2012

For the 1st Battalion this tour was once again in sharp contrast to the previous one. This time the battalion deployed as a formed battle group in its own right, considerably reinforced so that at times it had some nine rifle companies under command in the Nad-e-Ali area. The nature of the operations had changed considerably, being generally much smaller and proceeding step by step to a much greater extent than previously, reflecting small gains on a daily basis. They were also conducted almost totally in support of Afghan forces, at a lower level, so there were no large kinetic battle-group operations like those of operations *Silicon* or *Gharste Ghar* on *Herrick 6.* This reflected the changing nature of the conflict and the progress made towards handing over more responsibility for operations to the Afghan forces. The commanding officer, Lieutenant Colonel Mick Aston, MC, pointed out later that there was no single pivot point and that no one element of the battle group was decisive; rather, the success of the tour was shown in a steady day-by-day increase in the confidence of the Afghan forces, as they took on ever more ambitious and effective operations.

This gradual success is in the nature of counter-insurgency campaigns, but it is difficult to describe. During this time the British media chose not to tackle this aspect of operations in Afghanistan, continuing instead to look for sensational stories that would make headlines. Thus the press reported only so-called 'green-on-blue' incidents, where individual Afghans turned on their ISAF allies. As will be seen, 1st Battalion suffered no such green-on-blue attacks, but there was little reporting of the steady progress and consequent considerable success that was achieved. Each cleared compound, every small area of responsibility handed over to Afghan forces was a small brick of success.

Commanding officer bonding with the district chief of police.

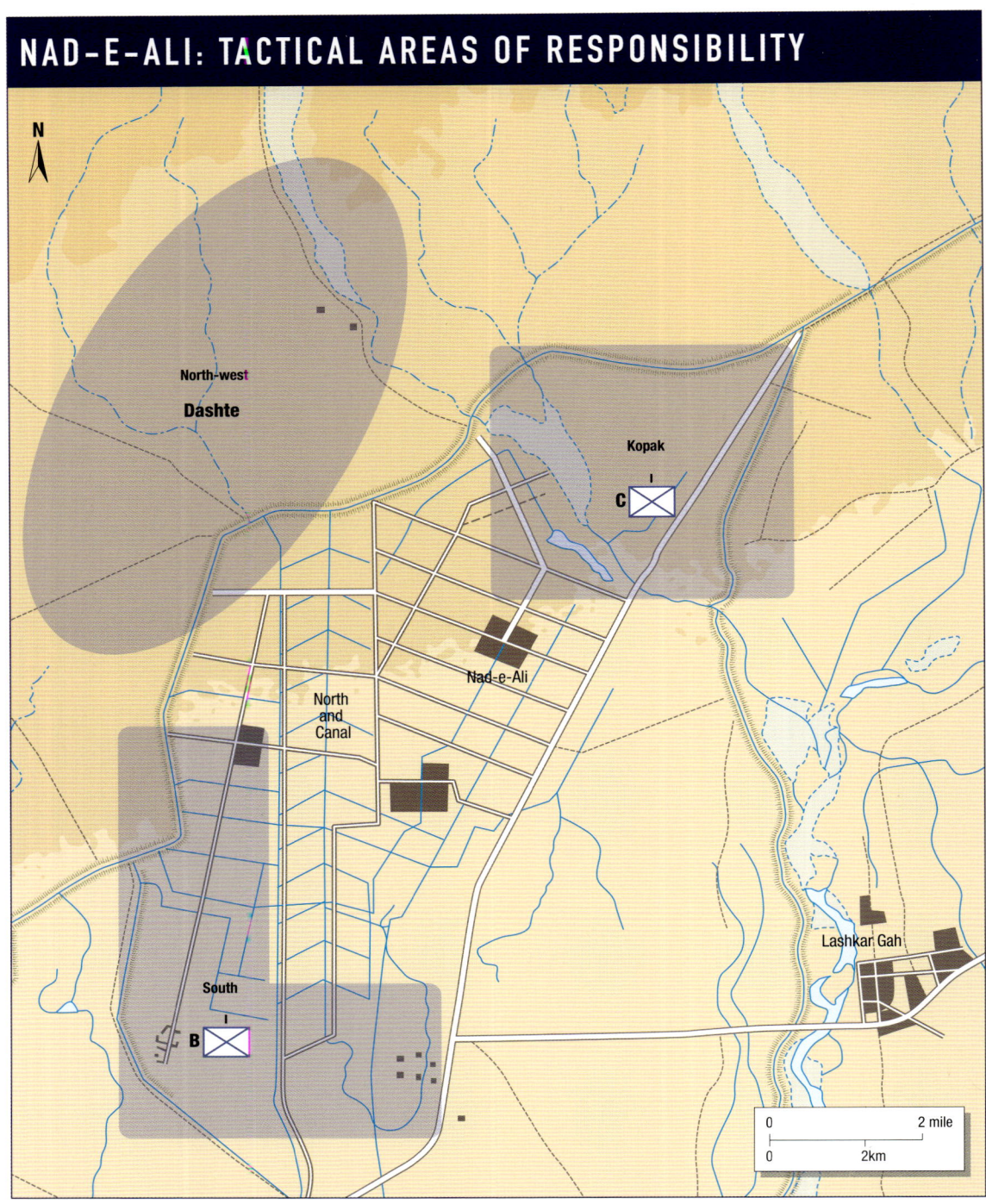

NAD-E-ALI: TACTICAL AREAS OF RESPONSIBILITY

Concurrent with these operations, the battle group continued to engage the Taliban when required. Although the overall battle group area remained the same, the company tactical areas of responsibility were changing on an almost weekly basis, producing a very complex picture, as indicated by the above map.

The Viking companies were initially deployed so that A (Norfolk) Company was Operations Company, tasked in the main with carrying out the larger, more deliberate operations across the whole of the battle group's tactical area of responsibility. B (Suffolk) Company was initially deployed into the southern area, but moved around a great deal; their tour will be described in more detail in a separate section. C (Essex) Company was deployed in the north-east in the Kopak area for the whole tour. The bulk of D (Cambridgeshire)

Company provided the Fire Support Groups for the rifle companies, with the mortar, reconnaissance and sniper platoons as battle-group assets as on earlier tours. Company headquarters provided the nucleus of the training and advisory effort and will be examined in more detail later.

Lieutenant Colonel Aston, MC later observed that, although he had been a company commander in both Iraq and Afghanistan, this tour was by far the most complex and challenging thing he had ever had to do, but it worked. Progress with this mission was quicker than expected, and also quicker than the Afghans were totally comfortable with.

Lieutenant Tomlinson and Corporal Taylor have a 'working lunch'.

Sangar living conditions in Checkpoint Tolo.

A Company on patrol.

The key was to maintain the momentum of transition, which Aston interpreted as to accelerate that rate of transition. There was so much friction, so many reasons to slow the pace, that if at any time the momentum was lost, the effect would spiral downwards. This encompassed everything from the timetable for handing over or closing bases, to police training, to the tempo of Afghan operations against the Taliban.

On arrival the Vikings took over 31 ISAF locations, but by the end of the tour they handed over just 11 – the closure of the others was a sign of the success achieved. Another feature of *Herrick 16* was increased campaign continuity between tours. The battle group therefore took over a scheme of manoeuvre and tactical design that required very little adjustment, so while the plan was tweaked during the six months, the direction of travel did not change. They very much took over a going concern from the 3rd Battalion The Royal Regiment of Scotland and benefited from the progress made in earlier *Herrick* tours, with the result that they were able to hand over a working scheme to the 1st Battalion The Mercian Regiment at the end of the tour. This was due to a variety of reasons: the situation was now more stable, the force density was probably right and the Afghan partners had more independent control than they had had previously. It also meant that, in order to ensure continuity of progress, right from the start the battalion was thinking ahead to what *Herrick 17* and *18* would look like.

It is worth looking at each of the four main areas or blocks of operation in turn.

SOUTH

In the south of the battalion's tactical area of operations, the conditions for transfer to the Afghan forces had already been met, so the main focus was to empower and enable them in order to protect the transition that had already been achieved. This was largely done through advisors, who took a step back so that the Afghans could more often take the lead in the planning and executing of operations. B (Suffolk) Company took the lead in this area.

In some sense the hard work of driving out the Taliban and allowing Afghan primacy had already been done in the south. The focus was always on the responsibility, authority and accountability of the Afghan forces, especially in the eyes of the civilian population. It was

B Company on patrol.

important that civilians perceived that the Afghan forces were delivering security rather than the ISAF forces. One of the ways to do this was actively to remove the Vikings from involvement in security, to take a step back and to close some ISAF bases. The question the Vikings had to pose was, 'What does transition look like?' This was sometimes quite hard to answer. Essentially, successful transition had Afghan forces in the lead, very light involvement from ISAF troops, good access to government services for the local population and tolerable levels of violence in the area. There were many possible measurements of effectiveness, but in the end Aston considered that their own military judgement of the situation was the most reliable guideline. The balance between maintaining momentum on the one hand and over-burdening the Afghan forces on the other was a difficult one, but was in the main achieved by allowing the confidence of the Afghan forces to grow steadily but continually.

NORTH AND WEST DESERT — THE DASHTE

The desert region, called the Dashte, to the north and west was where the previous *Herrick* operations had pushed the Taliban, into lower-quality land with a very low population density. There were insurgents in the Dashte, but so few locals that there was no insurgency as such, so the Vikings had a degree of freedom of action. The Vikings wanted to carry out operations to disrupt the Taliban in such a way that even when the insurgents responded, they would not be able to re-infiltrate the canal zone. The Vikings' intention was to act in support of the ANA, for whom this was an obvious task, but it became a source of some frustration as the local kandak (battalion) was unwilling to take the lead. Some of this was down to the personality of the kandak commander. The kandak had been in the area since 2009 and had managed to push the Taliban out of the populated areas into the Dashte. They

Estonian Sisu XA-180
armoured personnel carrier.

now wanted to maintain the status quo, rather than continue to stir up the Taliban. However, Aston saw this as a non-discretionary task: if it was not done, the insurgency would press back into the protected community.

Three additional checkpoints were constructed for the ANA in August in a major operation to help provide more of a screen or buffer between the protected area and the Dashte. Towards the last third of the tour, when B Company of the Estonian Scouts Battalion in their Sisu XA-180 series wheeled armoured vehicles were attached to the Viking battle group, the rate of disruption in the Dashte was increased. These were highly regarded, outstanding troops – fully armoured, highly mobile, with a very rapid response capability, and very willing to get on with the mission. Aston's aim was always to get ahead of the Taliban, but this usually required intelligence – often human intelligence – on Taliban intentions. This was rarely available, but nevertheless there were still some very good successes with strike operations into the Dashte, especially when the Estonian armoured infantry could be combined with aviation assets.

NORTH-EAST – KOPAK

Transition had yet to take hold in the area around Kopak in the north-east, as it had been cleared only about three months earlier. The region had been problematic because it had not been possible to generate the number of local men willing and able to be trained as local police. The Kopak area was thus still seen very much as ISAF-delivered hold – in other words, although Afghan forces had been in the lead during much of the clearing, the holding was done by ISAF. Kopak was therefore about 18 months behind the rest of the district, but it also had different dynamics, with less-developed agriculture, fewer bazaars, poorer roads and more recent memories of violence in the minds of the population.

It was clear to Aston that it would not be possible to transition Kopak fully during the tour, and he was determined not to try to bite off more than they could chew. However, some progress had to be made so that the transition could be targeted for *Herrick 17*. Higher ISAF-force density was required, so C (Essex) Company of the Vikings and B Company of the 1st Battalion The Royal Welsh, were deployed in the area throughout the tour. These were the only two companies that did not move bases during *Herrick 16*.

The effort to raise Afghan local police was continued, but this was a very stop-start process, essentially unsuccessful. Eventually, Aston decided to stop 'flogging the dead horse' and so instead persuaded the police to deploy more Afghan Uniform Police and some additional ANCOP into the area. Law and order was improved, but not to the point where it could be trusted to locally recruited police. One additional complication came from a lack of interest in the Kopak area from the civilian district government, so there was a constant effort to improve the profile of Kopak with the district governor.

The task in this area was thus about securing the north-eastern flank of the battle group, holding the gains made and not letting it slide back.

Major Guy Foden assumes command of AO Kopak from B Company, 2nd Battalion The Mercian Regiment.

TRANSFERRING CONTROL OF THE NORTH

This area – centred on the canal zone, between the south, the Dashte, and Kopak – was again something of a focus for the battle group. The aim was to reduce the ISAF involvement, encouraging the Afghan police to take on greater responsibilities. A great deal of re-balancing was done by the Vikings' battle group, with three companies moving in and out of this area

Corporal Strike of FSG-C in a Husky.

during the tour. The key was closing bases, which was a considerable logistics effort, with the return of equipment, restoring sites, liaison with landowners and even an element of gifting the land back to local ownership. These were highly complex operations, all done with a constant eye on any Taliban riposte.

The Vikings sought to keep the continuity of what had been achieved so far and also to maintain relationships with their Afghan counterparts, so everything had to be done step by small step. They were pleased to observe that the Taliban were unable to infiltrate back into the area, with the result that the confidence of the local population increased. This generated a positive spiral: local information networks started favouring the security forces, so that infiltration attempts by the Taliban would be reported early, allowing police intervention. When any larger attempts were made, the response from the district chief of police was effective and appropriate. These Taliban attempts were often carried out by small reconnaissance groups, but sometimes larger attacks were made. One checkpoint was almost overrun, with four policemen killed, but the Afghan police were able to respond themselves and put a stop to it. This in turn increased their confidence.

The plan was ambitious and bold, but it was delivered. Towards the end of the tour it was possible to go back to the district governor and report essentially 'Job done' – a major achievement by the Viking battle group.

Because of the gradual nature of these operations, this tour will be covered in a slightly different way. Given that A (Norfolk) and C (Essex) companies featured so heavily in Operation *Herrick 11*, the focus here is on B (Suffolk) and D (Cambridgeshire) companies. Rather than describing the myriad small operations, it is useful to look at the whole tour from company level, so B Company's time on *Herrick 16* is set out in chart form as an example. Some of D Company's smaller operations are examined in detail, one from a mentoring and training perspective, together with an especially successful ambush by the reconnaissance and sniper platoons.

B Company *shura*.

WEAPON MIX IN A MULTIPLE PATROL

The following quote from Lance Corporal Roberts gives an example of the weapon mix of a B (Suffolk) Company multiple patrol on *Herrick 16*:

> In our 12-man multiple, the lead man would have just an SA80, usually without the UGL, as he would also be carrying the Vallon mine detector. Next would be the secondary searcher, with a Vallon, and section commander, again both with SA80s but usually one with a UGL. The fourth man would be an LMG gunner, followed by two riflemen, one with SA80 and one with Sharpshooter rifle. Then the GPMG would be seventh, eighth would be another Sharpshooter, ninth another LMG, with three more riflemen at the rear. Generally the guys with the ECM would be 5 and 6 and 10, but this would vary. So this multiple had 7 x SA80, 2 with UGL, 2 x Sharpshooter, 2 x LMG, 1 x GPMG in total.

I Section of 6 Platoon on **Herrick 11** *showing their weapon mix.*

B (SUFFOLK) COMPANY OVERVIEW

B (Suffolk) Company, under command of Major Adam Wolfe, deployed on 12 March 2012 to patrol bases Kalang and Silab, an L-shaped patch in the southern Nad-e-Ali area. For 6 Platoon there was an element of déjà vu as they were returning to an area they knew very well from *Herrick 11* in late 2009–early 2010. The key challenge for the company was to transition control to the Afghan forces, starting as a ground-holding company, but with the aim of increasing the role of the Afghan forces as time moved along. To do this, the company later generated a number of company-level advisory teams, called Tolay Advisory Teams (TATs) from the Afghan word for 'company', and also Police Advisory Teams (PATs). Altogether the company generated three TATs and four PATs operating in an area 20km square. In May Company Sergeant Major Andrew Faupel, MBE handed over to Company Sergeant Major Hassan.

At the start of the tour the company group also contained Fire Support Group Bravo, led by Drum Major Eastwood in their Jackal vehicles, a Fire Support Team led by Captain Dawson and Sergeant Sobey of the Royal Artillery, which gave access to 81mm mortar, 105mm light gun and aviation support. The Apache or Cobra helicopter gunships were seen as the most useful form of fire support on this tour; in fact, the company did not call for mortar or artillery support at all. There was also a signals detachment and a small light aid detachment (LAD) of the Royal Electrical and Mechanical Engineers (REME).

The following table tells the story of the tour; the nature of the operations was many low-key, small steps, cumulatively making significant progress.

DATE (ALL 2012)	OPERATION	EVENTS	OUTCOME
12 March	Deployed in theatre	Advanced parties begin arriving.	
18 March	Arrival	Company group arrives in Camp Bastion.	In-theatre training starts.
28 March	Deploy to Nad-e-Ali	Company Group deployed to Kalang (Company HQ, 5 and 6 Platoons) and Silab (7 Platoon)	
2 April	Change of command	B Company assumes tactical command from A Company, 3 Scots.	
9 April	Quadrat	Whole company deployed north to Quadrat by helicopter. Manning tactical checkpoints and patrolling as part of a lager battle-group operation. In contact for entire day.	Company shakes out on its first major operation, experiencing first contacts of the tour.
17 April	Operation Tora Panchai	Search of Zaborabad; sweep, search and dominate the area. 60% ANA, 40% B Company cross boundary with USMC; insertion by USMC Osprey aircraft. Ends with massive lunch with ANA!	No finds; intelligence gathering on poppy fields and infiltration routes; deterring and disrupting insurgent activity. Good liaison with USMC. ANA practise planning and executing joint operations.
May	Several patrols into Mohamed Abed Dashte	Joint foot patrols with ANCOP to cut possible insurgent infiltration and exfiltration routes.	Consolidation and improved ANCOP confidence; some good ground intelligence gathered.
May	Across area	Lieutenant Tim Duncalfe focused on Afghan Local Police across the whole area.	Better understanding, training and intelligence.
16 May	Zaborabad	Another search of Zaborabad with ANA and ANCOP to sweep and dominate area.	No finds, but also no insurgents in the area – itself a minor success.
Mid-May	Tora Panchai 10 series rat-trap operations	Vehicle checkpoints (VCP) with ANA, ANCOP and ALP; 60 simultaneous checkpoints coordinated at junctions.	Lots of low-level intelligence on people movement, very popular with locals; improved confidence that they can move around safely.

23 May	Operation *Tora Sephah 59D*	With ANA and ANCOP into western Dashte, mainly on foot; compound searches.	Some weapons and ammunition found; successful test operation. Some contacts with insurgents; sporadic PKM fire at long range, but probably no insurgents killed.
3 June	*Shura*	Security *shura* as first step to handover of responsibility for security in Kalang. Also indicated strongly to locals that Kalang will be closed.	Improved cooperation with locals, better preparedness for handover.
June	Draw-down of Kalang	One 5 Platoon multiple sent to Bastion to re-train as police advisory team, later redeploying to Pimon in the north.	Command team of Lieutenant Thompson and Sergeant Stow trained as police advisors; this training cascaded to others.
30 June	Kalang exit	Civilian contractor brought in to level base; land handed back to three locals.	ISAF base closed.
June–July	Transition phase	New larger area of operations; Silab base handed over to ANCOP.	Re-balancing the company into a bigger area with more police and ANA advisory teams.
1 July	First Advisory Team	Reorganisation and redeployment to bases at Shawqat and Pimon.	Success: Afghan forces' confidence much improved.
Later July	Training	New recruits for Afghan Local Police (ALP).	Reinforced police advisory teams.
Later July		Many vehicle checkpoints and rat-trap operations.	Better intelligence on people movement, further improvement in locals' confidence to move around safely.
5 July	Operation *Tora Sephah 63A*	ANCOP and ALP search and find or detain policing task in Badullah Culp area.	Joint intelligence gathered but no contacts and no finds.
17 August	Operation *Qalb AZ 53*	Large operation mounted from Shawqat; preliminary move in vehicles (Mastiff and Ridgeback), Tac, 5 Platoon and FSG-B. Rendezvous with ANCOP and ALP in Sayedabad, then night move on foot; extensive searching with Vallon.	Large number of finds; four weapons caches found by Private Steven Carr, Sergeant Matt Wheeler and Major Adam Wolfe; important suspect detained; no contacts.
24 August	Operation *Qalb AZ 64*	Another cordon and search operation with ANCOP, but quite deep into the western Dashte area known as 'the Garden'. Vehicle insertion with attack helicopter support.	Some small finds for ANCOP. Major find for B Company of RPG with ammunition, small-arms ammunition and explosives. In contact throughout operation.
Late August	Repeated *Qalb AZ*	Joint cordon and search operations.	ALP training improved all the time.
Mid-September	Deliberate intelligence-led operation	Contacts in the Mohammed Abed Dashte.	Beginning to mount intelligence-led operations to deny insurgents freedom of movement in Dashte.
Late September	Cordon and search operations	Mounted in northern Dashte in conjunction with Estonians.	Some contacts, but much improved Afghan training and confidence in evidence.
3 October	Handover	Handover command to A Company, 1st Battalion The Mercian Regiment.	End of B Company tour; staging back via Cyprus to 'decompress'.

Above left: B Company Tac under fire.

Above right: B Company standing by to board a US Osprey on Operation *Tora Panchai*.

D (CAMBRIDGESHIRE) COMPANY OVERVIEW

D (Cambridgeshire) Company is a complex organisation that used to be known as Support Company. During Operation *Herrick 16* the company provided three Fire Support Groups, A, B and C, more or less permanently to each of the rifle companies. In addition, the mortar, sniper and reconnaissance platoons were deployed to provide fire support. They were grouped as battle-group assets but would be deployed in detachments to different companies for particular operations. The sniper and reconnaissance platoons were grouped together for much of the tour and some of their operations will be looked at in detail below. The company

Captain Crosbie confers with the ANA.

headquarters element formed the nucleus of a Kandak Advisory Team (KAT). This had smaller Tolay Advisory Teams (TATs) under command. The advisory team task was a challenging one at all levels. It required diplomatic, negotiating, influencing and persuasion abilities in addition to the more usual soldiering skills.

Major Allen advising.

Led by Major Bev Allen, the KAT had some five subsidiary TATs under its command. Due to the complexities of the deployment, this organisation was detached from the Vikings' battle group and placed under command of the 3rd Battalion The Rifles during the tour, despite their being co-located with the Vikings' battle group headquarters in Shawqat – all potentially rather confusing. This was a mobile role and they would often be on the ground with the ANA's 1/3/215 Kandak, or out visiting their TATs.

An ANA lunch on Operation *Shafuq*.

The KAT mounted three large operations with the 1/3/215 Kandak. The first, Operation *Shafuq*, was a large cordon and search on foot. The second, Operation *Atash*, involved a night helicopter assault into highly contested space; although there were few small-arms contacts, many IEDs were encountered, one of which killed a Tolay commander. The third, Operation *Azadi*, was very kinetic and is described below.

One of the key challenges to the advisory teams was to achieve their mission but also to manage the

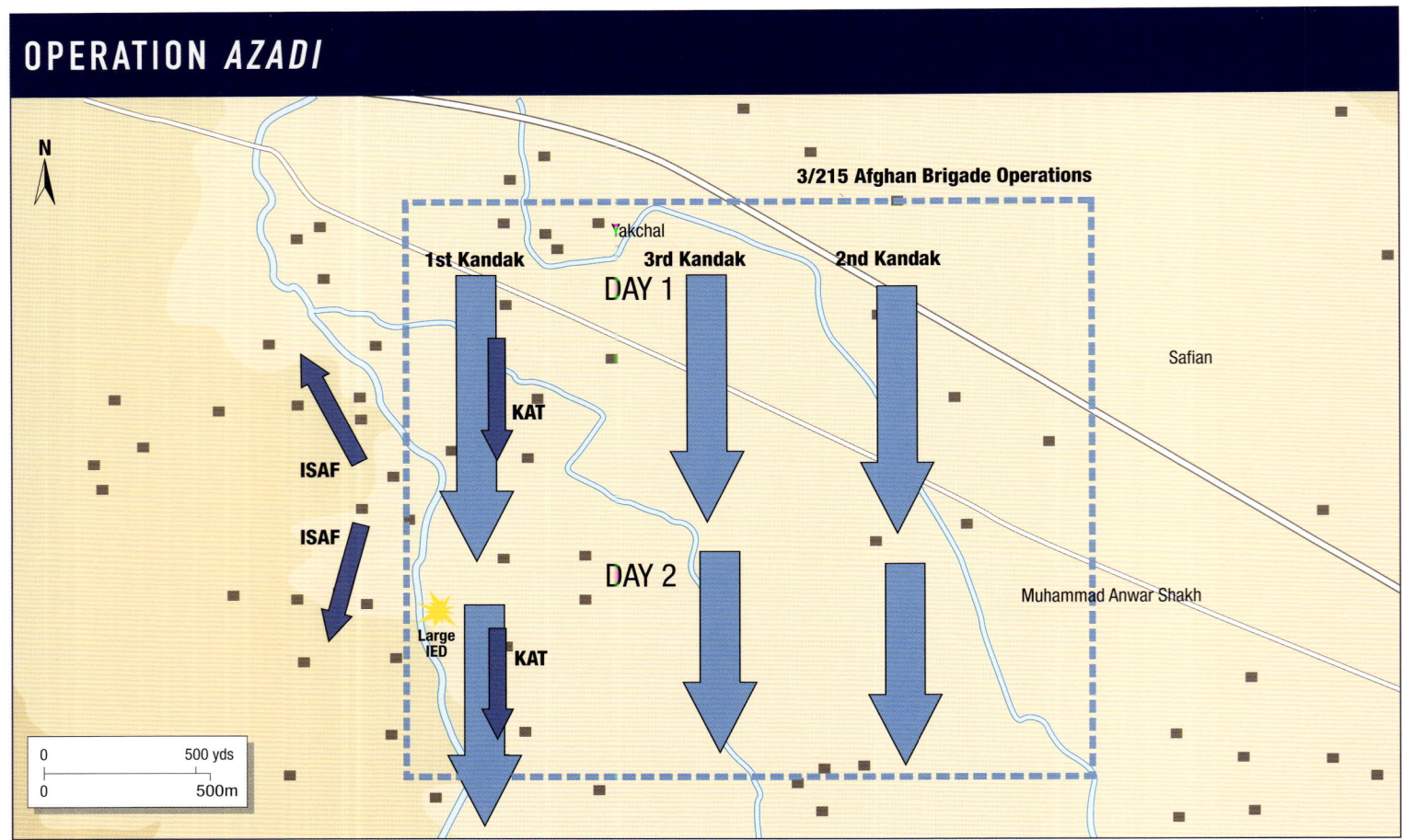

threat of any 'green-on-blue' incidents. There was a difficult line to tread between encouraging and influencing the Afghan forces – on occasion also leading from the front – but not pushing them too far. Captain Nick Denning, the company second-in-command, explained later that it was a huge puzzle. Both he and Major Allen spent a great deal of time alone with the Afghan forces, but they never really felt that they were in serious personal danger. The key was the ability to maintain good relationships with their Afghan counterparts in all situations.

One delicate situation arose on Operation *Atash* when the Tolay commander was killed by an IED. Captain Will Otridge was threatened by the highly stressed Afghans immediately after the explosion; understandably, they wanted a casualty evacuation under way, and also just wanted to make something happen. The medic, Private Farrow of the Royal Army Medical Corps, could see that the commander was already dead but he dressed his wounds anyway. Staying calm and professional, Captain Otridge was able to organise a 'Pedro' Black Hawk casualty evacuation helicopter and gradually the Afghans calmed down. The supporting Viking multiple, led by Sergeant Willan, was also able to help defuse the situation by insisting that the Vikings kept their weapons pointing down and by not reacting to Afghan provocation. Overall, though, this was seen as an anomaly in the otherwise excellent relationships between the KAT and TATs and their Afghan counterparts. It was therefore a shock to hear later that Captain Denning's successor was killed in a green-on-blue incident in the following tour.

Operation *Azadi* took place towards the end of the tour, between 13 and 17 September 2012 in the area of Yakchal. It was a very large ANA brigade-level operation involving Kandaks 1/3/215, 3/3/215 and 2/3/215 of the 3/215 Afghan Brigade. The mission for the whole of Task Force Helmand was to provide the 'wrap' around the ANA operation – in other words, they formed a kind of outer screen or cordon around the operational area to help secure it so that the ANA could operate almost alone. Apart from the KATs and TATs, there would be no ISAF forces inside this so-called 'operations box'. This was an important step in improving the ANA's confidence and ability to conduct operations essentially on their own, albeit with distant ISAF support.

The 3/215 Brigade was to sweep on foot from the north to the south, three kandaks across. The Viking KAT, led by Major Bev Allen with the role of advising the kandak commander, was with the most westerly kandak, 1/3/215, with their right flank against the river. Beyond the river was the Dashte desert – essentially an ungoverned space – so their right flank was going to be a concern.

The first day's sweep was relatively uneventful – just two IEDs that were easily dealt with – and the Kandak HQ and their KAT took over a compound for the night, having reached their first day report line. The second day was much more eventful, even though much less ground was to be covered. Within the first 200m an IED was found. As this was being dealt with, a second IED was discovered close to the first, at which point the brigade commander ordered a halt.

Meanwhile, to the rear, other members of the ANA were conducting 'biometric enrolment' – attempting to identify insurgents using various classified biometric techniques. Some eight suspects had been thus identified and loaded into

IED explosion.

an armoured Humvee vehicle, which was travelling south in a convoy, when a massive explosion was heard. It was a large command-wire IED and it essentially destroyed most of the vehicle. Major Allen described how they heard this explosion some 2km away to the north, at which point many of the Afghans started 'legging it to the north'. Arriving at the horrific scene, Allen saw body parts strewn all around the crater. The Taliban then opened fire from across the river.

Simultaneously with this attack, another tolay to the south-east came under fire. The Vikings' 1st TAT was with them, under Captain Andy Emerson who was hit, probably by an underslung grenade fragment. Fortunately, Company Sergeant Major Love was with the 1st TAT conducting a resupply with Mastiff and Husky vehicles, so he was able to help directly. Major Allen recalls a very hectic time as he tried to ascertain how bad the wounds were, organise a helicopter casualty evacuation for Captain Emerson, advise the kandak commander on the large IED incident and stop some of the Afghan troops spraying the area with fire, all the time under sporadic fire from Taliban across the river. Within 15 minutes the 'Pedro' Black Hawk helicopter was inbound and Company Sergeant Major Love had

D Company vehicles.

organised the move of Captain Emerson by Husky to the helicopter landing site. Just as the situation seemed to be coming under control, there was a radio message from the Husky driver reporting that it was bogged down and at that precise moment the contact was resumed, with more quite accurate fire from across the river. Responding quickly, Love had the presence of mind to get to the Husky and quickly tow it out with his Mastiff vehicle so that the casualty was at the landing site in time for the Pedro's arrival.

Major Allen having a
Lawrence of Arabia moment.

Meanwhile, back at the IED site, Afghan soldiers were still looking for the Humvee, which, it later transpired, had been blown off the road into the river. Major Allen recalls the surreal sight of some ANA soldiers stripped and diving into the river to try to ascertain the fate of their two colleagues in the vehicle, while others continued to return fire at the Taliban across the river. By about lunchtime the two men were still missing, which was having a very negative effect on Afghan morale. Major Allen suggested to the kandak commander that he could task a Royal Engineers diving team to help with searching the river, and the kandak commander very readily agreed.

The Viking KAT spent the night in a nearby compound, which Allen remembers had an adjacent pomegranate orchard – perhaps a memorable place in which to have your first taste of a fresh pomegranate.

The Royal Engineers diving team was brought in the following day, Day 3, but by the time they arrived the Afghan improvised divers had already located the lost vehicle and started to pull it out. The Humvee was almost unrecognisable as an armoured vehicle and the two crew had stood no chance of survival. Even though the Royal Engineers did not so much as get their feet wet, the fact that the KAT had been able to task them and deliver on the promise counted for a lot. The rest of Day 3 was spent clearing the area of the large IED. By this time the contacts had stopped because the ISAF wrap had moved in closer, inhibiting Taliban movement and preventing further contacts.

A D Company sharpshooter scans some open ground.

MIFFY THE MASCOT

Many soldiers have had mascots over the years, which have accompanied them on operations. This is the strange story of a toy rabbit, named after the children's book character Miffy, who became a mascot. While skiing before an Operation *Telic* tour in 2008, Major Bev Allen found the toy on the ground under a ski lift, obviously dropped by her real owner; he nobly retrieved the rabbit and stuck her on the outside of his day sack in the hope that her owner would spot her. By the fourth day of the trip, nobody had claimed Miffy so, as Major Allen was going to Iraq the next day, she went with him. Miffy was much photographed in Iraq, and she has accompanied him on every operation since.

Well-armed mascot Miffy.

Captain Nick Denning and Miffy. There was a growing concern that Captain Denning became rather too attached to Miffy on Herrick 16.

On Day 4, the brigade commander re-shaped the operation so that the 1/3/215 Kandak was redeployed far to the south together with their Viking KAT in Warthog vehicles. They had a clearance task, going through the Dashte to act as a southern screen, and eventually they moved to Taparigi, an ANP checkpoint.

This was a long, complex and tricky operation for the ANA, and it was not typical, most of their operations were far less eventful. The D Company KAT had achieved all that it set out to do, helping to ensure that the ANA could build on this difficult experience and turn it into increased confidence that they could mount ever more ambitious operations more or less on their own.

HERRICK 16 RECCE AMBUSH, 13–14 AUGUST 2012

This operation provides an example of another method through which ISAF could counter the unusual threat of an especially skilled sniper, although the IED threat remained the principal concern. This sniper was nicknamed 'Nowzadi' and was suspected of killing two and injuring eight ISAF soldiers, as well as several others in the ANA, in just one five-day period in early August 2012. He was using a Dragunov SVD 7.62mm sniper rifle with a telescopic sight. He was clearly becoming a cause for concern, generating a cumulative psychological effect on ISAF troops in the area. Most of these engagements were single

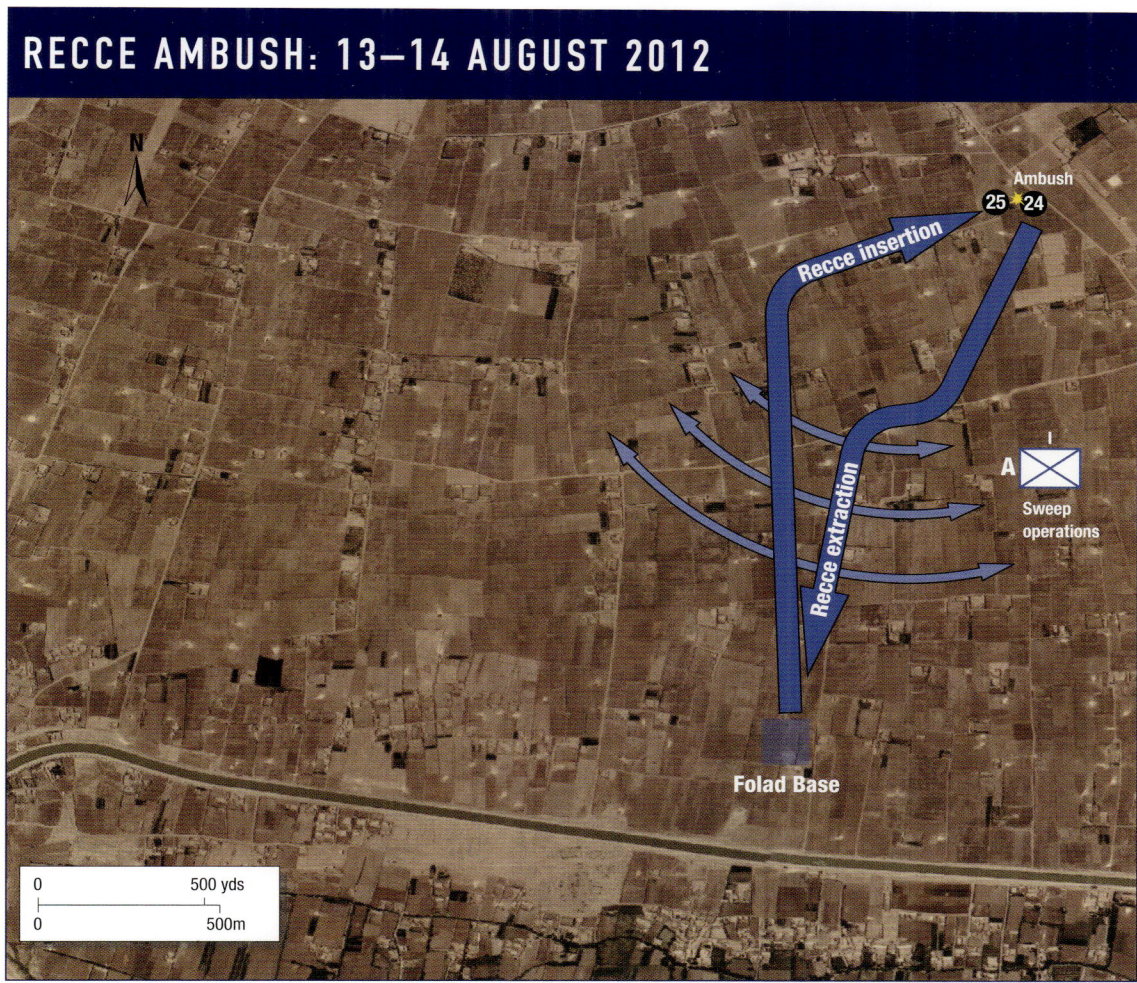

RECCE AMBUSH: 13–14 AUGUST 2012

N

Ambush
25 ★ 24

Recce insertion

Recce extraction

A ☒
Sweep
operations

Folad Base

0   500 yds
0   500m

shots at over 600m, sometimes up to 900m, and he seemed able to avoid the body armour of his target.

The area of operations was on the northern edge of the Nad-e-Ali area, centred around a prominent bend in the main road between bases called Quadrat and Folad, which had been a hotspot for the placing of IEDs for some months. To counter this, a string of new temporary checkpoints were being built in order to keep both sides of the road bend under continuous observation. C Company of 3 Rifles were providing the close-in, almost static, protection role, with A (Norfolk) Company (as operations company) deployed as outer protection in a more mobile role. The main Taliban approach into the area was from the north, so these operations were designed to disrupt their approach.

At this time Recce's primary task was to set counter-IED ambushes in this area. The Taliban were tending to place them in daylight when they could blend in with civilian activity, making the troops' task much more complicated. Recce, however, was still tasked with night ambushes, and having to take considerable risks during some of them.

Recce was ordered to carry out a counter-sniper operation to try to remove Nowzadi as a threat. Discussing the options at length with the team, Captain Mark Garner, the Recce platoon commander, decided that in order to catch someone as skilled as this sniper they would have to get into the location unseen. 'Kenno [Sergeant Paul Kennedy] and I were sat in the smoking area and I remember discussing it saying we can't keep going out, walking into ambush positions, somebody is going to get killed. Kenno said that on *Herrick 11* Recce did these ambushes from compounds, can we replicate that here?'

Recce was under pressure to have an effect quickly, but they thought that a carefully researched and planned, well-executed operation would have the highest chance of success. Essentially, they were to plan what was called a deliberate active counter-sniping operation. Knowing where the next compound operation was to take place and where A Company would be positioned, they conducted a ground appreciation to deduce the most likely approaches by the Taliban and the options for ambushing this approach. They then picked a series of compounds, and had the whole platoon watching all the available surveillance feeds to generate a pattern-of-life study so that they became familiar with the behaviour of the locals. One of these feeds showed a weapon being cached in Compound 24, which was on a route previously well-used by insurgents, so this was a strong indication that the Taliban might use it.

There was a long discussion about whether to set the ambush in Compound 24, or whether to use Compound 25 – 70m to the west – as the base for the ambush. It was decided that the latter course was more likely to be successful and Recce began to plan the operation in detail. They knew a family and their animals were living in Compound 25, but they were not very active outside the compound. By occupying Compound 25 they knew they would eventually be compromised, but they deduced, correctly as it turned out, that they might be able to mount the ambush for 24 hours or maybe longer before local curiosity gave away their location.

Once the plan was complete they conducted rehearsals before heading out from Base Folad on the evening of 13 August. Local activity died down after 23.00, so the large Recce multiple of 18 men headed out just before midnight into the warm, moonless night. The 2km approach was uneventful and they went over the walls of Compound 25 by around 01.00.

Having secured the compound, the multiple then talked at length to the resident family, who decided to spend the time in a corner room, although it being summer they would normally sleep outside in the middle of the compound. They were concerned for their animals, but otherwise reasonably cooperative. The multiple then set about preparing the compound for the ambush, a work phase which mainly involved carefully and quietly carving out firing apertures in the compound walls. The main gate was barricaded with logs and 14-gauge wire. The longer-ranged sniper weapons were deployed facing long vistas to the north and west, while the shorter-ranged shoot towards Compound 24 was covered by the other weapons. The apertures were completed before first light, by 04.30, the ambush

View through the aperture.

was set and the multiple settled into a routine for what was to be a long and very hot day. They were organised into three groups at this time: 'gates and goats', tasked with looking after the gate and animals; 'ambush group' based along the eastern compound wall; and 'command group' in the centre of the compound.

Between 05.00 and around 08.00, A Company conducted a sweep-type operation to the south of Compound 25, with another between 11.00 and 13.30, this time with Jackal vehicles. Recce had an awkward moment when some children banged on the compound door in the early afternoon, but without a response they headed off. Two young men walked past the compound a short time later, but did nothing. At this time, in the sweltering 40°C heat, Recce was beginning to think that they might have been compromised.

Recce on *Herrick 16*.

At 14.30, medic Private Corbett, who was on guard duty, saw two armed men on motorbikes approaching from the north. The ambush group quickly set themselves, two at apertures and three at ladders along the eastern compound wall. The men got off their bikes at the north-west corner and walked towards Compound 24 with their weapons. After confirming their rules of engagement, the ambush team prepared to open fire, four with 7.62mm sniper support weapons and one with an SA80 with underslung grenade launcher. Two further Taliban fighters came out of the compound at this point, also armed. On a count of 'Three, two, one' queued from Captain Garner at the aperture, as each Taliban fighter picked up their weapons, the three ladder men stepped up and opened fire over the compound wall, each firing about ten rounds and the 40mm underslung grenades. At only 70m range, this burst of fire dropped the four Taliban immediately. Soon afterwards three more appeared from the compound and picked up the dropped weapons, prompting a second burst from Recce. These three also fell.

As this second engagement was under way, one of the youngest members of the team, Private Stevens, called out 'Stop, stop, stop!' He could see a group of women and children who had left Compound 24 from the far side and who were now approaching the area of the firing. The other members of the team could not see them, so it was very fortunate that Stevens had spotted them and shouted the check fire just in time. The ladder men stepped down, but the apertures continued to observe.

The Taliban in Compound 24 did not seem to know where the fire had come from, a fact which was confirmed as the interpreter listened to the communications intercept radio. Captain Garner then had a difficult decision to make: whether to hot pursue into the Taliban bodies or remain secure within Compound 25. He decided on the latter, as there would be little advantage in a pursuit; the damage had been done and the Taliban were still unsure where the fire had come from. Within about a minute of the check fire, while the pursuit was being considered, a group of women all dressed in turquoise robes appeared and quickly started to carry away the bodies in wheelbarrows, still seemingly unaware of Recce. The Taliban's uncertainty probably increased the impact this operation had on them – it would have generated considerable fear.

CORPORAL JOE WARREN'S RECOLLECTION OF HIS WOUNDING ON *HERRICK 16*

Corporal Joe Warren of B (Suffolk) Company recalls his wounding during Operation *Herrick 16*:

I stood up, turned and followed on the rest of the patrol; I took about five steps and then snap. My arm felt like it had exploded from the inside, a big cloud of red mist sprayed out in front of my face, with a white mist centre, I began to spin and fall to the ground, the round had hit me in the left arm, then exited and smashed into my sniper rifle scope causing me to spin 180° before I hit the ground. As I fell through the air I remember my thought process being very fast, 'you're going home. I'll get some good compensation for this one, no more heat sweat and work, you can let your guard down, that white mist looked like bone'. I even had time to look at my arm as I fell, realising it was just my arm, and that I wasn't in too much trouble. As I landed I looked at the rest of the patrol who were now returning fire as the enemy continued to engage, I wasn't in much pain as I noticed that no one had seen me go down, and instead of shouting 'man down', I just let out a scream that they would expect from an injured soldier and sure enough they started to shout 'man down'. Someone shouted to Private Holland to get to me as he was the closest guy.

One of the two soldiers next to me began to help. Blood was squirting out of my arm as he began to tighten the tourniquet, it was then that the pain really came, I mean really came. The white mist I saw was bone, in fact the bullet had shattered around 6cm of my radius and the tourniquet was now forcing that broken bone down into my pulverised arm. It seemed like only seconds had passed as Lance Corporal Bargery [the medic] ran over, driving a morphine syringe into my leg as he took a knee beside me and began to go to work. The fire-fight was now raging as the boss turned and shouted, 'Woz can you walk?' I looked at my arm, then tried to stand up, my arm touched the ground and I collapsed in excruciating pain as I shouted 'NO, I don't think I can.' Before I knew it I was on a stretcher and being evacuated as the rest of the lads peeled along beside us, giving a heavy weight of covering fire. The pain was quite intense, I found that swearing and laughing hysterically took the edge off.

On the stretcher, I raised my head and looked back at the Platoon Sergeant's multiple as they covered us. I saw two of our boys in a ditch as a UGL landed in it with them, they disappeared into a cloud of kicked-up dust and I waited for the shout of man down, however it did not come, they had somehow escaped without injury and carried on engaging. Watching the fire-fight as I was being extracted was very strange. I could see the whole battle as I left the area, every bit of dust that was being kicked up, and the UGLs coming down around the other multiple. For want of a better word, it was pretty epic. Soon I was in relatively safe ground, with two medics checking me over and giving me more morphine, which I still couldn't feel. I felt more dehydrated than ever as I shouted for water. Private Holland ran over to me with his camelback straw in his hand; as he got to me he accidently kicked my wounded arm. I sat up, opened my mouth to shout, but before I did he stuck the straw in my mouth and I drank instead. Come to think of it he still owes me a beer for that. With the fire-fight easing off I heard the blades of a helicopter and was soon being loaded onto it, a familiar ride for me as I have been casevaced twice before.

Joe Warren eventually recovered from his injuries, but had to leave the Army in 2013.

Corporal Joe Warren being prepared for casevac after being wounded.

VIKING ON *HERRICK 16* WITH L129A1 SNIPER SUPPORT WEAPON

Company Sergeant Major
Clark hands out new
shoes to local children on
Operation *Herrick 11*.

Nothing further happened until, at about 17.30, the local imam came to the compound and asked that the family be allowed to leave, clearly indicating that the location was now compromised, but the family actually asked to stay until it was dark. The multiple left Compound 25 after last light at around 19.30, swiftly patrolling the 2km south back into Base Folad. Much of the route was covered by the base, so they could move reasonably swiftly and were back by 21.30. They had run out of water during the sweltering day and by the time they got in, Corporal McCall remembers, 'We were clagging hard, so we went straight to the cookhouse, drinking loads of water straight away.'

Higher formation intelligence later confirmed that both the sniper Nowzadi and the local Taliban commander had been killed in this incident, together with three other fighters. Recce freely admitted that the appearance of Nowzadi in the ambush was really down to luck, but they had demonstrated that it is possible, at least to some extent, to make your own luck with a well-planned and well-executed operation.

SUMMARY

At the point of the Regiment's 50th anniversary the 2nd Battalion will have just returned from Operation *Herrick 19* and the 1st Battalion will be preparing to return to Afghanistan in early 2015.

The history of operations in Afghanistan amply demonstrates that The Royal Anglian Regiment is a fighting regiment. On *Herrick 6* the 1st Battalion engaged in what has been described as some of the British Army's most intensive infantry fighting since the Second World War. In doing so, the battalion took on the Taliban 2007 summer offensive, grabbed it by the horns and defeated it in over 350 fire-fights, inflicting massive losses. This achievement firmly imprinted the reputation of the Regiment across the wider army, but it also created a wave of public support, especially in the counties of East Anglia, that strengthened the Regiment's link with the wider population. This was shown by the impressive turnout for the battalion's post-tour parades in Norwich and Bury St Edmunds.

The *Herrick 11* tour was more complicated and difficult, with the battalion deployed in separate pieces under command of other units, operating jointly with the ANA and implementing the change in operational tempo to a firm emphasis on hearts and minds. At times it felt like they were fighting in a minefield, the heightened IED threat straining nerves and testing patience on most operations. Despite this, members of the Regiment were able to show not only implacable resolve when engaging the Taliban, but real compassion when handing out shoes to local children or listening to the concerns of the elders in *shura*s.

Herrick 16 saw the Vikings deployed as a large battle group once more, but this tour was different again. It was a story of many small steps, with a keen focus on the transition of authority to the Afghan security forces. In a complex series of smaller operations, the Vikings were able to press the momentum and again delivered major success. This complex tour required the extensive use of diplomatic skills in advising their Afghan counterparts.

Throughout these tours, the support and commitment from the Steelbacks has made a very real and positive contribution. Their ability to integrate quickly and seamlessly with their full-time colleagues has been a key feature of the Territorial soldiers' contribution, but they have also shown themselves to be committed and professional under that hardest of tests: enemy fire. This has given the 3rd Battalion an impressive leavening of operational experience, which is the envy of many other infantry units.

This tremendous achievement by the Regiment as a whole has been marked and recognised by awards for gallantry and distinguished service to many individuals, with one Commander of the Military Division of the Most Excellent Order of the British Empire (CBE), three Companions of the Distinguished Service Order (DSO), five Members of the Military Division of the Most Excellent Order of the British Empire (MBE), ten Military Crosses (MC) and one Queen's Gallantry Medal (QGM) and a number of other honours.

This success has come at a terrible cost – some 15 members of the Regiment have given their lives during these operations. Nine were killed on *Herrick 6*, five on *Herrick 11* and one on *Herrick 16*. We will remember them. In addition, a large number of members of the Regiment were seriously injured in Afghanistan – some 57 on *Herrick 6*, 42 on *Herrick 11* and 32 on *Herrick 16*. We wish them a good recovery and a positive future.

NOTES

1. Colonel Richard Kemp and Chris Hughes, *Attack State Red (Penguin, 2009)*; James Cartwright, *Sniper in Helmand* (Pen and Sword, 2011).
2. The story of the southern part of the operation is in Patrick Hennessey, *The Junior Officers' Reading Club* (Penguin, 2009), pp.179–90.
3. For a more detailed account of Operation *Silicon*, see Colonel Richard Kemp and Chris Hughes, *Attack State Red*, pp.36–98.
4. *Castle: Journal of The Royal Anglian Regiment* (Vol. 16, No. 1, June 2010), p.65.

IRAQ

A Viking mobile patrol in Az Zubayr.

Operation *Telic* was the British name given to the invasion and subsequent operations in Iraq between 19 March 2003 and 22 May 2011. The British involvement in Iraq was centred on the south-east region around the southern city of Basra. From the Regiment's point of view, deployment to Iraq started with the 1st Battalion, under the command of Lieutenant Colonel Eddie Thorne, MC, on Operation *Telic 6* in April 2005, when the situation had settled into a counter-insurgency mission in support of the Iraqi army and police. Although the battalion deployed with a Security Sector Reform (SSR) mission to improve the capability of the Iraqi forces, the tempo of operations against the insurgents in the area varied greatly, from intense action to some periods with few incidents. Some of the key events are shown in the table opposite.

A number of detention and search operations were undertaken. A (Norfolk) Company was deployed in two halves, split between Camp Driftwood at Al Faw in the south and Basra Palace. B (Suffolk) Company was deployed initially to Chindit Camp in the town of Az Zubayr, some 15km south-west of Basra. C (Essex) Company was initially detached from the battalion and placed under command of the Royal Hussars Battle Group, based at Al Muthanna, but later became the brigade reserve company. D (Cambridgeshire) Company underwent a complex reorganisation: contributing assets to form a brigade-level surveillance company and, within the battle group, a Security Reform Cell and a Command and Information System (CIS) platoon. Other anti-tank mortar and drums assets were grouped with the rifle companies. Major James Woodham was selected to command the Brigade Surveillance Company and was later awarded the Military Cross for his actions during an incident.

DATES (ALL 2005)	EVENT
26 April	1 R ANGLIAN Battle Group take over Basra Rural South area.
10 May	Remote-controlled IED at Topeka junction against ATO vehicle, no casualties.
30 July	Shaped-charge IED attack against a Foreign & Commonwealth Office convoy, two killed.
5 September	Shaped-charge IED attack against a brigade convoy at Az Zubayr, two killed.
12 September	Shoot at B Company patrol in Az Zubayr, no casualties.
12 September	120mm round remote-controlled IED attack on US private security company, no casualties.
13 September	Shaped-charge IED attack on US private security company, no casualties.
26 September	Shaped-charge IED attack on US convoy on a slip road, two killed.
27 September	Shaped-charge IED attack on UK convoy, no casualties.
28 September	Shaped-charge IED attack on US convoy at Safwaan, two killed.
28 September	Find of a large remote-controlled blast IED.
29 September	C Company patrol find a remote-controlled Claymore device.
29 September	Camp Chindit closed, handed over to Iraqi army.
1 October	Operation *Circumvent*, a battle group search operation onto a farm south-west of Az Zubayr revealed a large quantity of weaponry including launch frames for rockets, RPG rockets and two 82mm mortars.
3 October	US find a remote-controlled 152mm artillery shell IED.
13 October	Shaped-charge IED attack on a water convoy, one civilian killed.
15 October	Iraqi referendum.
27 October	1 R ANGLIAN Battle Group hand over Basra Rural South area to 9th/12th Lancers Battle Group.

Although there was violence between the Sunni and Shia factions in Basra itself in 2005, the main threat to the security forces came from the largest Shia insurgent group called the Jaish al-Mahdi (JAM), sometimes called the Mahdi militia or Mahdi army, who were nominally led by the cleric Muqtada al-Sadr. In reality they were made up of various disparate groups operating semi-independently. They formed in 2003 but were not very active until 2004, as their campaign began as a response to the attempted banning of al-Sadr's newspaper. With close connections to the Iranians and easy supply lines between Basra and the border, supplies of Iranian weapons flowed in. They managed to infiltrate a number of sympathisers into the rapidly recruited Iraqi police, and even some into the Iraqi army. Several attempts at arranging a ceasefire failed and the violence increased significantly, so by the time the Vikings arrived in 2005, they were a capable and well-supplied insurgent faction.

Supplies of improved RPGs also started to appear at this time. These were Iranian copies of former Soviet or Chinese designs together with indigenous Iranian designs, appearing under a plethora of names and in a number of variants, but one system called the RPG-29 or Vampir was definitely used. In addition to newly designed systems, more advanced warheads for the older RPG-7 were also being used.

The JAM became increasingly proficient at indirect-fire attacks on security force bases using mortars of 60mm, 81mm, 82mm and 120mm calibre and the 107mm rocket often called the 'Chinese Rocket'. This was based on the round used by the 107mm B-11 recoilless rifle, which could be fired from a range of improvised single or multiple launchers. The

JAISH AL-MAHDI WEAPONS

The Jaish al-Mahdi (JAM) was initially equipped with a range of small arms taken from former Iraqi army stocks, including the ubiquitous AK-47 assault rifle, RPK and PKM machine guns and the RPG-7. From around 2005–06 they began to obtain supplies of Iranian copies of the Heckler & Koch 7.62mm G-3 assault rifle; indeed the presence of this weapon was later to characterise JAM involvement.

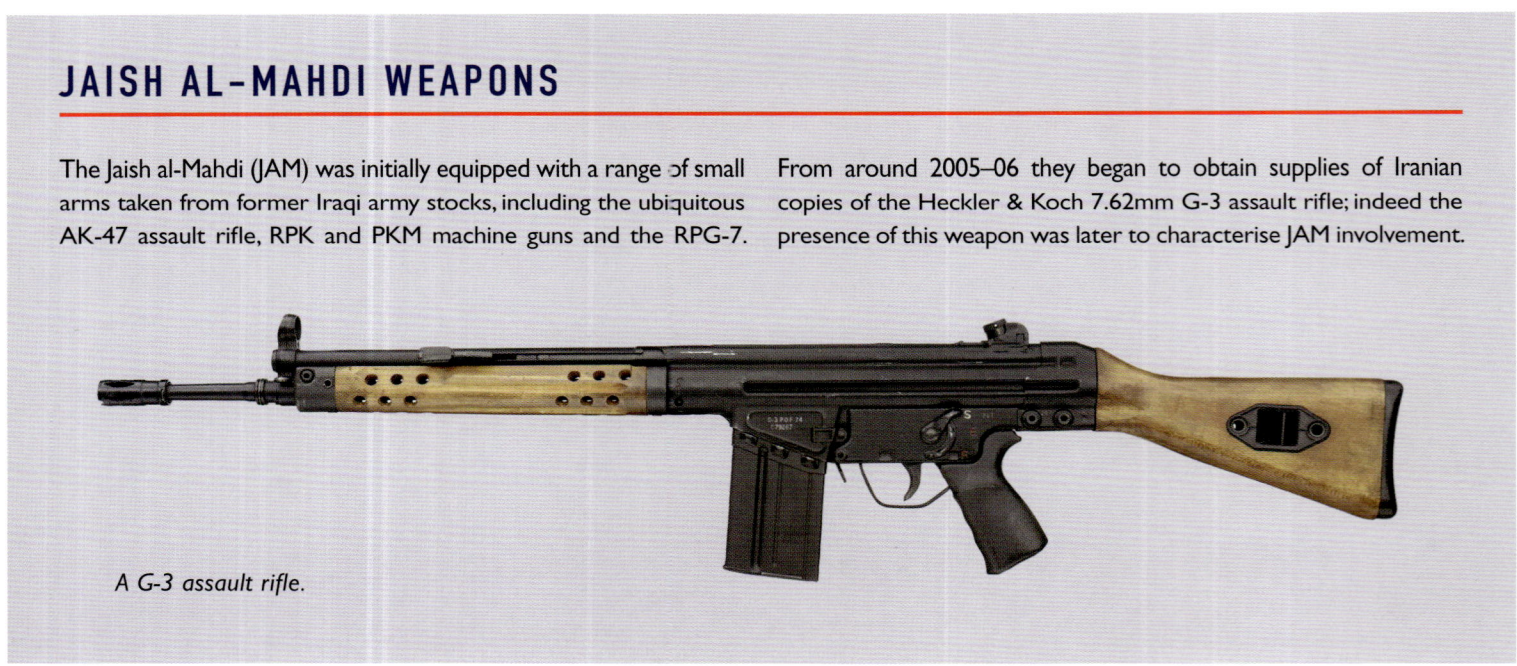

A G-3 assault rifle.

indirect-fire attack became something of a JAM speciality. Some attacks, using military-grade technology, proved highly effective, and the JAM continually improved the effectiveness and accuracy of these.

The JAM also had easy access to large quantities of explosive with which they could mount IED attacks. These varied greatly in sophistication, from simple artillery shells attached to a command wire to highly specialised anti-tank IEDs.

Captain Smit of the Vikings talks to the locals in a market in Basra.

OPERATION *TELIC 8*

Lieutenant Colonel Des O'Driscoll, commanding officer of the Poachers, conducted a reconnaissance of Basra in January 2006, when the Poachers were based in Clive Barracks in Tern Hill. Between then and their arrival in April 2006, the security situation in Basra deteriorated significantly. Not always a totally reliable source, the United Nations High Commissioner for Refugees (UNHCR) published an interesting report in August 2006 that described the period just before the Poachers' arrival:

> Relations between the British Forces and the local government soured after January 2006. After a series of arrests of corrupt police officials and following the release of a video appearing to show UK troops beating Iraqi civilians in Southern Iraq, the Provincial Council suspended relations with British Forces in February 2006. It was not until early May that local authorities agreed to formally resume co-operation.[1]

C Company of the Poachers with an arrested Iraqi suspect.

The force commander in Basra, General Cooper, had responded to a marked increase in the IED threat by ordering an immediate and strict 'Warrior Lead' policy. Every patrol had to be led by a well-protected Warrior armoured vehicle, which was highly successful because the insurgents expended great effort and ingenuity trying to destroy the Warriors. It became something of an obsession for the JAM, but their increasingly complex tactics were mainly rewarded with failure. The vehicle's excellent armoured protection meant that few soldiers were killed in a Warrior during Operation *Telic*, which effectively 'soaked off' and blunted the main insurgent IED effort.

Poachers in Snatch Land Rovers in Iraq in 2006.

ANTI-TANK IEDs

The Iraqi insurgents developed especially clever IEDs designed specifically to attack armoured vehicles. One such design used an effect called an Explosively Formed Penetrator (EFP). A shaped sheet of explosive was added to the back of a dome-shaped metal plate. As the explosive detonated and the blast wave unfolded, a phenomenon called the Misznay-Schardin effect caused the blast to shape the metal plate into a slug and project it forward at very high velocity. This explosively formed penetrator then hit the armoured vehicle at high speed, which might penetrate the armour or cause other damage. They have limited range, but at close range as IEDs they were sometimes highly effective. The Warrior proved remarkably tough as it had been up-armoured, and it was rarely penetrated in this way.

Many different designs of these IEDs were encountered, often very ingeniously concealed in walls by the side of roads. However, their technical complexity meant that they did not always work correctly. Properly functioning devices tended to indicate supply from Iranian sources rather than local manufacture.

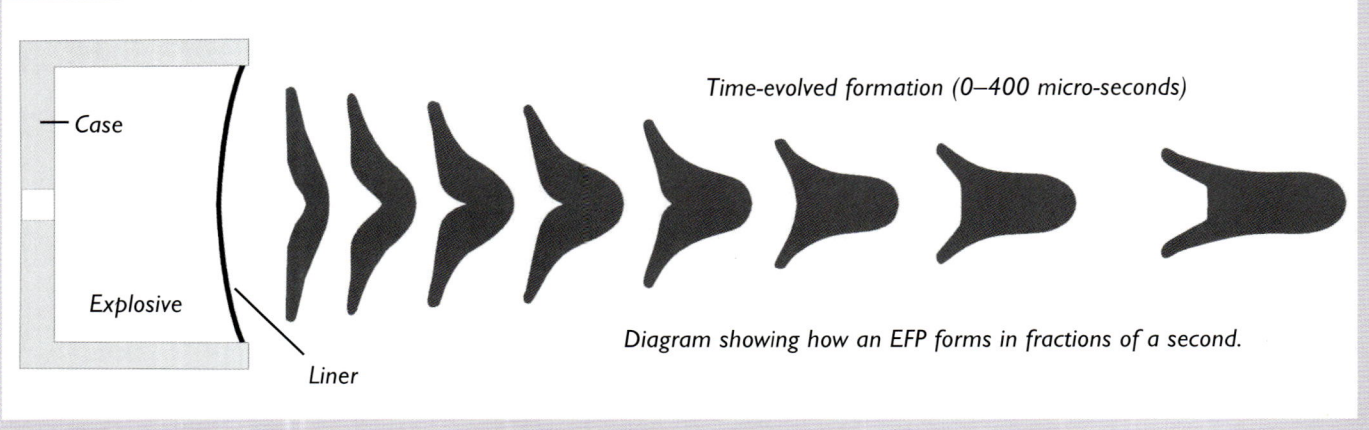

Case

Explosive

Liner

Time-evolved formation (0–400 micro-seconds)

Diagram showing how an EFP forms in fractions of a second.

The Poachers deployed into this awkward security situation and were designated as the Security Sector Reform battle group, which meant that they had a focus on developing the Iraqi forces' capability, capacity and credibility so that they could better protect the emerging government structures. As such they were mainly dismounted infantry, but they did use the Snatch Land Rover and other vehicles. On arrival, A (Lincolnshire) Company, under the command of Major Stuart Nicholson of the Royal Regiment of Fusiliers, was based in Basra Palace. B Company, under the command of Major Paul Leslie, was based in the Shatt al-Arab Hotel in the north, working mostly with the 1st Battalion The Light Infantry (1 LI). C Company, under the command of Major Mark Nooney of the Princess of Wales's Royal Regiment, was based in Shaibah and designated brigade reserve (also often called strike company); they provided a search and arrest capability. D (Fire Support) Company, under the command of Major Nigel Johnson, was also based in Shaibah initially, with a range of tasks including base security, but they later moved to the Shatt al-Arab. At this early stage, there was perhaps less engagement between the Iraqis and the British Army than might have been hoped, as there was still suspicion that some Iraqi organisations might have been infiltrated by terrorists and there had been some recent incidents, one of which involved Iraqi police firing on British troops.

The tour was very busy and dangerous right from the start. Sadly, two Poachers, Privates Joseva Lewaicei and Adam Morris, were killed on 13 May by an insurgent bomb, which also seriously injured Private Lionel O'Connor. In June a helicopter was shot down, and then in July there was a significant redeployment of the Poachers Battle Group into the city due to the deteriorating security situation in the city centre.

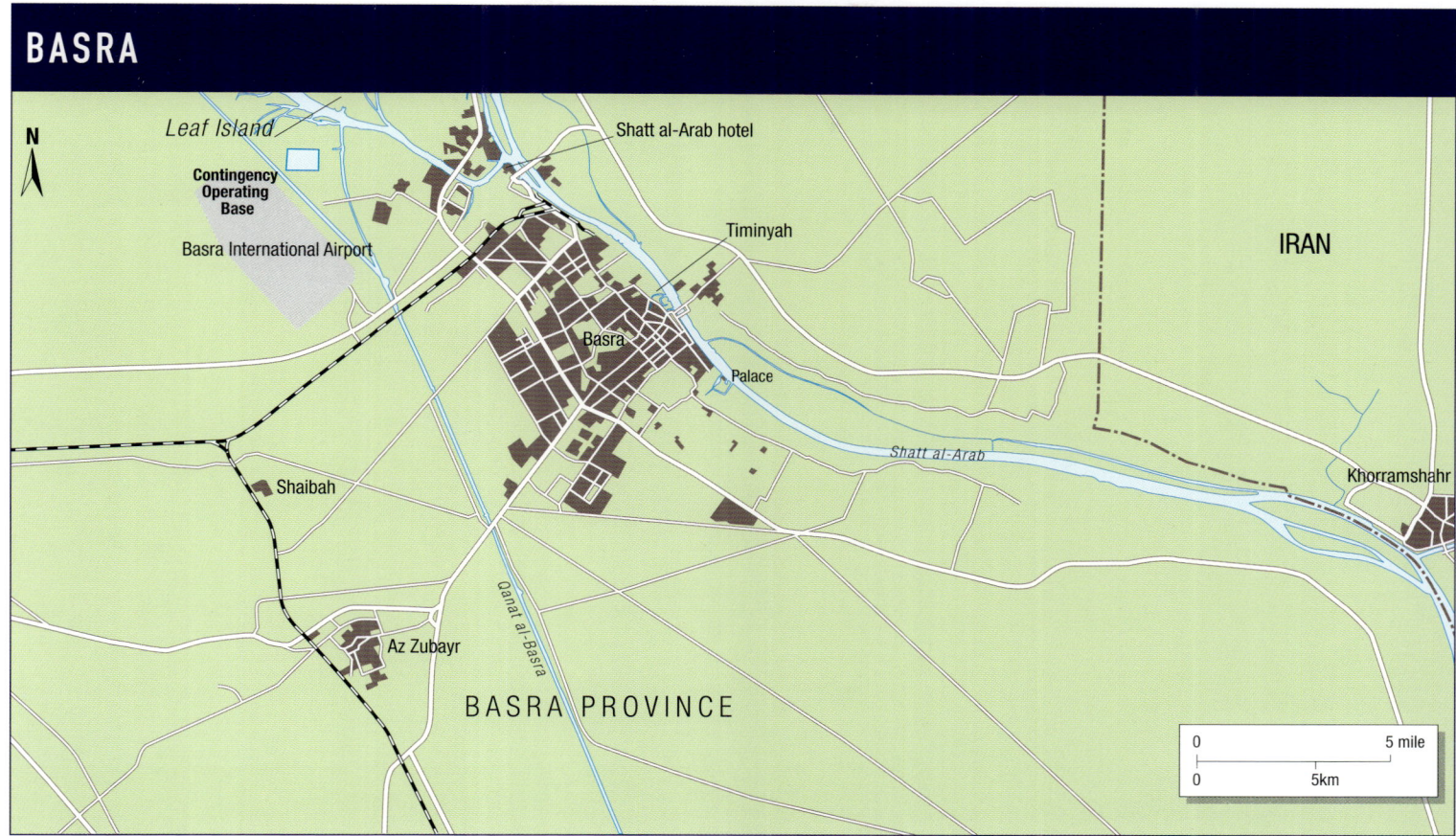

Battle Group Headquarters were deployed into the centre with the commanding officer also designated as advisor to the chief of police, with A (Lincolnshire) Company on foot and B Company of 1 LI with their Warrior armoured vehicles. They also had 17 Battery of 26 Regiment Royal Artillery (RA) under command. They quickly established a high level of patrol activity with a series of surge operations, in which large numbers of troops were deployed. They tended to patrol entirely on foot, or with Warrior armoured vehicles leading foot patrols at this time of high threat. These operations often also involved C (Northamptonshire) Company of the Poachers too, which was the Brigade Strike Company, although they were not under direct command. The detailed threat was mainly from a difficult combination of shootings, indirect fire and IEDs. It was a busy tour. Operation *Harlequin* will be examined in detail as a memorable example of the many undertaken by the Poachers.

OPERATION *HARLEQUIN*, 18 JULY 2006

This operation was originally called *Snail*, but the name was later changed to *Harlequin*. Intelligence had been received indicating that there were some indirect-fire weapons stashed in a house near a map feature called Red 30. It was right in the centre of Basra city, on a small peninsula called Timinyah which protruded into the main river, with tributaries either side.

Organised with A Company in Snatch Land Rovers, B Company 1 LI in Warriors, and 17 Battery RA in Snatch Land Rovers, they were allocated a Royal Engineer search advisor, a Royal Engineer search team and an Ammunition Technical Officer (ATO) team. The initial warning for the operation came in at around 14.00. The operation was due to start at

The peninsula of Timinyah in central Basra, location of Operation *Harlequin*. Note the densely built-up nature of the area.

Private Goodman of 2 Platoon stands next to the breach in the wall of the main building in the northern part of the Timinyah peninsula.

21.00 but the intelligence situation was changing during the afternoon, which meant that some hasty planning and briefing was required. There was not a great deal of detailed information available, and Lieutenant Colonel O'Driscoll had to undertake some improvisation with a laptop to get the briefing done in time.

After hasty orders, the battle group set off at 19.30, arriving shortly after in the Old State Building base, used as a holding area. Final briefings were being conducted in the Old State Building when the Poachers were told to pause. More intelligence had become available to higher formation, and there was an opportunity to strike at many additional targets. This 'pause' lasted several hours as 20 Brigade deployed many more troops.

While in position at the Old State Building, the insurgents targeted the battle group and started to mortar them with 60mm mortars at around 00.30. Fortunately, there were no casualties but the barrage damaged five vehicles and a container, with 2 Platoon losing four of its six Snatch Land Rovers due to damage. There was a blind (an unexploded mortar bomb) in the courtyard that had to be cleared by the ATO. Andy Rainey, the Poachers' regimental sergeant major, supervised some fairly hectic cross-kitting as 2 Platoon had to swap all the equipment from their damaged vehicles with some undamaged 1 LI vehicles.

The start time was slipped again, initially to midnight then to 03.00, when the Poachers were given the go ahead and they headed rapidly into the Timinyah peninsula. De-bussing and securing the area fast, they arrived at 03.30 and started searching the buildings. There was a minor problem as one of the Warriors threw a track on the way in, but this was quickly fixed and recovered at 03.58. After dismounting there were several traffic jam dramas, with over 40 vehicles manoeuvring in the narrow streets of a very small area, as Regimental Sergeant Major Andy Rainey remembers:

It was total carnage, trying to turn Warriors around in streets that were about as wide as they were, then all the Land Rovers

Some of the weapons found on Operation *Harlequin*.

milling about. Anyway we sorted that out. We then heard on the radio the code word Aladdin which meant they had a find.

2 Platoon made a breach in the wall of the main building in the northern part of the peninsula and gradually the scale of the find became clear. There was a feeling of the *Marie Celeste* about the buildings, with a meal found abandoned on one table and other evidence of a hasty departure by the insurgents. With the ATO and the engineers checking for booby traps, A Company worked their way through the houses. Lieutenant Johnny Lanham, 2 Platoon wrote in *Castle*:

> With 2 Platoon's Sergeant Greenhill and his multiple forming the inner cordon, the other half of the platoon with myself was able to batter its way through the external wall to gain access. Clearing through the house it quickly became apparent that whoever lived there had fled. However, unlike the familiar fairy tale of the three bears, it was not bowls of porridge that had been left behind but rather two tons of mortars, bombs, rockets, shells and further devices in the Aladdin's cave of weaponry.

Lieutenant Colonel O'Driscoll had deployed A Company and 17 Battery, as a close inner cordon with the search teams, and with B Company 1 LI at the base of the peninsula as his insurance policy, to ensure they could exit and did not get cut off. The Warriors also circled the outer cordon, acting as a deterrent and looking for potential targets, a tactic that the Poachers called 'Swimming Sharks'.

A Company formed a human chain and began to move the finds out of the buildings from about 04.00. It took a long time and was heavy work, especially as the temperature was still around 40°C. There was a vast array of mortar bombs, rockets, explosives and assorted other equipment to man-handle onto the vehicles, and it became increasingly difficult to cram it all onto the vehicles, so the men had to improvise, strapping equipment onto the outside of the vehicles. It was a strange time, eerily quiet on the Timinyah peninsula, but with a lot of firing going on in other parts of Basra. At 04.31, Brigade suggested to the commanding officer that

Sergeant Greenhill adopts a
fire position.

he make best speed, given the complex situation that was unfolding across the rest of the city
with several incidents under way.

The Poachers came under fire at 05.21, as dawn broke, and it was initially very difficult to
see where it was coming from. Mainly of 7.62mm calibre but also from heavy machine guns,
intermittent automatic fire initially came from the south, but then also from the north and
east, placing the Poachers on the peninsula under fire from three sides. They were also being
fired upon at very close range by insurgents on the roofs of nearby buildings. Fire was
returned from a number of different angles, mainly from teams of Poachers positioned on
the roofs. Next, a series of RPGs were fired from the south, across the inlet leading to the
main river. Lieutenant Colonel O'Driscoll had to ensure that his exit from the peninsula was
secure, discussing this with B Company 1 LI in their Warriors; it meant that they had to
continue to take this type of intermittent fire until the loading was completed.

Communications were proving a persistent issue – the battalion was using the newly
introduced 'Bowman Light' secure communications and experiencing a series of teething
problems. The Personal Role Radios (PRR) and an additional private mobile radio system
tended to work well enough, but only at close range in built-up areas and as they were not
secure, there was a risk of being overheard. O'Driscoll received a report that numbers of
insurgents were approaching, and with the rest of the brigade busy, the danger was increasing.
With the loading more or less complete and the volume of incoming fire increasing, it was
time to get off the peninsula. They had earlier considered trying to destroy all the ammunition
in situ, but it was not a viable option.

O'Driscoll was determined not to leave anyone behind, but in the confusion, and with
communications proving problematic, the only way to ensure this was to have the
commanding officer and regimental sergeant major physically running along the column of
vehicles from opposite ends, checking that everybody was accounted for. Two Warriors
arrived as escorts, and the sound of their returning fire with their chain guns was very
reassuring, providing a major boost to morale.

They all set off at about 05.40, and went about 50m before stopping. The Warriors leading
the column could not be seen and were out of communication, so the column had halted
without a 'Warrior Lead'. The Regimental Sergeant Major went forward to find out what

was going on, got to 2 Platoon leading the column and spoke to Sergeant Jay Greenhill. Lacking communications, the Regimental Sergeant Major with Sergeant Greenhill and Corporal Ollie Hartshorne moved forward to investigate. Under constant fire, Corporal Hartshorne moved up to a wall then got onto his knees and peered around the corner. He managed to locate the Warriors, so headed back and started the column. It later transpired that the Warrior had gone forward to Red 30 to eliminate an active insurgent 12.7mm DShK heavy machine gun – called a 'Dushka'. For his cool bravery Corporal Hartshorne was later Mentioned in Despatches.

With the Warriors now located, the rest of the battle group headed out of Timinyah. A Company came under contact at the bridge en route to Basra Palace. Lieutenant Lanham described the engagement:

Warrior vehicles at sunrise.

> While the company attempted to secure the far bank of the bridge, an attempt was made to ambush the company by a number of gunmen. These were soon dissuaded by Lance Corporal Davidson's call of 'watch my tracer' guiding a Warrior armoured fighting vehicle's chain gun onto the target to stress the point that the gunmen should go home, in the process demolishing the house they were hiding behind.

Lance Corporal Davidson was Mentioned in Despatches for his actions at the bridge. The vehicle column lost communications again and became separated at 05.47, so O'Driscoll halted around Point 29 to confirm that all vehicles were out. Due to a misunderstanding, compounded by the communications failure, 17 Battery had switched to the emergency route and headed off along the riverbank, rather than follow O'Driscoll's Tactical Headquarters. He had no communications with them or A Company at this time and could not be sure they were all out. It was eerily quiet around Point 29, as O'Driscoll remembers:

> I had one of those terrible moments; I could not release Dickie [Major Dickie Head, commanding B Company 1 LI] until I was absolutely sure that A Company and 17 Battery

The courtyard of Basra Palace from the roof.

were out and complete, and we had still not heard from them. It took another 10 minutes before we had confirmation. Then my signaller finally got the message: A Company all out and clear, 17 Battery out and clear. At that point I could start to withdraw B Company [1 LI]. It was only when we got the message that A Company were back in Basra Palace and complete that I knew we would not have to go back into the peninsula counter-attacking, a huge sense of relief.

On arrival at Basra Palace at 06.27, Lieutenant Colonel O'Driscoll tasked the regimental sergeant major with personally checking that everyone was accounted for. Andy Rainey recalls:

Weapons find from Operation *Harlequin*.

> I always remember standing in that dusty little car park, watching all the vehicles coming in, with flat tyres, windows and optics smashed by the intense fire-fight the battle group had just taken part in.

Vast numbers of small arms were fired at the battle group during this operation, together with over 100 RPGs, which were mostly fired at the Warriors but also at the Snatch Land Rovers. When all troops were safely back in their bases with no casualties at 06.50, the find could be catalogued and processed. At over two tons of material, including mortar bombs, rockets and explosives, it was the largest find in Iraq at that time. In O'Driscoll's opinion:

> The key was the Warriors of B Company 1 LI, they did a sterling job; communications were disappointing, but the team working was excellent. Everyone did their bit. The big worry for me was leaving somebody behind. We lifted a load of kit, but nobody was killed on our side.

POACHER IN IRAQ

Brigadier James Everard, Commander 20th Armoured Brigade, described Operation *Harlequin* as 'British Infantry at their best', later saying:

> The operation was intelligence based, well planned and highly successful in achieving the objective. Multi National Forces will combat the threat from terrorists and this is an example of the measures we will take to meet our commitment.[2]

The Poachers went on to conduct many more cordon and search and arrest operations, to a high tempo and completed *Telic 8* with their reputation considerably enhanced. Fortunately no other Poachers were killed during the tour although there were many serious injuries. In addition to six Mentions in Despatches, Major Mark Nooney of the Princess of Wales's Royal Regiment, but commanding C Company of the Poachers, was awarded a Military Cross, Lieutenant Colonel O'Driscoll and Private Lee Walters were awarded the Queen's Commendation for Valuable Service and Lance Corporal Michael Wilkinson was awarded a Queen's Gallantry Medal.

OPERATION *TELIC 12*, MAY–NOVEMBER 2008

Private Staines of the Poachers provides top cover on an early morning patrol.

While the Poachers, now under the command of Lieutenant Colonel Simon Browne, MBE, were undertaking pre-deployment training, a major operation in Basra heralded a sea-change in the operational emphasis of *Telic 12*. Operation *Saulat al-Fursan* ('Charge of the Knights') was launched in Basra on 25 March 2008. The initial operation involved US and Iraqi forces. The British Army became involved after the initial phases, and by the end of 'Charge of the Knights' the JAM insurgents in the city were largely defeated. Although Basra became much safer after this operation, it demonstrated, to Iraqi eyes at least, that the British Army had become as much part of the problem as part of the solution. The main reason for this was that local Iraqi forces felt they were now in a better position to develop consent with the local population that would deliver better security, mainly because they fully understood the culture in a way British forces never could. As a consequence the emphasis on Operation *Telic 12* had to be shifted quickly and decisively to supporting the Iraqi security forces by improving their capabilities through training, mentoring and coaching so that they could lead on all types of operation as soon as possible. At the same time, the combat role of British forces would need to be scaled back, and adopt a more supporting role, so that in the main Iraqi forces would be seen by the local population to be providing the security. This new role came to be called 'MiTTing', from Military Transition Team, and it triggered a rapid reorganisation of the Poachers, which actually happened during their pre-deployment leave. Despite the last-minute changes, they arrived on *Telic 12* ready for this more complex and challenging role, which they were to carry out most successfully. As also seen in Afghanistan, these tours in Iraq demonstrate the great operational flexibility of the Regiment

The Poachers' Regimental
Sergeant Major, Tony Bartlett,
briefing the Commanding
Officer's Tactical
Headquarters in the mud
prior to an operation.

– the same battalion fighting hard in difficult, full-on combat operations such as *Harlequin* then, just some 18 months later, undertaking a complex and difficult training and mentoring role, and achieving both successfully and with remarkable skill.

At this time there was no large body of experience in the Army of this type of training and mentoring role, so the Poachers were on their mettle and had to some extent learn by doing. Operation *Lightning 2,* which took place on 25 June 2008 and involved the Iraqi 52 Brigade, which was mentored by the Poachers' Battalion Headquarters, will be examined as a good example of the MiTTing work that went on during Operation *Telic 12.*

Although there was still an IED threat in mid-2008, it was greatly reduced, and the main problem faced by British forces in southern Iraq was the continued use of indirect fire onto bases that had been such a feature of Operation *Telic 8.* The use of mortars of 60mm, 82mm and even 120mm calibre, coupled with 107mm unguided rockets, still posed a considerable threat, particularly to the Basra airfield base, which was called the Contingency Operating Base or COB. Part of this equation was the arrival of the Mastiff armoured vehicle, because they were resilient against most types of IED seen at that time. The Poachers therefore felt that the IED threat was no longer the constraint it had been on Operation *Telic 8,* although they never had quite enough Mastiffs. Furthermore, it was clear to Lieutenant Colonel Browne that the political tolerance for casualties was much lower than it had been on earlier tours. As casualties were most likely to be caused by indirect fire, the countering of this became a top priority. There were 16 such attacks at the start of the tour, but very few towards the end as British forces finally got to grips with the threat. However, getting to this situation was a real challenge because the Iraqi forces were not really concerned with attacks on the COB, which they did not tend to consider their problem. Early on in the tour Browne was under pressure to develop a strategy that reduced these attacks, a tricky diplomatic position that would be difficult to manage.

THE RANGES OF THE INDIRECT-FIRE WEAPONS THREAT

Some element of skill was required to set up and fire accurately the 107mm rockets, called colloquially 'Chinese rockets' even though they were probably manufactured in Iran. These were originally designed to be fired from the Russian B-11 recoilless gun (see page 34), but were later found to be handy and easy for insurgents to use so they were fired from a range of tubes or even simply off the ground.

Depending on elevation and how they were fired, some could reach a range of almost 9km.

A mixture of different mortars were used, from small but easy to conceal light 60mm through the so-called medium mortars of 81mm and 82mm (see page 34), to the heavy 120mm mortar. Their ranges varied greatly depending on size and the charges used, but typically 6–8km could be achieved.

The Iraqi 14th Division was the lead formation in the Basra area. After the conclusion of *Saulat al-Fursan*, two of their brigades looked after the city itself leaving their third brigade, the 52nd, to look after the whole of the rest of the division's area of operations. This was an extensive, largely rural area of responsibility, more than 120km by 80km in size, which meant that troop density was very low. Of the Iraqi 52nd Brigade's three battalions, one was based in Qarmat Ali, the northern suburbs of Basra, another in Al-Qurnah to the north, at the confluence of the rivers Tigris and Euphrates, supposedly the site of the biblical Garden of Eden. This left the third battalion and the Brigade Headquarters based in Camp Sa-ad, roughly halfway between the two, in all very few troops to conduct operations across an immense area. The terrain was mainly flat, a mix of desert and marshland cut by a myriad of small and larger waterways, the largest of which was the Shatt al-Arab, flowing south after the confluence. Towns and villages were dotted around, mainly on the waterways. The Battalion Headquarters of the Poachers were based in Camp Sa-ad MiTTing the Brigade Headquarters, with the three battalions of the 52nd Brigade mentored by teams drawn from B (Leicestershire) Company under the command of Major Pete Smith. The nub of the problem was that all the indirect fire coming into the COB seemed to originate from the north, from a feature known as Leaf Island – although not strictly an island, the surrounding waterways shaped it into a perfect leaf. At around 6–8km from the COB, it was at ideal range for the insurgents' indirect-fire weapons.

The Iraqi 52nd Brigade was at the time by some distance the worst brigade in the 14th Division. They had been thrown into the fighting in Basra straight from training – not fully trained or equipped and with little experience. Consequently they suffered heavily during *Saulat al-Fursan*, taking many casualties and being effectively defeated repeatedly by insurgents. In Arab, and consequently Iraqi military culture there is a concept known as *Wastah* – which is an amalgam of pride, self respect, machismo, or even mojo. In the eyes of many Iraqis the 52nd Brigade had quite simply lost all their *Wastah*. They were looked down on by others, which was why they had been marginalised and sent to the rural area of responsibility. When Browne arrived with the Poachers MiTTing team, he found the 52nd Brigade low on self esteem and confidence, with Brigade Headquarters consisting of the brigadier himself, one officer and one white plastic table.

The brigadier was a difficult character, a former Ba'athist who tended to hold his cards very close to his chest and who was slow to trust anyone. While this trait had enabled him to survive the fall of the Ba'ath regime, it made everything difficult initially for Browne, who had to build up a rapport with him. Furthermore, the brigadier was very used to getting his

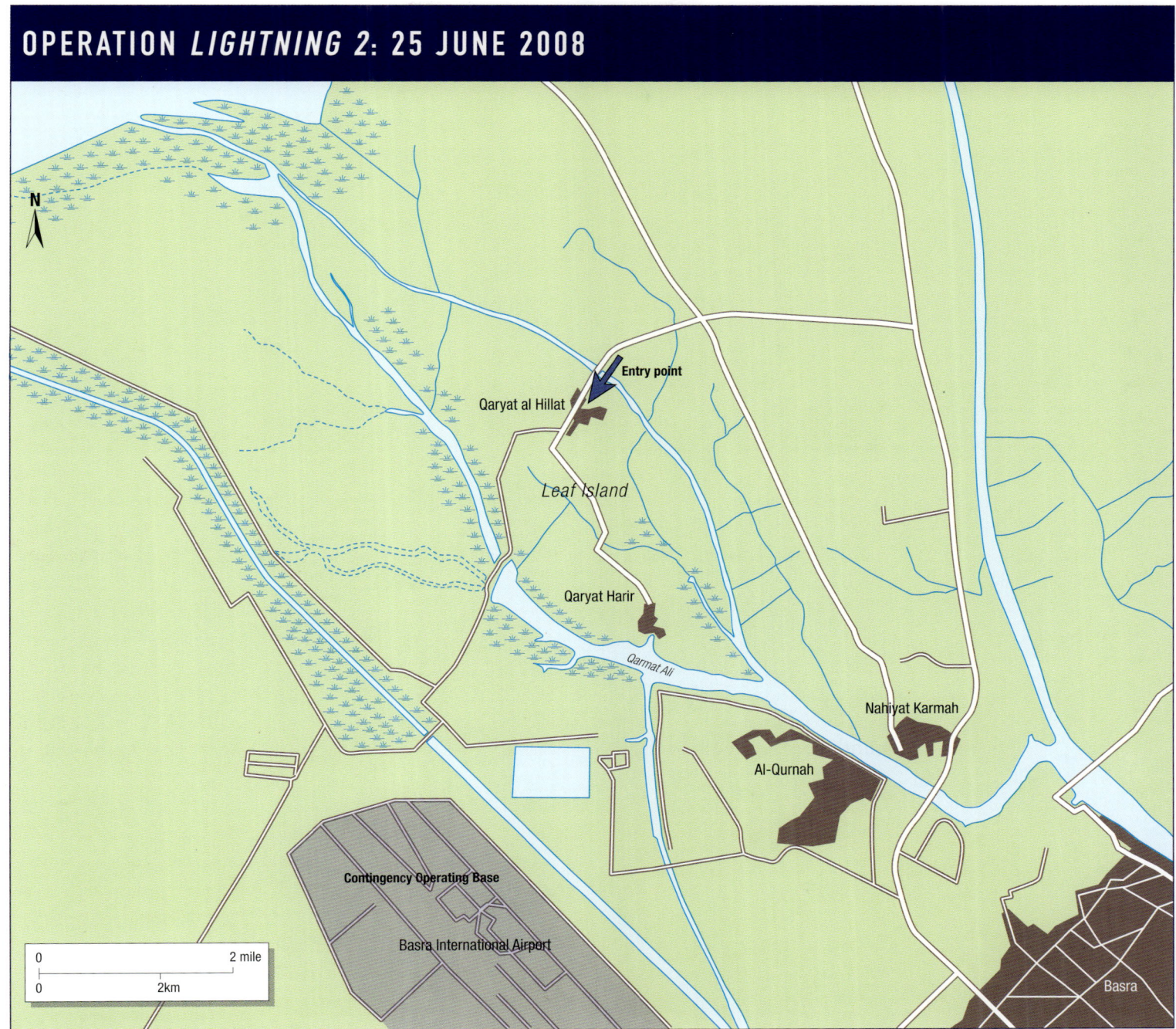

OPERATION *LIGHTNING 2*: 25 JUNE 2008

N

Entry point

Qaryat al Hillat

Leaf Island

Qaryat Harir

Qarmat Ali

Nahiyat Karmah

Al-Qurnah

Contingency Operating Base

Basra International Airport

Basra

| 0 | 2 mile |
| 0 | 2km |

own way, and Browne worked out that he could slowly nudge the brigadier along, get him to mount operations, but could only really get him and his formation to improve by a process of 'I told you so' when things went wrong. Persuading him to act was largely done by offering him opportunities to regain his *Wastah*, pointing out that only if he were to be seen doing things would Browne to able to attract resources into the brigade. In particular, despite having very good human intelligence sources, there was a tendency to rush to action without confirmation, a trait made worse by the brigadier's almost total reluctance to plan ahead, as this would involve sharing information with his troops, which he felt reduced his control over them. However, after a series of very obvious planning failures, the brigadier started to take notice of Browne's advice. But as one problem was solved, another complication would arise; for example, there was an almost total lack of map-reading skills in the brigade.

Brigade Headquarters and
the white plastic table.

Despite a good knowledge of the ground, the inability to relate this to a map seriously inhibited the brigade's ability to plan ahead. There was a cultural element to this, as anyone with skills that the commander lacked could be seen as a threat, consequently Arab commanders did not like skills being passed on. It became clear during helicopter reconnaissance flights that the brigadier both knew the ground very well and read maps very well, but he did not want this skill passed to his subordinate commanders. Despite some reluctance, the Poachers' Regimental Sergeant Major, Tony Bartlett, a former Sandhurst colour sergeant instructor, delivered a series of map-reading lessons, which were very well received, although he had to start with the very basics – it was quite a sight to see a warrant officer in the British Army trying to teach a full colonel in the Iraqi Army how to do 4-figure grid references.

The first in a series of operations directed against the indirect-fire threat was called *Lightning 1*, but this was something of a failure, mainly due to a total absence of planning. After an exercise in 'I told you so' from Browne, the second operation, *Lightning 2*, was much better planned. It involved a cordon and search of Leaf Island, and was sparked by the brigadier receiving some human intelligence that there was 'a heavy machine gun under some grass' on Leaf Island. The information was unconfirmed and from a single source; nevertheless, under pressure to get something under way, Browne persuaded the brigadier that it would be useful to conduct an operation, so as to be seen to be doing something. Together they worked out a plan involving over 600

Poachers with Mastiffs near
the bridge onto Leaf Island.

soldiers, drawn from all three of their battalions, that would eventually go in, after several postponements, on 25 June 2008.

After much discussion, the first phase involved the securing of an obvious choke point, the bridge over the river onto Leaf Island from the north-east. A simple convoy plan or movement table would be needed to get all 600 men over a single bridge in a reasonable time. Because the Iraqis were reluctant to do so, the Poachers had to lead from the front early on and with the assistance of just the regimental police staff, six Mastiffs and a supporting MiTTing team (a total of around 35 Poachers), Browne with the regimental police secured the bridge personally. This allowed the deployment of some surveillance assets such as a Desert Hawk, a small unmanned aerial vehicle. Later on, despite the Poachers' best efforts, there was the inevitable massive Iraqi traffic jam, but at least the area of the bridge was secured.

The Iraqis eventually arrived in the area of Qaryat al Hillat, dismounted from their vehicles and the search got under way. Although their approach seemed haphazard and was never systematic, some of the Iraqi search teams had an uncanny knack for making finds. After a somewhat chaotic process, a machine gun was found beneath two haystacks, which tended to indicate that the intelligence had been correct. It was a 14.5mm heavy machine gun of Russian design called a KPV, but probably made in China or Iran. Cleverly concealed, it was very carefully broken down and packed in oiled rags, suggesting that whoever hid it intended to use it again. This was a cause for concern for the Poachers because, although their Mastiffs were proof against any but the largest IED, they might not offer total protection against a 14.5mm machine gun firing armour-piercing ammunition or armour-piercing incendiary (API) ammunition, both of which were also found in the cache. It was certainly possible that insurgents had positioned this weapon in preparation for an attack on Mastiffs or Coalition helicopters.

Just as the heavy machine gun find was being processed, there was another great commotion, provoked by a find that was initially described by the interpreter as 'some other stuff'. On closer examination, this turned out to be a very large find of old artillery shells of

Launching the Desert Hawk.

Elements of the 14.5mm heavy machine gun find.

Poachers with the artillery shell and mortar bomb find.

152mm calibre, mortar bombs and cordite charges. Although this sort of older explosive could be, and had been, re-used for making IEDs, it was more likely to be a stash dating from the Iran-Iraq War rather than material hidden by insurgents. It was the sort of material that a Marsh Arab village headman might hide away 'just in case', possibly for decades, but probably not a direct threat. Nevertheless, it was still more than a ton of explosive material, and it was good to take it out of circulation.

Meanwhile Lieutenant Colonel Browne was trying to explain a search technique called 'Winthrop' to an Iraqi search team. This technique, developed in Northern Ireland and named after the inventor, involves looking at a piece of ground from the insurgent's point of view to see how he might describe the location of a cache to someone else, for example perhaps working from where a fence meets a track as a reference point. As Browne was explaining, he pointed to a derelict building with a wall junction, next to a patch of disturbed earth as a good example. As he started scraping at the earth on one side of the wall an Iraqi soldier went to the other side and started doing the same thing. Much to everyone's surprise he pulled a hand grenade out of the ground. Digging further, more grenades were found together with some very professionally buried magazines for a G3 automatic rifle. In this part of the world, the 7.62mm G3 meant only one thing – Iran, because their armed forces are equipped with unlicensed copies of this reliable German Heckler & Koch-designed assault rifle. The magazines were wrapped in oiled cloth, the inner tube of a tyre and then plastic wrapping, which indicated a professional insurgent cache. Working around this area, several small caches together made a significant find, this time almost certainly linked to insurgents.

Just as this latest find was made, there was yet another commotion and the interpreter said to Browne, 'I think they have found your rockets'. Another Iraqi search team had uncovered a massive find of the much sought after 107mm rockets, with a four-tube launcher, various mortar rounds, fuses, initiation cord and other related equipment. This find was tremendously significant as it was directly linked to the current threat on the bases. Some of the rockets had twin flex wire attached, which was a strong indication that this cache belonged to an insurgent indirect-fire team. The wires meant that they could be fired simply by touching the other ends of the wire to a battery. Some of the rockets were found still in the factory packaging with a rudimentary paper range chart attached representing an 'idiot's guide' for any firer giving

F2 hand grenade.

G3 magazines.

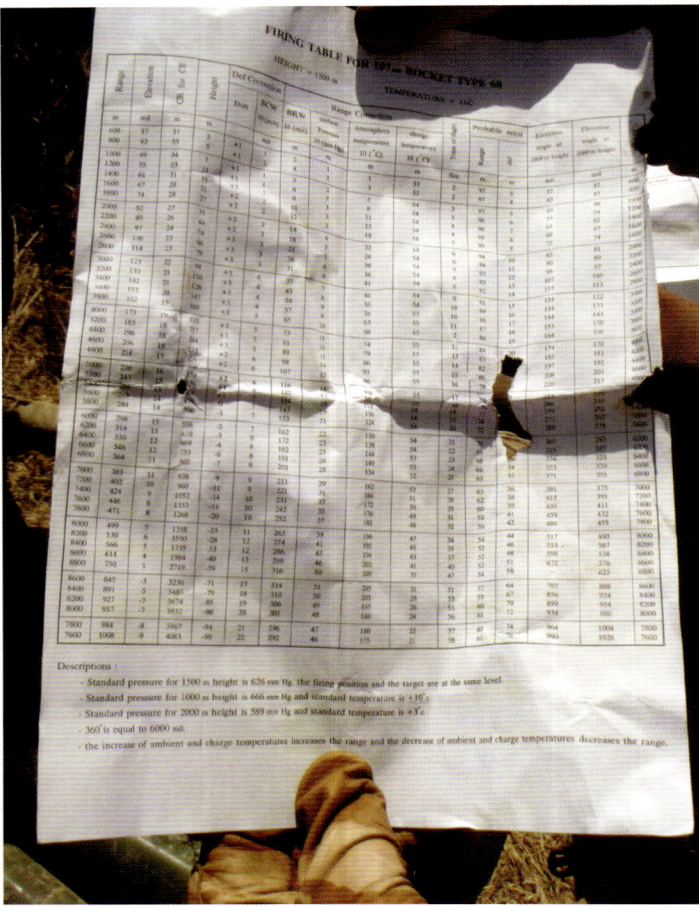

Insurgent 'Idiot's guide' range chart.

different elevations for different ranges and temperatures. The finding of 30–40 fuses – the final part of the rockets' firing system – was also very important. Further investigation of the area revealed that in the main the 107mm rockets were simply placed on an earthen bank or berm at the correct angle and pointed in the direction of the COB, then fired remotely using the wires. There were even some primitive delayed-initiation timer devices, enabling the insurgents to make good their escape well before the rockets actually fired.

There were also a range of tubes that were protective carrying cases for mortar bombs, recently manufactured. The smaller 60mm bombs appeared to have been made originally in Portugal, but the larger 81mm, 82mm and 120mm were consistent with examples known to have been made in Iran. The mortar barrels were not found, but they were relatively easy to transport to where the ammunition was cached, which was within range of the COB. There were even some anti-tank grenades, of Second World War-vintage Russian design with a drogue chute in the handle to ensure they landed on the target at the right angle. These may also have been intended for use against the Mastiffs.

Eventually, all of the finds were shipped back to Camp Sa-ad, where the brigadier was persuaded to make the most of the media opportunity presented by such a success. Soon both local radio and television arrived to interview the now clearly delighted brigadier. The divisional commander was also called in to be shown the finds, and soon it became apparent that the brigadier's *Wastah* had been considerably enhanced; indeed he was later promoted. The success of Operation *Lightning*

The four-tube rocket launcher.

107mm rockets with
initiation wire.

2 helped to build the relationship between Browne and the brigadier so that although future operations would never be described as going like clockwork, they were undertaken frequently and with an ever-increasing degree of sophistication and even an element of planning.

It emerged in the follow-up from this operation that the insurgents had long been using the network of small canals and waterways, navigated by small fishing boats, as the main supply route into their firing areas on Leaf Island. Later a riverine capability that

Mortar bomb canisters.

The finds from *Lightning 2* being photographed.

could intercept shipments along the small waterways was developed. Coupled with this, the Poachers augmented the 'stick' with a bit of 'carrot' with the aptly titled Operation *Grimsby* that was initiated to rebuild the vital fish market at Al-Qurnah. This included the provision of refrigeration and hygiene facilities which enabled the Marsh Arabs to sell their fish efficiently. This reduced the financial pressure they were under, thereby reducing their motivation to smuggle arms for money. This eased their financial problems and brought significant goodwill that the Iraqi security forces were able to exploit to gain significant intelligence about the insurgents' use of the waterways.

Operation *Lightning 2* had a remarkably similar result to Operation *Harlequin* – the discovery and recovery of a sizable find of insurgent equipment – but it had been arrived at

Below left: Mortar bombs on display later in camp.

Below right: Lieutenant Colonel Browne with a 107mm rocket.

in a very different manner. The reputation of the Poachers for their flexibility, patience and raw success with their MiTTing approach was greatly enhanced during the tour so that the whole of *Telic 12* was seen as a great success. Lieutenant Colonel Browne was awarded an OBE for this tour.

STEELBACKS IN IRAQ

As we saw in Operation *Herrick*, the Steelbacks of the 3rd Battalion provided a very useful contingent of 20 people on Operation *Telic 12*. Led by Sergeant Ian Pugh, they were fitted into various jobs, based on rank, mainly within 1 and 3 Platoons of A Company of the Poachers.

NOTES

1. UNHCR, *Basrah Governorate Assessment Report August 2006*, p.9, accessed at www.unhcr.org/459ba6462.pdf

2. Quoted from the MOD Defence News website, now in the National Archive: http://webarchive.nationalarchives. gov.uk/20060719044939/http://www.mod.uk/DefenceInternet/DefenceNews/MilitaryOperations/ UkTroopsUncoverHugeArmsCacheInBasra.htm

NORTHERN IRELAND

Corporal Isom and Lance Corporal Firman of the Poachers in a 1975 riot.

The roots of the conflict in Northern Ireland go back several centuries, but the involvement of the Regiment came following the outbreak of the 'Troubles' in the late 1960s. The Catholic civil rights movement in Northern Ireland – opposed to Unionist dominance – grew in both numbers and militancy through the 1960s. By the latter part of 1969 – following anti-Royal Ulster Constabulary (RUC) riots in both Belfast and Londonderry – the situation in the Province had deteriorated to such a degree that it was considered necessary to deploy British troops in support of the RUC. They would remain there for more than 30 years, part of the longest campaign in British military history.

The 1st Battalion was one of the earliest units to be involved in the long and at times vicious Troubles, and the Regiment would have an almost unbroken presence in the Province up until the Good Friday Agreement in 1998, and beyond. Individual members of the Regiment were deployed before this time, and Lieutenant General Sir Ian Freeland, KCB, DSO, Colonel of the Regiment from 1971 to 1976, was General Officer Commanding, Northern Ireland from 1969 to 1971, overseeing the early deployment of troops on the streets.

Politicians on both sides tended to view all aspects of the Troubles as purely political and there was no shortage of political disagreements. However, the issues were and are much more complex than this, comprising a mix of religious, economic and sociological aspects that interacted to make any form of political solution complex and invariably impossible to implement. The Catholic and Protestant communities in Northern Ireland had lived in close proximity for centuries, but as two mutually reinforcing sub-cultures that had drifted a very long way apart by 1969.

THE BRUTAL STATISTICS

By way of an overview of the whole conflict, the following chart shows the brutal statistics of most of the conflict*:

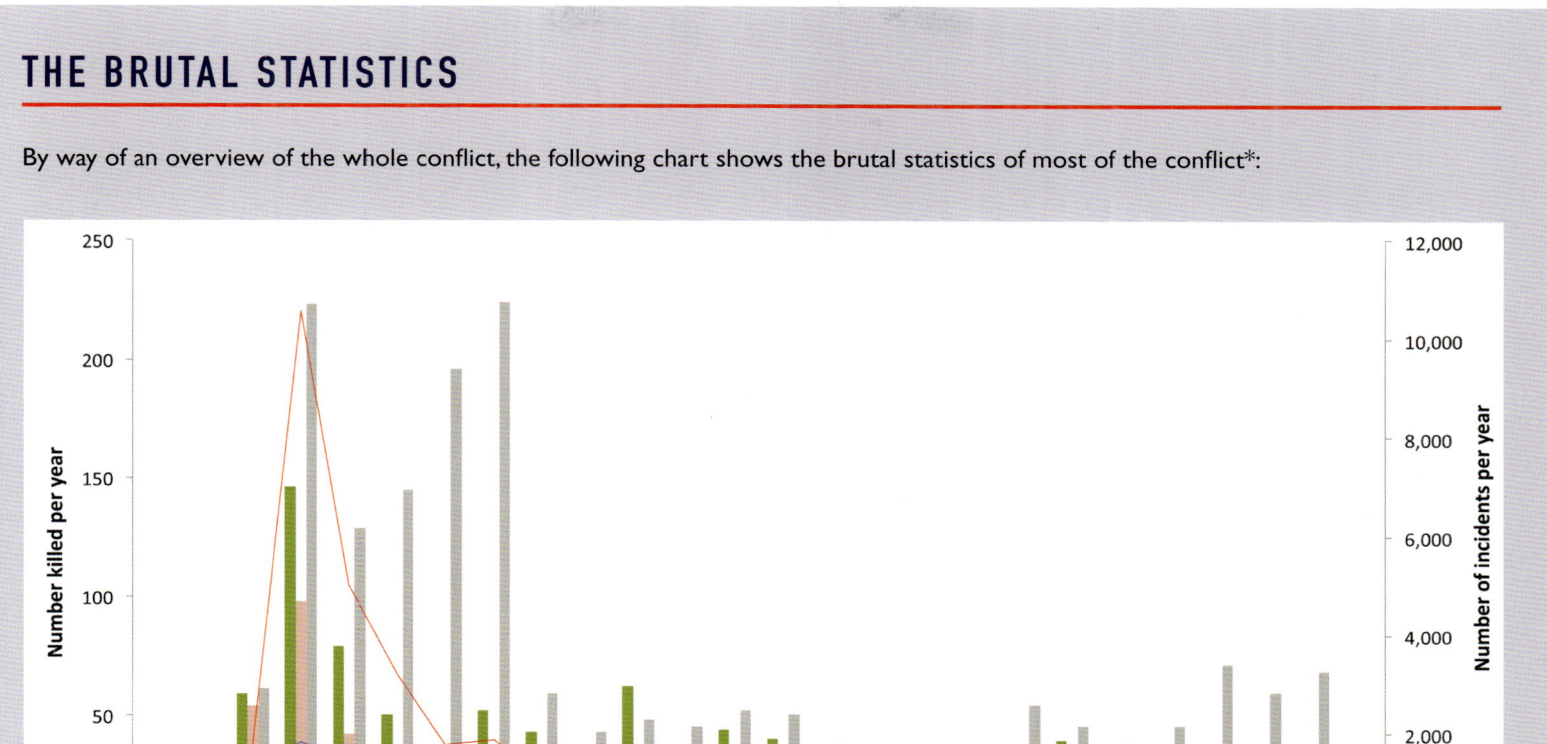

*Data taken from Michael Dewar, *The British Army in Northern Ireland* (Arms & Armour Press, revised 1996), Appendix I.

Most historians, for example Dewar and van der Bijl, tend to describe the build-up of violence purely in terms of political move and counter-move.[1] For those deployed at street level, it was clear that there were more fundamental factors in action. There was also a great deal of wishful thinking at the time about how the escalation of the Troubles could have been avoided. Given the depth and complexity of the issues, however, it is doubtful that it would ever have been possible to avoid the slide into violence in 1969 and 1970. From the Regiment's point of view, the four regular battalions watched the situation unfold with unease from their bases in Catterick (1st Battalion), Felixstowe (2nd Battalion), Aldershot (3rd Battalion), and Bahrain (4th Battalion).

With three battalions deployed in Northern Ireland at some time in the 30-year conflict, there is more than enough history to fill a whole book. However, a simple chronological narrative runs the risk of becoming very dull reading, so instead we will illustrate the totality of the Regiment's deployment and describe some operations in more detail. Between 1970 and 1998 the Regiment was involved in all aspects of the conflict – from altercations on street corners to major riots, shootings and bombings. Terrorist attacks became increasingly sophisticated and complex as the years went on, often involving multiple incidents in urban and rural settings.

The following table shows the deployments of the regular battalions throughout Operation *Banner*, the name the British Army gave to the whole operation:

BATTALION	DATE	LOCATION AND DETAILS
1st Battalion	July 1970–March 1972	Ebrington Barracks, Londonderry (Residential)
2nd Battalion	October 1970–February 1971	Belfast
3rd Battalion	April–August 1972	Belfast
2nd Battalion	August–December 1972	Belfast
3rd Battalion	March–July 1973	Londonderry
2nd Battalion	July–November 1973	Londonderry
Tiger Company	March–July 1974	East Tyrone/Armagh
1st Battalion	September–December 1974	Armagh
3rd Battalion	November 1974–March 1975	Londonderry
2nd Battalion	August–December 1975	Belfast
2nd Battalion	March–June 1977	Belfast
3rd Battalion	May 1978–November 1979	Palace Barracks, Holywood (Residential)
1st Battalion	May–September 1979	Belfast
2nd Battalion	January 1981–January 1983	Ebrington Barracks, Londonderry (Residential)
1st Battalion	August 1981–January 1982	Fermanagh
1st Battalion	December 1984–January 1987	Ebrington Barracks, Londonderry (Residential)
2nd Battalion	January–February 1986	Fermanagh, Tyrone, Armagh
2nd Battalion	April–September 1986	South Armagh
3rd Battalion	November 1986–March 1987	Belfast
2nd Battalion	January–June 1989	Belfast
1st Battalion	August 1989–January 1990	South Armagh
1st Battalion	April–November 1991	Fermanagh
3rd Battalion	May 1991–August 1992	Ebrington Barracks, Londonderry (Residential)
2nd Battalion	December 1992–July 1993	East Tyrone
1st Battalion	December 1993–June 1994	East Tyrone
1st Battalion	November 1996–May 1997	Belfast
1st Battalion	May 1999–May 2001	Ebrington Barracks, Londonderry (Residential)
2nd Battalion (D Company only)	November 2000–May 2001	Belfast
2nd Battalion	June–December 2002	Belfast, Omagh
1st Battalion	December 2002–June 2003	East Tyrone (four platoons only)
2nd Battalion	February 2004–December 2005	Shackleton Barracks, Ballykelly (Residential)

As Operation *Banner* progressed, the regular army units undertook both residential and roulement tours. The residential tour involved a battalion stationed in the Province (an alternative term for Northern Ireland) for a longer period of time. This varied, tending to be around 18 months in the early years but extending to more than two years in the later years of the conflict. Resident battalions took their families with them, with married soldiers living in quarters which, by and large, were rarely attacked by terrorists. Typically, they would run a monthly or six-weekly rotation which saw one and sometimes two companies deployed on operations, one or two companies on standby or reserve tasks and one on leave and training.

This varied a great deal during the Troubles. At busy times all companies would be deployed on operations; indeed this ability to rapidly surge the numbers deployed, which only the residential battalions could provide, was a major tactical advantage to the Army as a whole.

The other type of tour was called a 'roulement' tour from the French for rolling or rotation. In the early years they lasted four months, but this was extended to six months in later years. These tours were usually deployed in the more dangerous areas and could be very intensive. Deployed 'unaccompanied' – without wives and families – most personnel were able to take one short period of leave during the tour, but were otherwise constantly deployed on operations for the whole length of the tour. In addition to the forecast roulement tours, there were a number of occasions when the force reserve, often called the 'Spearhead Battalion', was deployed, generally at very short notice. These deployments could vary in duration from a few weeks to several months.

Although some individuals deployed on occasion, the Territorial battalions of the Regiment were never deployed to Northern Ireland.

TERRORIST ORGANISATIONS

In accordance with their republican ideals and their desire to promote reunification, Irish Republican Army (IRA) terrorists took advantage of the deteriorating situation in the Province in 1969 to provoke violent outbursts whenever possible. Initially, they were the Official IRA (OIRA) but they drifted into two factions from 1969 with the final split in 1972. At some risk of generalising a very complex situation, the Official IRA were seeking a more political approach but the Provisional IRA, hereafter PIRA, headed off along a more radical and violent tack. Both were occasionally affiliated with various Marxist and anarchist groups, but the main aim was always a united Ireland. PIRA made all the later running so that the OIRA faded away in the military context.

From around 1974, the PIRA eschewed their previous military-style hierarchy and instead adopted a cellular organisation, using a collection of small active service units or cells, and became much more effective. They acquired new weapons at this time, such as AK-47s and RPG-7s from Colonel Gaddafi's Libya but also Armalite assault rifles and M60 machine guns from US sources. PIRA and their Sinn Fein political arm were heavily supported throughout the conflict by funds raised in Irish communities in the United States. This embarrassing fact is often brushed under the carpet in recent times, but fundraising and political support in the US were crucial in turning the PIRA into such an effective terrorist force. It powered great increases in their technical and operational competence during the 1970s so that by the 1980s they were seen by many as by far the most effective and capable terrorist organisation in the world.

They perfected a range of attack types – generally bombings, shootings and mortars. For bombings they used a variety of command wire, radio-controlled, timed and booby-trap type initiators. The larger bombs, some weighing more than a ton, usually consisted of explosives that were home-made from fertilizer, but the acquisition of Czech-made Semtex high explosive from 1981 made them much more dangerous. Ever more sophisticated but audacious bombings were developed, probably culminating with the narrowly unsuccessful attempt to assassinate Prime Minister Margaret Thatcher in the Brighton bombing on 12 October 1984. The car bomb was a prominent feature, which initially tended to be detonated by timers. Car bombs were often delivered by non-terrorists under duress, these were known as proxy bombs. The terrorists would hold the family of the unfortunate driver hostage, and then instruct him to drive the bomb into a base, checkpoint or police station, threatening that failure to follow instructions would result in the family coming to harm.

Private Fred O'Rourke and Corporal Larry Sadler of the Poachers on an RUC support patrol, Divis Flats, 1975.

IRA shootings were initially rather impromptu, random and therefore costly affairs, but they became much more carefully planned in later years. Shootings tended to be of three types: the traditional single sniper shot, usually at long range and relying on the skill of the shooter who would use the difficulty of locating a single shot for concealment and to enable his escape; cross-border shootings, often involving multiple heavy weapons such as machine guns, usually at very long ranges – the border prevented the Army from pursuing so allowed a relatively easy escape; and the close-range attack, designed to overwhelm a small group of Royal Ulster Constabulary or Army personnel with heavy close-range firepower delivered by assault rifles. The sniper and cross-border shootings persisted and developed as a threat throughout the conflict. In contrast, the close-range attack was rare, and became even more so as the conflict progressed, but could never be discounted. In addition to these shootings at the security forces, a range of armed robberies, knee-cappings and sectarian murders were also carried out with firearms.

The third type of PIRA attack was the mortar, usually fired at an army base or police station. Various home-made projectiles would be assembled, typically in pipes on the back of a flat-bed lorry, then concealed. Mortar attacks could be devastating, but many more mortar attacks were aborted, failed to fire or detonate or simply missed their target than actually worked. However, these low probability-of-success mortar attacks were still considered worthwhile by the PIRA as they occasionally gave spectacular results.

The largest single event to increase support for the PIRA was Bloody Sunday on 30 January 1972, but the politically motivated hunger strikes of 1981 also significantly increased PIRA support and funding. PIRA's growing affiliation to its Sinn Fein political wing on the one hand made it ever more dangerous, because it tended to add an element of political legitimacy to their supporters, but ironically this very affiliation was to prove crucial in the negotiations for an end to the conflict.

There were several other smaller and more volatile republican terrorist groups, most notably the Irish National Liberation Army (INLA). Founded by Seamus Costello during the OIRA–PIRA split, they claimed a strong Marxist affiliation but quickly established a highly unpredictable reputation for themselves. Some of the more appalling terrorist attacks were attributed to the INLA, who were occasionally very problematic, but were always in very small numbers and lacked popular support.

Protestant terrorism grew in strength through the 1970s, mainly as a response to republican terrorism. There were more than 17 different organisations at different times but the main two were the Ulster Volunteer Force (UVF) and the Ulster Defence Association (UDA). Generally they did not attack the security forces. The Protestant terrorists were almost exclusively concerned with sectarian violence, targeting and killing Catholics, often as carefully calculated acts but also sometimes with a startlingly random element. Although they were an important feature of the conflict, they were only rarely a threat to the Regiment's soldiers so they will not be covered in any further detail.

POLICE RELATIONSHIPS

Success in a counter-insurgency of this nature very much depended on the effectiveness of the local police force. This was understood by the government, police and Army from the outset. The initial deployment of troops was necessitated by an escalation of violence. The majority of the RUC in 1969 were unarmed and regularly set upon when they attempted to patrol in the Catholic estates. The extent and pace of the civil unrest escalated to a level where it could not be ignored, but the RUC lacked the resources to respond appropriately. Although the initial deployment of troops was clearly in support of the RUC, the Army took the lead on many aspects of security in the early years. So in addition to riot control, the Army undertook community relations programmes and began to collect their own intelligence on local terrorist suspects. Practical understanding of police cooperation and police primacy tended to vary from unit to unit, particularly in the early days of the campaign. Success to a great extent depended on how far real cooperation was achieved. The lead in intelligence services was especially important, but it was difficult to get the balance between RUC and Army right in this area.

It is probably fair to say that the early attempts by the RUC to reassert full primacy in the 1974–78 period were somewhat premature, requiring a resurgent response from the Army. By around 1983 the RUC were able to realise full police primacy and from then on the security forces were able to exert a steady concerted pressure to gradually reduce terrorist activity. This was necessary in order to enable the population to begin a return to a more normal way of living, which tended to hinge on the level of violence that both communities would find acceptable. The aim was to slowly but surely push the terrorists into a no-win position, by making violence increasingly unacceptable, which the troops called 'keeping the lid on'. It was recognised throughout the campaign that there was no purely military solution; the security forces were containing the problem until a political solution could be achieved.

The military component was just one strand of the campaign. Applying criminal law to terrorist crimes, improving employment prospects, housing and social infrastructure, economic development and following the terrorist 'money trail' were all important. In addition, an increasingly effective intelligence effort started to achieve results; an example of this was the 'Supergrass' informant phenomenon. This in turn laid the groundwork for the peace process, which eventually came to fruition with the Good Friday Agreement, albeit after a fairly rocky road.

NORTHERN IRELAND

LONDONDERRY, 1970–72

In July 1970 the 1st Battalion, under the command of Lieutenant Colonel Roy Jackson took over Ebrington Barracks, Londonderry from the Royal Navy. It was to be their home for the next 18 months.

They arrived into a situation that had deteriorated rapidly into sporadic civil violence at a level beyond which the exhausted police could control. The civil disorder was centred on the perimeter of the Bogside and Creggan Catholic estates, IRA territory and home to large numbers of unemployed youths. In these early days the Vikings were only involved with stone-throwing youths who occasionally mobilised in greater numbers to riot and build barricades. The actions of the Vikings in dispersing the 'aggro', as the troops were to call stone throwing, had a significant initial effect. The opportunity for the Vikings to deploy aggressively so early in their tour did much to boost confidence, and the situation was soon under control. The battalion rotated between city and country duties with the other major unit, 2nd Battalion The Royal Green Jackets (2 RGJ) based at RAF Ballykelly, about eight miles from the city.

Although there were significant but well-forecast riots linked to the traditional marching season in August, by December both estates had calmed down and were again policed by the RUC, at that time unarmed, but closely covered by the Army. The situation was considered sufficiently stable so that by early 1971 both the Bogside and Creggan estates were placed in bounds to off-duty soldiers and a range of community relations schemes started. Fraternisation between members of the battalion and local girls resulted in a series of later marriages. *Castle* described the A Company view of this situation:

> Looking back over the last six months it is possible to see a pattern to most events. While the weather was warm and the evenings light, it could be almost guaranteed that as soon as the local pubs shut or dances were over there would be a spate of stone, bottle and eventually petrol bomb throwing. Usually by 0230–0300 hrs all was quiet.

However, from May 1971 when the situation deteriorated rapidly in Londonderry, there was little spare time for anyone, other than on block leave.

Belfast flared up in February 1971, when most of the Vikings' companies were deployed to the Clonard estate working directly to the 2nd Battalion – a rare event in the Regiment's history. The atmosphere in Belfast was markedly more aggressive than in Londonderry, but on their return to the city, they found hostilities there also increasing. The situation worsened as the months slowly passed. In May, Private Larter was shot in the hand when escaping from three armed men who attacked him as he said goodnight to his fiancée in the Bogside. His fiancée was later tarred and feathered and had to be rescued by the Vikings. In July the IRA started to escalate the situation by increasing the frequency of shooting incidents, some 140 rounds being fired at the battalion over the next few months. A *Sunday Times* report from 21 November 1971 described the situation:

> By the night of 7 July 1971, rioting had been going on for four days and the Royal Anglians had been fired on 60 times by their count. It says a good deal for the firm discipline of this Regiment – the Anglians have a reputation for unusual coolness and restraint – that only three shots were fired in reply.

On 8 July a Viking soldier shot at a man carrying a rifle, hitting his femoral artery and causing heavy bleeding. Later identified as Seamus Cusack, he was put into a car and driven across the border to Letterkenny Hospital, where he subsequently died due to loss of blood. Had he not been driven away, immediate treatment with a tourniquet might have saved his

B Company of the Vikings in action in a riot.

Newspaper article claiming that early treatment would have saved Seamus Cusack's life.

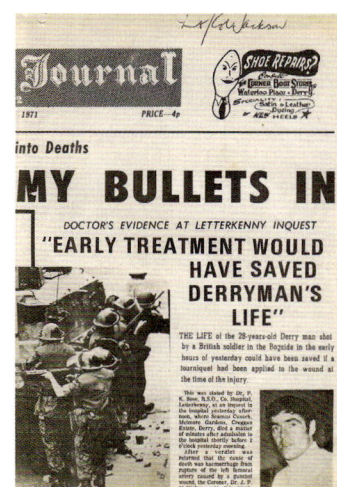

POACHERS IN BELFAST, 1970–71

The 2nd Battalion, the Poachers, undertook their first short tour in Northern Ireland from October 1970 to February 1971, in West Belfast. The Poachers were notably successful on this tour. Under the command of Lieutenant Colonel Dick Gerrard-Wright, they encountered a series of serious riots as West Belfast was more violent than Londonderry at this time. These riots escalated during the tour, meaning that the Poachers had to learn how to deal with heavy riots the hard way, by actually doing it. Petrol bombers made their first wide-scale appearance, requiring the development of new tactics in response. This included the use of CS gas, the use of baton guns, flanking manoeuvres and snatch squads.

life. A second man, Desmond Beattie, was about to throw a nail bomb when he was shot and killed by the Vikings. From then to the end of the tour the situation deteriorated markedly with rioting and stone throwing becoming an almost daily occurrence, augmented by frequent sniper attacks.

THE REGIMENT'S WEAPONS IN NORTHERN IRELAND

Throughout the first two decades of the conflict, the British Army used the FN FAL 7.62mm calibre automatic rifle, known as the Self-Loading Rifle L1A1, the SLR. In British Army service the fully automatic fire function was removed, so it fired repeated single shots automatically from a 20-round magazine. The SLR originally had a wooden butt and stock, which gave a distinctive brown appearance, but these were progressively replaced by black plastic during the late 1970s. Most teams on urban operations would carry only the SLR, supplemented by baton guns. On rural operations the GPMG was usually carried on a scale of one per four-man team.

SLRs were normally used with the iron sight built into the weapon, but from the early 1970s an optical x4 magnification sight called the Sight Unit Infantry Trilux (SUIT) sight was introduced. The SUIT sight gave a better view of the target, especially in twilight conditions and at longer ranges. At around the same time a first-generation image intensification sight was also introduced, called the Individual Weapon Sight (IWS), which could be fitted to various weapons. This large, heavy and clumsy sight enabled a soldier actually to see in the dark. Image intensification sights worked by using charge-coupled devices to amplify the ambient light to generate a green monotone sight picture.

First used by the Vikings on their 1989 South Armagh tour, the 5.56mm SA80A1 and Light Support Weapon (LSW) replaced the SLR, and were used on all subsequent operations.

Baton guns – sometimes called rubber bullet guns or riot guns by the press – underwent a series of developments during the conflict. The first weapon used was the Gun, Riot 1.5in L67A1, of 1.5 inch (38mm) calibre. It went through several minor changes but was used until the early 1990s, when it was replaced by the Heckler & Koch L104A1 37mm Baton Gun with a new set of baton rounds.

In the early 1970s actual rubber bullets were fired, but these were changed in 1979 to a PVC (polyvinyl chloride) plastic round.

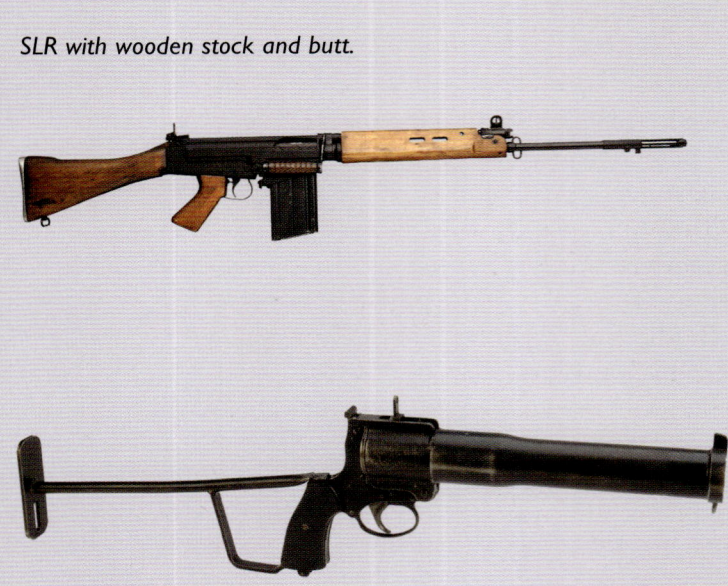

SLR with wooden stock and butt.

L67A1 baton gun.

Soldiers from the Poachers fire baton rounds at rioters during 'hunger strike riots' in Bogside, Londonderry, 1981.

It was nearly impossible to catch and arrest these stone-throwing rioters unless they were outflanked, and the battalion became experts in doing this by deploying the 'Derry Hook'.

The first member of the Regiment killed on operations in Northern Ireland was Private Roger Wilkins, aged 32, who was shot while on duty in a sangar in the Brandywell on 27 September. He died of his wounds on 11 October 1971. Several others were wounded at this time, and then on 9 November Lance Corporal Ian Curtis, aged 23, was shot and killed on a patrol securing the route from Craigavon Bridge to the Brandywell.

On 9–10 August 1971 the huge, province-wide Operation *Demetrius* was mounted, more widely known as internment. As some of the intelligence was flawed, certain key terrorists probably had wind of the operation so that few of the real players were arrested but some innocents were. This tended to fuel resentment against the troops and boosted the violence still further.

The Vikings' final rotation into the city ended on 21 December 1971 with the commanding officer handing over the keys to the city to Lieutenant Colonel Ferguson of the 22nd Light Air Defence Regiment of the Royal Artillery.

By the end of January 1972, the battalion's tour was coming to an end. As they made preparations for their move to Cyprus, to which many were greatly looking forward, one of the pivotal events in the conflict took place in the Rossville Flats area of the Bogside on the afternoon of 30 January – forever afterwards to be known as Bloody Sunday. Some 26 protestors were shot by the 1st Battalion The Parachute Regiment. Thirteen died. This tragic incident occurred during a large-scale operation called Operation *Forecast* that was devised to deal with a planned march from the Bogside to the city centre.

Lieutenant Colonel Jackson's testimony to the Saville Inquiry is preserved and is a remarkable open source on the difficult position of the Vikings on this fateful day.[2] It is clear from paragraphs 36–39 that the commanding officer was less than pleased with the way

Lance Corporal Ian Curtis.

Lieutenant Colonel Roy Jackson (right) hands over at Roaring Meg, a historic cannon on the Londonderry Walls.

Operation *Forecast* had been shaped without his involvement. In paragraph 40 he describes his actions:

> Immediately after the O Group, I asked Brigadier MacLellan if I could speak with him in his office. There was no-one else present and the meeting lasted a few minutes. I told him that 1 PARA should not be used in Londonderry: they did not know the area and would go in blind. I said that I should be given the role of 1 PARA and they could take over the blocking role allocated to 1 R ANGLIAN and that this would be more acceptable all round. (As the Province Reserve battalion, the Paras had operated in all areas of the Province other than Londonderry. From my understanding, they seldom operated for any length of time as we resident battalions in Londonderry. As I have explained above, Derry and Belfast were as different as chalk and cheese, and our job in Derry at the time was to maintain a containment line, albeit in an aggressive manner, which was so different to the role required of units in Belfast.)

On 30 January, the Vikings spent a busy day holding the Craigavon bridge and were stoned and shot at as usual in the Brandywell estate area and some parts of the city centre. However, no Vikings were directly involved with the terrible events in the Bogside on Bloody Sunday. Jackson's testimony further records (paragraph 55):

> During 30 January 1972, 1 R ANGLIAN had been fired on eight times (16–18 rounds) and had returned fire on six occasions (18 rounds) and claimed four hits; one additional hit was confirmed later. We had expended nine baton rounds during the day and made seven arrests.

After Bloody Sunday the whole atmosphere in Northern Ireland changed for the worse, with many formerly indecisive or uncommitted supporters flocking to the IRA. Attacks on soldiers now became their aim and the level of violence peaked still further.

The Vikings spent the rest of February on countryside operations, then moved to Cyprus in March, individually by air. Lieutenant Colonel Jackson notes (paragraph 63):

Commanding Officer's Tactical Headquarters on Bloody Sunday, 30 January 1972.

1 R ANGLIAN left Londonderry in March 1972. We had buried two soldiers murdered by terrorists, four more were wounded by gunfire and a further eight soldiers were seriously injured (two of whom were seriously injured during our visit to Belfast in February 1971) and one soldier had his married quarters damaged by a bomb; fortunately neither he nor his family were injured. We took with us to Cyprus 69 young Londonderry ladies who had married 1 R ANGLIAN soldiers.

The previous commander of 8 Brigade, Brigadier Alan Cowan, MBE, had recommended Lieutenant Colonel Roy Jackson for an operational award of the OBE, which was later granted, the citation for which stated: 'his personal example and calm and fearless leadership had been of a very high order, often under exceptionally difficult and trying circumstances, throughout sixteen arduous months'.

Vikings in action with a Humber Pig.

NORTHERN IRELAND ORGANISATION

The Regiment deployed to Northern Ireland almost always organised as four companies, usually each consisting of three platoons plus a headquarters. Three of these companies were provided by the rifle companies and the fourth provided by D or Support Company converted from their normal heavy weapons to the counter-insurgency role. All companies were commanded by majors, assisted by a company sergeant major of warrant officer class 2 rank and a second-in-command, usually a captain who would often double as a company operations officer.

Platoons were usually led by an officer, a lieutenant or second lieutenant, sometimes by a colour sergeant and in the early days would consist of a platoon headquarters of four or five men and three sections each of eight men. This organisation was soon found to be inappropriate for Northern Ireland so was changed first into four-man teams, initially called 'bricks', in 1971. Later the name was changed to 'team', and these were usually grouped into three, which was then called a multiple. Each multiple would thus normally consist of 12 men, in three teams of four men. Platoons would usually be able to deploy two multiples, one led by the platoon commander, the other by the platoon sergeant. Each of the teams would normally be led by a corporal or lance corporal. Vehicle patrols would often consist of just two teams, each in its own vehicle.

These organisations could vary a great deal and be changed for particular operations. For example, Support Company of the 1st Battalion in 1986 often used multiples of five to seven teams, of mixed foot and vehicle-mounted teams, even on routine patrols.

Some companies were occasionally designated as Operations Company, which meant they did not have a company Tactical Area of Responsibility (TAOR) – often called a 'patch' – so they would be free from routine ground domination duties in order to plan and conduct specific operations.

RIOT TACTICS AND SNATCH SQUADS

During the early years of the conflict, the tactics of 'snatch squads' were developed, where small groups of very fit stalwart soldiers, often rugby players, would strip down for speed, carrying only a wooden baton each. On a signal, usually following a salvo of baton rounds, this team of just four men would dash out to grab and drag back rioters – ideally the ringleaders – who had been incapacitated by a hit by a baton round. The Poachers were instrumental in developing these tactics right from the start. Lieutenant Colonel Dick Gerrard-Wright, then commanding the Poachers, was recommended for an OBE for his contribution. The citation for his OBE stated that:

> In addition to his preoccupation with an endless succession of disturbances, Lieutenant Colonel Gerrard-Wright has been outstandingly successful in making contact with various subversive elements and extracting from them an immense amount of valuable information. There is no doubt that he has greatly improved the understanding which the Security Forces have of the subversive elements in this way, and this alone would have been a highly important contribution to the army's effort in Belfast. He has also done a great deal to maintain and improve relations between the army and the Royal Ulster Constabulary in his area. Finally, by his attention to the detailed tactical uses of small groups of soldiers in riotous conditions he has developed a method

of using snatch squads which has greatly increased the number of arrests made by the army during recent outbreaks of violence.[3]

B Company of the Poachers called their snatch squads 'Ham squads' as the first had been formed under Corporal Hampton. The Poachers also devised squads designed specifically to outflank rioters, using tactics similar to the Derry Hook. They were based on the Reconnaissance Platoon led by Sergeant Nugent who was awarded a BEM for his actions in a particularly difficult riot on 14 January 1971.

In the early days snatch squads were often highly effective but – always on the look out for a weakness – the rioters adapted their tactics so as to try to isolate a snatch squad away from its supports. After some nasty incidents, the use of snatch squads became less frequent in the later years of the conflict. It was relatively easy to send a snatch squad into the periphery of a riot, but the people snatched there would often be onlookers rather than ringleaders. It was much more difficult and dangerous to send a snatch squad into the middle of a riot, where the ringleaders were usually positioned. The tactics were still taught in training, but in actual riots a more cautious approach, often still involving flanking manoeuvres, regularly achieved better results. The accumulation of more than a decade of experience in this type of work by the Poachers was probably an important factor leading to their later effectiveness during the hunger strike riots of 1981.

BELFAST, 1972

As already seen, 1972 was a monumental year in Northern Ireland. In fact, it was to be the worst year of the conflict by all measures: there were more incidents, more deaths and more injuries than in any other year. Following Bloody Sunday, the level of violence escalated alarmingly to some 1,853 bombing and 10,628 shooting incidents during the year. During the year 467 people were killed – 103 regular army, 26 UDR, 17 RUC and 223 civilians, 95 Republican terrorists and three Loyalist terrorists. The total number of troops and security forces in the Province almost doubled, from 7,800 in 1971 to 14,300 in 1972, before peaking at 16,900 in 1973. Total deployments were as follows:

YEAR	REGULAR ARMY	UDR/ROYAL IRISH	RUC
1971	7,800	4,044	4,083
1976	15,500	7,645	5,253
1981	11,600	7,470	7,334
1986	10,500	6,408	8,234
1991	10,500	6,276	8,222
1996	11,815	4,855	8,424
2001	12,346	4,598	8,495

At this time both the OIRA and PIRA were experimenting with incidents designed to shock by killing and maiming large numbers of civilians, to demonstrate how they could disrupt normal daily life, almost at will. The car bomb made its first major appearance, in devastating fashion. Most car bombs were initiated with timing devices, as were many of the static bombs. Static bombs might also be initiated by command wires, but there was not yet a radio-controlled bomb threat. There were many shootings, often of an impromptu nature, not very well planned and involving a great range of firearms, many dating from the Second World War. These were called 'cowboy shoots' by the troops – perhaps a hasty act by teenagers or sometimes a drunken terrorist. They could be effective, although dangerous for the terrorist, which explains some of the many terrorist deaths during 1972. There were also plenty of other more carefully planned shootings. Rioting, vehicle hijackings, erecting barricades and stone throwing were daily events, with some 'minor aggro' by youths escalating alarmingly quickly into full-scale riots.

Stone-throwing youths.

Sectarian violence between Catholic and Protestant factions escalated during the year, and as a consequence in February and March various no-go areas were established in Catholic estates by the IRA. It took a major coordinated operation on 31 July, Operation *Motorman*, to clear these. This was seen as a success in that it removed the no-go areas with their barricades and re-established the rule of law, but it was at the cost of further alienating the Catholic population. The split between the Official and Provisional IRA was to widen during the year, further complicating an already baffling intelligence situation.

The summer was characterised by a government-led negotiation leading to a ceasefire, which was broken without warning by the PIRA, then punctuated by 'Bloody Friday'.

Into this violent situation, the 3rd Battalion, the Pompadours, deployed in central Belfast from their base in Paderborn, Germany. Assuming command from the 1st Battalion The Gloucestershire Regiment on 12 April 1972, their patch consisted initially of the Lower Falls, the Clonard area, the Divis Flats and the northern peace line between the Catholic areas and the Protestant Shankill estate. During the course of the tour their patch would change frequently and

Initial patch bounded by Shankill Road (north), Grosvenor Road (south), Upper Falls and Springfield Road (west) and Millfield and Durham Streets (east). Map dates from before the Divis Flats were built.

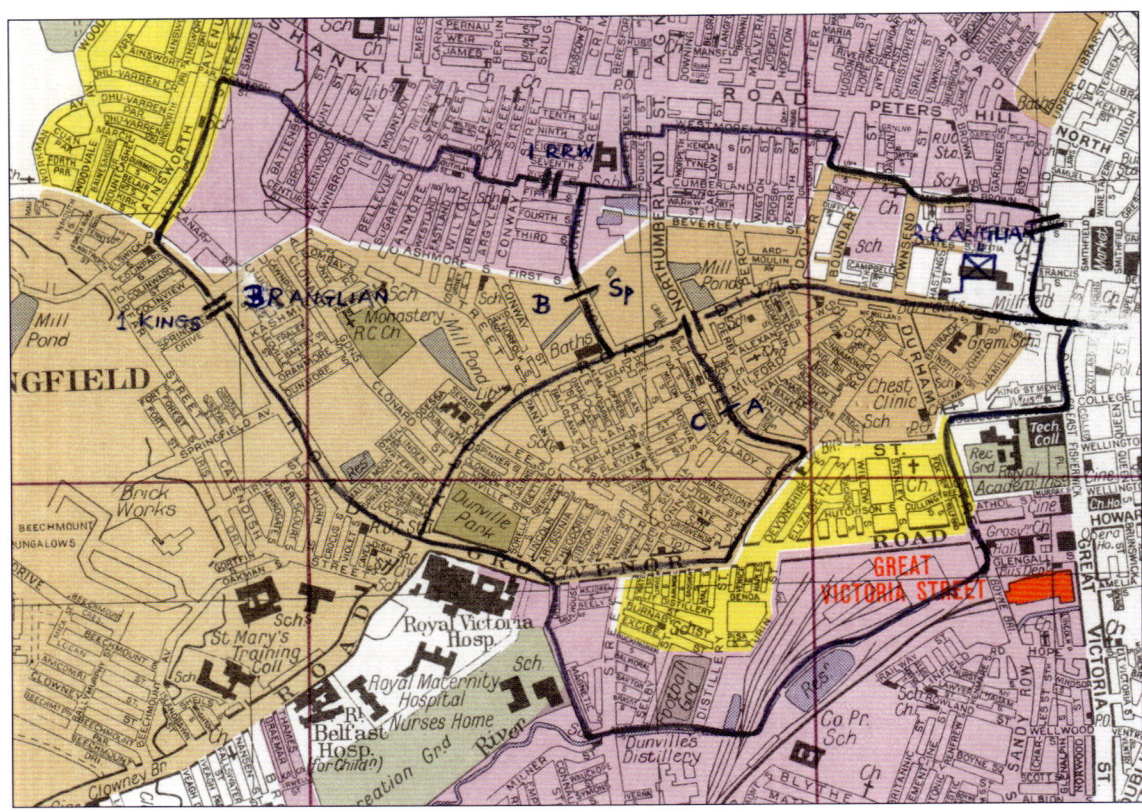

additional units would be attached; at one point the battalion had some nine companies under command from a range of other units. Under the effective leadership of Lieutenant Colonel Jonathan Hall-Tipping, the Pompadours were to experience a very testing time with some seven shootings, an armed robbery, three bomb hoaxes and two riots within their first 48 hours in command.

A famous composite from *Castle*, showing a Pompadour astride the Divis Flats.

The Pompadours were thrown straight in at the deep end with a violent and difficult time around the Divis Flats area in April. This was to become known as the 'Battle of the Divis Flats', which mainly involved A Company. The terrain of the Divis flats was unusual to say the least, as the fortress-like concrete structure provided a safe haven for the IRA and allowed them to dominate the surrounding area.

A Company, the Pompadours, under the command of Major Trevor Veitch, was based in Albert Street Mill, just across from the Divis Flats. He described the situation:

Within 4 days of our arrival we were faced with a large-scale insurrection and a result of the IRA commander Joe McCann being shot by 2 PARA [2nd

A riot in the Divis Flats.

Battalion The Parachute Regiment] on 15th April. This involved hundreds of people coming out of the flats and the Falls Road, building barricades, throwing stones and petrol bombs and burning vehicles and buildings.

Lieutenant Peter Dixon, the A Company Operations Officer at the time, recalled:

> It would start at about 3.00pm in the afternoon and then go on until one or two in the morning, day after day. The point was they were using the Divis Flats as a base from which to shoot at us, usually from the links – the joins between the blocks of flats. We were very vulnerable when coming out of Albert Street Mill base as it was completely overlooked from the flats.

The most violent day was 16 April, as an extract from the A Company operational log of the day records:

16.50   Very heavy fire from Divis Flats, press men and pedestrians scatter under hail of bullets. Troops return fire but no hits observed.
17.40   Barricade in Divis Street set alight.
17.55   Albert Street Army Post shot at and fire returned.
18.00   Communication on one death and three injuries to terrorists in Divis battle.
18.30   Shooting at Divis intensified.
19.00   Body reported found by civilian in St Congalls School in Divis Street, body head mutilated claim, body later disappeared.
21.00   Divis tower shrouded in smoke from burning vehicles. Divis Street deserted as snipers firing from flats.

This type of intense rioting mixed in with shootings went on for nine more days, finally petering out at the end of April. It tended to follow a pattern; Major Veitch and Lieutenant Dixon described how:

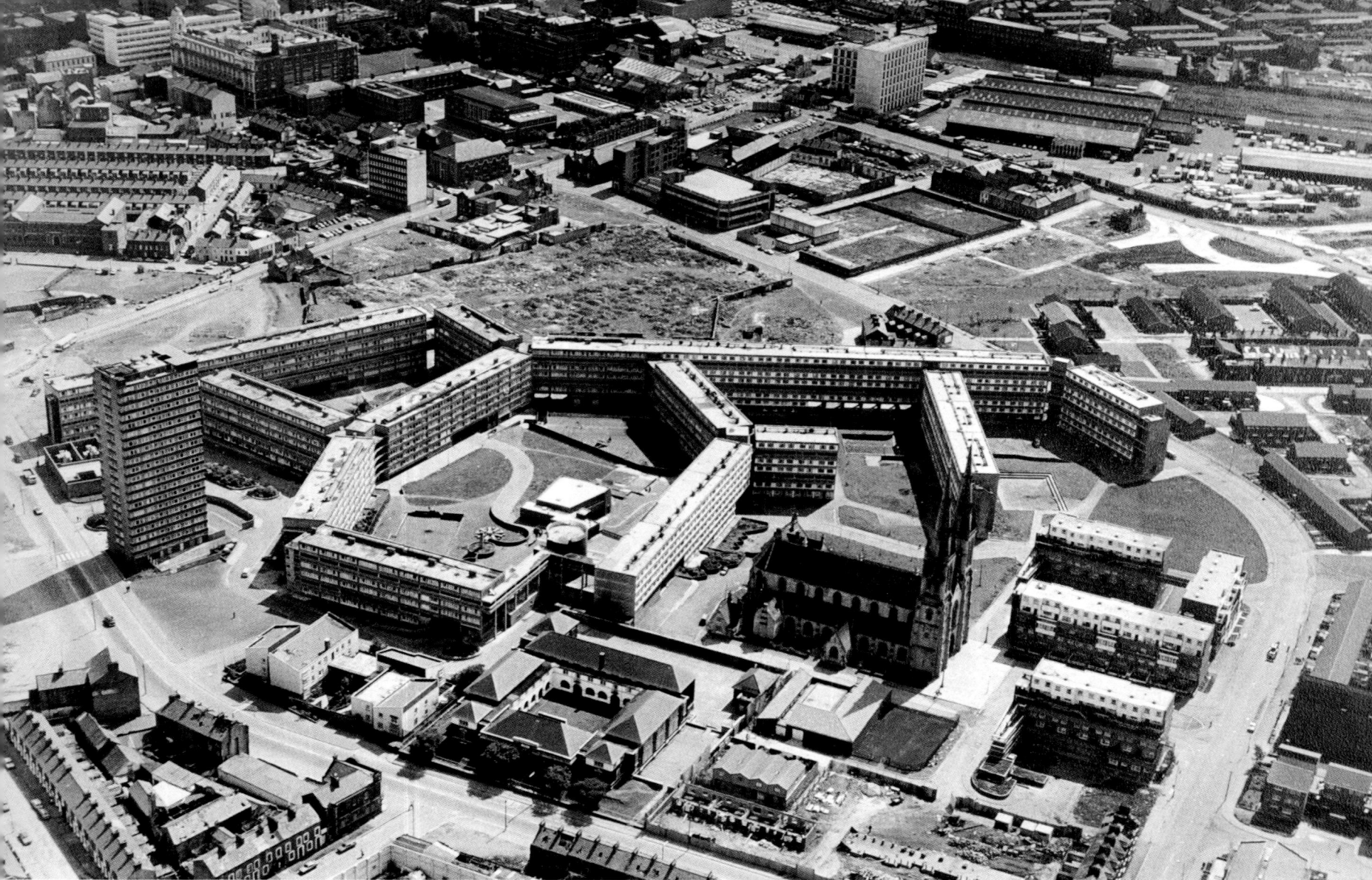

The Divis Flats from the air.

Opposite, top: Second Lieutenant Nick Hull.

Nothing would happen in the mornings because they did not get up until lunchtime. Then it would start with the younger youths stoning, and gradually during the afternoon the older youths would show up and start petrol bombing and building barricades and hijacking cars and setting them alight. Then towards the evening the shootings would start, interspersed with more rioting, burning cars, burning buildings, ripping down everything in the street, burning furniture from the buildings. We would respond by driving out in 'Pigs' with the bars on the front through the barricades, sometimes also using Engineer vehicles with diggers to remove them. It was escalated by the death of McCann but they would have tested us out anyway. Not only did we have to get used to the urban geography but also the extraordinary layout of the Divis Flats. If somebody fired at you it was very difficult to locate the firing point. This went on for 4 months, but this particular week was the worst

On 16 April the battalion suffered its first fatal casualty when Second Lieutenant Nick Hull of A Company was shot and killed while in a Pig armoured vehicle. A strange account of this incident has emerged from the other side, reported by Kevin Myers in his book *Watching the Door*:

Rioters took control over Divis Street, hijacking and burning busses, and erecting barricades. Fresh troops were arriving just as I did. I climbed up the stairs onto one of the balconies, where I beheld a vision from hell: fifteen-year-old boys with sub-machine guns and semi-automatic rifles. They were gathered beside one of the now disused lift shafts, and were receiving orders from some infant-Rommel …

Bullets were ricocheting everywhere, as these demented children emptied magazine after magazine into anything and everything, yet amazingly not themselves …

There were no soldiers left in view, just a single Humber Pig APC lumbering towards the flats. Hideous volleys of bullets from a dozen infant-held guns smashed against its side and nose, and indeed over half the street as well. It stopped, paused for about half a minute, and then reversed.

On the balcony, the children cheered, waving their huge rifles: inside the APC 2nd Lieutenant Nicholas Hull lay dying. Incredibly a chance round had passed through an observation slit and fatally injured him.[4]

On the following day, 17 April, Second Lieutenant Robin Chisnall was shot and very seriously wounded while investigating a bomb scare on the Falls Road. On 19 April some 177 rounds were fired at the battalion. The Pompadours were to suffer four fatalities in total during the tour, together with some 36 serious injuries.

THE HUMBER PIG

Although the six-wheeled Armoured Personnel Carrier (APC) the Alvis Saracen was used extensively during the first decade, including ambulance variants, the iconic armoured vehicle of the Northern Ireland conflict was without doubt the Humber Pig. This four-wheeled, lightly armoured vehicle had an especially pugnacious appearance. It could carry two teams, up to eight men, more at a squash and was very useful for carrying cargo too. There were many variants, most notably with fold-out riot screens or wings, inevitably called the Flying Pig. It had many drawbacks, mainly that it was not fully bulletproof; although its armour would stop most rifle calibre ammunition, it could be penetrated by specifically armour-piercing (AP) rifle rounds such as the .3006-inch Garand AP round. A second major drawback was poor visibility – when closed up with all the vision blocks shut, it was very difficult to see out, especially for the driver. Pigs accounted for very many vehicle accidents and collisions. This poor visibility meant that the troops would usually leave as many vision blocks open as possible, but this had the unfortunate effect of allowing in bullets, which then had a tendency to ricochet around inside the armour. Several members of the Regiment were killed and wounded in this way. Lieutenant Dixon said of the Pig:

You actually felt a lot more secure if you were outside your vehicle. You did feel if you were driving in that Pig that you were in a potential coffin. People were much happier outside.

In later years the opposing youths worked out the poor visibility and took to throwing paint bombs – gloss paint in plastic bags – at the vision blocks. The wipers had no chance of cleaning this off, forcing the crew to open the vision block, which could then be petrol bombed.

A Royal Anglian Humber Pig.

For his intelligent actions during two patrols in June, which led to the capture of a gunman and the arrest of a man carrying ammunition, Corporal Jephcote of B Company received the Military Medal.

Shootings, bombings and rioting were essentially daily occurrences in the spring, but as a result of the peace initiative, the OIRA declared a ceasefire on 29 May followed by the PIRA on 26 June. The violence subsided slightly, but not for long as the PIRA broke the ceasefire on 13 July with the killing of two Pompadours – Corporal Kenneth Mogg and Lance Corporal Martin Rooney – both shot in armoured Pigs. This was followed eight days later by Bloody Friday, Friday 21 July, when some 22 bombs, mainly car bombs on timers, were detonated in the Belfast city centre within about 80 minutes, between 14.10 and 15.30, killing nine and injuring 130, mainly civilians. The Pompadours were deployed at full stretch on that day, as the commanding officer described:

I remember that my Brigade Commander, Brigadier Dickie Lawson from 22 Armoured Brigade in Germany, was visiting me at the time and I was down with him visiting Bill Dodd's Company, C Company. There we were talking and we heard the bang-bang-bang of the bombs going off. I was in the C Company Operations Room; it was difficult to know what was going on, but we had our immediate action drills and at that point basically everybody with boots on turned out and deployed onto the ground. It was however basically a mop up operation, they were going off one after the other almost like fireworks. We knew they had placed the bombs in areas to make it difficult for us, we were very stretched, mainly in support of the police, but at that time although the police could operate in the Protestant areas, they could not go into the Catholic estates without us. So I deployed the whole Battalion to operate in the Leeson Street, Clonard, Falls Road and around Divis to try to maintain order and show a presence on the streets. There were a lot of people about shouting in support of the bombs, and I wanted to prevent the situation getting any worse. It was mainly about providing cover

A Humber Pig in a riot.

Above: A Pompadour
snatch squad.

Lieutenant Colonel
Jonathan Hall-Tipping, 3rd
Battalion (left), hands over
to Lieutenant Colonel
Dick Gerrard-Wright, 2nd
Battalion.

to the other emergency services, to provide as much of a presence on the ground as we could achieve. It was a bit like the blitz with ambulance, fire and police vehicles moving all around. Overall, however, we could only provide the presence and support the other services; it was essentially a mopping up operation for us.

The remainder of July was again very busy, with the battalion conducting a series of three large cordon and search operations, swiftly followed by full involvement in Operation *Motorman* on 31 July. A rare event took place when the 3rd Battalion handed over operational command of their patch in central Belfast to the 2nd Battalion on 2 August 1972. Commemorated by a famous photograph in *Castle*, it was one of only three operational handovers between battalions during the history of the Regiment, the next being in July 1973 when the 3rd Battalion handed over to the 2nd in Londonderry, the other one taking place in October 1982 when the 3rd Battalion handed over in Belize to the 1st Battalion.

POACHERS IN BELFAST, AUGUST–DECEMBER 1972

Led by the highly innovative and dynamic Lieutenant Colonel Dick Gerrard-Wright, the Poachers followed up from their 1970–71 tour and were back in Belfast again, taking over a very violent and difficult situation. A Company took over the Lower Falls, with B Company concentrating on the Divis Flats, C Company the city centre and Support Company on the peace line by the Shankill estate. The tour followed a similar pattern of responding to riots, shootings and bombings. The table shows the key events of the tour:

DATE (ALL 1972)	EVENT
17 August	Corporal Michael Boddy, aged 24, of the Drums Platoon killed by an IRA sniper while leading a patrol in Selby Street, off the Grosvenor Road in the Lower Falls.
14 September	Capture of IRA commander James Bryson by Sergeant Whitfield and Lance Corporal Ley.
23 September	Corporal John Barry, aged 22, shot by an IRA sniper while on a mobile patrol at the junction of Cyprus Street and McDonnell Street in the Lower Falls. He died of his wounds two days later.
25 September	Large battalion-level cordon and search operation in the Lower Falls bottle factory. Company Sergeant Major Greenfield wounded in the hand by a sniper round.
29 September	Corporal Sanderson's section shoot and kill IRA gunman James Quigley and recover his rifle in Albert Street while on foot patrol.
29 September	Private Ian Burt, aged 18, shot and killed by an IRA sniper in Albert Street, Lower Falls.
30 September	Corporal Wright engages and wounds a gunman at a range of 600m from the Divis Observation Post.
24 October	Private Robert Mason, aged 19, shot and killed by an IRA sniper in Naples Street off the Grosvenor Road.
28 November	The IRA fire an RPG-7 for the first time, at a vehicle commanded by Sergeant Whitfield, injuring the gunner Private Sanderson.

Opposite, middle: Picture of James Bryson from *Castle*.

Opposite, bottom: The team that captured Bryson, Sergeant Whitfield on the right.

14 SEPTEMBER 1972

This intriguing incident started when an alert C Company soldier in an observation post in the Post Office building on the Grosvenor Road saw a car being hijacked in Leeson Street, in the early afternoon of 14 September 1972, and reported it over the battalion radio net. The duty officer in A Company's operations room in Mulhouse base sent out the standby

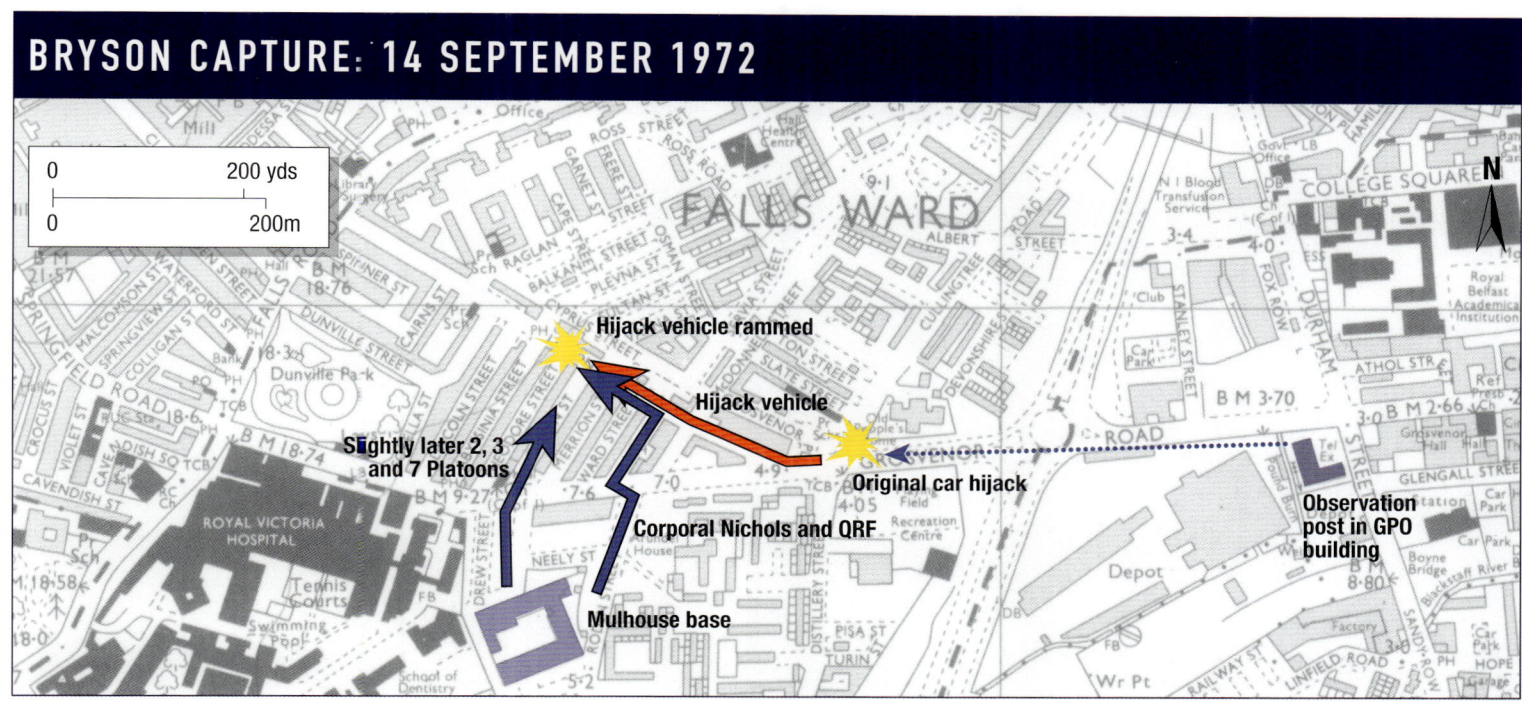

BRYSON CAPTURE: 14 SEPTEMBER 1972

Quick Reaction Force (QRF) under Corporal Nichols, into the Lower Falls, Leeson Street area to try to find and apprehend the hijacked vehicle, while the rest of A Company was stood to in support. As he reached the Grosvenor Road, Corporal Nichols spotted the vehicle in a queue of traffic and he followed it up to Leeson Street, whereupon the wanted vehicle reversed wildly before hitting a wall. As one of the terrorists raised a gun, Private Sentence, the vehicle gunner, shouted to the driver to ram the car. At the ramming, both gunmen debouched from the car and ran off, exchanging shots with the dismounting Poachers. One of the gunmen was hit and ran into a house. Meanwhile, the rest of A Company in the form of 2 and 3 Platoons were joining the chase, along with 7 Platoon from C Company, as a crowd of around 200 people started to gather in Leeson Street. Second Lieutenant Chris Groom and Sergeant

Arnold followed the blood trail from the yard of one house, over a 3m-high wall and into another house, where they found the wounded terrorist receiving first aid from three others. All four were apprehended.

Meanwhile a cut-off group, led by Sergeant Whitfield and Lance Corporal Codling, were climbing another wall when they came across the other terrorist pointing his pistol at a foot patrol. Hearing movement the terrorist ran – straight into the arms of Lance Corporal Ley and Private Amberton. Ley promptly brought down the terrorist with a rugby tackle and arrested him. Later, while this terrorist was being processed, he was recognised by one of the Poachers'

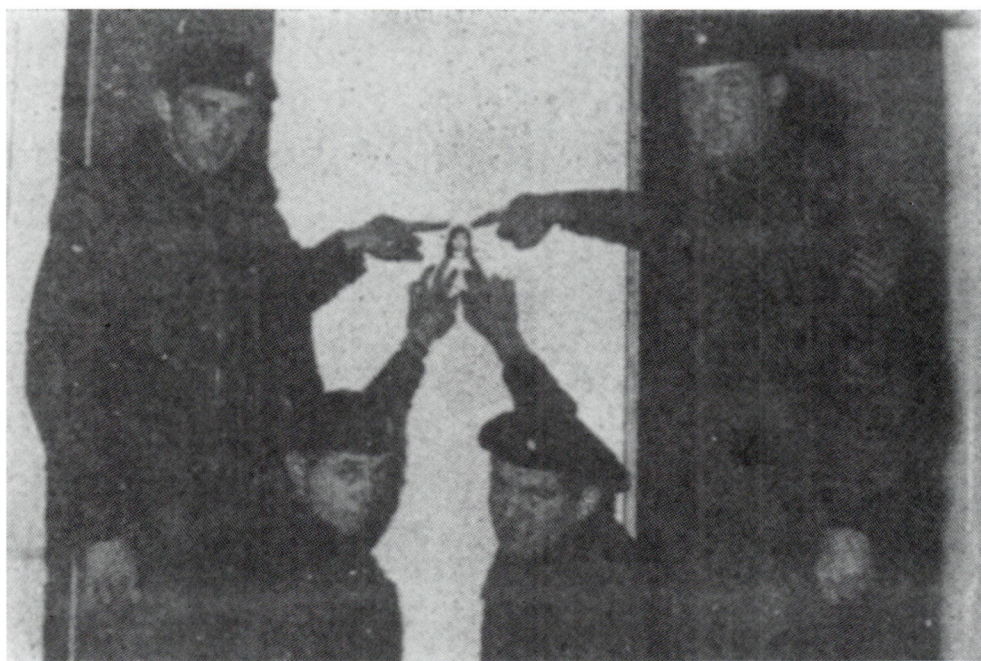

LANCE CORPORAL LEY IN ACTION

intelligence cell due to his crooked nose and thought to be a rather important catch. It was later confirmed by the Special Branch that the name he had given was false, and he was in fact none other than James Emerson Bryson, the commander of B Company of the PIRA and the most wanted terrorist in West Belfast.

That evening Mulhouse base was described as a 'happy place', but the operations room had been an occasionally frustrating place to be in the late afternoon, as it was not always clear what was happening. The A Company commander, Major Charles Barnes, remembers 'getting a little frustrated and banging the table at times', but it ended well for the Poachers and congratulations flooded in, including from Mr Whitelaw, the Northern Ireland Secretary. This was no fluke, however, but a direct result of prompt and decisive action by Major Barnes, in crashing out as many Poachers as possible to pursue the opportunity presented by an alert observation of the initial hijack. Major Barnes was awarded an MBE for this tour and Sergeant Whitfield a Distinguished Conduct Medal.

BELFAST AND LONDONDERRY, 1973–79

The difficult years of the conflict between 1973 and 1979 were characterised for the Regiment by a busy schedule of roulement tours. Pre-tour training for these tours would take two to three months and post-tour leave of one month was usually followed by re-training to the normal role, which took a further two to three months. The following table shows the schedule of urban tours for these years for the Regiment.

BATTALION	DATES	LOCATION
3rd Battalion	March–July 1973	Londonderry
2nd Battalion	July–November 1973	Londonderry
3rd Battalion	November 1974–March 1975	Londonderry
2nd Battalion	August–December 1975	Belfast
2nd Battalion	March–June 1977	Belfast
1st Battalion	May–September 1979	Belfast

Rather than recounting each of these tours in detail, we will look at one of them in the form of a photo essay.

POMPADOURS IN THE CREGGAN, 1973

This is recorded from the viewpoint of A Company, 3rd Battalion, the Pompadours, commanded by Major Kerry Woodrow, who recalls:

I was so lucky; I had some outstanding NCOs, Wysocki, Wilson, Wilkinson, Ramsey. They had all been in Belfast the previous year. I arrived from Staff College, green as hell but found that I had this superbly experienced company. Roy Brunning was a Company Sergeant Major whose whole life was the welfare of the soldiers. My platoon commanders were Tim Power, Jerry Monk ('the professor') and Colour Sergeant Joe Randall-Wood. The company boundaries kept changing throughout the tour. We were based in a base built in the old shirt factory between Bligh's Lane and Eastway; we called it Bligh's Lane.

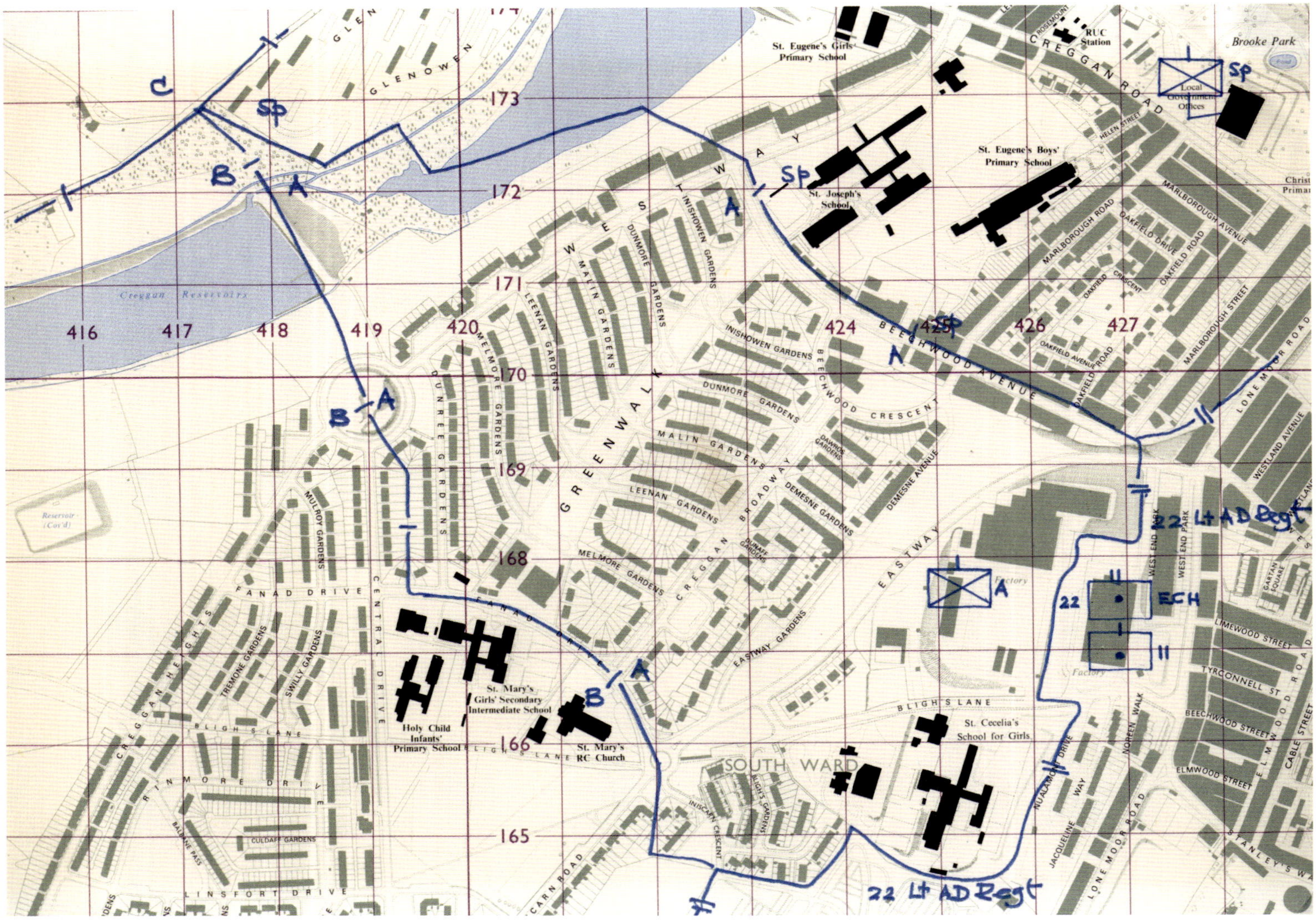

Above: Contemporary 1:10,000 scale map showing the A Company Tactical Area of Responsibility ('the patch') in the central part of the Creggan estate, Londonderry, at the start of the tour in March 1973.

Right: Air photograph of the patch with Bligh's Lane in the right foreground.

Above: Company Commander's group: Private Allen, Private James, Major Woodrow, Captain Rodney Corbett and Private Anthony Goodfellow, aged 26, who was killed by a sniper shot on 27 April 1973 while manning a vehicle checkpoint on the Westway.

Major Woodrow hosts a visit from the commander of 8 Brigade, Brigadier Mostyn, with Regimental Sergeant Major Stan Bullock in the background.

Barricade clearing on Fanad
Drive.

Company Headquarters
relax on their Saracen APC
inside Bligh's Lane camp.

A patrol setting out. Left to right: Lance Corporal Nelson, Privates Brazzill, Sephton, Howell, Schofield, La Pierre.

Sergeant Clive 'Zap-Zap' Mallett, a nickname earned on the Belfast tour of the previous year.

Beechwood Crescent in the
Creggan estate, with locals.

Beechwood shops in the
Creggan estate.

The junction of Central Drive and Fanad Drive in the Creggan estate, looking south.

STATISTICS to date	24 Jul
grenades, smoke	52
grenades, cs	102
cartridges, cs	445
rounds, 7·62	153
rounds, baton	2616
rounds, pvc	0
rounds, 9mm	0
lifts	42
arrests	128

A Company statistics, including ammunition used during the tour, on handover, 24 July 1973.

A typical confrontation with protesting locals.

Local boys throwing stones: 'minor aggro'.

BELFAST, 1978

The 3rd Battalion, the Pompadours, undertook a residential tour based in Palace Barracks on the north-eastern outskirts of Belfast from May 1978 to November 1979. Under the effective and cheerful leadership of Lieutenant Colonel Bill Dodd, MBE, the Pompadours were in good shape with high morale. At this time the residential battalions tended to be deployed in many small 'penny packets' of multiple (12 man) or platoon size, usually under command of the roulement battalions. Although this gave great flexibility and a surge capacity to the overall Army position in the Province, it was annoying for the troops themselves to be constantly switching between operational commands. They called their rotation 'rent a mob', but all companies were occasionally deployed together, for example on 12 July for the Orange Day parades. Despite these irritations, the Pompadours retained their excellent professional standards and earned a good reputation with those units they supported. Lieutenant General Sir Timothy Creasey, KCB, OBE, was the General Officer Commanding Northern Ireland at this time, an influential senior commander with his roots in the Regiment.

The violence was moving into a more calculated and in some ways more sinister phase as PIRA was now mainly targeting the Army. PIRA were experimenting successfully with new types of initiation for their bombs. New types of time clock, different and cunning command wires and the very dangerous radio-controlled initiators were beginning to appear in numbers. These were the early days of the radio-controlled device, often based on model aeroplane or car components, against which the Army had no real defence at that time. The radio-controlled devices were problematic because they gave the bombers much more flexibility – they could detonate at will, without warning and with almost no chance of their targets

Older youths throwing stones.

A picture of 5 Platoon, the Pompadours, from *Pompadour* magazine, 1978.

detecting the device. It also greatly reduced the risk to the bomber, who did not have to be anywhere near the device when it detonated. Other forms of detonation each had their own drawbacks: timers lacked flexibility and command wires meant at least a chance of detection.

Shootings were still a threat, but the hastily planned 'cowboy'-type shootings of earlier years were no more. By 1978 almost all shootings were meticulously planned. Some were single long-range sniper shots, but others were designed to overwhelm the troops at short range as PIRA now had automatic assault weapons, such as the AR-15 and AR-18 Armalites and AK-47 Kalashnikov and even RPG-7 rocket launchers.

A single incident will serve as an example of the many dangerous patrols and operations mounted by the Pompadours during their 18-month tour. It involved a 12-man multiple of 5 Platoon in B Company, the Pompadours, call-sign 21A, led by Lieutenant Paul Currell and Sergeant Allen Orton. They were deployed into the Catholic Clonard area of Belfast on a routine multiple foot patrol, under overall command of the 1st Battalion The Light Infantry, on a summer's morning on 25 July 1978. The multiple was moving south along Clonard Gardens and Clonard Street towards the Falls Road at around 11.15. As Lieutenant Currell was about 10–15m south of the Clonard Gardens–Dunmore Street junction, opposite the grounds of the Clonard Monastery, one of his team said that they could see wires in a lamp post. He told the team to keep back while he went to have a look, reporting the fact over the radio. This was in no way a rash act, it was in fact normal procedures for the time, as patrol commanders had to follow the four Cs – Confirm, Clear, Cordon, Control. It was necessary to confirm a possible device, because if a patrol reacted to every possible false alarm, it would never go anywhere or do anything. The Confirm stage required a form of calculated bravery from the patrol commander.

There were no locals on the street as Lieutenant Currell approached the lamp post. He was standing next to it and was putting his hand to his radio mic when the lamp post exploded at 11.28 – the lamp post contained a radio-controlled bomb, and the bombers, who had a narrow line of sight, were waiting for a soldier to get close.

THE FOUR Cs

The 4Cs – Confirm, Clear, Cordon, Control – became a standard operating procedure for the Army in Northern Ireland and later in other counter-insurgencies.

The challenge of **Confirm** was considerable and it was learned the hard way, through many hours wasted on false alarms. Early on there were many nuisance false alarms; a biscuit tin containing a battery, an old clock, some wire and plasticine could be enough to trigger a major security situation. Eventually, after losing some support from the population for all the disruption caused, a system of telephone code words was agreed between PIRA and the RUC. Ironically, the PIRA would actively discourage pranksters from making these fake devices in later years as they complicated the situation for all parties. It was therefore normal practice for the patrol commander to confirm a potential device, usually by getting close enough to look at it, never a comfortable task.

The **Clear** stage required that everyone in the danger area be moved out as swiftly as possible. The population learned to evacuate their premises quickly and without fuss, while the Army and RUC got better at clearing through experience. As the conflict wore on, the Clear stage of an incident became ever more ingrained.

The **Cordon** stage required that the movement of people around the area be stopped, preventing anyone re-entering the danger area. This would often require the stationing of teams for long periods on every surrounding road junction in urban areas. In rural areas the cordon might often dig themselves into trenches, sometimes for many days. Towards the end of the conflict, the clear and cordon phase was often the least problematic, but the ever-adaptive PIRA soon learned to use cordons as a way to predict where the troops might deploy, using an initial incident as a lure so that they could later attack the cordon.

The **Control** phase of an incident was often very busy for the incident commander. This was usually an officer or NCO, often a company commander for the larger incidents, who was charged with coordinating the range of agencies that deployed to incidents to carry out various tasks. These might typically include an ATO, search teams, and police with scenes of crime and other forensic specialists.

An Incident Control Point (ICP) was usually nominated – often a street corner or road junction. Again the PIRA would try to anticipate its location, as a favourite site for a secondary device. Operations rooms kept logs of ICPs so as to avoid setting predictable patterns, but it was not always possible to do so. A separate cordon commander was often nominated too; typically this might have been a multiple commander, charged with ensuring that the cordon was effective and stayed alert.

The explosion severed Currell's right leg and inflicted many other serious injuries on him. The rest of the four-man team, Privates Colin Davey, Paul Wale and James Blackburn, were knocked off their feet and concussed. The three ran to Currell's aid, where they were soon joined by the platoon medic, Private Ian Campbell, known as 'Jock'. Sergeant Allen Orton was calling the incident in on his radio as he ran around the corner, where he was confronted by a terrible scene: 'You never want to see that, something I can't forget. Lieutenant Currell was on the ground with his leg half way up the road and the three lads were moving towards him. There were no locals about then. I span around, but had no idea where the bombers were at that time, they could have been anywhere.'

Orton's training kicked in and he organised the securing of the area, deploying one team to the Monastery area slightly north, a second lower down Clonard Gardens to the south. Unwittingly, some of the second team members took cover in the factory doorway where the

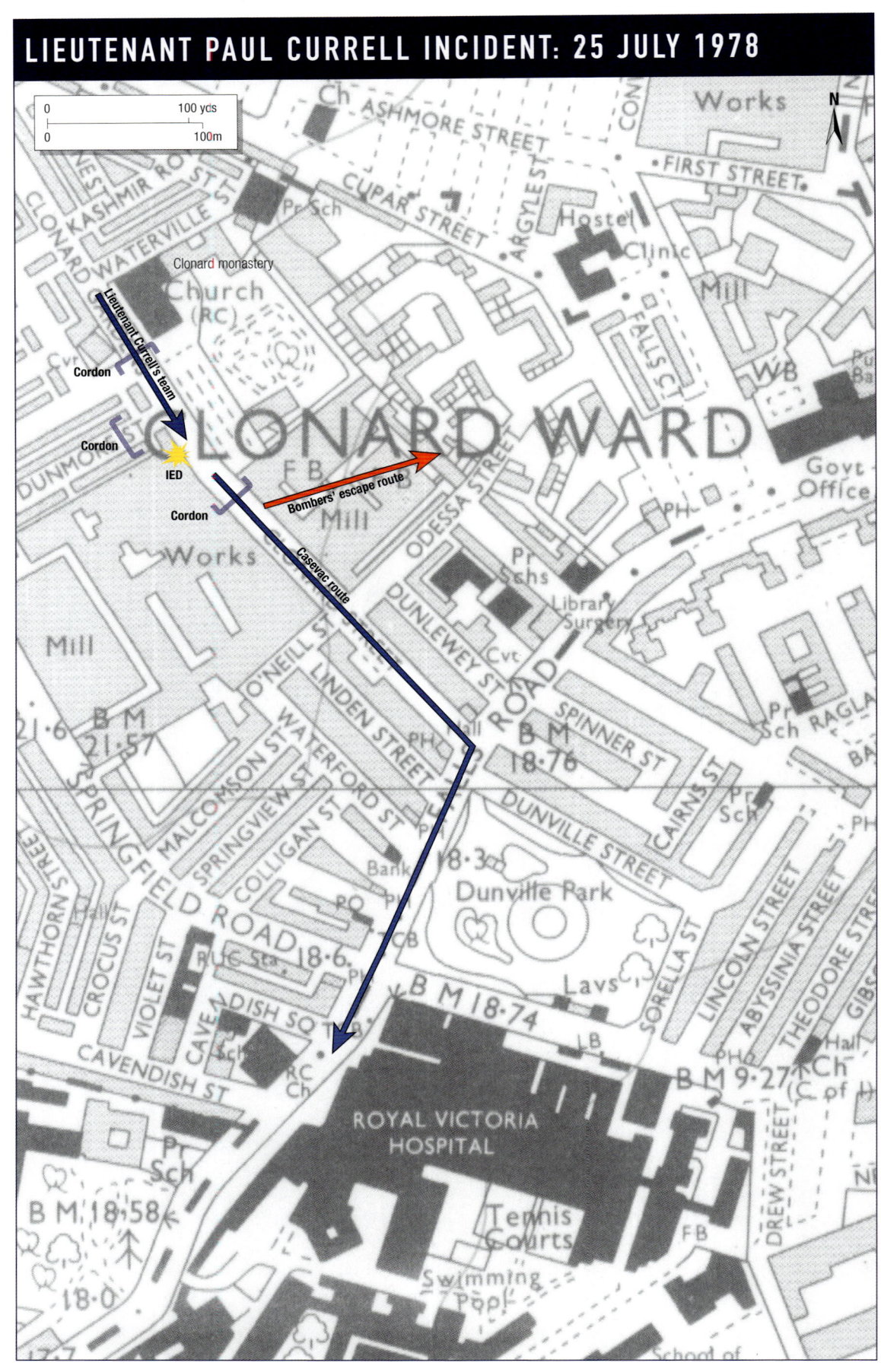

LIEUTENANT PAUL CURRELL INCIDENT: 25 JULY 1978

firing point was later to be discovered, but they could not have known that at the time. The third team secured the immediate area while Campbell worked on Currell's injuries. Orton described the scene:

> We were really worried that the boss might not make it, he had terrible injuries to his chest and was losing a lot of blood from the wounds to his other leg. He was unconscious. Campbell was doing a great job, good lad, he was later to receive a GOC's commendation for his actions but the injuries were really bad. Large numbers were gathering at both ends of the cordon, lots of people looking on but the lads kept them all back. They did really well.

A shout from a soldier on the northern cordon alerted Orton to a civilian at the cordon holding up a large first aid pack. Permitting the man to approach he ascertained that he was a local paramedic or doctor so let him assist Private Campbell. Using the supplies in the first aid kit, Campbell got a tourniquet on the severed leg and took care of the other injuries while the civilian managed to patch the serious chest wound so Currell could breathe more easily. Sergeant Orton observed:

> There is no doubt that the unselfish actions of this man, and possibly at no small risk to himself having been seen aiding a member of the security forces in a very staunchly Republican area, helped to save Paul's life. He must have quietly slipped away once the crash crew arrived and I never got the chance to thank him for what he did and for that I will always be truly sorry.

Only 50m away, the crowd was hostile, and growing, all trying to get a look at what had happened. No more than 5 or 10 minutes after the explosion the brigade medical crash crew arrived in two Saracen armoured ambulances, but it would have seemed like an age to those with Currell. Sergeant Orton remembered that the doctor in the crash crew looked deeply shocked by the extent of Currell's injuries as he got out of the Saracen. They carefully took up Currell and whisked him swiftly to the Royal Victoria Hospital, only some 500m away. There was still much work to do at the scene as the various agencies arrived, and Sergeant Orton was busy there for a few more hours. Investigations revealed that the bomb was probably about 5lb (2.2kg) in size and was initiated by radio control. The PIRA claimed responsibility. Their bomb team was probably concealed behind a factory door some 50 or 60m to the south and across the road from the lamp post. They had been watching through a very narrow gap in the door – it would not have been possible for the patrol to see the bombers or their likely escape route through the factory.

Although the incident in Clonard Gardens was soon over, it was not to be over for a very long time for Lieutenant Paul Currell.[5] On admittance to hospital, Paul was in a very bad way. There is footage of him being operated on in the BBC documentary *Man Alive*, and the surgeon described the injuries to the BBC reporter:

> He has lost his right leg and has very serious injuries to his left leg. Mr McGill is working at his left leg now and there will be an orthopaedic surgeon along soon. He has lost a great deal of blood and Dr Young, our anaesthetist, is giving him a great deal of blood, he has already had about eight pints. As well as that he has blast lung injuries to his chest and as well as that he has got, I think, a fragment through his skull. We are going to look at that now.

You do not need much medical knowledge to realise that Paul was in a very bad way. The average human body contains between 8.3 and 8.8 pints of blood and Paul had lost most of this before transfusion. Paul was in surgery within about 12 minutes of the explosion; he

Lieutenant Currell during his recovery.

Opposite: Paul Currell at the Officers' Mess dinner.

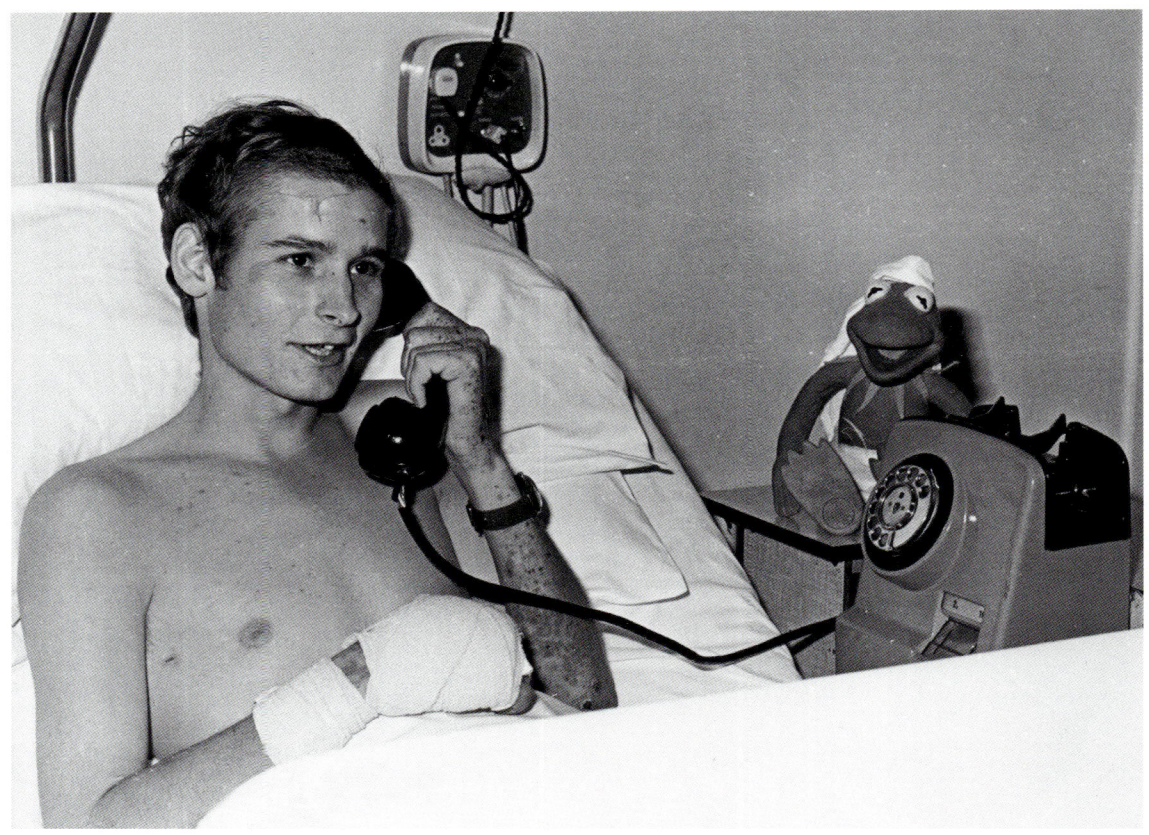

Opposite, far right: Front page from *The Belfast Telegraph*, 25 July 1978.

5 Platoon reunion with Lieutenant Currell.

remained there for more than two hours. Towards the end of the surgery, one of the surgeons said that he would be lucky to survive. At 12.30 that day, Headquarters Northern Ireland issued a signal confirming Paul's injuries and placing him on the Very Seriously Ill List (VSIL). Being on this list indicated that there was a high probability that he would not survive. It was not until 11 August that Paul was transferred to the Seriously Ill List, indicating that his life was no longer in danger; he was said to be 'making slow progress'. A week later he was transferred to Ulster Hospital, Dundonald, where he recuperated for a month before being transferred back to the UK via Musgrave Park Hospital, Belfast. At Queen Elizabeth Military Hospital, Woolwich, Paul was finally taken off the Seriously Ill List on 25 September, exactly two months since the explosion.

Paul faced several further operations on his remaining leg, and underwent extensive physiotherapy, to enable him to walk with a prosthetic leg. No one had to push him; if anything the physiotherapists had to hold him back. In the BBC documentary Paul said: 'early on I got

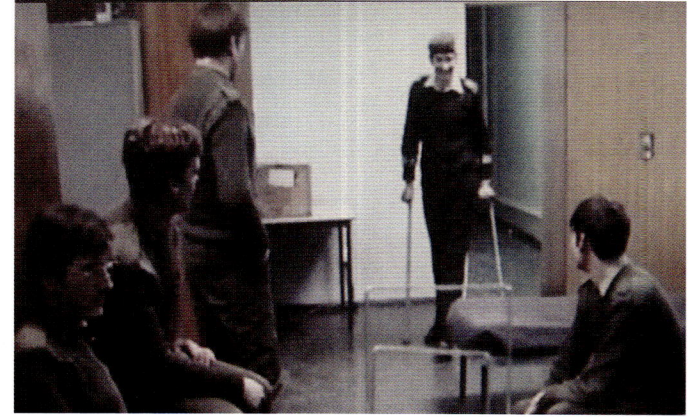

too much sympathy, sympathy is something I don't need, there is no reason to have it and I don't feel any sympathy for myself and it is something I want to avoid. When people see your attitude, that you don't want sympathy, then most people forget about it, they then treat you like another person.' Eventually he learnt to walk without crutches; and was able to again drive a car, albeit an automatic. In the documentary he was shown enjoying a day on the rifle range. He had some trouble getting into a prone fire position, but was then able to shoot as well as ever, and was quite pleased with his grouping of shots.

In February 1979 he returned to Belfast to a great welcome from the Pompadours, and attended an Officers' Mess dinner.

The reunion with his platoon was clearly an emotional event, despite the somewhat inhibiting presence of a BBC camera crew.

Paul said 'my biggest regret is never being able to command a platoon again, it was the thing I enjoyed most about being in the Army, it must be the best job in the Army, but one I could never live up to again.' He was posted to the Depot Queen's Division at Bassingbourn near Royston while he underwent further recuperation. His future remained in the balance as he had to wait until his recovery was more or less complete before a medical review could take place. Paul left the Army on 14

November 1981. The Colonel Commandant of the Queen's Division, Major General Dick Gerrard-Wright, CBE, and the Colonels of the Regiments of the Queen's Division bade Paul farewell at a ceremony. He was noted in the *London Gazette* (17 November 1981) as 'retired on retired pay on account of disability'. On leaving the Army Paul enjoyed driving fast cars and he was one of the first people in the UK to take up hang gliding and flying microlight aircraft. Sadly, he was killed in a microlight crash in France on 4 May 1985.

PAUL'S LETTER

From: Lt P B Currell

8

3rd Battalion
The Royal Anglian Regiment

Palace Barracks
Holywood
British Forces Post Office

Lt Col Murray-Brown
Regimental Secretary
The Keep
Gibraltar Barracks
Bury St Edmunds
Suffolk

04 | Sep 78

Dear Colonel

I enclose £5 which was sent to me by an Irish well wisher. I send it on to you as a donation to the Regimental Association. I feel that as I am still paid by the army and with some compensation for my injury likely at some stage in the future, this sum could be put to better use by the Association. I hope it will go to a soldier who is suffering from some hardship. I know in any case the money will be well used.

Colonel of Regt, ...

Yours sincerely

RO II ....
RO III (A) N
RO III (B) ....
Paul Currell t.o. MBR

While he was still in the early stages of his recovery, Paul received a donation from a well-wisher. However, he was uncomfortable with accepting it so he sent it on to the Regimental Association fund. A copy of his letter to Lieutenant Colonel Murray Brown, the Regimental Secretary at the time, is on file, dated 4 September 1978.

It is clear that Paul was still having trouble writing, as somebody had helped him to physically sign the letter. This letter shows something of Paul's outstanding generosity of spirit.

Soldier critical after Belfast blast

A SOLDIER was critically ill this afternoon after a booby trap attack in Belfast.

He was on foot patrol in Clonard Gardens outside St. Vincent's monastery when the bomb, hidden in a lamp post, exploded.

Three other people, one a 73-year-old woman, were injured. She and another man were treated for head injuries and shock. A second man was also treated for shock.

The soldier, a lieutenant in the Royal Anglian Regiment, was seriously injured.

A 14-year-old boy who was near the scene of the lunchtime blast said: "He looked in terrible shape, and it seemed as though his leg was blown off.

"His rifle looked just like a safety pin. It was all squashed up and blown into the grounds of the monastery, about 20 yards away."

This afternoon the soldier was in an operating theatre at the Royal Victoria Hospital undergoing an emergency operation.

Some windows in the monastery were blown in, and one of the two men taken to hospital is believed to have been a passenger in a passing black taxi.

The patrolling soldier was walking down Clonard Street towards Clonard Gardens, and took the full force of the blast.

Old people use the monastery, but according to early reports none of them were inside at the time.

CIVILIAN CASUALTIES

The members of 5 Platoon are emphatic that there were no civilians on the streets in the area at the time of the explosion on 25 July 1978. Indeed, this was normal as the locals often knew when to keep well away — the absence of locals was a common indicator that something was about to happen. However, *The Belfast Telegraph* reported that three civilians claimed injury, including a 72-year-old woman. It is possible that these civilians were injured indoors, but it also seems possible that the 'compensation culture' is not new and may have been in existence in Belfast in 1978.

LONDONDERRY, 1981–83

The 2nd Battalion moved from Montgomery Barracks in Berlin to Ebrington Barracks in Londonderry, assuming command on 27 January 1981. They stayed until January 1983 for a very busy residential tour that spanned the period of the PIRA hunger strikes. Under the vigorous command of Lieutenant Colonel Roger Howe, MBE, the Poachers adopted a monthly rotation of city tour, reserve and training tasks. The commanding officers handed over in October 1982 Lieutenant Colonel Julian Browne, MBE taking over. They had a large patch under command, covering what was then called the RUC 'N' Division. This not only contained the two large population centres of Londonderry (87,000) and Strabane (16,000) but also a large rural area containing 32 miles of border with the Republic and 42 crossing points. They had two companies of Ulster Defence Regiment under command, mainly responsible for the rural areas and a company of Royal Military Police that manned the permanent border checkpoints. The battalion's families were moved into married quarters next to Ebrington Barracks or in a small village on the outskirts called Campsie. The Poachers swiftly renamed their three family centres after their battle honours – Sobraon, Talavera and Hindoostan.

Major General Jack Dye, then Colonel of the Regiment, visits the Poachers on the city walls. Behind him stands the Commanding Officer Lieutenant Colonel Roger Howe; on the right is Major Brian Davenport.

This residential tour would see its share of shootings and bombings, but it would be characterised largely by civil disorder and rioting. The Poachers started by adopting a cycle of six weeks' duration, but after one complete rotation of the companies, they reduced this to four weeks for the remainder of the tour. The main operation was then a four-week city tour with Company Headquarters and one platoon in Fort George in the north of the city, a platoon in Rosemount base near the Creggan estate and a platoon in Masonic Lodge in the city centre. In addition to the usual trouble on various anniversaries, security activity at this time was also heavily influenced by the public response to the PIRA hunger strikers, who were led by Bobby Sands. However, the first major trouble occurred almost straight away on the anniversary of Bloody Sunday. A march of 1,000 people set off from the centre of the Creggan estate but swelled to more than 2,000 at a rally at the Free Derry Wall in Rossville Street. Some 150 youths started the stoning and petrol-bomb throwing that was to become an regular experience of the tour.

The hunger-strike rioting started on 16 March 1981, after which demonstrations and marches by small crowds in support of the hunger strikers became routine events. Although many passed off without incident, some of the larger demonstrations were orchestrated into riots. Indeed, building on their experience of earlier tours and the many demonstrations in 1981, the Poachers gained a reputation as being particularly expert at dealing with riots and civil disorder. Their patience and restraint in the early stages of the trouble often ensured that minor events did not escalate. However, once the serious rioting did start, a combination of resolve and controlled aggression dealt effectively with the violence.

A large 'day of action' was organised in support of the hunger strikes on 15 April which developed into an eight-day-long spell of rioting, one of the most sustained periods of disorder in the Province since the early 1970s. During this hectic period, most of the battalion was deployed most of the time. Over 900 petrol bombs, 20 acid bombs and six hand grenades were thrown at the Poachers, and some 64 vehicles were hijacked, of which 48 were burned, and most were also used to make barricades. In an especially fiendish twist, some of these barricades were wired up to mains electricity, making their clearance more difficult. The rioting and other incidents continued throughout a very busy summer, and as hunger strikers started to die in May, the rioting escalated further. This heightened level of disorder was to last right through to October, when the surviving H Block prisoners finally abandoned their hunger strike.

The Free Derry wall was the end of an old terraced house, painted with the slogan 'You are now entering Free Derry', which became something of an iconic landmark.

Mortar Platoon Warrant
Officer Class 2 Mick Draper
and Poachers at the back of a
Humber Pig.

HIT BY A PETROL BOMB

On 22 April 1981, the last day of the eight-day-long riots, Lieutenant Steve Brunt was commanding 2 Platoon in A Company. Reporting into Major Brian Davenport, the commander of D (Support) Company, before 2 Platoon took over base-line duties from the Mortar Platoon, Lieutenant Brunt recalls standing next to Major Davenport as the sky was filled with rocks, missiles and petrol bombs and saying to him, 'You've got to be joking haven't you'. Lieutenant Brunt continued:

It had only been a few minutes since I arrived on William Street and as I looked up I saw a petrol bomb spinning directly towards me. I felt frozen to the spot and the next thing I knew was that the petrol bomb had hit me smack on the forehead. I had a motorcycle type helmet on, and the visor was down. Instantly I was then engulfed in flames. I just thought, 'keep calm, stand still.'

I closed my eyes and stopped breathing and immediately pressed my gloved hands over my face under the burning visor. At that stage, and what seemed like an eternity, I could feel I was getting very hot and I briefly took my hands away to see if the flames were out – they weren't. It was then that I just began to sense panic as the flames were still all over me. But then in an instant they were out as those two men with the fire extinguisher did their job. While it felt that I had been engulfed in flames for ages, in reality it can only have been a few seconds – but that seemed long enough.

The one thing that had really irritated me was that as I rammed my hands over my face I had dropped my rifle. It was on a sling, with one end around my right wrist and the other attached to the butt. I felt really quite irritated with myself for dropping it. At the time I did not think that I was very badly burned so I stayed out with the platoon for the duration of the platoon's 'shift' on the base line. When I got back to Ebrington Barracks I went to see the Medical

Officer (MO) and the caring assurance of Sergeant Ali [the Medical Sergeant]. The Doc removed the blistering that covered most of my face including my eyelids and cheeks. My face was a nice big weeping open blister. They then took some photographs before covering my face with Flamazine [an anti-burn cream] and the MO said I could either go to the Medical Centre or go back to the Officers' Mess. I got back to the Mess and watched the riots and myself getting hit by the petrol bomb on News At Ten, I thought that it looked pretty impressive.

The next morning I went to the sink to wash and shave and then in the mirror I saw the state of my burned face. It was only then that I thought that this might be a bit serious. Everything that was not covered by the helmet had been burned. Fortunately the burns were only superficial and healed fairly quickly. Sergeant Ali had however done his stuff; the photographs taken at the time helped secure £2,000 of compensation with which I purchased a new Triumph Bonneville bike – thanks Sergeant Ali!

Lieutenant Brunt went on to make a full recovery and was only slightly scarred by the burn.

Rather than list all the riots experienced by the Poachers during this busy tour, we will look at a typical large riot, which started at 23.30 on 21 May 1981 as news of the death of the hunger striker Patsy O'Hara, a Derry man and member of INLA, reached the city. Riots broke out that evening across the Province with disturbances reported in Belfast, Newry, Dungannon and Lurgan. A large crowd soon gathered at 'Aggro Corner' at the junction of Rossville Street and William Street in the Bogside area of Londonderry. By midnight thousands of protesters and rioters had gathered and were stoning the police, so the Poachers were called in to help. The aim was to prevent the rioters moving into the city centre and damaging the many commercial properties there. D (Support) Company, under the command of Major Brian Davenport, deployed their Mortar and Drums platoons to form a base line with interlocking 2-metre Perspex shields, facing the rioters, with the Anti-tank Platoon in reserve and providing counter-sniper cover. The participants' recollections of the night are patchy because they experienced so many riots during the tour, and were also exhausted for much of that time, meaning that 30 years on the memories tend to merge together.

The rioters had set fire to 11 buildings, and a series of cars had been hijacked and barricades made. Major Davenport recalled that there was another company deployed, probably A Company and several vehicles, including at least three 'Flying Pigs'. One document written soon afterwards by Major Davenport recorded that 'The rioting was very severe – as severe as any in my experience of NI, which started in the Falls in Belfast in 1972, and there were hundreds of people involved. There was much stone throwing, petrol bombing and blast bombing from the crowd, as well as the erection of barricades.' Other estimates put the number of rioters as high as 3,000, but it was very difficult to estimate accurately the numbers of rioters in the dark, as small groups moved around, coalesced into larger groups, then split up again.

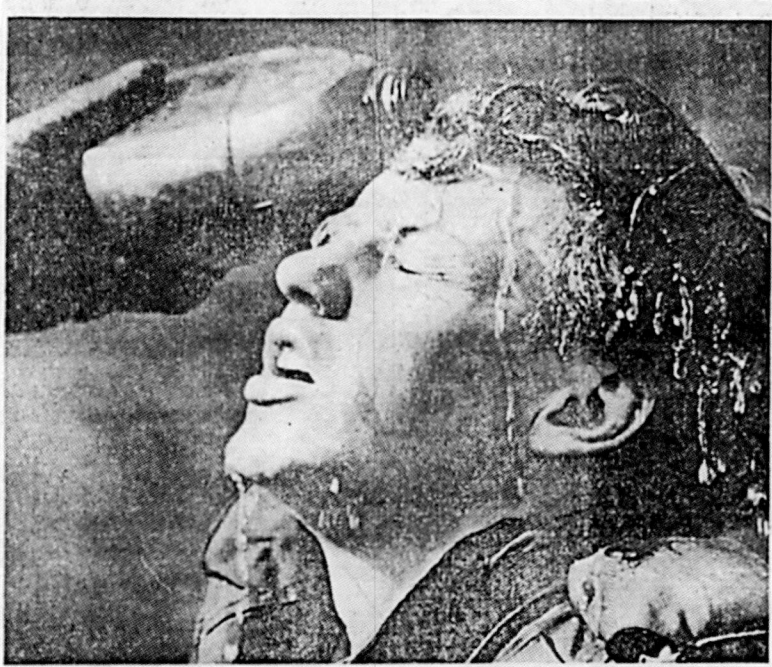

Victim of acid-bomb

A YOUNG soldier is given on-the-spot treatment after falling victim to the rioters' latest terror device — the acid bomb.

He was hit by one as he faced a mob in William Street, Londonderry.

A comrade pours water from his canteen to dilute the acid before it has time to burn and disfigure.

Within minutes the soldier is back to the front line again — facing the anger of Derry's youth.

More pictures — Page 11.

WEATHER

FORECAST for tonight and tomorrow: Mostly dry, but rather cold, with slight frost, tonight. Clear or sunny intervals. Min. temp. minus one C. Max temp. 8C. Light, mainly east to north east winds. Outlook for Saturday: Little change.

NORTHWEST

Today's news and advertising supplement is between pages 2 and 3. Rioters on the rampage again—P3. Pictures of the trouble—P11.

Lieutenant Brunt with water being poured over his face. The photographer or caption writer has assumed that Lieutenant Brunt was hit by an acid bomb, but this was incorrect: the picture is definitely the aftermath of the petrol bomb hit.

Aggro Corner, in the Bogside area of Londonderry.

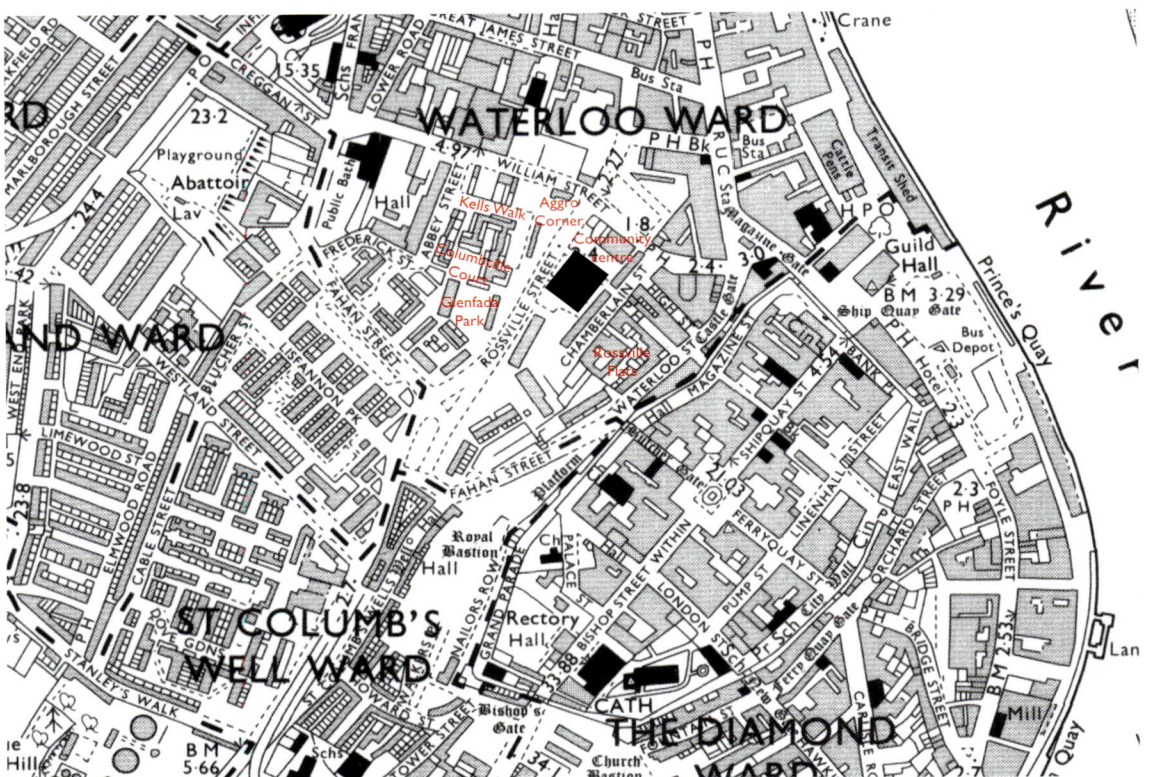

The riot surged back and forth for several hours. Small groups of youths would run up to the base line to throw stones and petrol bombs, then be driven off by salvos of baton rounds. The Poachers fired some 400 baton rounds that night.

A blast bomb or grenade injured four Poachers, and the heavy stoning injured several more including the company commander and company sergeant major, who were both clearly leading from the front. A short report described how 'One of the soldiers hurt during the Londonderry rioting … was CSM Dave Bausor of D Company, the 2nd Battalion The Royal Anglian Regiment. He was hit in the face by a brick thrown by a rioter in William Street, but was not seriously hurt'. Major Davenport recalled that it was largely a matter of containing the crowd rather than trying to make arrests, although he tried to get around the flanks occasionally to distract the rioters.

Aggro Corner in 1971, before the Community Centre was built.

Later on Major Davenport was injured, his report stating, 'One of the missiles, almost certainly a quite large stone, struck me in the mouth, causing me a deep cut between my mouth and nose and also breaking one of my front teeth. I was wearing a helmet and visor but had lifted the visor very slightly to speak to the soldiers, due to the difficulty of communicating properly with it fully down'. He received first aid but stayed in command until the riot subsided before visiting the battalion medical centre.

Five civilians and one policeman were admitted to the local Altnagelvin hospital for treatment for injuries sustained in the riot. Another source says some 20 people in total, including six Poachers, were injured, which is still a relatively small total given the more than four hours of heavy rioting by so many people.

Major Davenport's injury.

Describing such a large riot is very difficult, and few good photographs are taken in or of a night-time riot. The participants tend to remember just a few snippets or vignettes of the events together with an overall impression. One participant recalled the noise level of the riot on 21 May being somewhere between the roar of a waterfall and a number of locomotives, something like a big football match crowd. Major Davenport remembers:

Clipping from the *Belfast Telegraph*.

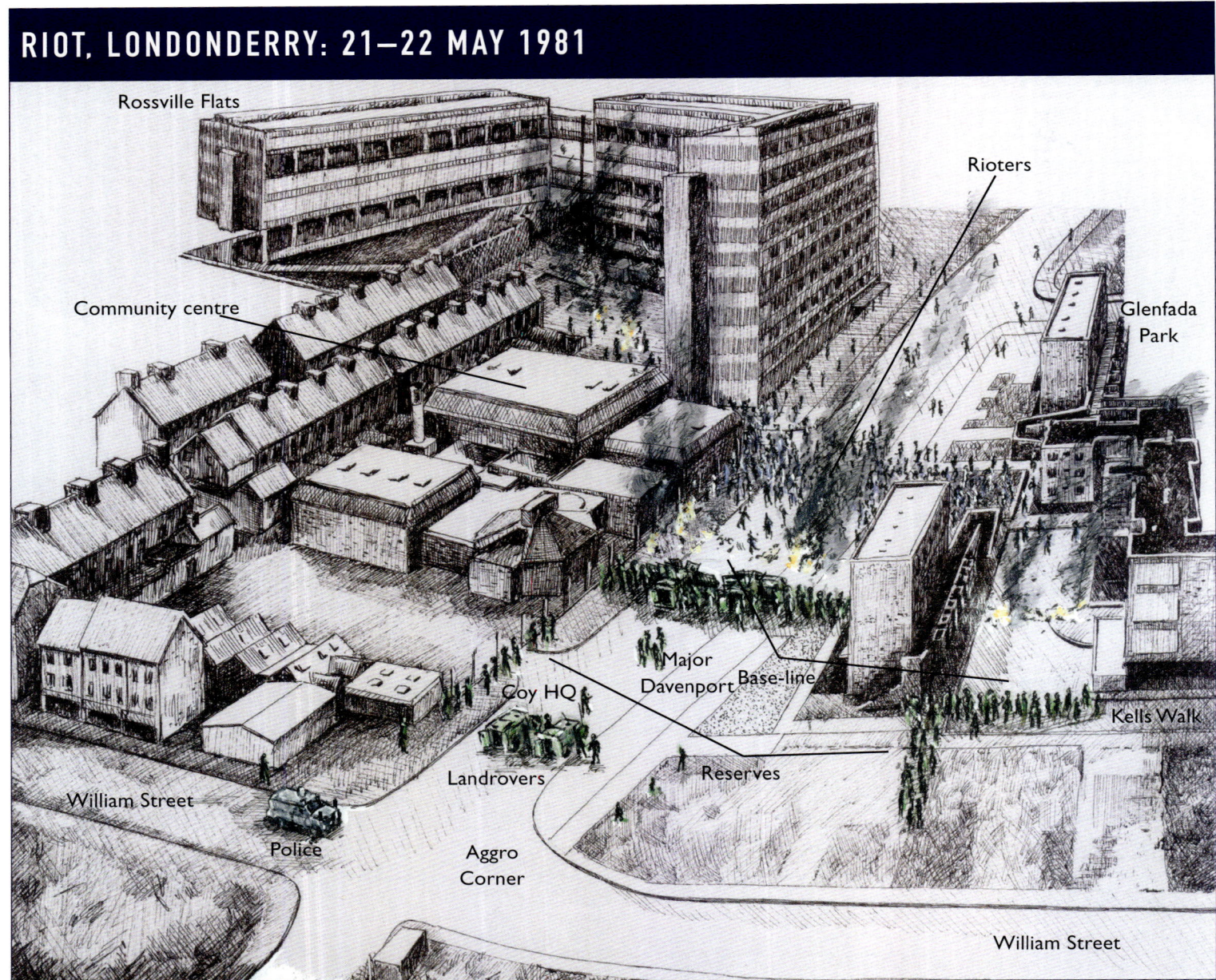

RIOT, LONDONDERRY: 21—22 MAY 1981

One of my remaining overall impressions is of the fluidity of a riot; so many things going on at one time, whether it was the ebb and flow of advancing and retreating rioters, from different places and at different times, their noise and anger, missiles of various sorts being thrown – petrol bombs, blast bombs, stones. Then the need to counter all that by keeping a steady line, by use of baton rounds, by positive action towards the crowd, by redeployment and augmenting of resources. All the time trying to keep some sort of reserve to deal with the unexpected, or just simply to plug a gap. Another remaining impression; how solid the boys were; they were unyielding and just toughed it out. They did everything I asked of them and more.

The Poachers went on to complete a very busy residential tour, facing so many riots that they became highly proficient at dealing with them. Indeed, they were able to maintain and enhance the reputation that the Poachers had gained in 1972 of great competence at dealing with riots, but they also faced many shootings and bombings and made many finds of terrorist equipment.

POACHER IN RIOT GEAR, 1981

C. Farmer '13

BATTALION-LEVEL INTELLIGENCE

A good understanding of an opponent is important for success in all operations, but in low-intensity conflicts – 'wars among the people' – it is essential. That understanding is gained by the activities of a variety of agencies and at several levels. In the course of the Northern Ireland campaign a sophisticated and effective organisation was, in time, developed to achieve that understanding and to inform decisions and the conduct of operations. An unspectacular but important part of that process was intelligence activity within battalions, and having a good understanding and the right approach to this aspect of operations was a major factor in overall success or failure.

However, the battalion intelligence organisation was only part of the overall effort. It was crucial that commanding officers, company commanders and more junior leaders understood the intelligence requirement and process and the relationship between intelligence and operations, even at the lowest level. In the absence of intelligence from higher levels and other agencies, it was necessary to glean as much background information as possible from carefully directed patrol activity as well as research, to collate this within the cells and draw deductions from careful analysis. This developed into a structured approach with intelligence briefings for each patrol and operation and a debrief for everyone immediately afterwards.

LONDONDERRY, 1984–87

The 1st Battalion moved from Oakington to Ebrington Barracks in Londonderry some three years later in December 1984 for what was to be a long residential tour, lasting 27 months, to January 1987. Under the command of the charismatic Lieutenant Colonel Mike Walker, OBE, the Vikings swiftly fitted into their routine of operational rotation under command of 8 Brigade, also headquartered in Ebrington Barracks. Some of the older Vikings

Lieutenant Colonel Mike Walker.

remembered their time there from 12 years earlier. The battalion's families were again moved into married quarters next to Ebrington barracks or four miles north-east in Campsie.

By 1984 the main operation was a city tour of one month's duration, where a company would deploy to three locations in the city of Londonderry. Some of the earlier bases had been closed down, so typically a single platoon would now occupy Rosemount and Masonic Lodge bases with a third platoon together with Company Headquarters at Fort George. A city tour was followed by a short leave of two weeks, then some time re-training before moving onto various reserve tasks. The rifle companies rotated their platoons between the three bases on respective city tours, but Support Company chose to keep the same bases throughout the whole time.

During the first year, reserve tasks could lead to deployment anywhere in the Province by platoons or companies, and they did deploy frequently all over. Province Reserve, as this task was called, led to some bizarre situations due to the rotation of troops. One memorable event found Support Company, the Vikings, deployed to Omagh, while troops from the 3rd Battalion The Light Infantry, then based in Omagh, were deployed to Londonderry. Lieutenant Colonel Mike Walker first argued for a change with 8 Brigade, who then persuaded Headquarters Northern Ireland to change the whole reserve rotation system. For the Vikings this meant that during the second year, 1986, the majority of reserve tasks led to deployment into the city of Londonderry itself, which by then the Vikings knew intimately. Their detailed knowledge of the ground and the local people was then a significant advantage during operations.

The conflict was entering a more political phase by 1984, with ever more complex incidents arranged by PIRA, often linked to some political objective and with a strong media management aspect. In 1985 PIRA mounted a concerted and province-wide series of attacks on police stations using large mortars, shootings and a new small weapon called the Improvised Projected Grenade (IPG). These attacks led to a military response that was called Operation *Counterpoint* which required that at least a multiple of troops be deployed within 300m of every police station in the Province at all times. Hardly very popular – the troops called it the '300m bungee' – this difficult-to-sustain operation eventually succeeded and the attacks on police stations ceased. It required a particularly firm discipline from the Vikings, who had to stay alert during the many long hours of patrolling around and around the same ground over and over again.

The annual calendar of parades and anniversaries also produced reasonably regular, orchestrated rioting in the city, together with shootings, bombings both large and small and hostage taking by the PIRA. Both radio-controlled and command-wire bombs were in use. Several command wires were discovered and acted on in various ways during the tour and it would be fair to say that the Army had the edge in electronic counter-measures at this time, so radio-controlled devices were quite rare. PIRA tactics began to resemble a game of paper-rock-scissors – they would tend to shoot at mobile patrols, use well-concealed command-wire bombs against foot patrols, but attack bases with mortars or proxy bombs.

The battalion was to deal with the following crimes in Londonderry over the whole tour, which gives an indication of the frequency and type of event.

IN PRAISE OF MULTI-ROLE DRUMMERS

The drums platoon in most battalions for most Northern Ireland tours performed multiple roles. Unlike bandsmen, drummers were trained infantry soldiers first and foremost, but they had a secondary, ceremonial role performing with drum and flute at various parades, Mess functions and the like, for which they had to practise regularly. In Northern Ireland they would also normally form a counter-insurgency platoon, usually organised like the other platoons fielding two 12-man multiples and performing all the same duties as a rifle platoon. In addition, many drums platoons also had a role as machine-gun platoons, operating between four and six tripod-mounted GPMG (SF), which presented a considerable training challenge. Yet they seemed to manage these multiple roles well, typically approaching each task in a cheerful manner and indeed benefiting from the variety. Some became extraordinarily proficient; for example the Viking Drums Platoon in 1985 won Northern Ireland GPMG (SF) shooting competition, Match 83. Under Drum Major Bokenham, they then went on to win it again in 1986 and then went on to win the Combined Services Shield, effectively beating the best in the rest of the Army.

Vikings Drums Platoon with their GPMG (SF) in 1986.

INCIDENT	NUMBER
Murders	7
Attempted murders	21
Explosions	30
Shootings	81
Arson attacks	17
House take-overs	37
Attempted house take-overs	7
Kidnappings	6
Robberies	46
Petrol bombs thrown	438
Vehicle hijacks	155
Attempted vehicle hijacks	21
Hoaxes and suspect devices	180
Booby traps and IEDs	31
Finds of weapons and ammunition	42

The Vikings became tactically more sophisticated too, mixing mobile and foot patrols, and became ever more adept at manoeuvring so as to threaten any terrorist escape routes. Intimate knowledge of the ground and PIRA tactics made this type of manoeuvre increasingly effective. The Vikings' ace tactician was Major Kevin Ryan, who developed highly successful tactical methods, often using the sudden deployment of large numbers of troops to swamp an area, discouraging any terrorist from actually going though with an attack by threatening his escape route. This type of swamping tactic was greatly enabled by the new reserve system in place from the end of 1985 as it allowed the deployment of Viking troops who were already familiar with both the ground and with this mode of operating. By 1986, although

The Viking Mortar Platoon on patrol in the city centre in 1985, led by Sergeant Phil Clarke.

LAND ROVERS AND ARMOURED PATROL VEHICLES

Throughout the conflict the Army used the ubiquitous Land Rover, both long- and short-wheel-based version. In Northern Ireland they were initially armoured with 'Makrolon', a rigid type of Kevlar armour. While this gave protection against hand-thrown projectiles, it did not make them bulletproof. The rear had a Makrolon carapace with a hatch for a standing top-cover soldier. They also sported a wire-cutting bar after yobs figured out the height of the top-cover soldier's head and strung wires across the street at this height. Mesh screens covered the windows. Many units removed the doors on their Makrolon Land Rovers to allow faster exit. In the 1980s several vehicles were fitted with a sniper-locating radar called Claribel, which gave an approximate indication of the direction of the incoming bullet, but these fell out of use as the last thing anybody did when under fire was to look at the Claribel indicator.

Viking APV patrol in Londonderry, with Corporal 'Boris' Davis of Support Company in command.

Starting in 1985, the Vikings introduced into service the new heavily armoured Land Rover called the Armoured Patrol Vehicle (APV), which was similar to what was later to be called the Snatch Land Rover. Featuring modern face-hardened armour and an armoured windscreen, the APV was much better protected, and the Vikings developed more aggressive tactics exploiting this feature. Most companies started practising a drill to have the top-cover man duck inside while driving full pelt at the firing point if shot at in APVs. The PIRA might have wondered about the protection level of this vehicle, as they did not shoot at them during this tour.

Viking Makrolon Land Rover.

there were still many standard patrols of a single 12-man multiple, troops were increasingly deployed in larger groupings for deliberate operations.

This was to produce a situation of move and counter-move, described by the commanding officer as like 'a very dangerous form of shadow boxing' as the tour progressed, such that at one point late on in the tour, the battalion received specific intelligence that PIRA was finding them very hard to kill. This was about as close to a compliment from PIRA as it was possible to get. These operations represent the long, boring grind of counter-insurgency, where the troops strove to 'keep the lid on' – trying to keep the level of violence down to a point where the public perception of what was acceptable reduced year on year.

On 22 February 1986, PIRA mounted a shooting attack on Fort George, but a quick-thinking C Company corporal caught them in the act and shot both gunmen in their car – Anthony Gough was killed and his accomplice was wounded and arrested, and both their assault rifles were recovered.

The introduction of a new, heavily armoured Land Rover in 1985 was an asset to the Vikings as this made their mobile patrols almost bulletproof. The availability of protection to the troops operating in Northern Ireland had been dramatically improved during the tour. The Vikings' main weapon was still the well-trusted 7.62mm Self-Loading Rifle, supplemented by the baton gun on urban operations and the GPMG on rural operations.

Fundraising, especially from the USA, was still highly important to the Republican movement at this stage of the conflict. The regular August visits by personalities from the US-based fundraising organisation, NORAID, produced a predictable string of incidents. Media coverage was also increasingly important and many terrorist attacks certainly looked as though they were set up to suit the media, with a strong element of stage management. The arrival of a TV film crew in the area was usually taken by troops to indicate that an incident was about to happen. We will next look at one complex string of incidents as an example of the type of events typical of this period of the conflict.

8–9 AUGUST 1986

On 4 August 1986, a large party of some 30 delegates from NORAID arrived in the Province for a 12-day visit. Starting in Belfast, they first toured rural areas in Fermanagh and Tyrone, then moved to Portadown and South Armagh.[6] The visit was organised by Sinn Fein and was supposed to be led by one Martin Galvin, the NORAID publicity director. As a terrorist fundraiser, he was at that time subject to an exclusion order from the UK, so he arrived into Dublin instead. The rest of the delegation was led by Richard Lawlor, Galvin's deputy. The delegation was due to visit Londonderry on Friday 8 August, so the Vikings were expecting trouble. Indeed, it started that afternoon when a command-wire bomb was discovered with several pounds of explosive in a gas cylinder on William Street. The area was cordoned off and the device defused and cleared by the ATO. Concurrently, various riots started to get under way. The arrival of a BBC film crew was a significant indicator that serious events were afoot. It was later claimed in *The Belfast Telegraph* that 'a number of civilians, including a BBC cameraman, were struck by plastic bullets'.[7]

During the afternoon, with Major Kevin Ryan in command, Support Company was fully deployed as the city company, with elements of A and B Company in support. The Vikings' Anti-tank Platoon, together with half the Drums Platoon under the command of Captain Steven Bowns, formed a base line across the open area around the junction of William Street and Rossville Street – 'Aggro Corner' again. This base line consisted of around 30 men with large 2m riot shields, supplemented by ten baton gunners who were also equipped with fire extinguishers. They were pelted with rocks and petrol bombs for most of the afternoon by a large crowd on Rossville Street. Strangely, the petrol bombs were less dangerous than the larger rocks, as they could be seen easily in the daylight in the open and, with extinguishers readily to hand, were quickly put out. Even some direct hits on the riot shields were easily dealt with. Seeing this, the rioters gradually faded away, only to be encouraged by ring leaders to make more attacks, in a surging riot that lasted into the evening. At one point in the early evening, members of a BBC camera crew approached the base line asking Corporal Kim Clarke for help because their car had been hijacked and set on fire. Suffice to say that after three hours of bombardment, which had seemed to them like it was largely for the benefit of the cameras, the Anti-tank Platoon were not especially sympathetic to this request. By around 20.00 the rioters had dispersed and the base line was packed up, the troops returning to their respective bases.

Also during the afternoon, part of the cordon around the William Street bomb, manned by the police and the Viking Mortar Platoon with elements of B Company in support, led by Captain Duncan Venn, was also under intermittent attack from rioters from the city centre from Butcher Gate and a feature called the Diamond. Later on, the Diamond was secured and these rioters driven off by the Mortar Platoon. During the early evening the commanding officer deployed to the Diamond with his Rover group, often referred to as call-sign 'Mike 9', to confer with the RUC commander there.

Concurrent with all this activity, Sergeant Paul Boucher, the Mortar Platoon sergeant, call-sign Tango 10B, was preparing to insert a covert observation post into the area. On his seventh tour of Northern Ireland, he was especially experienced in this type of work, and had spotted that if he could get four men onto the crenellated roof of a bakery in William Street, he would have an excellent vantage point over the area. It had taken him some time the day before to persuade Major Ryan to authorise it. With only four men, it was a dangerous and vulnerable operation, one that would not normally be allowed but was sanctioned because of Sergeant Boucher's experience and because there would be so many other troops on the ground. Sergeant Boucher, accompanied by Privates Harding, Parr and Rogers slipped into the back of the bakery by dropping off from a Mortar Platoon foot patrol; the remainder of the patrol then returned to their base in Masonic Lodge. Scrambling up onto the roof, Boucher remembers that they took a large pair of naval binoculars with them and they were soon well ensconced behind the 3-foot-high wall formed by the crenellations on the roof, with an excellent view into the area of William Street, a taxi rank and into the Rossville Flats.

Suspicious activity started at 00.20 in an alleyway adjacent to the junction of William Street and Chamberlain Street. Watching through the binoculars, Private Harding reported that 'there is a bloke down there in the taxi rank stood about, not getting into a taxi.' He was still there half an hour later. A taller man appeared and started pointing with his arms as though he was indicating an arc of fire, then put on a pair of gloves before ducking back into an alley. Boucher reported this on the radio, and continued to watch through the common weapon sight on his rifle. The other man came out wearing a balaclava and Boucher deduced they were waiting for a vehicle to enter their arc of fire, so reported this on the radio.

One of the suspects fiddled with something by a concrete post at the end of the alleyway before moving up to orchestrate a small crowd in William Street. A vehicle was heard starting up, and the suspect started 'bobbing' – jumping about. Boucher had the suspect in his sight, and was just waiting until he could see a weapon or an explosion, in line with the rules of engagement in force at the time. Just as the vehicle was approaching the crucial point, Boucher's sight went blank as the battery gave out. He switched batteries as fast as he could but the replacement battery was also dead so he pulled the sight off his weapon, but he could not then see the suspect without it. As Private Parr had a SUIT sight – a magnifying optical sight which worked well in twilight conditions – on his weapon, he could see the suspect. Switching to the naval binoculars, Boucher could then see the suspect again, and confirmed with Parr that he too had a clear line of sight on the suspect as he primed the device. As the Land Rover approached the spot, Parr opened fire but simultaneously an 'almighty flash' came out of the alley way at 45°, and the suspect flew backwards. Boucher asked 'Did you hit him?' 'I don't know,' replied Parr, 'I could not see the strike'. Reporting the contact over the radio, a Quick Reaction Force (QRF) was deployed in support. As this was going on, the Land Rover, an RUC Hotspur, stopped and a policeman got out, kicked something then got back in and they drove off. Actions unfolded quickly, and the QRF from the Drums Platoon, led by Sergeant Les Lay, call-sign Tango 20A, was in position on the street next to the bakery within a few minutes. Normally the platoon sergeant, Lay was acting as Drums Platoon commander as Drum Major Bokenham was away. The troop deployments were later further adjusted so as to form a cordon to cover the ATO as he dealt with the remains of the device in the alleyway.

It was now 02.00, and as this and other incidents unfolded, Major Ryan was sure something more was afoot and that he needed more troops in the area. Calmly giving radio instructions from the operation room, Captain Tony Powell, the Support Company operations officer soon had most of the company deployed and a large number of reinforcements, mainly from A Company, under way. A small riot of about 150 youths was kicking off at the base of the Rossville Flats and the presence of another TV crew did not augur well. This riot escalated and moved around, until a large crowd, mainly inside the Columbcille Court area, was stoning Sergeant Lay's multiple, which was deployed with two APVs in the open ground around Eden Place. By 02.16, Sergeant Lay reported that his multiple was being pelted with stones, now by around 250 youths, who were moving around from the base of the Rossville flats and from derelict buildings across the street.

The Anti-tank Platoon had also deployed a large 20-man multiple across the waste ground just off William Street and the Sackville Street area, forming the northern outer cordon as call-sign Tango 30A under Captain Bowns. A 12-man multiple from 1 Platoon, A Company under command of Lieutenant Alan Wylie, call-sign November 10A, was deployed on the first floor of Block 2 of the flats, receiving stones from the rioters and firing baton rounds down into them. There was another multiple from 2 Platoon, A Company, under the command of Lieutenant Frank de Planta, call-sign November 20A, in Block 3 of the flats, also on the first floor.

At 03.06 a whistle was heard to blow from Glenfada Park and all the stone throwing stopped suddenly. Sergeant Lay reported; 'the hairs on the back of my neck stood up, I knew something was about to happen'. At 03.15 three bursts of 5.56mm Armalite fire came from the top northern corner of the flats (Block 1) on the fourth storey. The first burst was of four single shots that went off to the right of Lay, hitting a wall well above Captain Bowns, Corporal Clarke and Private Fox's heads, but none of them could see the firing point. The next burst, also of four single shots, went over to Lay's left, possibly into a chimney near Sergeant Boucher's position. The third burst, this time of ten rounds of automatic fire, might have been aimed at Lay's multiple itself but again it went very high, way over their heads into the area of the Post Office buildings. Lay and Lance Corporal Smith immediately returned fire with six rounds each, including tracer, into the top corner of the flats, while Sergeant Boucher's team fired five.

The 1 and 2 Platoon multiples in the flats also returned fire as they had seen muzzle flash, which, it later transpired might have been reflected off the concrete walls in the top of the stairwell at the upper corner of Block 1. They fired more than 100 rounds of 7.62mm from their SLRs up into the top corner stairwell, which stopped the gunmen firing further. At the time they thought they had hit the gunman, and they subsequently found bloodstains. It only became apparent later that the gunmen had survived, probably by hiding behind a large concrete block, which was hit by most of the rounds fired by 1 and 2 Platoons. It was possible that the gunmen had been injured by concrete fragments that were shot off this block.

Major Ryan called over the radio for all call-signs to halt and not to conduct hot pursuit into Block 1 of the flats. It was normal procedure to attack any located firing point in 'hot pursuit', but with many flights of stairs and a riot to get through, there was little point as the gunmen would be long gone. Major Ryan also suspected that the shoot might have been a lure to draw troops onto yet another bomb, which might explain the ineffectiveness of the Armalite fire. At 03.40 the riot picked up again but this was eventually dispersed, so that by about 04.00, with so many troops on the scene, the area quietened down.

As dawn came up, with investigations under way, it emerged that nobody on either side had been killed in any of the night's events. The device that Sergeant Boucher observed turned out to have been an improvised bomb on a short command wire, although there was some uncertainty that an IPG might also have been involved. There was also some possibility that police had opened fire during the gunfight, adding to the confusion. There were later

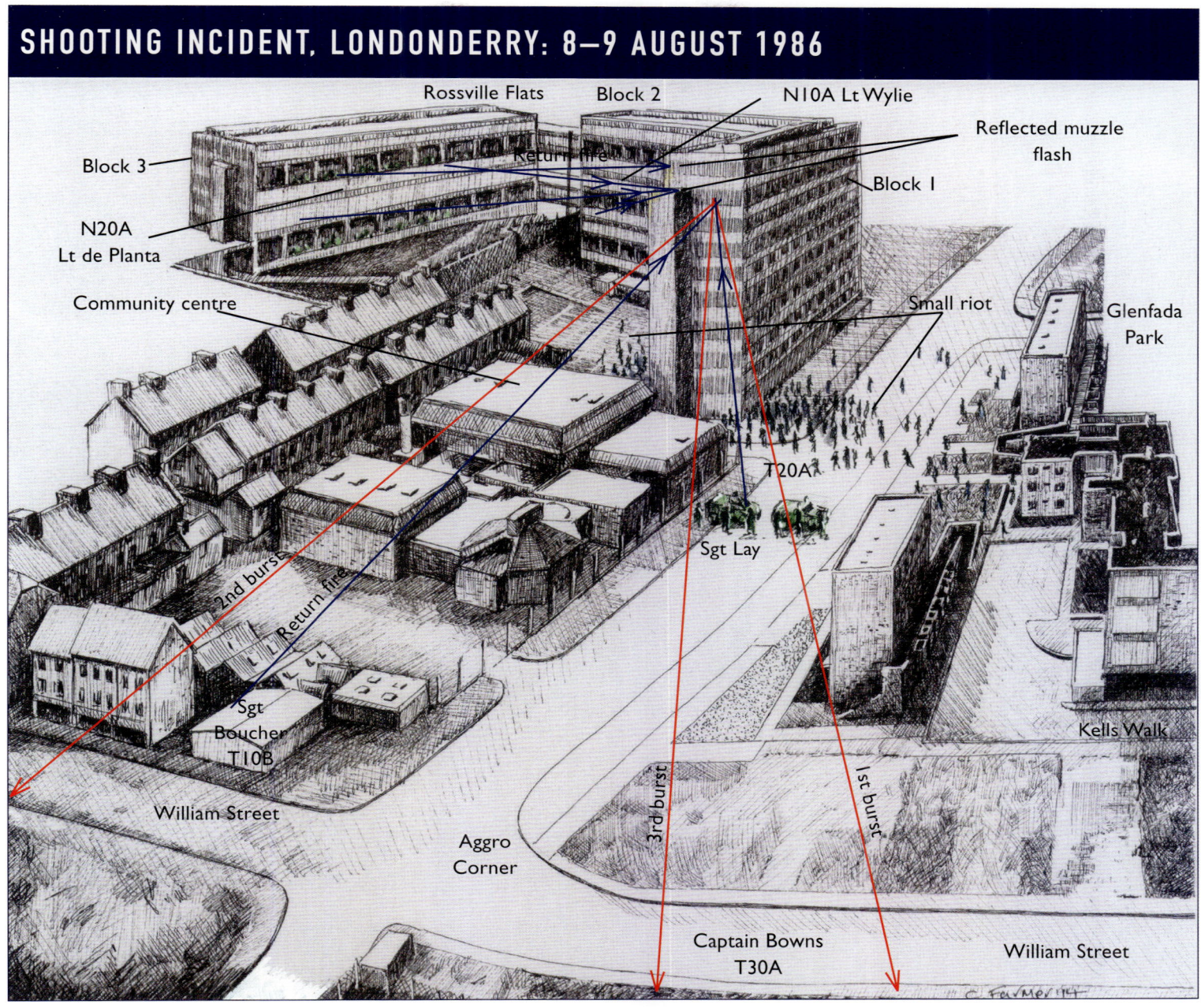

SHOOTING INCIDENT, LONDONDERRY: 8–9 AUGUST 1986

Rossville Flats
Block 2
N10A Lt Wylie
Block 3
Reflected muzzle flash
Return fire
Block 1
N20A
Lt de Planta
Community centre
Small riot
Glenfada Park
T20A
Sgt Lay
2nd burst
Return fire
Sgt Boucher T10B
Kells Walk
William Street
3rd burst
1st burst
Aggro Corner
Captain Bowns T30A
William Street

rumours that two PIRA men had received medical treatment for wounds that morning in Letterkenny Hospital, across the border in the Republic, but these were never confirmed. Nobody ever figured out why the gunmen had fired so high; possibly they did not know of the phenomenon of 'plunging fire'[8] or they may have only intended to lure troops into Block 1 of the flats from a safe firing point.

Thus ended a fairly typical incident for the middle and later phases of the conflict – 'dangerous shadow boxing' indeed. It was a hazardous and complex string of events that could have come to a much worse ending for the Vikings. Good tactics and professional conduct were important, but a little luck was also needed on occasion. Major Ryan was fond of saying that you could make your own luck, and perhaps that was the case with this incident. For his ingenuity and courage in this action, Sergeant Boucher was later Mentioned in Despatches. Major Ryan was awarded an MBE for his outstanding overall contribution to this long and very successful residential tour by the Vikings.

VIKING BY THE ROSSVILLE FLATS, 1986

THE RURAL TOURS

While the Regiment's overall experience of Northern Ireland was dominated by the urban tours in Belfast and Londonderry, there were several important rural tours undertaken during the course of the conflict:

BATTALION	DATES	LOCATION
Tiger Company*	March–July 1974	East Tyrone/Armagh
1st Battalion	September–December 1974	Armagh
1st Battalion	August 1981–January 1982	Fermanagh
2nd Battalion	January–February 1986	Tyrone, Fermanagh and South Armagh as Spearhead Battalion
2nd Battalion	April–September 1986	South Armagh
1st Battalion	August 1989–January 1990	South Armagh
1st Battalion	April–November 1991	Fermanagh
2nd Battalion	December 1992–July 1993	East Tyrone
1st Battalion	December 1993–June 1994	East Tyrone

*When the 4th Battalion was disbanded in 1970 it did not disappear entirely as it was reduced to a company-sized organisation called Tiger Company. In 1974 they undertook a four-month roulement tour of East Tyrone then Armagh, under command of several different units, initially 3rd Battalion The Royal Regiment of Fusiliers.

The main distinctions between an urban and a rural tour were the terrain and the far lower population density in rural areas, which meant the experience of soldiering was very different. Rural counter-insurgency work was much more like conventional soldiering, with the field craft – patrolling, use of ground and concealment in the countryside – following more familiar and traditional lines. Some members of the Regiment preferred this aspect, many participants saying that a rural tour in Northern Ireland was more like 'proper soldiering'. However, the rural setting was still a dangerous place, especially South Armagh, which was often described as 'bandit country'. The PIRA was especially active in this area throughout the conflict. The presence of the border with the Republic meant that they were often able to escape pursuit as troops were not allowed to physically cross the border, although they were allowed to shoot over it. In all rural areas the threat of well-concealed, large IEDs was significant. These might be detonated by command wire, radio control or by the use of various 'booby trap' initiation methods. It was vital for the troops to avoid setting patterns, in order to avoid walking into these devices. They could not use any obvious gate, track or gap in a hedge. Most rural areas featured a particularly thick and difficult type of hedgerow – the blackthorn hedge – and many members of the Regiment will recall the trouble they had repeatedly fighting their way through such hedges to avoid using an obvious gap.

The improvised mortar, often on the back of a flat-bed lorry, was used in rural areas, typically to attack a patrol base or police station. Due to the low population density, the PIRA tended to use larger IED devices and mortars in rural areas. Shootings were also a constant threat but, especially in South Armagh, they might also involve the use of PIRA's heavier weapons such as M60, GPMG and even M2 .50-calibre machine guns at long range, often cross-border, in addition to more usual sniper-type shootings.

Typical security-force operations involved routine patrolling to dominate the ground and to keep an eye on the border; vehicle checkpoints to monitor vehicle movement; and often large cordon and search-type operations to search for terrorist weapons and equipment or to deal with a located terrorist device. Troops would often spend many days at a time on

Above: Major Andrew French
in South Armagh.

Above, right: Private Leddie
of 2 Platoon, the Poachers in
South Armagh.

these types of operations, living in the field, often in concealed hides of different types or
even in trenches. The use of helicopters to deploy forces was often vital in rural areas where
the IED threat to vehicles could be very high. After the large device at Warrenpoint killed
18 soldiers of The Parachute Regiment on 27 August 1979, helicopters became the primary,
and sometimes only, means of transport in high-threat rural areas, other than moving on
foot. Most units would also feature a quick reaction force on immediate standby in
helicopters on the ground, ready to take off immediately, called the Airborne Reaction
Force (ARF), often consisting of eight men in a Lynx helicopter.

In 1986 the Poachers had an especially arduous time. While Spearpoint (standby) battalion
they were deployed province-wide in January and February on Operation *Caracara* to help
guard against the spate of attacks on RUC stations described earlier. They then returned in
April for a full six-month roulement tour in South Armagh, which was especially dangerous
at this time. Sadly they lost a company commander, Major Andrew French, killed by a large
IED on 22 May in the Miltown Bridge area, just outside Crossmaglen. Two more Poachers
were killed on 9 July – Private Carl Davies, aged 24, and Private Mitchell Bertram, aged 20
– by an IED hidden in a van in Glassdrumman near Crossmaglen.

KILNASAGGART BRIDGE, 8 NOVEMBER 1989

As it is not possible to examine each of the many rural incidents experienced by the Regiment over the years, we will look at a single large rural incident by way of example. The incident concerned the 1st Battalion, the Vikings, in a cross-border shooting in South Armagh on 8 November 1989 in an area called the Kilnasaggart Bridge.

The rationale for the operation concerned the main Dublin–Belfast railway, which crosses the border by a village called Jonesborough. The PIRA had been placing a series of convincing hoax devices on both the railway and also on the main A1 Newry–Dublin road which crosses the border nearby. The hoax devices caused disruption and inconvenience, but the main reason for placing them was to force the security forces to react, as they had to clear the device in order to get the trains or traffic running again. The PIRA could then closely observe the security force's behaviour to look for patterns that they could exploit in a later attack. It was inevitable that, no matter how careful the security forces were, some patterns would eventually be set if enough hoaxes were placed. In the months before November 1989, there had thus been a long series of hoax devices around the area where the railway line and A1 road crossed the border, and following careful observation and analysis, the PIRA had prepared an attack, having effectively drawn the security forces into a place of their own choosing.

The constant disruption did generate some local irritation. In an article in the *Newry Times* on 4 November 1986, Councillor Sean Gallogly was quoted as saying; 'I can tell them that all they succeeded in gaining was the outrage of the local community and the public road users. Our feelings and our sympathies must lie with the many local residents who were moved out of their homes late on Friday night/early Saturday morning'. The PIRA was unconcerned by any irritation caused – they were focused on an attack on the Vikings. The

Vikings on ARF duties in a Lynx helicopter in South Armagh.

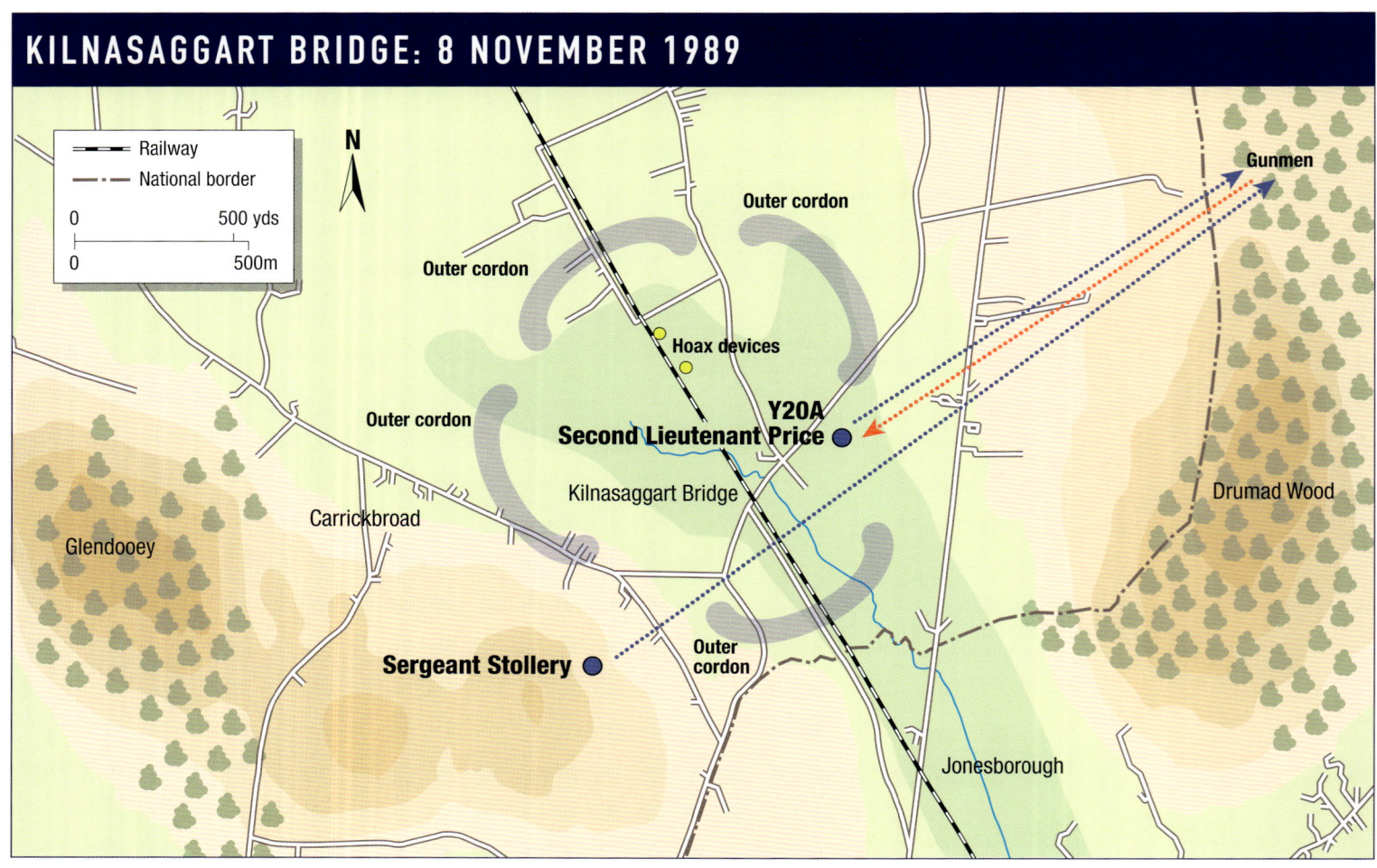

KILNASAGGART BRIDGE: 8 NOVEMBER 1989

Railway
National border

0   500 yds
0   500m

N

Outer cordon

Outer cordon

Outer cordon

Hoax devices

Gunmen

Y20A
Second Lieutenant Price

Kilnasaggart Bridge

Drumad Wood

Carrickbroad

Glendooey

Sergeant Stollery

Outer cordon

Jonesborough

The original photograph of
the incident area.

latest in a string of hoaxes was a batch of suspect devices on the railway line between Grants Bridge and Kilnasaggart Bridge that the PIRA called in by telephone using the correct code word. Later a railway employee 'line walker' saw them and reconnaissance confirmed their locations, together with the locations of a possible command wire. C Company, the Vikings, under the command of Major Ian Hall, was operations company, and was tasked with clearing the railway line between the two bridges.

Major Hall and Captain Nigel Spinks, the battalion operations officer, devised a deliberate four-phase operation that would take several days. Phase 1 was a night insertion of a large cordon by helicopter, then Phase 2 was a reconnaissance phase, once the cordon had secured the area. Phase 3 would be the actual clearance of the devices, with Phase 4 being the extraction. It was essential to secure the area before reconnaissance, otherwise terrorists could remove or place further devices after reconnaissance was complete.

The whole of C Company, together with various reinforcements, would deploy with an outer cordon of six multiples from 10 and 11 Platoons and the Heavy Platoon, with 9 Platoon providing the close protection to ATO and the Royal Engineer Search Teams. The Heavy Platoon was a composite of half the Reconnaissance Platoon and half the Drums Platoon, formed specifically for this tour. The Garda (Irish Republic Police) and the Irish Army were to

Second Lieutenant Andy
Price.

provide cover in the corresponding areas close to the border on the Republic side. Bizarrely, the operation was to be named Operation *Alcoholic*, such were the vagaries of the way the names for operations were allocated at this time.

We will follow the story of one multiple, that of Yankee Two Zero Alpha (Y20A) led by Second Lieutenant Andy Price, who had arrived in the battalion just a few months earlier straight from Sandhurst to assume command of 10 Platoon. His four-man team also contained Lance Corporal Frankie Freeman with an SA80, Private Aidy Dack with a GPMG in the light role, and Private Dave Adan armed with an LSW. The other two teams in the multiple were similarly armed, and commanded by Corporal Sudderby and Lance Corporal Steward.

This multiple deployed by helicopter into a field to the east of and quite close to the Kilnasaggart Bridge from 00.45 of 7 November, quickly shaking out to their cordon locations and commencing to dig three trenches, one per team.

These trenches formed a secure base for each team, but they had to dash out to the road in order to control traffic, so the Y20A trench was facing the road, to the north-west. The trenches dug, the multiple concentrated on controlling traffic, working to their defence routine. On the second day, at 17.07, just as Private Dack was starting to eat a can of chicken curry rations, a burst of about 20 rounds of automatic fire came in over the back of the Y20A trench from across the border. The team heard the crack of the bullets going over their heads. Quickly switching to the rear of the trench, they returned fire. Initially Private Adan fired into a building nearby but as a further burst of another 20 rounds came in, they spotted the firing point. Private Dack fired an initial burst from the GPMG, but then swapped it to the

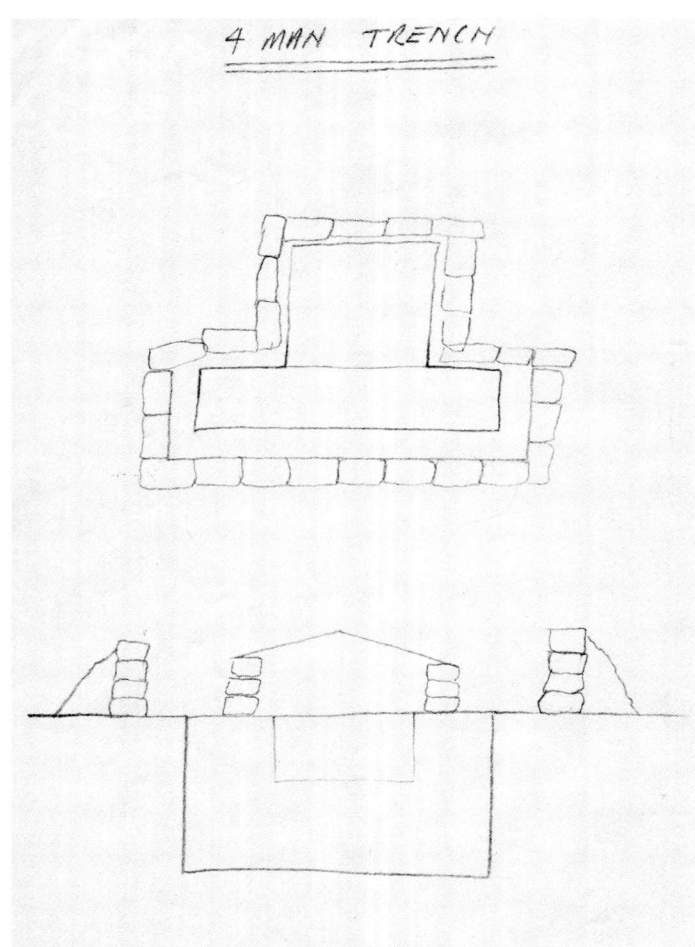

4 MAN TRENCH

Above: The original diagram that Second Lieutenant Price used to describe the trenches shows that they were quite large.

Right: Initial firing positions of Y20A at Kilnasaggart Bridge, November 1989.

other side of the trench as Lance Corporal Freeman had a better view of the firing point, so he fired the subsequent bursts from their GPMG.

The two-man PIRA gun team was on a wooded hill feature called Drumad Wood, just over the border, more than 900m from the trench. They were also firing a 7.62mm GPMG, together with an AKM assault rifle. Second Lieutenant Price, now firing from the sleeping bay end of the trench recalls:

I remember distinctly that in the middle of this, I saw a line of bullets heading towards me, kicking up little 'V'-shaped splatters of earth, just like you see in the films, just as the line of rounds got to me I ducked my head down below the parapet and the last round either hit the trench or went just over my head. I can close my eyes now and see that sequence, it has stuck in my head like a You Tube clip, as clear as day.

At the same time, two Heavy Platoon machine-gun teams with tripod-mounted GPMG (SF) further to the south on a hill feature called Slievbolea had also spotted the firing point. The platoon second-in-command was Sergeant Kevin Stollery, call-sign Echo 20B, who had just been doing his round of the position, checking sentries prior to last light. Fortunately, both guns were pointing in the direction of Drumad Wood and were manned by the highly experienced Lance Corporals Peter 'Five Tours' Fleming and 'Roscoe' Robinson.

They had been issued with a new, long-range tracer round, which burned out to 1,800m range but it was possible to shoot still further, out to 2,400m or more if the strike of the rounds hitting the ground could be observed, even after the tracer had burned out. Their first two bursts went low, however, and Sergeant Stollery recalls:

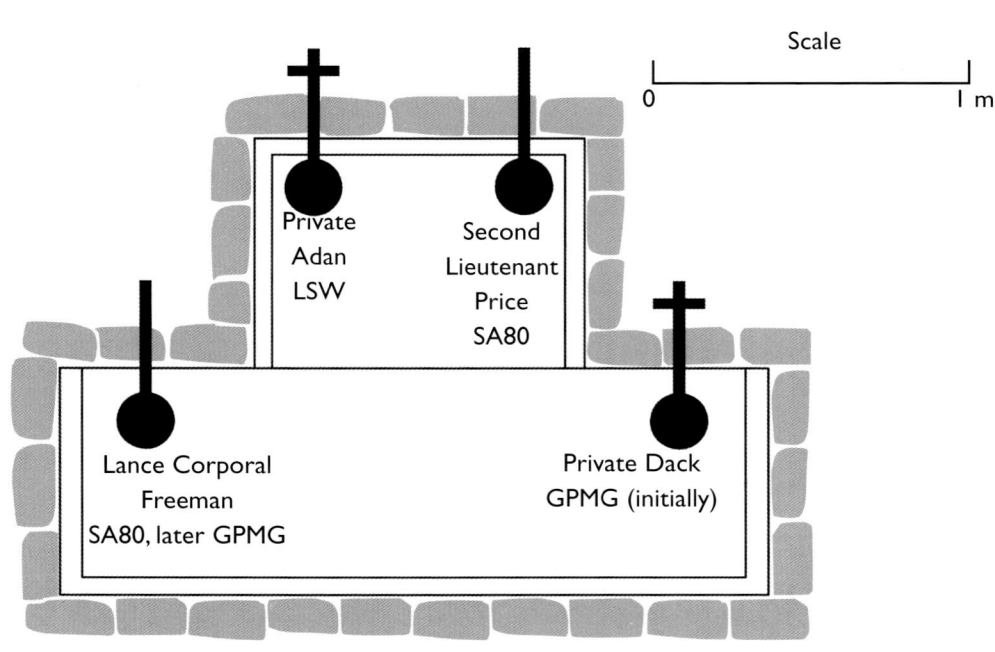

Scale

0   1 m

Private
Adan
LSW

Second
Lieutenant
Price
SA80

Lance Corporal
Freeman
SA80, later GPMG

Private Dack
GPMG (initially)

Lance Corporal Peter
Fleming on one of his earlier
tours, Londonderry 1985.

We could hear the gunmen firing between our bursts so it was quite exciting; although the first
bursts were low, we could see that so we were quickly onto the target and I am pretty sure the
third long burst hit. They stopped firing about then anyway. Just then Pete Fleming's gun had
a stoppage so I ran over to that trench to help clear it and we carried on firing. We fired more
than 400 rounds as I remember, counting the brass [empty cases] later.

It was all over very quickly, however, as the PIRA gun team stopped firing, probably as a
result of return fire either landing close or hitting them. The guns carried on firing to ensure
the PIRA gun team was suppressed, and also to inhibit their escape. It was later discovered
that the range from the guns on Slievbolea to the target on Drumad Wood was at least
2,200m, an impressive piece of shooting.

Back at the Y20A trench, Second Lieutenant Price remembers: 'I saw the SF fire sweeping
across our front in a perfect arc of tracer, the Drums were very fast in returning fire and the
first long burst seemed to go straight smack into the firing point.'

Apart from being covered in spilled curry, the Y20A call-sign were unharmed by the
incident. An immediate follow-up was under way by the Garda, and Sergeant Stollery
remembers hearing their sirens approaching from the south. As the firing point was clearly
inside the Republic, there was little else the Vikings could do but watch. The PIRA gun team
had a well-concealed escape route south through the woods, it was well out of sight from the
cordon and they managed to evade the Irish Army and Garda's follow up.

One early report stated that the Vikings had returned fire with some 287 rounds at the
firing point, but the actual total was higher when the information from the guns came in,

Kevin Stollery on an earlier tour, also Londonderry 1985.

Second Lieutenant Price's GOC's commendation certificate.

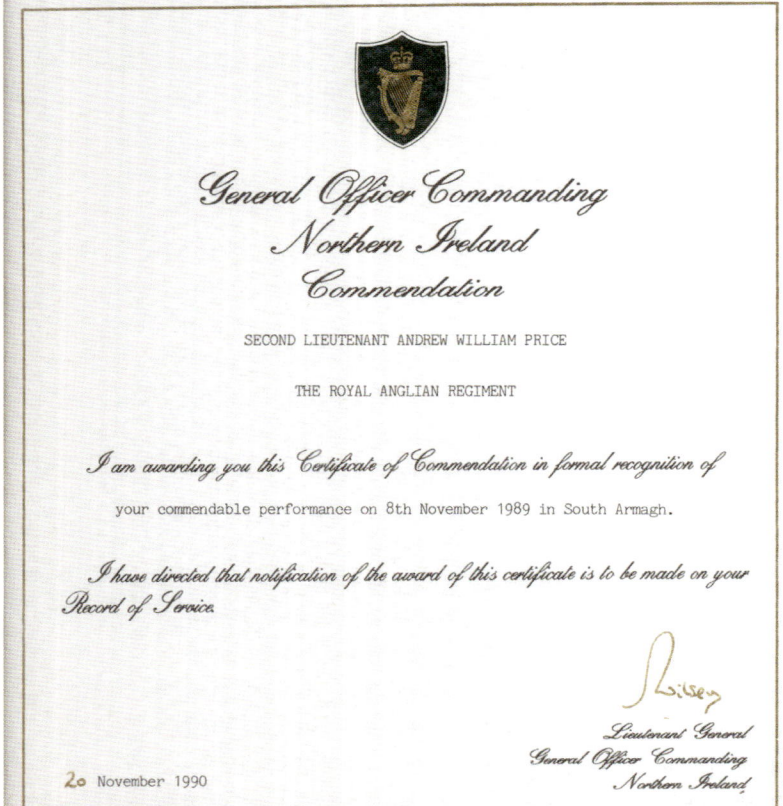

probably more like 600 rounds. A later investigation by the Garda found that there were many hits close to the firing point – 27 rounds had punctured some silage bags that the PIRA gun team had used as cover. There was also a report of blood on the firing point suggesting that the PIRA team had been hit, but this was never confirmed. It is always difficult to know what effect security-force behaviour had on terrorists, but it seems likely that such rapid and accurate return fire, straight into their distant firing point, would have discouraged somewhat the PIRA from making further similar attacks.

The cordon remained in place until the hoax devices were cleared by ATO and the company then extracted some days later without further incident. Second Lieutenant Price was to receive a commendation from the General Officer Commanding Northern Ireland for his 'commendable performance on 8th November in South Armagh'. Major Ian Hall was Mentioned in Despatches for the tour.

JOB DONE

The last soldier of the Regiment to be killed by terrorist action in Northern Ireland was Private Nicholas Peacock, 2nd Battalion on 1 February 1989, who was aged 20. He was killed by a remote-controlled bomb hidden in a drainpipe, while on a foot patrol on Rockmore Street in the Falls area of

VIKING ON PATROL IN SOUTH ARMAGH IN 1989 WITH GPMG

Belfast. As it moved into the third decade, the conflict was not yet over, but the number of casualties started to reduce. The tours continued, as shown in the following chart:

BATTALION	DATES	LOCATION
2nd Battalion	January–June 1989	Belfast
1st Battalion	April–November 1991	Fermanagh
3rd Battalion	May 1991–August 1992	Londonderry
2nd Battalion	December 1992–July 1993	East Tyrone
1st Battalion	December 1993–June 1994	East Tyrone
1st Battalion	November 1996–May 1997	Belfast
AFTER GOOD FRIDAY AGREEMENT		
1st Battalion	May 1999–May 2001	Londonderry
2nd Battalion (D Company only)	November 2000–May 2001	Belfast
2nd Battalion	June–December 2002	Belfast and Omagh
1st Battalion	December 2002–June 2003	East Tyrone (four platoons only)
2nd Battalion	February 2004–December 2005	Ballykelly

In the 1990s, the PIRA were suffering from significant penetration by the intelligence agencies. The secret war had waged throughout the conflict, but first came to the public eye with the supergrass phenomenon of mid-1980s. There were further significant penetrations such as the so-called 'Death on the Rock' event in 1988. This attack targeted the Vikings' Mortar Platoon and Band and Drums, but was foiled by superior intelligence; its failure sent shock waves through the PIRA. They again reorganised and revised their security procedures, which led to a reduction in the type of routine attacks that they could mount.

There were the following deaths in the whole conflict in the 1990s:

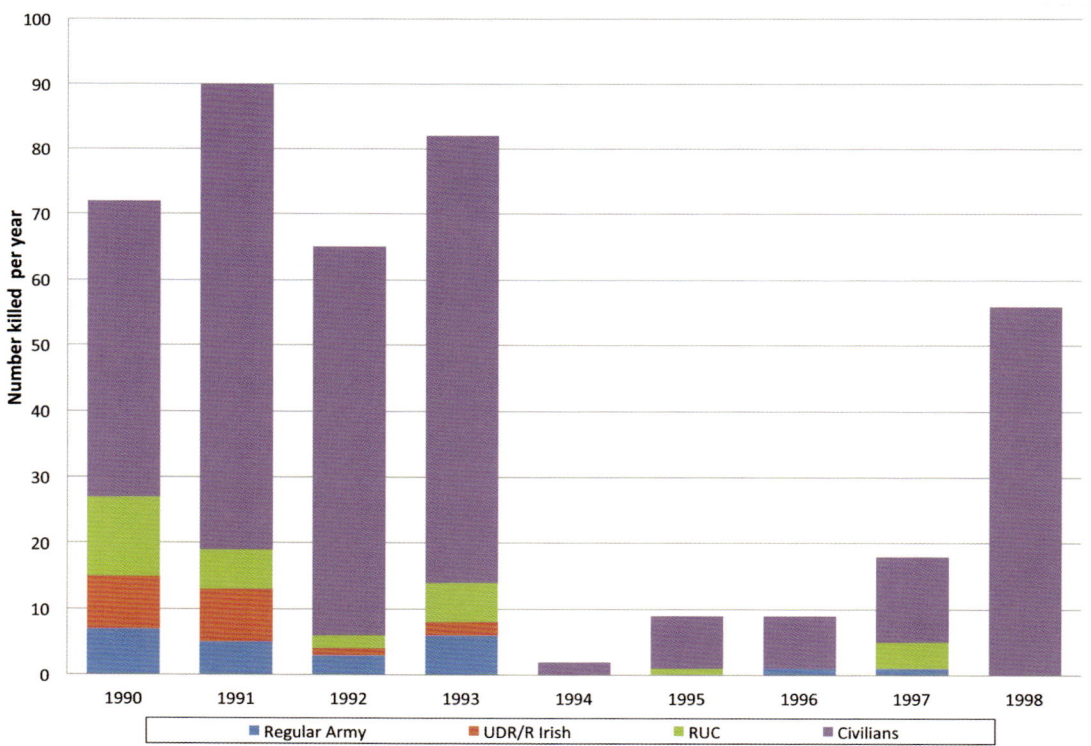

Figures from http://cain.ulst. ac.uk/sutton/chron/index. html

The Province was still a dangerous place for the battalions serving there, but not as dangerous as it had been. The PIRA switched its main effort to more spectacular attacks, such as the destruction of the Buncrana permanent vehicle checkpoint near Londonderry by a proxy bomb, which killed six and the proxy bomb's driver on 24 October 1990. Partly in response to the intelligence penetration, the PIRA now undertook only a few operations, but these had to be large and spectacular to be worth the risk. Their next attempt, however, went badly wrong on 23 October 1993 when they were trying to attack a meeting of Loyalist paramilitaries in a chip shop on the Shankill Road. The paramilitary meeting had been rescheduled, and the device exploded prematurely, killing the bomb team and nine civilians. In the next years they switched to attacks on the UK mainland, using newly formed active service units, with an attempted mortar attack on Heathrow airport in March 1994.

The trend of terrorist violence was, however, clearly and significantly a downwards one, mainly as a result of political pressure being exerted on the PIRA by their supporters. Much of this pressure came because the population were prepared to accept far less violence and disruption to their lives than in the earlier years of the conflict. Much of this arguably came about because of the efforts of the security forces to 'keep the lid' on over the years. On 31 August 1994 the PIRA announced a ceasefire, as what was eventually to become known as the Good Friday Agreement peace process got under way, although it was to be a bumpy road. Despite the ceasefire, PIRA detonated a massive bomb on Canary Wharf on 9 February 1996, then another in Manchester city centre on 15 June and then undertook a bomb attack on Thiepval Barracks in Lisburn on 7 October. At this time the 1st Battalion was just about to move to Belfast, under the command of Lieutenant Colonel Dick Harrold, OBE. He recalls why the tour was an important one:

Vikings on patrol in West Belfast.

After the latest ceasefire came to an end with the Thiepval Barracks bomb, the IRA wanted to go back to war; the method they chose was to have a special operations team. Rather than going back to war with everything, they wanted to mount a series of clever, spectacular attacks. Thiepval Barracks was the first of these. In October 1996 the RUC managed to arrest most of that special operations team, just before the Vikings arrived in Belfast. So when we arrived, it was almost like a phoney war, cease fire or not cease fire? Just after we arrived, the PIRA decided to activate all their active service units, so not long after, we were back into war. It was interesting because for some reason that I do not know, this part of the conflict centred in Belfast. South Armagh did not kick off, nor did Londonderry; it was very much focused on where we were in West Belfast.

With all my experience in Ireland, I would say that if they wanted to kill a soldier in South Armagh, they would probably manage it, but I did not think that was the case in West Belfast in late 1996 because the urban environment was utterly different. I was convinced that if we did it right in the urban environment, we could deter an attack. What you had to do was to sow that seed of doubt in the opposition that their escape route was not clear, because they were not suicidal. I set the main effort of the battalion as deception, because if the opposition did not know where we were or where we would pop up next, they would find it very hard to mount an operation. By combining foot patrols, vehicles and helicopters we had enormous flexibility. I set the task on my company commanders to try something new, do something different, sow a seed of doubt, use different sizes of multiples and so on. This was the whole essence of it and

Corporal Tim Newton supervising his team in the loading bay.

they did a bloody good job. I got one piece of feedback from intelligence where the IRA scout went out, observed us, went back and said 'scrap it boys, the Brits are doing it right', so they called off the attack.

There were attacks mounted against us once a week, which was a very high rate because they were desperate to get a kill. One example happened on the 6th March 1997 when Corporal Tim Newton (later to be RSM of the 1st Battalion), was in the Ballymurphy when the IRA laid on a pretty shoddy command wire IED attack, with a relatively short wire. They detonated it. Corporal Newton and his team were blown off their feet but he got up and went straight into pursuit. It was absolute textbook, he pursued into depth and he caught the bomber red handed, brilliant. It was just textbook. Towards the end of our tour, around May 1997, a sort of unofficial ceasefire came in, with an election coming up, and after that they declared the second ceasefire. Now, I don't want to say that peace in Northern Ireland was thanks to 1 R ANGLIAN, but I am convinced that one of the reasons in their going into this ceasefire was because they had had a go but failed. They had tried for four months solidly, an attack a week, but got nothing; in fact they had taken casualties in terms of arrests and finds. That must have been a part of their thinking in going into the ceasefire again. I do not want to be melodramatic, but if you wanted to finish the story of the Regiment in Northern Ireland, I think that would be a very good place to finish.

Viking Saxon patrol in the Falls Road.

The last British soldier to be killed on Operation *Banner* was Lance Bombardier Stephen Restorick, Royal Artillery, killed by a sniper on 12 February 1997. On 20 July 1997 PIRA reinstated its ceasefire; this time it was to hold, and peace came to Northern Ireland on 10 April 1998 with the signing of the Good Friday Agreement. As always with Northern

Ireland, there was a twist in the tail, as the splinter group called the Real IRA exploded a huge car bomb in Omagh on 15 August, killing 29 people and two unborn babies, but despite such a tragedy, the peace process held.

From the Regiment's point of view it had been the defining operational experience in the middle years of its life. Eighteen members of the Regiment were killed in action – their average age just 23 – and more than 100 were seriously wounded, but through the grinding tours The Royal Anglian Regiment established a superb reputation as being professional, firmly disciplined, and hard to kill, but even-handed, fair, cool and restrained. The Regiment made a very significant contribution to Operation *Banner* across the three decades and those who served in Northern Ireland can look back with considerable pride and say 'job done'.

NORTHERN IRELAND AWARDS

The gallantry and distinguished service of individual members of the Regiment in Northern Ireland has been marked by a considerable array of awards over the years. The totals are shown in the following table:

AWARD	NUMBER
Commander of the Military Division of the Most Excellent Order of the British Empire (CBE)	4
Officer of the Military Division of the Most Excellent Order of the British Empire (OBE)	16
Member of the Military Division of the Most Excellent Order of the British Empire (MBE)	27
Distinguished Conduct Medal	1
Military Medal	4
Queen's Gallantry Medal	2
British Empire Medal	7
Mentions in Despatches	89
Queen's Commendation for Bravery	4
Queen's Commendation for Valuable Service	10

NOTES

1. Colonel Michael Dewar, *The British Army in Northern Ireland* (Arms & Armour Press, 1985 and revised 1996); Nick van der Bijl, *Operation* Banner (Pen and Sword, 2009).
2. http://webarchive.nationalarchives.gov.uk/20101103103930/http://report.bloody-sunday-inquiry.org/ (accessed 8 May 2014).
3. National Archives, record from 1971. Online at http://discovery.nationalarchives.gov.uk/SearchUI/Details?uri=D7632129.
4. Kevin Myers, *Watching the Door: Cheating Death in 1970s Belfast* (Atlantic Books, reprint, 2008), p.77.
5. His recovery can be followed in detail because there is remarkable primary source material available, both from a contemporary television documentary from BBC News, *Man Alive: Fighting Back* (1980), and the casualty file from Regimental Headquarters which has survived intact and contains copies of all relevant correspondence. (The BBC programme also covers the recuperation of Trooper Keith Thompson from head injuries.)
6. 'Noraid delegates are taken on a border tour', *The Belfast Telegraph* (4 August 1986), p.11.
7. 'IRA in Gun Battle', *The Belfast Telegraph* (Saturday 9 August 1986), p.1.
8. Plunging fire occurs where weapon sights that are adjusted for normal flat trajectory do not work properly when firing downwards at a steep angle. As gravity is working on the bullet in a different way, using normal sights in plunging fire produces high shots. The correct counter to this is to aim very low, but perhaps the terrorists had not thought about it, did not know about this effect or were anyway staying out of line of sight.

BOSNIA

The ethnic and religious conflicts in former Yugoslavia had deep and complex roots. With the collapse of the former communist state in 1990, and as the communities fractured, fighting broke out and ethnic cleansing took place, which saw communities separate on ethnic lines. In 1992, some would say somewhat belatedly, the United Nations deployed peacekeeping forces to Bosnia-Herzegovina as part of what was to be known as UNPROFOR, the United Nations Protection Force.

Operation *Grapple* was the name given to the British participation in UNPROFOR from 1992 and the Poachers, under the command of Lieutenant Colonel John McColl, OBE formally took over from the Coldstream Guards on Operation *Grapple 4* on 8 May 1994. They trained for a mission focused on escorting humanitarian aid convoys, but it swiftly became clear that the actual mission on deployment would be quite different and more complex. Between the training brief and deployment, the situation on some parts of the ground deteriorated rapidly, with the war between the Bosnian Serbs and Muslims on the periphery of their deployment area intensifying alarmingly. However, there was a fragile peace just in place between the Bosnian Croats and the Bosnian Muslims in the central area.

The Poachers deployed as armoured infantry, equipped with 45 Warrior mechanised infantry combat vehicles, eight Scimitar reconnaissance vehicles and a quantity of FV432 armoured personnel carriers from their base in Celle in Germany. The handover period was marred from the start as Captain Steven Wormald was killed and Corporal Nick Davey was seriously injured when their Land Rover ran over an anti-tank mine in the

Gornji Vakuf area on 29 April. The bulk of the battalion was deployed to Vitez, with Battalion Headquarters, C Company under the command of Major Andrew Wadman and D (Support) Company under the command of Major Richard Clements deployed there. A Company Group, under the command of Major Richard Kemp, MBE, included the Recce Platoon. It initially deployed to Zepce, then later moved north to establish additional bases in the area of Jelah and Tesani. The Poachers had a host of attached units under command, the largest of which was A Squadron of the Light Dragoons, under the command of Major Alex McKenzie, deployed to Tomislavgrad. They also had a range of support elements under command, including 5 Field Squadron, 32 Armoured Squadron and 61 Field Support Squadron of the Royal Engineers, together with Military Police, tactical air control, logistics and medical support. B Company of the Poachers, under the command of Major Alasdair Wild, was initially deployed in Gorni Vakuf, but under the operational control of the Duke of Wellington's Regiment. They had two serious incidents very early in the tour, which it later transpired were essentially due to banditry, rather than the war.

WARRIOR MICV

With considerable extra firepower and protection capability over previous armoured personnel carriers, the first true Mechanised Infantry Combat Vehicle (MICV) was the Russian BMP-1, which entered service in 1967, followed by the German Marder in 1971. The British Army was therefore relatively late in introducing an MICV, as the Warrior entered service in 1988. However, this time was put to good use as the Warrior proved to be of an excellent design, a highly successful vehicle that has been upgraded and improved significantly over its long lifespan, as it was still in service in 2014. A relatively large vehicle, it is armed with the highly effective 30mm Rarden cannon with a coaxial Hughes chain gun – so-called because of the novel design of its reloading mechanism. It has an excellent sighting and surveillance system, which has also been repeatedly upgraded over the years. The large turret carries a two-man crew of commander and gunner, with a driver positioned in the front left hull and a rear compartment with sufficient space for up to seven dismounting infantry. The major feature of the Warrior, however, has been its protection, especially as it has been repeatedly up-armoured, more recently with advanced novel armours. The robust and capable Warrior has proved to be very hard to destroy, yet packs a considerable punch, making it a highly popular vehicle with the troops.

A Warrior of 6 Platoon, the Poachers in Gornji Vakuf, Bosnia in 1994.

These groupings on deployment did not last long, however, but the Poachers showed their customary flexibility through the frequent changes of organisation and deployment that followed. The mission required the manning of many checkpoints, and vehicle and foot patrols, especially along the many buffer zones between factions. There was also a novel concept called the 'Active Site', which involved locating and corralling all the Bosnian Muslim heavy weapons – such as tanks, artillery and mortars – into an area so that their use could be monitored. This monitoring was necessary because the Muslims and Serbs were still at war, but the use of these weapons against the Croats could have caused a breach in the fragile Muslim–Croat peace. Never an easy task, the Poachers were nevertheless able to verify the elevation and bearing of the weapons before they were fired. The Poachers had to perform a range of other diplomatic tasks, from hosting various meetings between factions, through negotiations about water and electricity supplies to building a refugee centre.

During their tour the Poachers achieved dramatic improvements to the initially fragile security situation, especially in the central area. The number of ceasefire violations dropped from 40–50 per day in May to fewer than four or five incidents daily by September. The number of routes that allowed civilians to cross the confrontation lines was increased from eight to 11 over this time, which allowed trade to restart and restored at least an element of normality to civilian life. This was not achieved without fighting – some 417 small-arms rounds were fired at the battalion, as well as 54 mortar and artillery rounds, by Serbs, Muslims or Croats.

As an example of the sort of engagements that took place we will look at an incident on 12 July 1994, which concerned 3 Platoon, A Company, the Poachers. Under the command of Lieutenant Steve Russell, 3 Platoon deployed with four Warriors to a village called Sije.[1] At this stage in the tour, the well-protected vehicles were providing most of the capability so they were only normally manned – in addition to the normal crew of commander, gunner and driver – by two dismounting infantry called 'dismounts', rather than the full complement of an infantry section. The platoon's mission was to observe the Bosnian Serb Army to discourage them from breaking a newly negotiated ceasefire. Lieutenant Russell dismounted from his vehicle so that he could oversee the positioning of the other three. Deploying along a mountainous ridge near the village, the white-painted Warriors had some difficulty in finding good hull-down positions, such that Corporal Andy Rainey, in command of the 3 Section vehicle, call-sign 33, had to push forward through some foliage and over the crest line in order to get a decent view into the valley that formed part of the buffer zone.

Corporal Rainey took the best choice available, using the foliage to provide some camouflage, although his task was not helped by the Warrior's colour scheme. It was not yet dark when the vehicle was finally in position, and Corporal Rainey told his gunner Private 'Spike' Howie to rig a Union Jack so any Bosnian Serb Army observers would be in no doubt that it was a British vehicle. Privates 'Handbrake' Hambridge and 'Bungalow' Fulton, the two dismounts, were outside the vehicle covering the rear. They were discussing whether to display the flag from the radio antenna or to lash it to the engine deck when Corporal Rainey and Private Howie heard a swishing noise above them. They were both wearing active noise cancellation headsets as usual, so they did not immediately recognise that the swishing was in fact incoming rifle fire. A radio message from Sergeant Athroll, the platoon sergeant, confirmed that they were under fire. Quickly dropping into the turret, they battened down their hatches and attempted to locate the source of the fire. The initial few shots soon escalated to full automatic fire and they could see the incoming tracer. Both Corporal Rainey and Spike Howie were observing, soon joined by Private 'Ron' Hills, the driver. Hills located smoke coming from some farm buildings, and Corporal Rainey with his x8 sight then identified that the source of the fire was a narrow firing slit in a boarded-up window. This was a legitimate target in self-defence under the rules of engagement and Corporal Rainey was concerned that the fire could hit his dismounts so he gave the fire order to Spike Howie: 'Coax 800 – building in farmyard at bottom of valley.'

HULL-DOWN

'Hull-down' is a term used for the preferred siting of armoured vehicles when they are observing, firing or static in defensive positions when only the top of the turret and main gun are visible to the enemy, usually just over a crest line. Ideally the turret should also be concealed in foliage or with cover behind it so that it is not silhouetted against the skyline. The advantages of hull-down positions are many as the tank is hard to see and presents only a small target while the bulk of the vehicle is protected from the enemy view and direct fire. However the position can be difficult to achieve as it is not always known where the enemy may be observing from, and when in place, the view from the tank, particularly downward, can be restricted by the crest line. When observing from a height down into a valley, as at Sije, there is inevitably a compromise between the protection of a hull-down position and the ability to properly observe the area and so complete the mission.

Good tactics required a series of hull-down positions to be used – adopting one for a short time then reversing and moving into another – this was usually called 'jockeying'.

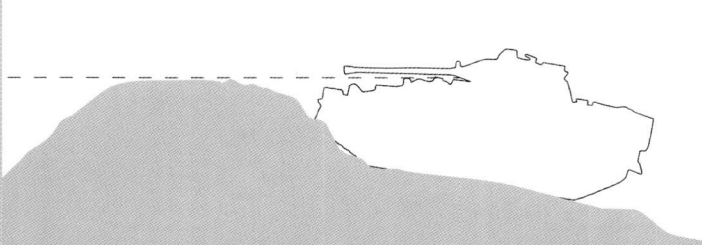

The first burst of the coaxial chain gun went low, so with an 'Add 200' the next burst hit spot on, disintegrating the boarding on the window and ending the incoming fire. Nothing happened for several tense minutes and the crew of Warrior 33 remained quiet, intently observing the valley, then all hell broke loose. Several weapons across the valley fired at once: 20mm automatic cannon, a Bofors 40mm anti-aircraft cannon, a large 85mm anti-aircraft gun and machine guns in direct fire, together with 82mm and 120mm mortars and howitzers firing indirectly. Warrior 33 was hit repeatedly and many rounds fell behind into the village.

Corporal Rainey gave a precise contact report over the radio, specifying the targets and their grid references. Several large rounds then landed very close, one mortar bomb exploding so close that it showered the hatches with earth. This gave Corporal Rainey cause for concern. Although the Warrior was well-protected frontally with Chobham armour, its position on the forward slope, pointing downhill, meant that the more vulnerable turret roof and engine deck were exposed to the fire of enemy heavy weapons – a hit could mean disaster. He therefore ordered Private Hills to reverse the Warrior back over the crest into dead ground, a wise choice as even as they reversed over the crest, some enemy rounds ricocheted off the belly plates. Although they were now in dead ground to the direct fire, it became clear that an enemy spotter had a line of sight onto them as the indirect fire continued to fall and got closer and closer.

Meanwhile Lieutenant Russell brought up his Warrior 30. He initially occupied the position that 33 had been in, then jockeyed to a new and better hull-down position by pushing through a hedgerow, but the Warrior was promptly hit by a hail of tracer fire that destroyed the commander's sight. Warrior 33 had now returned to the crest line providing mutual support and firing at identified targets with its chain gun. Spike Howie proved his gunnery skills; using longer than usual bursts, he suppressed or destroyed several targets while 33 took several hits from small-arms fire.

Reporting into Company Headquarters, which was itself under artillery fire, Major Richard Kemp, MBE was able to arrange a close air support demonstration (CAS demo) using his satellite telephone. A CAS demo was a low-level over-flight by a fully armed NATO F-16 or Harrier – such a demonstration of firepower had proved to be effective in dissuading the factions from further firing without the aircraft having to use their weapons at all. Major Kemp also despatched the quick reaction force and forward air controller to Sije to support 3 Platoon.

Corporal Rainey had again withdrawn 33 back from the crest line where he saw the bizarre sight of some Bosnian Muslim soldiers firing their pistols then running into some woods, but it later transpired that they might have found the Bosnian Serb Army artillery spotter, so were chasing him off. Immediately after this, a quick succession of 30mm automatic grenades from an AGS-17 landed around Warrior 33. It was now around 19.50 and with darkness falling Lieutenant Russell was ordered to withdraw, so he gave orders for the platoon to do so. There was some protest – Corporal Rainey pointed out that their excellent night sights gave them the advantage in the darkness, but he followed orders. As the withdrawal got under way another concerted barrage of 120mm mortars fell around the vehicles, but without inflicting significant damage. Withdrawing was rather tricky as the vehicles had to reverse along a narrow track with a sheer drop of 10m (33 feet) on one side, for about a kilometre. Corporal Rainey found this almost the most dangerous part of the incident, and despite the shellfire he opened his hatch and leaned out in order to better direct Ron Hills along the last 500m.

When the platoon finally got out of contact at their emergency rendezvous, the crew of Warrior 33 were able to inspect the vehicle. They were disappointed to find very little

CORPORAL ANDY RAINEY IN HIS WARRIOR TURRET

Corporal Rainey with Lance Corporals Rob Hill and Oggy Ogden just after the tour.

battle damage, just a few bullet impacts, shattered mirrors and a scorched hole through the Union Jack. They had fired some 167 rounds of 7.62mm chain gun during the incident. The following day Corporal Rainey discovered that some Bosnian Muslim armoured vehicles had previously been painted white to try to fool the Bosnian Serb Army into thinking they were UNPROFOR vehicles, which might have been why Warrior 33 had been fired on in the first instance. For his coolness under fire and quick effective decision-making during this incident, Corporal Rainey was awarded a Military Cross.

Overall the Poachers had a very successful tour, demonstrating that they could fight hard when needed but they also had the patience, intelligence and humanity to carry out the complex range of diplomatic tasks required by the mission. This tour of Operation *Grapple 4* is a fine example of what these characteristics can achieve; they are widespread throughout the Regiment, but were exemplified by the Poachers in 1994. Sadly, the cost of these achievements was one fatality to the Poachers and others to the supporting elements in their battle group and several serious injuries, mainly from anti-tank mines. Some of their contribution was recognised by the award of the Military Cross to Corporal Rainey and an MBE to Major Alasdair Wild. Lieutenant Colonel John McColl, OBE was Mentioned in Despatches, and Major Richard Kemp, MBE, Lance Corporal Shaun Ollerton and Sergeant Dale Robinson each received a Queen's Commendation for Bravery. Captains Simon Etherington and Paul Leslie together with Major Simon Porter received the Queen's Commendation for Valuable Service.

VIKINGS IN CROATIA

The 1st Battalion, under the command of Lieutenant Colonel Roger Brunt, MBE, deployed as a brigade reserve to Ploce in Croatia from August to October 1995, as the situation in Bosnia-Herzegovina deteriorated. By August, the political tensions had eased and the release of some UN hostages was achieved through diplomatic efforts. NATO air-strikes were intensified and the likelihood of a ground operation increased, although no actual deployments were undertaken.

At the end of September freak storms hit the Croatian coast and heavy rain caused much of Ploce Camp to be flooded. Consequently, the decision was taken to move the Battalion to an alternative site at Rastevic Camp, a UN base located in the Krajina area of Croatia. The situation in Bosnia began to improve with the United States' diplomatic initiatives having some effect. A ceasefire was announced and by the end of October a peace conference, eventually leading to the Dayton Accords, had been called. The Vikings returned to the UK in October 1995 having suffered no casualties.

NOTES

1. See also Simon Dunstan, 'Rainey and "Reggie": A Poacher's MC in Bosnia' (*Osprey Military Journal*, 2000); www.ospreypublishing.com/articles/modern_warfare/poacher_MC_in_bosnia/

ADEN

After annexation by the British in 1839, Aden became part of the network of re-fuelling ports required by ships travelling between the possessions of the British Empire. By the mid-20th century, although still an important naval base with a major Army HQ and garrison and RAF Khormaksar, the writing was on the wall. Re-fuelling was no longer important, and the ripples of decolonisation and independence had been growing in intensity since the late 1950s.

The port of Aden in 1962.

Prior to 1963, Aden consisted of the port itself and immediate hinterland including the suburb of Crater; Little Aden some 8km along the coast where a British Petroleum oil refinery was located; and the Arab township of Sheikh Othman some 6km to the north.

In January 1963, as a move towards eventual independence, Aden was incorporated into a collection of 15 small tribal states that lay between Aden and the Yemen border. These states occupied a huge inhospitable and mountainous area, with poor communications and sparse population, part of which was known as the Radfan. The resulting federation was named the Federation of South Arabia. Just a few months later, an insurgency broke out against British administration, and in 30 November 1967, after a protracted and bloody struggle, the Federation gained full independence as the People's Republic of South Yemen.

There were a number of insurgent groups operating during this period, some motivated by simple self-interest or tribal agendas, but most seeking to speed the way to full independence. All of them were supported to a greater or lesser extent by Egypt. At this time President Nasser of Egypt was calling in military aid from the Soviet Union. His attempted nationalisation of the Suez Canal in 1956 had prompted the Suez Crisis, with an invasion

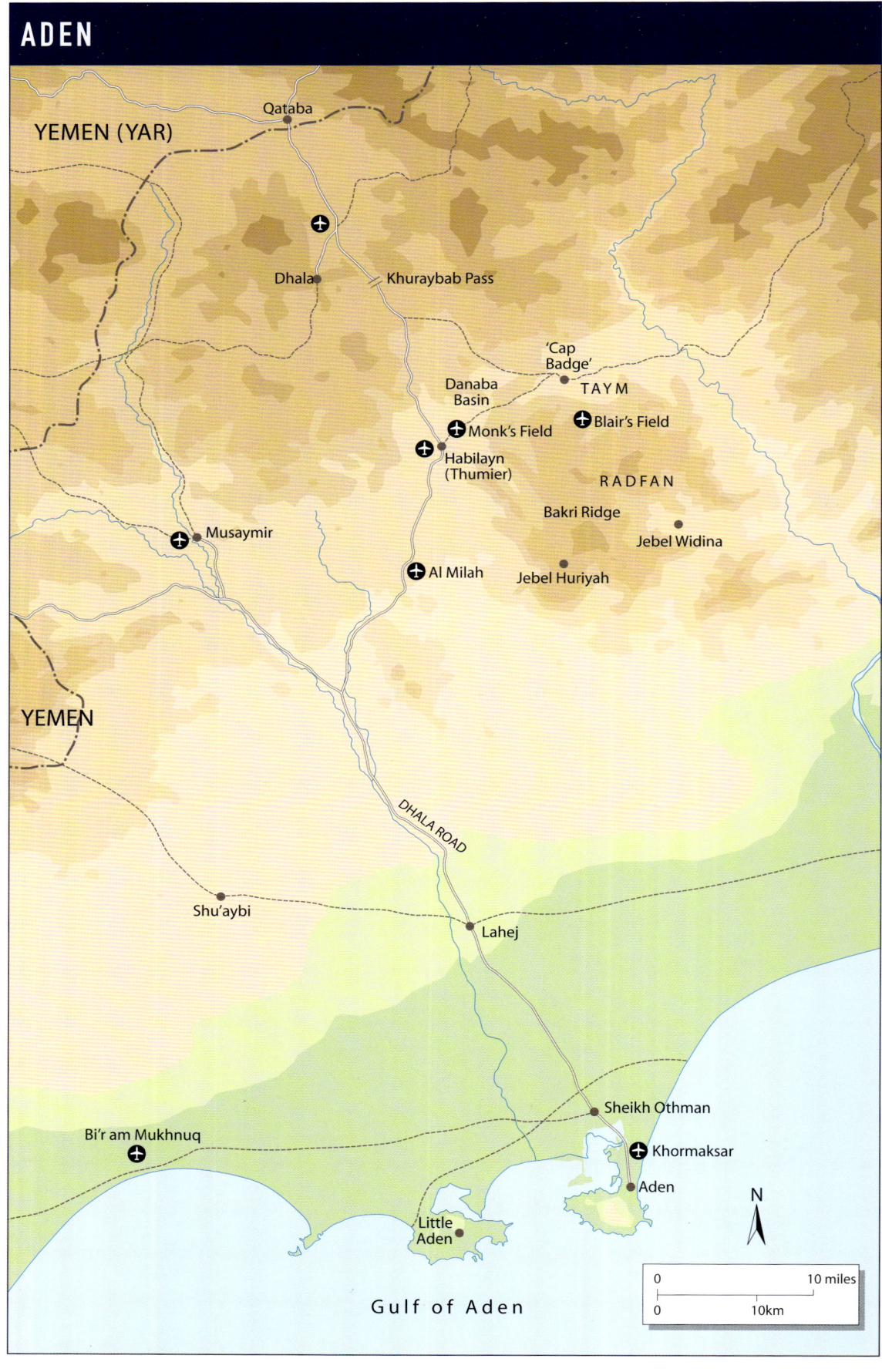

ADEN

YEMEN (YAR)

Qataba

Dhala   Khuraybab Pass

'Cap Badge'

Danaba Basin   TAYM

Monk's Field   Blair's Field

Habilayn (Thumier)

RADFAN

Bakri Ridge   Jebel Widina

Musaymir

Al Milah   Jebel Huriyah

YEMEN

DHALA ROAD

Shu'aybi

Lahej

Sheikh Othman

Bi'r am Mukhnuq   Khormaksar

Aden

Little Aden

N

Gulf of Aden

0   10 miles
0   10km

by British and French troops, so he was no friend of the British Army. It suited him to stir up as much trouble as possible for the British in Aden, so Egypt offered active support to the independence movement.

There were two main insurgent organisations, the National Liberation Front (NLF) and the Front for the Liberation of Occupied South Yemen (FLOSY). The two joined forces in 1966 but this alliance broke down within the year and they fought each other from time to time. Neither were homogenous organisations, rather they were both coalitions of different smaller groups with similar interests. They were all supplied with Egyptian weapons to supplement the stocks of Second World War-vintage and captured small arms that they had accumulated over the years. Light machine guns of various types were reasonably common and the occasional anti-tank weapon, such as the RL-83 Blindicide (an 83mm calibre Belgian-made Bazooka-type weapon), was deployed sometimes. Egyptian military training was offered to insurgents, and at different times some Egyptian military 'advisers' were thought to be operating in Aden, although FLOSY was more committed to Egyptian control than the NLF. These insurgents presented a range of threats to the troops. One of their specialities in towns was the military hand grenade, thrown from short range, over a wall or around a corner, with the 'Cairo Grenadier' as they were called by the troops, making his escape by ducking along narrow streets and into alleyways. The insurgents were able to combine grenade attacks with shootings, including the occasional sniper shot but more often involving a range of automatic weapons to generate a barrage of fire. Another favourite form of attack was the land mine, usually using Second World War-vintage mines. Both anti-tank and anti-personnel types were in frequent use and the troops had to undertake an extensive mine-clearing effort to negate the threat and to enable the safe movement of military vehicles around the area. The British troops in Aden were supported by locally raised forces, the Federal Regular Army and police.

3rd Battalion soldiers patrol past FLOSY graffiti on buildings in Aden.

Below: Looking down on the Crater district of Aden.

Below, right: A 3rd Battalion terrorist weapon find, a British .303 Bren gun, two German 9mm MP38 sub-machine guns and various ammunition, grenades, explosives and equipment.

PORT OF ADEN

Barracks

Sheikh
Othman

Al Mansoura

Khormaksar
airfield

Waterloo Lines

ADEN HARBOUR

Steamer Point

Tawahi

Ma'alla

Government
House

Jebel Shamsan

Spion Kop

Crater

0   1 mile

0   1km

N

All battalions of The Royal Anglian Regiment fought in Aden at various times, shown in the following table:

UNIT	DATES
1st Battalion	January 1964–September 1965
4th Battalion	February–August 1965
B Company, 2nd Battalion	May–July 1966
3rd Battalion	October 1966–May 1967
C Company, 4th Battalion	January–March 1967

Aden was important because right from its formation the Regiment was actively involved in operations. Each battalion's story has already been told by Michael Barthorp,[1] so rather than simply repeating his work, we will seek to add to it somewhat by focussing on some different aspects and by describing some specific operations in more detail, dealing with each battalion in turn.

1ST BATTALION, FORMATION TO SEPTEMBER 1965

By the time the Regiment was formed on 1 September 1964, the 1st Battalion had been in theatre conducting operations for some nine months, having arrived as the 1st East Anglian Regiment in January. At that time the situation within the Federal States had deteriorated to such a degree that the vital Dhala Road had become bandit country and inter-tribal squabbles threatened the stability of the whole area. In April an ad-hoc brigade was formed to stabilise the Radfan and secure Aden Port's hinterland. By the end of April, a firm base had been established about 65km up the Dhala Road, later to grow into Thumier Camp. They next secured the giant Wadi Misrah, the most populous area, surrounded by mountains and dominated by three peaks, the largest of which was Jebel Huriyah. As the brigade progressed across the Misrah, two fortified forward bases and airstrips were built – Monk's Field and Blair's Field – which were to play a key role in future operations. By early May two of the peaks had been secured by a Marine commando, leaving just Jebel Huriyah.

On the night of 10/11 June, after a protracted and difficult approach march, 1st Battalion began the assault on Jebel Huriyah. By dawn it had been captured with little resistance, and the lights of Aden could be seen glimmering in the far distance. Having pacified the Radfan, they were then rotated back into Aden itself meaning that Formation Day was a fairly straightforward affair, marked by a parade in Waterloo Lines. The commanding officer, Lieutenant Colonel Jack Dye, MC, recalled at interview some 50 years later:

> We had been conducting the Radfan campaign in the summer of 1964. When I left in February 1965, I handed over command to Tim Creasey, so I was commanding officer of the 1st Battalion The Royal Anglian Regiment for some 5 months, although I had been in command of the 1st East Anglian Regiment for two years.
>
> We had quite a big parade on formation day; we had come down from the Jebel and the Commander-in-Chief, General Sir Charles Harrington handed out the new cap badges. We had been in scruffy uniforms for weeks so we put on our white uniforms and had an evening parade. That is the beginning of The Royal Anglian Regiment.
>
> I think one of the factors that made it easier was that we had all been through a previous amalgamation of the Norfolks and Suffolks, which was awful. We were in Germany then; [the

1st East Anglian officers on the peak of Jebel Huriyah on 11 June 1964, shortly after its capture. The battalion returned to Aden from this operation to become 1st Battalion The Royal Anglian Regiment. Back row from left: Nigel Lewis, Bill Deller, Richard Wilson, Jack Dye, Rodney Cotton (RA), Alex Turnbull, Hugh Horrex, Frank Fleming, John Churchill, Doctor, Patrick Stone, Richard Abbott, David Clarke; front row from left: Tony Calder, John Child, Willie Hawkins, Ian Pearce, John Keep, David Voy, Rupert Conder.

Suffolks] had to come out and join us, it went on and on. We had to make certain that if the first commanding officer was a Norfolk then the second one had to be a Suffolk and so on. If the CO was a Suffolk then the 2IC [second in command] had to be a Norfolk and all that kind of thing. I remember I was the senior Norfolk officer on that parade, we marched on in two formations. Bill Murray Brown the CO marched on but I then had to march off.

In Aden it was much easier. On 31 August I was commanding the 1st East Anglian Regiment, the next day I was commanding the 1st Battalion The Royal Anglian Regiment. The only thing that happened was we had a parade, the soldiers took their hats off and changed badges and I was still commanding the same soldiers. There was none of that inter-leaving and nobody minded this. I think they preferred the title of Royal Anglian to East Anglian, it had a better ring about it and we had no trouble at all with people absorbing the Royal Anglian cap badge. Compared with putting two regiments together this was a doddle. This is why we got off to such a splendid start, and we were on operations which also helped.

Following formation, there was a brief respite to organise equipment and then the 1st Battalion was back on operations with companies rotating into bases at Dhala and Mukeiras. The battalion was then back in the rugged Radfan terrain at the end of 1964, with casualties suffered on 31 December due to a land mine. Private Walter Frazer was killed and Corporal Andrews and Private Barrell were wounded. The terrorist violence increased as 1965 wore on, especially in the town of Sheikh Othman and in the Crater part of Aden town. The Crater, or Seera in Arabic, a long-extinct volcanic crater, was a poor district of the town of Aden, at the time a hot bed of insurgents.

There were a series of 'close shaves' in the early part of 1965 including grenade attacks and the firing of a Blindicide rocket at 7 Platoon in Sheikh Othman on 12 March, which seriously injured two Vikings.

We will look next at one later incident in more detail. Just after dark at 19.30 on 19 June 1965, two terrorists threw two grenades that injured five British civilians – two men, two women and a child – near the Seamen's Mission at Steamer Point in Aden. Second Lieutenant Willie Hawkins had just visited the guard at Government House when he heard the explosions, so he stopped his Land Rover. Rounding a corner he saw a light-coloured car, stopped by the Seamen's Mission. It started to roll forward slowly, two Arabs jumped in and it sped away. Running to his Land Rover he told the driver Private Richardson to give chase. Showing considerable skill in driving through the narrow streets of the Tawahi district in the dark, Richardson closed in on the car. Realising they were being pursued, the Arab car accelerated, violently twisting and turning, but Hawkins told Richardson to stay with them at all costs, and they continued the chase through a shopping centre

Satellite image of Tawahi district, showing the maze of narrow streets through which Second Lieutenant Hawkins and Private Richardson pursued the suspects.

then a series of narrow back streets. Their persistence paid off as eventually the Arab car stopped. The three men started to run off, but Hawkins was able to grapple with and detain one of them. Drawing his pistol, Hawkins sat on the suspect's chest and instructed Richardson to go and fetch help in the Land Rover. Hawkins was left alone, sitting on the prisoner as a hostile crowd started to gather. The *London Gazette* noted his courage in doing this:

> He remained there alone for some ten minutes in sole control of a delicate situation.
>
> Throughout the whole incident Second Lieutenant Hawkins and his escort were unable to use their weapons as the current rules forbid this, in spite of the probability that the occupants of the car were terrorists with weapons. He was therefore in the position of an unarmed man pursuing and capturing armed men. In the situation, Second Lieutenant Hawkins showed a high degree of alertness, courage, discipline and tenacity. His actions resulted not only in the overpowering and arrest of a terrorist who had been involved in the wounding of five British persons but also in the uncovering of information which has proved of great importance to the Security Forces.[2]

THE 'BIG RED A' NICKNAME

General Dye recalled: 'I am not entirely sure, but I think that the title 'Big Red A' for A Company was coined by Bill Deller in the period around 1965–66, and it seemed to stick.'

It was mentioned in *Castle* in 1966 and interestingly this title was still in use some 40 years later at a reunion event in Norwich called 'Big Red A Reunion'. It was only superseded as a nickname by the county title A (Norfolk) Company in 1994.

A great deal of useful information was recovered from the car and from the prisoner, leading to several arrests. Six months later, some of the information recovered led to the complete break-up of a terrorist cell. For his cool and calculated bravery in this incident, Second Lieutenant Hawkins was later awarded an MBE and Private Richardson received a Commander-in-Chief's Commendation.

After many more operations and incidents, and following an especially intensive spell enforcing a curfew during their last week, the 1st Battalion finally left Aden on 21 September 1965, handing over to the Prince of Wales's Own Regiment of Yorkshire. They had been in Aden more than 18 months and during these operations had converted to Royal Anglians.

2ND BATTALION, MAY–JULY 1966

The 2nd Battalion, the Poachers, were never deployed to Aden as a full battalion; however their B Company did complete a short tour. The battalion was based in Alexander Barracks at Dhekelia in Cyprus from October 1964 to July 1967. B Company, under the command of Major Geoffrey Yates, deployed to Khormaksar airfield in May 1966. Between then and July they undertook a range of security duties including cordon and search operations, personnel searching and lots of guard duties. Writing in *Castle* in October 1966, one anonymous author of B Company described a range of incidents:

> Rows of sleeping bodies on either side of the smelly street. Time 0200 hrs. The charpoy sleepers of Crater City. We wake them one by one, search and take them away. A few hours later they are all back in place making up for lost sleep. Five hundred and fifty assorted troops and airmen took part. No rattles, no sound. DMS boots.

BOOTS, DMS

DMS (directly moulded sole) boots were gradually introduced into service from 1958 to replace the previous leather-soled 'ammunition boots' also called 'Boots, General Service' which had equipped British infantry since the 1880s. As the soles were made of rubber, the key advantage of the DMS boots was that they were quiet. However, this feature was disliked by drill sergeants, as their troops no longer made the distinctive crunching noise during drill practice. For example, Lieutenant Kerry Woodrow recalled:

> They were issued to 3rd Battalion in Berlin in 1966 just before Allied Forces Day and the big Allied Forces Parade. The Americans and French troops taking part had studs and metal heel plates so their marching 'crunched' while we marched silently. Our CO, Peter Leng, ex-Scots Guards, got the Regimental Sergeant Major, Robbie Blood I think, to see if we could nail studs and metal heel plates onto Boots, DMS so we too marched 'properly'. Disaster. The experiment was a complete failure as all the studs and heel plates fell out within yards, so we marched with Boots, DMS as issued!

Normally worn with woollen puttees, Boots, DMS stayed in service until replaced by Boots, Combat High (BCH) from 1982. Interestingly the 1st Battalion conducted a rocky terrain trial of the new BCH in Cyprus in January 1984, when nearly every pair that was issued fell to pieces during some hard use on exercise in the rocky Akamas peninsula. As a result of this and other failures, the synthetic material used in the trial batches of BCH was changed back to leather before they were issued more widely.

Boots DMS.

Above: Private Fred Holt of the Poachers on vehicle patrol, RAF Khormaksar.

Above right: Poachers conducting cordon and search operations.

In another incident:

Scene Maalla Bandar roundabout.
Time 6.15 p.m. daylight

A ragged man throws a bottle across the road. American Ford stands on its front bumper (good brakes). A mini runs into the back of it (not very hard). SCLI [Somerset and Cornwall Light Infantry] Land Rover patrol ... click, click, click ... cock rifles. Screech of tyres, thump of heart ... prickle of sweat ... Ragged road cleaner stuffs paper into a sack unaware of how close he was to death. Relax, smile, on we go. Mini driver looks at scratches but does not complain. American Ford already out of sight.

B Company suffered no fatal casualties during their short but busy tour, returning to Cyprus in July 1966. Some interesting information on the order of battle of B Company, the Poachers from October that year has survived:

B COMPANY, 2ND BATTALION THE ROYAL ANGLIAN REGIMENT
Officer commanding: Major G. R. Yates
Company Sergeant Major: Warrant Officer Class 2 C. McColgan
Company Quarter Master Sergeant: Colour Sergeant B. Philips

5 PLATOON	6 PLATOON	7 PLATOON	8 (SUPPORT) PLATOON
Officer commanding: Lieutenant G. W. M. Hipkin	**Officer commanding: Second Lieutenant P. P. Rawlins**	**Officer commanding: Second Lieutenant R. P. D. Price**	**Officer commanding: Lieutenant G. I. G. Brett**
Platoon Sergeant: Sergeant D. Taylor	Platoon Sergeant: Sergeant G. Hewitt	Platoon Sergeant: Sergeant A. Love	

Private Dick Styles of the Poachers talking to a local.

3RD BATTALION, OCTOBER 1966–MAY 1967

The Pompadours, under the command of Lieutenant Colonel Peter Leng, MBE, MC, deployed to Aden in October 1966 for a nine-month tour. Based in the tented Radfan Camp in the desert to the north of Aden town, the battalion was responsible for Sheikh Othman and Al-Mansoura, both some 6km north of Aden, and for patrolling the Scrubber Line, the name given to the boundary between Aden State and the hinterland.

From the start it was a busy tour, with the advance party finding themselves caught up in incidents while taking over from the outgoing Somerset and Cornwall Light Infantry. The battalion sadly suffered its first casualty within a week of arriving when Corporal Richard Watson was shot dead on 24 October 1966. Shortly afterwards the commanding officer's Land Rover was mined, fortunately with no serious casualties, just before he handed over to Lieutenant Colonel John Dymoke, MBE.

This set the pattern for the following months, with Radfan Camp itself being mortared in December. Initially, there were restrictions limiting the battalion's ability to take the initiative, but this changed early in 1967 when the civil police were placed in support of the Army instead of vice versa. This presumably followed Whitehall's realisation that neither FLOSY nor the NLF would accept a peacefully negotiated independence; they wished to be seen as having taken it by force.

The pace of incidents escalated seriously in April when a three-man United Nations delegation visited Aden, and the terrorists determined to show them that they controlled the colony rather than the security forces. They tried and failed to make Sheikh Othman and Al-Mansoura 'no-go areas', and both towns became hotbeds of trouble during the visit. In early April there had been some freak flooding in Sheikh Othman. The situation was compounded by five days of general strikes, and by 6 April the streets in the town were covered in rubbish and litter. FLOSY was using the detritus to conceal mines, making it virtually impossible to drive through the town. The Pompadours were tasked with clearing the streets to enable vehicular access, and 13 Platoon of C Company, under the command

The Commanding Officer's
Land Rover with his driver
Corporal Alex Keep.

Opposite, bottom: Lieutenant
Brian Harrington-Spier.

Below: 3rd Battalion soldiers
on patrol – probably in
Sheikh Othman.

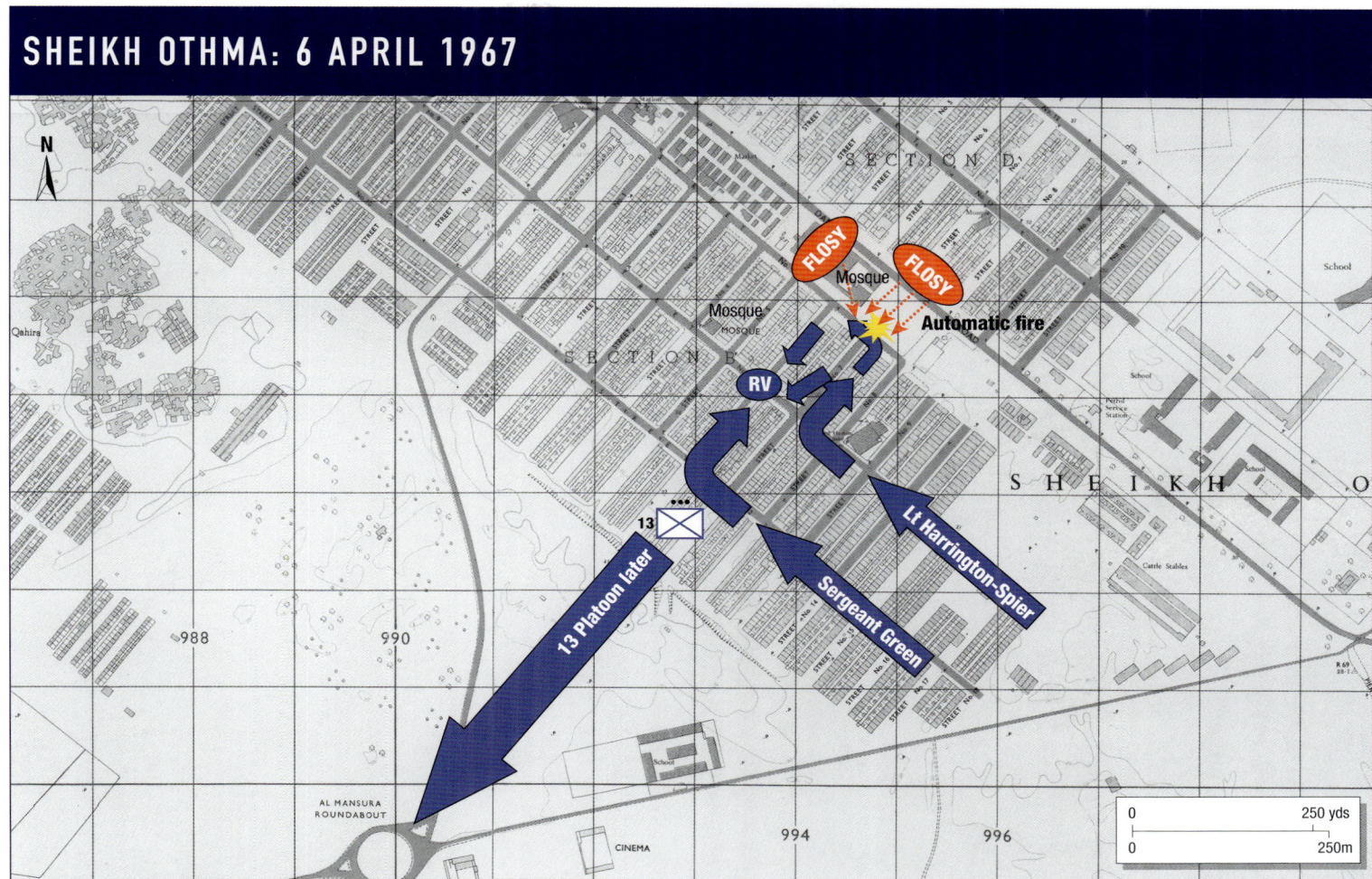

SHEIKH OTHMA: 6 APRIL 1967

of Lieutenant Brian Harrington-Spier, received orders to lead his platoon into Sheikh Othman at 07.00 on 6 April 1967.

Although the actual task was to clear the roads of rubbish to allow vehicular access, it was also necessary to dominate the town as it was thought that Egyptian commandos were stirring up the local FLOSY insurgents. The platoon was divided into two halves, one under Sergeant Green with two sections under Corporals Turner and Kenneth Mogg, the other under Lieutenant Harrington-Spier with Platoon Headquarters and Corporal John Valentine's section. The two halves were to patrol in parallel, with Sergeant Green on the more southerly track. As Lieutenant Harrington-Spier's half-platoon turned the corner towards the mosque, a couple of grenades went off and Private Anderson was slightly wounded. Corporal Valentine's section promptly shot the grenadier but he escaped wounded into the mosque. At that time troops were never allowed to enter mosques, so they could not follow up. The platoon carried on, and they passed a small public lavatory building, Lieutenant Harrington-Spier remembers:

All hell broke loose, there was a pile of Coca-Cola crates when all this automatic fire came down on us, I took cover behind the crates and Corporal Lemmon, my radio operator had to take cover behind the

Looking south over Sheikh Othman, with a large mosque prominent in the left foreground.

Right: Pompadour radio operator with SMG.

Opposite: Looking south-west along the central blocks of Sheikh Othman. Between the two main roads can be seen the police station, the market and beyond that a large mosque. In the distance can be seen the desert which surrounded the town.

lavatory. The fire was coming from across the road. As I hit the deck, the weight of fire was unbelievable; I remember thinking that there was nothing in *The Infantry Platoon in Battle* [the tactics pamphlet of the time] about this. So I took my helmet off and raised it on my rifle above the crates and there was an enormous burst of fire, all these shards of Coca-Cola crate went all over. There were 8–10 weapons firing, mostly automatic fire. I shouted to Corporal Lemmon to get over here; hoisting his radio on his back he took a couple of paces towards me when the road in front of him just boiled, a huge burst of fire, so he fell back into the cover of the lavatory. Shouting across, I told him to get on the radio to get a Tango [armoured vehicle] down here.

The platoon was spread out and under heavy fire, so Lieutenant Harrington-Spier shouted to reorganise them at a rendezvous he had sited in Street 10.

Corporal Valentine described the action in *Castle:*

Reorg in Street 10. The order came from the platoon commander, with the news that a Saracen APC and Saladin armoured car would be covering our move. We regrouped at the end of Street 5. Counting the men, I found that two were missing, Theophile and Butcher.

The platoon withdrew back and collected at the rendezvous, together with Sergeant Green's half. The Queen's Dragoon Guards were supporting the Pompadours at this time, and a troop of armoured vehicles, commanded by Lieutenant George Streatfeild, was on its way. The fire had come from the area of the large mosque and large grey building on Damascus Street. On arrival at the rendezvous, still under sporadic fire, the platoon discovered that two men were not with them. Lieutenant Harrington-Spier recalls:

Privates Theophile and Butcher of the Pompadours.

My heart sank when I realised they were not with us, I thought they were dead. I then thought, I am not going to have my soldiers strung up on a lamppost and mutilated, I am going to get their bodies out. By then two armoured vehicles had arrived, a Saladin and a Saracen. The Saracen was from C (Support) Company. We drove back and they started firing at the Saracen; the door was slightly open and you could hear the rounds bouncing off. Then two or three grenades went off behind us. The three of us were not hurt but I took Lanaghan, McCormick

3rd Battalion Tactical Headquarters, left to right: unknown, Captain Kerry Woodrow, Lieutenant Colonel John Dymoke and Sergeant Tatlock of the Royal Signals who later transferred to become a Royal Anglian.

and Anderson with myself on foot, to pick up the bodies and put them in the back, planning to use the Saracen to transport them out. As we went down the road, we were shielded by the Saracen, we were running behind it. As we ran along I was shouting 'Butcher – Theophile', I was not sure why I was shouting because I thought they were dead. Then I heard ''Ere Sir, I'm over here, Sir'. My relief was enormous, it was such a lift to know that they were both alive.

Both had survived the heavy fire by taking cover – one in a small coffee shop entrance, the other at the back of the shop, in the shadows where they could not be seen. Both were recovered using the Saracen, and they all made their way back to the rendezvous, still under sporadic fire, but this all took more than an hour. Lieutenant Harrington-Spier discussed the situation with Lieutenant George Streatfeild in the Saladin:

I got George in his Saladin to go back into the killing area to neutralise those guns so that my guys could get out. I set off on foot, alongside the Saladin. They weren't allowed to use the 76mm gun in towns, only their Brownings (coaxial machine gun). I could see the muzzle flashes of the enemy guns in the upper window so I pointed these out to George and he hammered away with the Browning. I was quite elated, his machine gun was very effective.

They were also able to engage and return the fire coming from the corner turrets – the minarets – of the mosque. This effective suppressive fire from the Saladin allowed the remainder of 13 Platoon to extract south-west out of the area without casualties or further incident. By this time every one of them was completely soaked, their khaki drill uniforms dark with sweat.

NUMBERS AND ORGANISATION

A detailed order of battle for the 3rd Battalion in 1966 has survived as part of an insert in *Castle*, and it shows some interesting features. At this time, 3rd Battalion unusually had C Company as its support company with Recce, Mortar and Anti-tank platoons. A Company had platoons numbered 1, 2 and 3 with B Company's platoons numbered 5, 6 and 7. The third rifle company was D Company, which had platoons numbered 13, 14 and 15 and it seems with the band attached.*

*The sources conflict in that Lieutenant Brian Harrington-Spier is shown in the *Castle* order of battle as commanding 13 Platoon in 1966, and that is certainly his own recollection, but the citation for his decoration from the *London Gazette* has him commanding a platoon numbered 15 at Sheikh Othman.

SALADIN AND SARACEN ARMOURED CARS

The Alvis Saladin was a six-wheeled armoured car with a large turret armed with a 76mm L5A1 main gun that could fire high-explosive and high-explosive squash-head ammunition. It also had coaxial and roof-mounted .30in Browning machine guns and was usually fitted with smoke dischargers. This was a useful vehicle, well armoured and liked by the crew.

The Saracen was the armoured personnel carrier version, based on the same chassis but with a higher armoured body to accommodate eight troops, and armed with just a small machine-gun turret.

Examples of Saladin in Aden.

Captain Kerry Woodrow in front of a Pompadour Saracen in Aden.

For their part in the incident Lieutenant Harrington-Spier was awarded an MBE for gallantry and Corporal Valentine a British Empire Medal for gallantry (published in the *London Gazette,* 22 August 1967). That wasn't the end of the action for 13 Platoon that day. There was quite a large operation going on in the town at the time, and once Lieutenant Harrington-Spier had made his report and been debriefed by the intelligence officer, the platoon was sent out to a new location.

In the end the battalion's tour was cut short and the Pompadours returned to Tidworth six weeks earlier than planned. During their time in Aden they had logged some 450 incidents, suffered nearly 200 casualties of varying degrees of seriousness and been awarded two MBEs for gallantry, two BEMs and four Mentions in Despatches.[3]

4TH BATTALION, FEBRUARY–AUGUST 1965

Above, left: A Beaver light aircraft on Monk's Field.

Above, right: Monk's Field camp.

In February 1965, in response to the deteriorating security situation in the colony, the 4th Battalion, the Tigers, under the command of Lieutenant Colonel Alan Cowan, MBE, were despatched on a six-month emergency tour to reinforce the Aden Brigade. Initially employed on the counter-insurgency tasks of patrolling on foot and by vehicle, manning checkpoints, guard duties and cordon and search, the battalion quickly found itself responding to grenade attacks, shootings and follow-up operations after the not infrequent assassinations of local officials, often special branch policemen. Barely a month after arrival, the battalion was sent into the rugged Radfan area to join 24 Infantry Brigade in their operations to cut off the insurgents' supply lines to and from their safe havens in Yemen and to prevent them from attacking the bases and airstrips at Thumier and Monk's Field. There they were responsible for picketing mountain passes, patrolling wadis (dried river beds) and keeping roads free from mines, which was achieved by extensive patrolling. As the situation worsened, the 4th Battalion found itself employed on bigger cordon and search operations and on imposing curfews in the Crater district of Aden, as well as increasing the intensity of vehicle checkpoints and random vehicle and personnel searches. This tour has been described in more detail in Michael Goldschmidt's recent book *Marching with the Tigers*,[4] so here we will delve deeper into one typical low-level incident.

The incident concerns a composite platoon drawn from the 4th Battalion's C Company in March 1965. C Company was deployed to Monk's Field, a small airfield outpost in the Radfan area, north of the town of Habilayn (also called Thumier) with two small fortified camps nearby. It was not much of an airfield, just a compacted rock chip and aggregate strip, but light aircraft like the Beaver observation plane could use it with ease, and in good weather others could try, including the large Beverley transport aircraft on occasion, if not without some risk.

The water bowser in the wadi near Monk's Field.

The two camps were pretty rudimentary affairs constructed of rock walls, with some sandbags, barbed wire and tents for shade. One was run by the Royal Artillery, the other by C Company of the Tigers, supported by the 10th Hussars with Saladin armoured cars.

Modern satellite image of Monk's Field airfield.

Water was scarce in this arid rocky region and the nearest water source was a well, drilled into a nearby wadi. Water had to be drawn each day by the Pioneers, pumped into a bowser then taken back to the camps, but as the water source was outside the camps, patrols had to be mounted near or around it almost every night.

This was less than an ideal situation, but it was not possible to drill through solid rock to build a water point inside the camp; neither was it feasible to fortify the dried river bed, as it was liable to flash flooding. Frequent patrols were therefore the only answer, and were necessary as there was a concern that the FLOSY insurgents might try to poison the water supply in the dark. Water was a vital commodity in the arid landscape, and lack of water would not only severely constrain operations but could determine how long the bases could be occupied.

Twenty-year-old Second Lieutenant Andrew Dexter had arrived in C Company straight from Mons Officer Cadet School just three months earlier. In command of 9 Platoon, it was his turn to lead a patrol near the water point in the wadi on the evening of 6 March 1966. He remembers that the patrol on this particular evening was of about 12 drummers. With Drum Major West as second-in-command, the patrol headed out of the camp as soon as it was dark at around 20.00, and Second Lieutenant Dexter led them down into the river bed in single file.

It was only possible to patrol in single file in the dark as the ground was very rocky and gravelly, covered in spiky, thorny plants. At this time there was no night vision equipment, although normal binoculars might sometimes help a little. Depending on the moonlight, without illumination, visibility could be down to a few metres and hearing was usually more important than vision. The patrol was armed with the L1A1 SLR but Second Lieutenant Dexter had to take a Sterling sub-machine gun (SMG), somewhat reluctantly. Officers were required to carry the Sterling in 1966. Second Lieutenant Dexter takes up the story of the patrol:

> I remember that navigating in this basin was difficult, but that a local called Ali Nasser had a
> wooden tower which had a red light on top. Now, when the light was on it was possible to

THE STERLING SUB-MACHINE GUN

The Sterling was a 9mm calibre sub-machine gun, developed from the famous Sten gun of Second World War fame. Introduced into service in 1953, the Sterling was considered to be more accurate and more reliable than the Sten, but that did not say much. It was of the blowback design, which had the main breech block 'blown back' in recoil by the explosion of a round. As it went back, the breech block pressed against a spring which then later drove it forward again, collecting the next round from the magazine, housing the round then striking it with a fixed firing pin, so the cycle was repeated. A short weapon, it had a curved 32-round magazine, a folding metal stock, a sling and a rarely used bayonet. It had a theoretical maximum (cyclic) rate of fire of some rounds 550 per minute, much less in practice, with an effective range of around 200m in skilled hands. The best

features were that it delivered automatic fire and was relatively lightweight at some 6lb (2.7kg) so it was supposed to be carried by radio operators and officers. There was a later variant with a silencer for covert operations.

Because the magazine stuck out from the left of the weapon at a right angle, it often got in the way; indeed the Sterling seemed to have protrusions in all directions, making it a decidedly awkward weapon, despite being reasonably short. On top of this it had a reputation for being unreliable, as it was prone to not generating sufficient recoil force to fully complete the blowback cycle, especially with lower quality ammunition. Consequently, stoppages on the Sterling were rather more common than would be desirable. All in all it was an unpopular weapon; soon after Aden, all officers would carry the SLR instead.

The wadi next to Monk's Field.

navigate around the basin quite well, but when the light was off, it was always difficult in the pitch dark. Ali Nasser always turned the light off whenever there was firing of any sort in the basin; there was no other artificial light at all, you could just make out the silhouettes of mountains which we called 'Coca-Cola' and 'Pepsi Cola' and there was a wadi that ran past Monk's Field. On this particular evening I was heading down towards the water hole in the wadi, it was a few hundred yards from the camp perimeter. The water hole was a good reference point and I think the red light was on, but behind me to the left so not especially relevant. The basin was not entirely flat but there was a series of folds in the ground. I was not far from the water hole and I was standing on a miniature spur some five feet high, the surface of which was convex. Then I heard sounds to my left, so I lay down and signalled to the rest of the patrol. I could see people, five or six, moving across my front left to right, which meant they were moving towards the water hole and the camp. We were lying prone for about 30 seconds before the next event.

Prone on an exposed spur in the pitch black, yards away from the enemy and with the rest of the patrol behind in single file so unable to fire forwards, everything rested on the

Monk's Field camp.

shoulders of a young, inexperienced second lieutenant. Andrew Dexter admitted to being pretty frightened at the time:

> Anyway, I fired and the figures in front of me scattered, melted into the dark. There wasn't time to pass word to everybody in the patrol that there were enemy to the front. I think I also whispered in addition to the hand signal that there were enemy. I was on this rock feeling very exposed when the gun jammed, I had fired probably between six and eight rounds, and was expecting to receive incoming fire any second, but I managed to clear the stoppage.

Clearing a weapon stoppage in the pitch dark with enemy so close at hand is no simple task, requiring a certain coolness. Dexter continued:

> I am not sure what the next step was precisely, but the people in the camp had heard me fire and I remember them shouting 'Stand To'. I could hear the sergeant in charge of the Saladin armoured car and his crewman start up their vehicle in preparation to fire a Defensive Fire (DF) task [pre-programmed Defensive Fire tasks were called DFs], brave and fortunate chaps, these, because some days later, when they escorted us and the District Officer on a 'flag waving mission', they survived the blowing up of their Saladin when it struck a double-banked anti-tank mine. I could also hear the mortar crews making ready to fire their DFs. I remember

Tigers on convoy escort to Thumier.

thinking that these were all welcome signs that fire support was coming to our aid and that we would give the dissidents something else to remember us by. I gave a quick run down on the incident to Captain Richard ('Dick') Robinson, C Company Commander, on the radio. It was agreed that the patrol should withdraw back to the camp, where we were debriefed. Hindsight is a wonderful thing, but I have a feeling that had we been doing all this today, our basic military skills and instincts would have been supplemented by a dynamic combination of technology and massive fire power to win the day. As it was, we were modern in our time; and we won in our way.

With the insurgent patrol scattered and the camp stood to, this incident was effectively over. At first light the following morning the patrol and others returned to the scene to investigate, but there was essentially nothing to see. The SMG empty cases were still in place, but that was all. There were no blood trails in evidence but it was thought that one insurgent was wounded. Later in the morning, C Company had a visit from a Colonel Richard Mathie for a debrief; he talked to Dexter at length, probably for intelligence purposes. From Andrew Dexter's point of view, this was just part of life in the Radfan at that time, however he did take some learning points from the experience:

> Some days later on another night patrol I bounced a sangar-building party from the Federal Regular Army (Local Aden Forces). With the benefit of hindsight brought about by my waterhole incident, I knew that if you were going to shoot somebody in the dark you had better be up close. Consequently, I got up close to the sangar-building party and did not shoot anybody, because I discovered who they were. That was a very important lesson for any soldier to learn because it saved lives.

Their tour in the Radfan lasted barely three weeks before the 4th Battalion returned to Aden. The 1st Battalion was also there at the time, nearing the end of their two-year tour, so there was willing co-operation between the two. For much of the Tigers' time it was usual to have one company under command of the Vikings or occasionally vice versa. The Tigers completed their tour without suffering any fatal casualties, returning to Watchet in the UK in August 1965. All those who served for more than 30 days in theatre earned a General Service Medal with the clasp 'South Arabia'.

Overall Aden was important because it gave all four regular battalions of the nascent Regiment operational experience. Although it represented a British withdrawal from the region, Aden was a reasonably successful counter-insurgency campaign and all the regular battalions of the Regiment played an important role in the success. This contribution came at a cost, however, with the deaths of five members of the Regiment: Private W. F. Frazer, 1st Battalion on 31 December 1964; Private L. E. J. Wallace, 1st Battalion on 4 July 1965; Corporal R. Watson of 3rd Battalion on 24 October 1966; and 3rd Battalion suffered two fatalities in 1967, Corporal J. E. Herbert on 3 March, and Private C. Rogers the following day. Many others were wounded.

4TH BATTALION SOLDIER ON PATROL IN ADEN

POSTSCRIPT

Jack Dye was awarded an OBE for his time in command of the 1st Battalion, and he personally continued to make a significant contribution to the stability of the region subsequently, in command of the South Arabian Federal Regular Army, 1966–67. This was described in his obituary in the *Daily Telegraph* on 1 July 2013:

> The Federation was composed of 17 states in what would become South Yemen, and Dye had the daunting task of carrying out policy decisions against the background of the impending British withdrawal from Aden, tribal rivalries within the Army and virtually no support from the weak federal government to whose ministers he was responsible.
>
> Despite being subjected to pressures from many quarters, he never lost sight of the importance of keeping his force intact as the single stabilising factor in the fluid and volatile state of affairs in South Arabia. His men were dangerously susceptible to the propaganda of the extremists but, with an adroit mixture of firmness and tact, he managed to achieve a balance between the opposing factions within the Army.
>
> Nonetheless, on the morning of June 20 1967, elements of the Army mutinied. They burned down their barracks and broke into the armoury. It is a measure of Dye's success that the rest of his force remained loyal and played a vital role in helping to restore order.
>
> The welding of the FRA into an effective force was achieved at considerable personal risk. Deprived of the support from above and below which a commander could normally expect, Dye lived a lonely and at times dangerous existence. He was appointed CBE at the end of his tour.

Major General Dye, CBE.

NOTES

1. Michael Barthorp, *Crater to the Creggan: The History of the Royal Anglian Regiment 1964–1974* (Leo Cooper, 1976), pp.33–48.
2. Quoted from the MBE citation in the *London Gazette* (19 November 1965, No. 43818).
3. A full account of this tour appears in Michael Barthorp, *Crater to the Creggan*, pp.43–48.
4. Michael Goldschmidt, *Marching with the Tigers* (Pen and Sword, 2009), pp.143–63.

OTHER OPERATIONS

Tigers advancing up a wadi in Fujairah.

We will look briefly here at some of the other operations that the Regiment has carried out in Bahrain, the Falkland Islands, Sierra Leone and Kuwait.

TIGERS IN BAHRAIN, 1969

The 4th Battalion, the Tigers, under the command of Lieutenant Colonel Terry Holloway, deployed for a nine-month tour to Bahrain in August 1969. An island in the Gulf, Bahrain is now linked to the shore by a causeway, but this was not built at the time of the Tigers' tour.[1] The battalion was based at Hamala Camp in the centre of the island with a mission of counter-insurgency support for the King or *Hakim* of Bahrain. This meant that one company, the Alert Company, was on standby to deploy at short notice, so was confined to camp. The rifle and support companies deployed in sequence to train in the deserts and mountains of the Trucial States, the small states on the mainland such as Abu Dhabi and Dubai. Platoons travelled overland to Oman on small-scale 'hearts and minds' patrols and the battalion conducted two large field training exercises on the mainland, combining with RAF Wessex helicopters and Royal Naval amphibious vessels, such as the Landing Ship Logistic *Sir Bedivere*. Although the Tigers trained hard in the heat of Bahrain, they were not called upon to conduct any counter-insurgency operations and suffered no casualties, and returned to Gillingham in May 1970. The British garrison finally left Bahrain in 1971.

THE FALKLANDS, 1989–2009

The Regiment was not directly involved in the Falklands War of 1982, but in July 1989 C Company of the 3rd Battalion, under the command of Major David Bayliss, was deployed for a six-month tour of the Falkland Islands as the Falklands Islands Resident Infantry Company. The Pompadours' Reconnaissance Platoon also deployed to the bleak outpost of South Georgia under command of Major Richard Clements as the garrison commander. At that time the Argentinean president, Carlos Menem, had just been elected to power and had promised to regain the 'Malvinas', 'by blood if necessary'. The Pompadours' mission was to defend the Falklands, especially Mount Pleasant Airport, until large-scale reinforcements could arrive from the UK. This involved patrolling, helping to guard the important radar and Rapier surface to air missile sites and also providing a quick reaction force on immediate standby.

The company group was 190 strong, including a fire support platoon with mortar and anti-tank detachments. The Pompadours soon settled into a busy routine of patrolling, training, guards and reserve duties. Although this was an operational tour, in the event there was no further Argentinean invasion. This tour came to an end with their return to Colchester in November 1989.

B (Leicestershire) Company of the 2nd Battalion deployed to the Falklands for a similar tour in March 1999. The company group was 150 strong with an enlarged headquarters, three fully manned rifle platoons, and a quartermaster platoon to deal with the large stock of equipment. This was to enable the rapid reinforcement by a battalion with support weapons, should the need arise. Their tasks were as before and they undertook a large exercise called *Purple Strike* towards the end of their tour which involved working with close air support aircraft and naval gunfire support.

Pompadours Corporal Redding, Lance Corporals Gardiner and Cunliffe and Private Homes occupy the remains of an Argentine sangar on Mount Tumbledown.

A similar tour was carried out by D (Bedfordshire & Hertfordshire) Fire Support Company of the 2nd Battalion, under the command of Major Paul Muncey in May 2009. The 'reassure and deter' functions were carried out through the conduct of often isolated and demanding, yet popular, section-level patrols across the islands. Sections were delivered by air to remote parts of the islands with enough supplies to last a week. During these patrols visits to isolated settlements took place, spending a day or so providing manpower to farmers, and some visits even provided a night out of the South Atlantic winter in a barn.

Opposite, top: Poachers on patrol in the Falklands, 1999.

POACHERS IN SIERRA LEONE:
OPERATION *BASILICA*, JUNE–JULY 2000

Sierra Leone is a small country, about the size of Northern Ireland, on the west coast of Africa. A former British colony, it received independence in 1961. Since then it has undergone a series of military coups, then a long-running civil war between the Sierra Leone Army (SLA) and a loose grouping of insurgents and rebels called the Revolutionary United Front (RUF). This savage war has caused the death of an estimated 50,000 people and the displacement of around half the population of six million. As the war was petering out in October 1999, the UN deployed an 8,000-strong peacekeeping force of contingents from Jordan, Nigeria and India, called the United Nations Mission in Sierra Leone (UNAMSIL), to help to enforce a peace of sorts and to disarm the RUF. However, the situation then deteriorated further as the RUF advanced on the capital of Freetown, and despite increases in the UN force to 11,000 then to 13,000, by May 2000 it was deemed necessary to evacuate the British and other foreign nationals from the country. This triggered Operation *Palliser*, where elements of the 1st Battalion The Parachute Regiment deployed to secure the main airport at Lungi, and helped to evacuate some 500 people safely. While this was taking place, Foday Sankoh, the leader of the RUF, was arrested, which combined with increasing pressure from SLA led to the disintegration of his force. At this point, despite the dangers of possible mission creep, the government decided it was worth the risk to deploy more troops to help to train the SLA, so that together with the UNAMSIL they would be better able to enforce the peace.

This was the situation into which the Poachers, under the command of Lieutenant Colonel Alasdair Wild, MBE, deployed, at short notice in early June 2000, on an operation called *Basilica*. The bulk of the combined security and training mission would be carried out by B (Leicestershire) Company group under the command of Major Nick Nottingham. However, several other elements of the battalion also deployed, with the commanding officer taking over the role of deputy commander of the British forces in Freetown, with Major Paul Leslie as chief of staff and Captain Steve Romilly as staff officer, operations. Other headquarters and liaison elements were also deployed; for example, Captain Brian Rayment took on the role of liaison officer between B Company and local SLA and UNAMSIL forces.

Numbering some 250, the B Company Group was reorganised to provide a training team, made up mainly of NCOs from C Company, with the rifle platoons performing the security role around the camp called Benguema and the surrounding area. The quartermaster, Captain Alf Todd, did a superb job in setting up the camp and improving the challenging logistic situation of this deployment. The training team took on an enormous challenge – receiving 1,000 'recruits' and training them into an effective SLA brigade within a six-week programme. Most of the recruits had actually been in the army before, mostly unpaid; some had seen considerable action, but most had very rudimentary military skills. Training started with the basics and progressed onto live firing and

Opposite, bottom: Poachers mortar firing in the Falklands.

Sergeant Coyler instructing the SLA.

B Company WMIK patrol in Sierra Leone.

platoon-level tactics. One enduring memory seems to be of the SLA troops singing, especially during runs and route marches. Concurrently, the training team had to develop the organisation, identifying leaders and evolving the groupings into sections, platoons and companies as the training continued. By the end of July, the new SLA Brigade was, relatively speaking, well trained – an astounding achievement given the circumstances.

Meanwhile, the rifle platoons conducted a range of security tasks, including securing the camp and various patrol tasks in the surrounding areas. The patrols often used WMIK Land Rovers fitted with GPMG or .50in Browning heavy machine guns to insert, then combined with foot patrols into villages. Low-level intelligence was gathered and reassurance to the local population seemed to be effective. There were several incidents, however, that required that challenging mix of diplomatic and soldiering skills that are now almost a hallmark of the Regiment. Making sure that the patrols were always secure, but could also carry out their reassurance mission was a constant difficulty that required consistently good judgement by junior leaders. There were several armed militia-type groups operating in the area, but some were more like armed criminal gangs than insurgents. One such group, the West Side Boys, later became infamous by their capture of 11 members of the Royal Irish Regiment, six of whom were then rescued in the spectacular Operation *Barras* on 10 September.[2]

The Poachers suffered no casualties and had no hostages taken in their highly successful delivery of Operation *Basilica*. They received much praise for achieving the complex and difficult task of training swiftly an effective brigade of the SLA and providing security and reassurance. This was a great help in the process called 'Disarm, Demobilisation and Reintegration' that took place across Sierra Leone over most of the following year. This in turn was so successful that the British forces were replaced by an international force in 2001, and Sierra Leone enjoys a peace of sorts to this day.

Major Nick Nottingham and Company Sergeant Major Rich Bredin running the SLA through a training exercise.

OPERATION *GRANBY*: THE GULF, 1991

The Regiment was not involved directly in Operation *Granby*, the Gulf War of 1991. However, several individuals from the Regiment did serve, some with considerable distinction, for example, Brigadier Mike Walker, OBE was awarded a CBE for his service as Chief of Staff HQ 1 (BR) Corps, the headquarters responsible for mounting the operation. Captain Richard Kemp deployed as the 7 Armoured Brigade commander Brigadier Cordingley's tactical operations officer, and Captain Nigel Spinks deployed as operations staff officer in the 1st Armoured Division Headquarters.

The Viking Band, under command of Bandmaster Wallis, deployed in their wartime role of casualty handling following an intensive period of medical training in October and November 1990. Moving to the site of a field hospital in Al-Jubail in Saudi Arabia, their first task was to help in the building of the hospital, a vast array of tents of all sizes that had to be equipped to handle chemical casualties. There were many other infantry bands also deployed here in this role; the Viking Band were given the specific task of casualty reception, which focused on documenting the arriving casualties then moving them to the various departments at the right speed. By December 1990, after a series of exercises, they were well prepared to receive casualties. During the initial air-war phase

The Viking Band on
Operation *Granby*.

Corporal Grouse and Lance
Corporal Coupe in Doha,
Kuwait ferrying tank drivers.

in January 1991, under threat from Iraqi Scud missiles, they suffered many alarms but no actual hits. In the ground-war phase, thankfully there were no massed casualties, so the Viking Band were not overly taxed during the war. They returned to Colchester on 17 May, ready to get back to their music practice.

On 23 March 1991, A Company of the 2nd Battalion, under the command of Major David Whitehead, deployed to Al-Jubail in Saudi Arabia to take part in the logistic recovery operation after the war. The remainder of the 2nd Battalion then left its base at Celle between 3 and 11 April, at very short notice. It arrived in Al-Jubail and moved with A Company to Kuwait where it established itself with artillery, armoured squadrons and supporting elements in a vacant bonded warehouse complex at Doha to the north-west of Kuwait City. The Poachers' battle group role was to maintain a British military presence in support of mainly American forces remaining in Kuwait. The battalion was equipped with Warrior armoured vehicles. On 11 June the battle group returned to Al-Jubail leaving one company in Kuwait. There was a major ammunition fire incident in Kuwait on 11 July 1991, for which Lance Corporal Plant was awarded a Queen's Gallantry Medal and Warrant Officer Class 2 Rimmer a Queen's Commendation for Brave Conduct.

In Al-Jubail its task was primarily as a guard force for the remaining logistic installations. The Poachers then returned to Celle in July 1991.

NOTES

1. The story of this tour is told in more detail in Michael Goldschmidt *Marching with the Tigers* (Pen and Sword, 2009), pp.234–49.
2. See William Fowler, *Operation Barras* (Orion Publishing, 2004) and Damien Lewis, *Operation Certain Death* (Arrow Books, 2005).

SECTION 3
DEPLOYMENTS AND THE COLD WAR

Poachers in Cyprus.

BRITISH ARMY OF THE RHINE

Pompadours working with the Bundeswehr near Paderborn in 1971.

The experience of serving in West Germany as part of the British Army of the Rhine (BAOR) has been a significant feature in the life of the Regiment. The title of BAOR was actually first used in 1919 by the forces occupying Germany after the First World War, and was reprised in August 1945 as BAOR formed from the British 21st Army Group. Its original role was that of occupation but as the Cold War progressed, this soon changed to one of defending West Germany from a possible Warsaw Pact attack, as part of the NATO conventional defence. When it was founded in 1949, the Federal Republic of Germany did not have any military forces, but this soon changed with the formation of the Bundeswehr in 1955. This bolstered the NATO position and allowed a reshuffling of forces, so that the 1st British Corps, the main fighting formation of BAOR, was progressively reorganised and its deployment concentrated on the north German plain. By the time of the formation of the Regiment in 1964, and with the end of national service, the strength of 1st British Corps had fallen from an earlier 77,000 in 1960 to 55,000, organised into four armoured divisions with an additional, roughly brigade-sized infantry field force. Lieutenant General Sir Richard Goodwin, KCB, CBE, DSO, subsequently Colonel of the Regiment, commanded the 1st British Corps from 1963 to 1966. The 1st British Corps was again reorganised in 1983 into three armoured divisions (1st, 3rd and 4th) with an additional infantry division, the 2nd, based in the UK and centred mainly around Colchester Garrison. After the end of the Cold War, the Headquarters of the 1st British Corps and BAOR evolved into the Allied Rapid Reaction Corps (ARRC).

GERMANY

National capital ★
Intra-German Border ━━━
Barracks
Training area

DENMARK

Baltic Sea

N

SCHLESWIG-
HOLSTEIN

MECKLENBURG-
VORPOMMERN

HAMBURG

Hamburg

POLAND

Soltau

BREMEN

Bremen

Soltau

NEDERSACHSEN

BERLIN
(WEST)

EAST
BERLIN

NETHERLANDS

Celle

Hannover

BRANDENBURG

Minden

Osnabrück

SACHSEN-
ANHALT

Sennelager

Schlagen

EAST GERMANY

Münster

Paderborn

Essen

Leipzig

NORDRHEIN-WESTFALEN

Dresden

SACHSEN

THÜRINGEN

BONN

HESSEN

BELGIUM

WEST GERMANY

Frankfurt am Main

CZECHOSLOVAKIA

RHEINLAND-
PFALZ

LUXEMBOURG

SAARLAND

BAYERN

Stuttgart

FRANCE

BADEN
-WÜRTTEMBERG

Munich

AUSTRIA

SWITZERLAND

0   100 miles
0   100km

The following chart summarises the time that the three regular battalions spent based in BAOR. The 4th Battalion did not serve in BAOR, and TA units were always based in the UK, although some had operational commitments to deploy to BAOR in event of war.

BATTALION	DATES	LOCATION	DURATION (MONTHS)
1st Battalion	October 1965–February 1968	Trenchard Barracks, Celle	29
1st Battalion	August 1978–May 1982	Trenchard Barracks, Celle	46
2nd Battalion	May 1971–June 1976	Oxford Barracks, Münster	62
2nd Battalion	March 1987–February 1996	Trenchard Barracks, Celle	108
2nd Battalion	August 2007–August 2010	Trenchard Barracks, Celle	37
3rd Battalion	December 1970–August 1975	Alanbrooke Barracks, Paderborn	57
3rd Battalion	January 1984–February 1989	Elizabeth Barracks, Minden	62

From this table it can been seen that the experience of the battalions in BAOR varies, with the 1st Battalion having spent some 12.5% of the 50 years there, the 3rd Battalion 19.8%, and the 2nd Battalion the longest time, some 34.5%. These calculations are based on the number of months that the battalions were based in a BAOR location, ignoring the time spent deployed on roulement tours of Northern Ireland. However, both 2nd and 3rd Battalions also spent time in Berlin, which strictly speaking was not part of BAOR. If time in Berlin is included, then the proportion of time over the 50 years rises to 39.5% for the 2nd Battalion and 23.8% for the 3rd. Clearly the Poachers spent significantly more time in Germany than the other battalions, especially since before formation – as the 2nd East Anglian Regiment – they had been based in Osnabrück from May 1961 to June 1964. If this time is included, then the Poachers' figure rises to 43.1% of their life spent based in Germany, quite a surprising proportion. The table also indicates the long-standing connection between the Regiment and the town of Celle near Hannover on the north German plain.

For most BAOR tours the battalions were mechanised infantry, mounted and deployed in the FV432 Armoured Personnel Carrier. However, in their 1987–96 tour the Poachers were armoured infantry, mounted in Warrior Mechanised Infantry Combat Vehicles. This placed additional skill requirements on all members of the battalions, but especially on commanders. Every vehicle had to have a commander, who ranged in rank from lance corporal to lieutenant colonel.

The skills that the battalions required to operate as mechanised and armoured infantry included vehicle maintenance and recovery; communications and signalling; map reading from vehicles – which was significantly different from dismounted navigation; enemy armoured vehicle recognition; operating in Chemical, Biological Radiological and Nuclear (CBRN) environments; vehicle dismounting drills and tactics; and new weapon skills when mounted in Warriors. On top of all this, the more traditional infantry skills had to be maintained.

Soldiering in BAOR had a range of distinctive features – common to all battalions across the life of the Regiment – which we will look at, rather than describing each of the battalions' tours as a narrative.

TEN LITTLE SOLDIER BOYS

This poem appeared anonymously in *Castle* in May 1969 and gives a flavour of soldiering in BAOR in the earlier years.

Ten little soldier boys
Fighting in the line,
One forgot to count his
   rounds,
And then there were nine.

Nine little soldier boys,
In a war of hate,
Respirator didn't fit,
Alive but breathless, eight.

Eight little soldier boys,
At war and not Rheinsehlen,
Driving badly – threw a track,
Then there were seven.

Seven little soldier boys,
Alone and in a fix,

Fiddled with a trip flare,
And then there were six.

Six little soldier boys,
Hoping to survive,
A forgotten password on
   patrol,
And then there were five.

Five little soldier boys,
The light was getting poor,
A match struck to light a fag,
Crack! There were four.

Four little soldier boys,
Shooting SMG,
Fingers in the working parts,
So easy: that made three.

Three little soldier boys,
Swimming 432s,
Hull plugs had not been
   checked,
Then there were two.

Two little soldier boys,
Prone behind their gun,
One couldn't clear a jam,
And then there was one.

One little soldier boy,
Left on his tod,
He fell asleep on guard,
Silly little fellow.

ALL ARMS COOPERATION

One of the most important features of soldiering in BAOR was the requirement to cooperate with other parts of the Army and with the armies of other NATO countries. Usually referred to as 'All Arms Cooperation', this mainly involved working with armour, artillery, engineers and a range of supporting services. Depending on the brigade and the time, the sub-units of infantry and armoured units would be swapped, so that an infantry battalion headquarters might have one or two armoured squadrons under its command, while sending some of its infantry companies to an armoured regimental headquarters. Usually called battle groups, these formations would also have artillery and engineers attached, and several – usually three or four – such battle groups would form a brigade. Sometimes, especially in the earlier years, this principle was applied further down so that company-sized 'combat teams' would swap platoons, resulting in, for example, two infantry platoons and an armoured troop working to a company headquarters. Working in this way required soldiers to be skilled at cooperating with other units, which in turn sometimes required the subjugation of regimental pride in order to get the job done well, especially on larger exercises. By and large, the Royal Anglian sub-units were comfortable both under command of other units and when commanding other arms.

   All battalions of the Regiment have had a persistent reputation for professionalism and an easy cooperative style that has enabled them to get along well with most other units in BAOR. There was inevitably an occasional source of friction; for example, certain cavalry regiments sometimes seemed to want to emphasise their perceived social superiority, their 'smartness', rather than focussing on the job in hand, but these occasions were few and far between. This type of friction was often dissipated by the sheer professional conduct and good sense of humour shown by the Regiment.

For many members of the Regiment, All Arms Cooperation added an interesting aspect to soldiering as it meant working with and learning about different vehicles, weapons and equipment, with a wide and varied range of people, in many different settings. There were also many opportunities to work with different armies in NATO, adding further variety to tours.

NAMES AND FORMATIONS

One persistent source of confusion to the uninitiated is the variety of names used for sub-units. The following table offers a translation of these different names:

INFANTRY SUB-UNITS	ARMOURED EQUIVALENT	ARTILLERY EQUIVALENT	ENGINEER EQUIVALENT
Battalion	Regiment	Regiment	Regiment
Company	Squadron	Battery	Squadron
Platoon	Troop	Troop	Troop
Section	Section	Section	Section

WORKING TO HIGHER FORMATIONS

To some extent, this theme applies to all military situations as infantry battalions are rarely deployed alone. However, the higher formation aspects of soldiering in BAOR were perhaps the most marked as this is where most of the armoured brigade, division and corps headquarters were located. In practical terms, what this meant for most Royal Anglian commanders was an emphasis on communications, and for everybody it meant a tendency to spend a lot of time waiting around. As a general rule, the higher the formation mounting an exercise, the more time spent waiting around for orders or for something to happen. This was a natural feature of the processes that were used, especially the orders cascade and battle procedure processes. Consequently, a company-level exercise would normally involve much less waiting around than a brigade or divisional exercise.

The emphasis on communications was taxing because every vehicle commander had to use at least two and sometimes three communications networks. One would be the vehicle intercom, commander to driver and to a speaker in the back of the vehicle, so the commander could talk to his section. The next would be his platoon or company radio network. The third might then be his company or battalion radio network. To listen to and understand messages and speak on two or three networks simultaneously was not a trivial task, stressful and almost impossible at busy times. This difficult challenge was supposed to be met by the use of a piece of equipment called the Commander's Position Unit (CPU). Suspended from a strap around the neck and resting on the chest, the CPU had a switch that allowed the commander to select which network his microphone was broadcasting on, and allowed the different networks to be heard in different ears. One complication, however, was that although speaking on a radio network required the use of strict radio voice procedure, any language was permitted on the intercom as it was not broadcast. This meant that the radio networks were inevitably

NATO ROYAL ANGLIAN SOLDIER, *c.* 1965

sometimes peppered with intercom rather than radio voice procedure, with commands such as 'take a left, yes down that track', often laced with swear words. This difficult set of communication skills was acquired through constant practice, meaning that battalions that had been in BAOR for a long time were noticeably more slick with their communications. Indeed, a battalion's professionalism was often judged on the slickness of its radio networks.

GENERAL DEPLOYMENT PLAN AND ACTIVE EDGE

The General Deployment Plan (GDP) stipulated the geographic positions to which the battalions would have deployed had a third world war started. Commanders down to platoon level were shown their GDP as part of a regular reconnaissance process, but they had to be kept secret. The management of the GDP plans within a battalion was especially serious, requiring considerable staff and clerking effort to keep these plans up to date and secure. It was especially chilling to be shown the GDP, as it forced soldiers to imagine what they would be expected to do in the event of an attack by the Warsaw Pact, and really brought home exactly why they were deployed in West Germany. Perhaps more than most therefore, the members of the Regiment who served in BAOR have particular good reason to be thankful that an attack never came.

Deployment for war had to be practised frequently. For security reasons the actual GDPs were not used in practices, so mock locations were used. These practices were often called 'Active Edge' – after the code word used to initiate them – for much of the Regiment's time in BAOR. These practices imposed a considerable burden as, by and large, a battalion was judged by higher formation on its performance during an Active Edge call-out. A good performance required that all elements of the battalion worked well together, as failure of one small aspect could have a knock-on effect.

The process started with the impromptu receipt of the code word by the duty officer – at this point higher formation would start their stopwatches. The first action was to contact key commanders, then a recall process would begin. Everyone in barracks had to be roused and all those living in married quarters contacted so they could get into barracks fast. With the clock ticking, anyone who was out of contact for whatever reason – perhaps seeing a girlfriend – stood a serious risk of getting into trouble. Once assembled, the battalion had to handle large quantities of ammunition and stores into their vehicles. War stocks of ammunition were rarely issued as they could not be re-packed once unpacked making the exercise rather wasteful and expensive, but all weapons and personal equipment needed to be issued and packed into the vehicles. Once the commanding officer was content, the battalion departed from barracks in their vehicles to the given mock location, usually called an assembly area. Higher formation would only 'stop the clock' once the bulk of the battalion was in the assembly area with the correct equipment.

These call-out practices were an important feature of serving in BAOR as they practised the war role, but they did impose many restrictions on the more normal life of a battalion. Postings and individual training courses away from the battalion were restricted as there had to be sufficient key personnel left to mount a call-out when needed. This required careful management. Married members of the battalions had to be near a designated telephone, so even simple visits to other people's houses might be curtailed. For most of the earlier years in BAOR, there were no mobile telephones, so the recall system had to work around fixed telephones with known numbers and even messengers. Single people suffered even more restrictions, as they could only go out at certain times and might have to be back in barracks for a particular time; again all this had to be managed.

Another aspect of BAOR was regular Annual Readiness of Unit (ARU) inspections, which covered all necessary skills from shooting to fitness, vehicle maintenance to navigation. By and large the battalions of the Regiment performed well in their ARUs, leading to the Regiment steadily building up an excellent reputation for military competence.

NUCLEAR: SITE GUARDS AND ESCORTS

In the middle years of deployments in BAOR, most infantry units had to participate in a task to assist in guarding nuclear sites and escorting the movement of nuclear convoys. The sites were the locations where nuclear warheads were stored, usually for tactical nuclear weapons such as the British Honest John surface-to-surface rocket. The convoys arose when these warheads had to be moved for a variety of reasons. They were normally a large section or half-platoon sized task, often commanded by a corporal, that came around by rotation. They were serious jobs, as live ammunition was issued, there were many rules and regulations that had to be learned and adhered to, and some rather tricky rules of engagement to be absorbed. For much of the time, it was expected that a Warsaw Pact attack would be preceded by special forces like the Spetsnaz attacking the nuclear sites to prevent their use. This gave a Nuclear Site Guard a particular edge. Many of these tasks would be for five to ten days' duration, but different units managed them in different ways.

When the Poachers moved to Münster in 1971, they were under the command of 4th Armoured Brigade for administration and training, but their operational role was to be the Nuclear Convoy Escort Battalion. As such they worked closely with the then 8 Regiment Royal Corps of Transport, also based in Münster, who were responsible for transporting nuclear ammunition between the special ammunition sites where it was stored in peace and moving them to field sites and user units in time of war. The battalion deployed companies to defend the field sites and platoons to escort individual convoys against the threat from the Warsaw Pact. The role was exercised regularly, involving United States communication units and custodians. Rigorous inspections were conducted by NATO-level international inspection teams in barracks and on field exercises to confirm the readiness for role.

CHEMICAL, BIOLOGICAL, RADIOLOGICAL AND NUCLEAR TRAINING

Chemical, Biological, Radiological and Nuclear (CBRN) training is the modern term for what many older members of the Regiment will remember as Nuclear Biological and Chemical (NBC) training. It was an important aspect of soldiering in BAOR because it was expected that the Warsaw Pact would use their arsenal of what later came to be known as weapons of mass destruction in the event of war. This posed a significant threat, especially from their chemical and battlefield tactical nuclear weapons. Training to cope in such an environment was very demanding. Fortunately, the British Army had probably the best CBRN equipment of any nation for most of this period. The equipment consisted of an over-suit made of absorbent charcoal-backed fabric, together with rubber over-boots and gloves and a respirator of various designs. There were also various detection devices to become familiar with, and alert procedures, decontamination procedures to be learned and so on. As it was an extra layer of clothing, the suit, called a 'Noddy Suit' by the troops, meant that overheating in summer was a common consequence, but its extra warmth could be an advantage, especially in the cold German winters. By far the most taxing item was the respirator because, although it was well designed and much better than other nations' equivalents, it was still very irritating to wear for long periods. Everything became more difficult in a respirator: breathing, seeing, speaking, eating and drinking, while sleep became

Pompadours training to decontaminate their FV432 in 1988.

more or less impossible. Wearing the full equipment – usually called 'State Black' – for long periods caused tempers to fray and the CBRN training was one more additional requirement, something else to learn, another set of skills to acquire. CBRN was never popular, but it was seen as an unpleasant necessity.

TRAINING AREAS

Life in BAOR was mostly spent undertaking training. Members of the Regiment would have spent many months on training areas like Sennelager and Soltau if they were based in BAOR. Most of the live firing ranges were at Sennelager, a large training area of some 116 square kilometres, north of the town of Paderborn and roughly between the towns of Augsburg, Detmold and Schlagen on the edge of the Teutoburg forest. It comprises fairly flat rolling countryside, dotted with woods. Since it is in central Germany, it rains reasonably frequently and it gets very cold in winter, below -5°C on occasion, with conditions made worse by a biting wind.

Tanks and FV432s of the Pompadours battle group on Soltau, 1988.

The 4,600-hectare Soltau training area was on the Lüneberg Heath, well to the north of the town it was named after. This training area had a sandy soil and was more densely covered with vegetation than Sennelager, with trees, scrub and shrubbery dotted about most of the

Poacher FV432 being
recovered from the Soltau
mud, 1988.

area, and it seemed to rain a great deal. Battalions based in Celle undertook many exercises
on Soltau. A description in *Castle* of one such three-week exercise in 1981 noted that:

> Not a single day passed without rain – never less than the odd shower, but frequently a number
> of heavy showers and on occasion 24 hours without stopping! The word 'mud' took on a new
> meaning but at least the Soltau mud brushes off quite easily and doesn't set like concrete as the
> Salisbury Plain mud does.

With German reunification and rising environmental concern, manifested in some local
protests, training on Soltau was first restricted in 1990 then ended altogether in 1994. It is
no longer used for military training.

Starting in 1972, battle groups from BAOR regularly took the opportunity to train on the
Canadian prairie on a huge training area called BATUS, from British Army Training Unit
Suffield, near the town of Medicine Hat. It is not easy to get accurate figures for the size of
the training area, but estimates come in at around 2,500 square kilometres – about the size
of Luxembourg. Since the winter temperature can dip below -40°C, BATUS is only active
between May and October each year. The process of deployment was made easy in that the
people moved but the vehicles stayed put, so units would take over a full battle group set of
vehicles on arrival and hand them over on departure. There was and is a permanent training
team established to look after more than 1,000 armoured vehicles and to assist in mounting
exercises, with most training packages lasting for around six weeks. The rolling prairie,
although undulating and cut by streams, has almost no trees; a single prominent tree in the
centre of the area is nicknamed 'Lone Tree,' a military joke that stemmed from target
indication orders, which often used the expression Lone Tree. All the battalions of the
Regiment stationed in BAOR have exercised repeatedly on BATUS, and most have found it
a very enjoyable experience because the size of the training area meant that the exercises
allowed the full use of mechanised mobility and usually culminated in a very realistic,

Vikings at BATUS in 1980.

large-scale, live firing phase. More recently these large-scale events have been called Tactical Effects Simulation Exercises, or TESEX.

VERY LARGE EXERCISES IN GERMANY

Several very large exercises took place in the middle years of the Regiment's time in BAOR. We will look at one in detail. As its name suggests, Exercise *Crusader 80* took place in 1980, the largest exercise ever mounted by NATO at that time. Designed to test the ability of the UK-based forces to deploy to BAOR over a short period of time, it was made up of a series of subordinate exercises called *Spearpoint* and *Jog Trot*. Overall some 30,000 British troops took part in this multinational exercise, including approximately 10,000 regulars and 20,000 territorials. The 1st Battalion took part in Exercise *Spearpoint*, but having just returned from BATUS, it was to some extent just another mechanised exercise for them, so we will focus on the NATO-committed 5th and 7th TA Battalions, for whom *Crusader/Spearpoint* was a very important event. It was one of the very few occasions upon which they were able to practise their war role. At this time the 6th Battalion had a home defence role, so did not take part in the exercise.

The 5th Battalion's training had been building up all year to their deployment on 16 September 1980. On deployment some 506 members of the battalion spent most of the time occupying a large wood. *Castle* (1981) recorded that:

> We were fortunate that we all saw some battle which many did not. Without a doubt the Exercise was well worth all the preparation and effort with many valuable lessons learnt at all levels. The best point of all was the way everyone buckled down to their tasks on the Spearpoint Exercise in spite of some initial problems. In particular the trenches dug wearing NBC suits in warm conditions were excellent and both the Umpires and Enemy commented as much.

On their way out to the deployment area, the 523-strong 7th Battalion met up with the 3rd Battalion in Rheinsehlen camp for a brief exchange of hospitality before deploying forward for the main exercise phase from 18 to 23 September 1980. The 7th Battalion had two companies

7TH BATTALION ON EXERCISE *CRUSADER*, IN FULL CBRN EQUIPMENT

Overleaf, top left: Number 1 Suffolk Company Assault Pioneers of the 5th Battalion on Exercise *Crusader*. Left to right: Privates Paul Knight and Stephen Burt, Colour Sergeant Ian Burnett and Private Colin Crawford, who were all from Great Yarmouth.

Overleaf, top right: Lance Corporal Williams, Private Grieve, Sergeant King and Private Houle from Hertford, 5th Battalion with their Wombat, enjoying a brew at the end of Exercise *Crusader*.

Overleaf, bottom: 7th Battalion on Exercise *Crusader* – five minutes to make tea.

forward defending bridges with two depth companies in villages. Their main mock battle took place on the 23rd, and was watched by a host of important visitors. *Castle* recorded that:

many regular officers who had no direct contact with the TA before, could only stand the TA in good stead – if everything went right! It did! To clouds of smoke, explosives detonation, small arms fire and the thunder of engines on land and in the air. The big demonstration exercise was followed immediately by great numbers of VIPs inspecting the Battalion positions of A and B Coys. [Both of which incidentally coped admirably with the situation]. A remark overheard from the Inspector General of the German Army – 'Very good – I wish the German Reserves were of the same standard.'

The 3rd Battalion, the Pompadours, then based in Colchester with a NATO reinforcement role, also deployed on this exercise, initially to guard a reserve demolition of a bridge over the River Leine. Having been relieved in their initial location by two companies of the 7th Battalion and one company of the 5th Battalion, they were later joined on their main defensive position by the 1st Battalion. At one point therefore, there were four Royal Anglian battalions in the 1st Armoured Division. The rumour was that the commanding officers of the 1st and 3rd Battalions discussed re-naming the division as the Royal Anglian Armoured Division.

Many of these large-scale exercises and a large proportion of battalion- and company-level exercises took place on 443 areas, so called after the number of the form on which the application to train was made. This enabled troops to train over normal countryside and farmland, giving a much more realistic feel to the exercise than if it had been confined to a training area. Following the end of the Cold War the facility to use 443 areas was withdrawn.

INFANTRY ANTI-TANK WEAPONS

Infantry anti-tank weapons were an important feature of the battalions in BAOR as they were expected to face large numbers of Warsaw Pact armoured vehicles in the event of war. Within the rifle companies, the Carl Gustav 84mm recoilless anti-tank weapon was the mainstay in the earlier years. The M2 variant of this bazooka-type weapon was already in service when the Regiment formed. Known to the troops as the 'Charlie Gee', this heavy but quite accurate medium anti-tank weapon had a range of around 300m against moving targets, more with a skilled gunner or against static targets, and it packed a

Lieutenant Colonels John Hart, MBE, of the 1st Battalion (left) and Robin Drummond, OBE, of the 3rd Battalion discuss renaming the Royal Anglian Armoured Division, September 1980.

reasonable punch with the 84mm HEAT warhead. From the late 1970s it was supplemented by a light anti-tank weapon called the M72, which was purchased from the United States. This small, disposable lightweight 66mm-calibre rocket launcher, usually called the '66' by troops, was handy and generally useful as a supplement, although it lacked range and punch.

From 1987 the new and much heavier 94mm LAW 80 came into service. It was perhaps euphemistically called a light anti-tank weapon as, weighing in at 10kg, it was actually heavier than the Carl Gustav. This disposable launcher had a 9mm spotting rifle built in, to check the range prior to firing the main round, which was supposed to make it accurate to beyond 400m. Although its advanced HEAT warhead packed a considerable punch, the LAW 80 was awkward to use, especially the spotting rifle, which meant it was never a very popular weapon. It is still in service in 2014, but not deployed on actual operations, where the AT-4 and Javelin are used instead, and it is being replaced by the New Light Anti-tank Weapon (N-Law). The N-Law is even heavier at 12.5kg, but has a range of more than 600m, since it is a fire-and-forget guided missile rather than an unguided rocket. It packs a huge punch against armoured vehicles since it can deliver an overflying top attack or direct attack, like the Javelin.

In addition to these weapons that were deployed in the rifle companies, the battalions in BAOR have also always had specialist anti-tank platoons, equipped with heavier weapons. In the early years all the Royal Anglian anti-tank platoons in BAOR and elsewhere were equipped with six Wombat 120mm calibre recoilless guns. The name Wombat came from Weapon Of Magnesium Battalion Anti-Tank. This was one of the largest recoilless anti-tank

ARMOURED VEHICLES

Learning to live in vehicles and acquiring a mechanised mobility mindset was always a challenge for soldiers trained as infantry, but one to which the Regiment was able to rise when called upon to do so. For most of the time, the mainstay of the mechanised infantry was the FV432 armoured personnel carrier. The scale of issue of FV432s changed at different times, but by and large each section of eight men had their own vehicle, so four in each platoon and 14–16 per company. A battalion would have around 70–85+ FV432s. This tracked armoured box had certain advantages in that it was easy to drive, had plenty of room in the rear and best of all had a boiling vessel in the rear door. The 'BV' as it was called, was by far the most popular feature of the vehicle as hot water was almost always available, meaning that a brew was never far away. The disadvantages of the FV432 included an annoying tendency to shed its tracks, particularly when driven around corners without sufficient care – they seemed to shed tracks much more easily than other armoured vehicles. Getting the heavy track back on by hand, usually in mud, in the dark and pouring rain was never an easy task. Other disadvantages were that it was under-armed, with just a pintle-mounted GPMG, although an armoured GPMG turret was later introduced to some vehicles. They were also relatively thinly armoured, but this potential vulnerability was fortunately never put to the test. From 1987 the Poachers were equipped with the much better protected and armed Warrior.

Mechanised infantry battalions had a range of other vehicles, including specially adapted support versions of the FV432s for firing 81mm mortars and Wombats and for recovering other vehicles. For most of the period a mechanised battalion was equipped with eight Scimitar Combat Vehicle Reconnaissance (Tracked) or CVR(T). Sometimes mis-named a light tank, the Scimitar was and is an excellent reconnaissance vehicle, indeed it has been so successful that it was still in service in 2014. With good acceleration and manoeuvrability, plus an effective and versatile 30mm Rarden cannon and a very useful thermal sight called the Battlegroup Sight, the only real limitation of the vehicle is that it is lightly protected. This can be overcome by careful fieldcraft and tactics, although those Scimitars deployed to Afghanistan have now been up-armoured. At various times mechanised battalions also had a handful of Ferret scout cars, used for liaison and reconnaissance tasks, the Stalwart amphibious truck and a range of other trucks.

All mechanised battalions had a company-sized unit of Royal Electrical and Mechanical Engineers (REME) known as the Light Aid Detachment (LAD) attached to them. They provided expert advice and skill in maintaining the vehicles.

Lance Corporal Thorpe of the Poachers in command of his FV432 in BATUS in 1988; note the GPMG turret.

Poacher Warrior, 1999.

Lance Corporal Colton and Private Thompson of the Poachers with their Scimitar in 1987.

guns ever fielded; other nations tended to use the US 106mm or the Soviet 107mm. The large calibre allowed the Wombat to fire a High-Explosive Squash Head (HESH) warhead, which comprised a bag of plastic explosive and a base fuse. On hitting the target armoured vehicle, a 'cow pat' shape was formed by the explosive, which when detonated from behind by a fuse in the base formed huge shock waves which scabbed off pieces of armour from the inner face, sending them flying around inside the vehicle. Even if this did not happen, detonating such a large amount of explosive on the target vehicle did a great deal of other damage: shaking up the crew, knocking off antennae, shattering sights and breaking tracks. The Wombat used a .50in spotting rifle to check the range, and was effective out to 600m, but only at shorter ranges against fast-moving targets. The Wombat was popular with its crew; despite the large back-blast which made it hard to conceal, it was reasonably portable with a crew of three or four, could be mounted to fire from the FV432 and above all was appreciated for the impressive effect of the large warhead. Some units in the early years used the Wombat's obsolescent predecessor, a similar 120mm weapon called the Conbat, from Converted Battalion Anti-Tank. Between 1974 and 1978 the 1st Battalion had a short encounter with the Vigilant, an early but unsuccessful anti-tank guided missile. The Vigilant was never deployed to Germany, however, and was taken out of service by 1978.

Poachers with a Carl Gustav in the 1960s.

In September 1978 the Viking Anti-Tank Platoon, then under command of Captain Jonathan Borthwick, was the first unit in the British Army to adopt a new anti-tank guided missile called Milan. Milan was the first semi-automatic command to line of sight system in service with the British Army. To fire it, the operator just had to keep his cross hairs on the target, the system did the rest. Initially deployed with a 103mm HEAT warhead, Milan was later upgraded with an advanced-technology 115mm warhead. It had a maximum range of 1,950m, but needed a minimum range of about 400m for the system to gather the missile.

Poachers firing a LAW 80.

Viking Wombat live firing in 1966.

The real advantage of Milan over previous systems was that it could consistently and easily hit moving targets that other weapons could not, especially at longer ranges. With a crew of just two, it was man-portable and easy to conceal with a small firing signature. Soon after introduction into service, an early thermal image sight called the Milan Infra Red Adaptor was added. This was the first thermal sight deployed to the battalions and it gave an additional surveillance capability that was much used and much appreciated. It was a great weapon, the only drawbacks being a long flight time of 12 seconds to maximum range and later a problem with enemy decoy counter-measures. This popular weapon stayed in service for almost 30 years until it was replaced by the Javelin in 2006. Milan platoons increased in size until, with a maximum of 20 ground-mounted and four vehicle-mounted firing posts deployed, they were almost the size of a company.

A smiling Private Charles with an entrenched Viking Milan in 1997.

Mechanised battalions received a vehicle-mounted version of Milan from 1984 which had a turret with two ready-to-fire missiles mounted on a Spartan chassis, called Milan Compact Turret or MCT. This vehicle was meant to add anti-tank capability to the forward screen, so was usually deployed with the Reconnaissance Platoon, forward of a battle group. One tricky feature of the MCT was that the commander had an image intensifier night sight but the Milan gunner had a thermal sight, which meant that they were literally looking at the world from different viewpoints or wavelengths. There were therefore many comedy conversations between MCT gunner and commander along the lines of: 'You must be able to see it, right on the corner of the wood?' 'No, I am looking at the wood and there is nothing there'. This was resolved by training and practice.

SOCIAL LIFE

One final but important point on soldiering in BAOR concerns social life. Flights back to the UK and days on leave in the UK were restricted so that most time off-duty was spent in Germany. The role of the NAAFI and the Corporals', Sergeants' and Officers' messes as the focus of social activity was therefore relatively more important than when soldiering in the UK. It has to be said that to some extent this was fuelled by the fact that no tax was paid on alcohol or cigarettes consumed in these institutions, making 'booze and fags' around half the price they were in the UK and around a third of the price they were in Germany. Many members of the Regiment nevertheless enjoyed many nights out in German towns, especially in Celle where the long-standing connection with the Regiment meant relations were good. There was always an element of hazard, however, as the German police were notably unforgiving, and the language barrier could cause some issues. Some of the married quarters were on army 'patches' but many others were often integrated into estates in German towns. This meant that married men were generally more 'at home' in Germany than single soldiers, especially as so few members of the Regiment spoke German.

BERLIN AND GIBRALTAR

Sergeant Alf Todd leads
7 Platoon of the Poachers
route marching in the 1981
Inter-Platoon Competition.

BERLIN

Throughout the Cold War period, Berlin was a geographical anomaly, a Western enclave right in the heart of East Germany. This situation stemmed from the Potsdam Conference during the Second World War, which mandated that at the end of the war the occupation of Berlin would be divided between Britain, USA, the Soviet Union and France. The three Western powers cooperated between their sectors, and later the Berlin Wall separated them from the Soviet sector. As relations between West and East cooled after the war, the Soviets cut off all land communications to the city from 24 June 1948, resulting in what came to be called the Berlin Blockade. The Western response was the Berlin Airlift, which daily flew in 4,700 tons of supplies needed by the population of over three million, a considerable logistical achievement.

Both the 1st and 3rd East Anglian Regiments served in Berlin, the 1st in 1960–61 and the 3rd in 1964, so they became Royal Anglians while in Wavell Barracks in Berlin. By this time the political situation was more stable, and although there was a requirement to train for operational deployment should the Cold War go hot, the role in Berlin also had a significant ceremonial component. There were just two postings to Berlin for the Regiment, the 3rd Battalion forming there in 1964 and departing in August 1966 and the 2nd Battalion in Montgomery Barracks from August 1978 to January 1981.

Each of the Western countries contributed an independent brigade to the defence of Berlin with the British Brigade being made up of three infantry battalions, an armoured squadron and various support units. Understandably, the Berlin Brigade tended to specialise in fighting

BERLIN

FRENCH
ZONE

Tegel ✈

1

2

13
Wavell
Barracks

12

3 4

BRITISH
ZONE

5 6 7

EAST
BERLIN

Gatow ✈

Tempelhof ✈

Montgomery
Barracks

8

AMERICAN
ZONE

9

10

11

Schönefeld ✈

1.	Bomholmer Straße/Bösebrücke West Berlin and BRD citizens	8.	Sonnenallee West Berlin citizens
2.	Chauseestraße/Reinickendorfer Straße West Berlin citizens	9.	Walthersdorfer Chausee West Berlin citizens and foreigners to Schönefeld Airport
3.	Invalidenstraße/Sandkrungbrücke West Berlin citizens	10.	Checkpoint Bravo/Dreilinden/Drewitz Autobahn transit to BRD
4.	Friedrichstraße Railroad station	11.	Griebnitzsee/Wannsee Rail transit to BRD
5.	Checkpoint Charlie/Friedrichstraße Foreigners and diplomats	12.	Heerstraße Non-autobahn transit to BRD
6.	Heinrich-Heinestraße/Prinzenstraße BRD citizens	13.	Staaken/Spandau Rail transit to BRD
7.	Oberbaumbrücke West Berlin citizens	14.	Stolpe/Heiligensee Autobahn transit to BRD

● Crossing points
◉ Crossing points existing in 1961
✈ Airport
▬ The Wall

in built-up areas (FIBUA) and both the Pompadours and Poachers developed considerable expertise in this role during their time there. Due to the location, tension was always rather high and Warsaw Pact troops could often be seen, in some cases just across the street. There were a number of incidents over the years as East Germans were killed while trying to escape to the West, which put a hard edge on the situation. The battalions always had their war stocks of ammunition available at short notice and underwent frequent practice call-out deployment exercises, the largest of which was called *Rocking Horse*, after the code word used.

Although the main training areas were in Berlin's many forest parks such as the Grünewald, in later years there was also the use of a FIBUA training village in the US sector. There were many opportunities to train with US and French infantry and armour, which added an element of variety, as the battalions and indeed the Berlin Brigade in general had a reputation for training very hard. There were also many training competitions that tested the full range of military skills of all the units and the battalions were also able to train regularly outside Berlin, normally as companies, by rotation at least once each year.

A Pompadour Ferret scout car by the frontier in 1966.

Lieutenant Dick Tewkesbury leads 1 Platoon of the Pompadours through the Grünewald during the 1966 Berlin Brigade Test Competition.

FV432 with Fox Turret.

The battalions were not mechanised, being dismounted 'leg infantry' better suited to FIBUA, but at various times some armour was included. In the earlier years this consisted of Ferret scout cars and Saracen armoured personnel carriers. In later years, it included a novelty in the form of the FV432 Fire Support Vehicle. This was an FV432 armoured personnel carrier with the 30mm gun-armed turret from a Fox armoured car on top. All the armoured vehicles in Berlin sported a unique camouflage scheme consisting of rectangles of grey, white and brown, which was specially adapted to their FIBUA environment.

Because of its location in the middle of East Germany, there was a requirement for all the Western troops in Berlin to show the flag regularly, so a large and important ceremonial occasion was created: Allied Forces Day. This large parade was held annually in June, and over the years an element of competition built up, with not only national pride but regimental pride in the drill at stake. Many members of the Regiment will remember the rather 'relaxed' style of some US Army drill contrasting with their own. During one drill rehearsal in 1979, a US master sergeant was heard to ask a Poacher company sergeant major, 'Gee, how do you get your guys to stand so still all the time?' The reader can perhaps imagine the response.

Christmas was usually very cold in Berlin and seems to have been especially memorable. After training so hard, the battalions also seemed determined to play hard when not on duty. *Castle* records the Pompadours' Christmas 1964 celebrations:

In Berlin, Christmas festivities, which began on 15th December, were now in full swing. A Battalion concert, organised by Colour Sergeant P. South, provided three hours of hilarious entertainment. Other activities such as an All Ranks Dance, Civilian Staff Parties, the Sergeants'

ELEPHANTS AT THE BERLIN WALL

About six months before the 1979 Berlin Tattoo, a major British biennial event, each of the resident battalions was asked to submit an idea for an act, featuring either their history or culture. Lieutenant Colonel Patrick Stone, the commanding officer, discussed this with his command team and the consensus emerged to propose an idea that was so outlandish that it would be turned down flat. Eventually they decided to propose a re-enactment of the role played by their forebears the 10th of Foot at the decisive battle of Sobraon in the First Anglo-Sikh War of 1846, featuring massive fortifications, huge artillery pieces towed by elephants, and as a finale, the gigantic main gates of the fort smashed to pieces by the elephants. Sadly, they had grossly underestimated the financial and engineering resources available to the Berlin Tattoo, and the ambition of Michael Parker, the experienced event organiser. To the Poachers' horror, the proposal was accepted with alacrity.

A few months later the first rehearsal took place on the Montgomery Barracks hockey pitch, when six nervous elephants were introduced to 60 equally nervous Poachers. The Poachers were under command of Major Colin Groves but the elephants were commanded by Bobby Roberts, elephant master supreme, and were oblivious to orders from anyone else. The lead elephant was a canny beast named Maureen. The fact that the hockey pitch was located immediately adjacent to the Berlin Wall and overlooked by a large Soviet guard tower was only to dawn a little later.

The idea of this first rehearsal was to introduce the two gun-towing elephants to their special harness and then carefully hitch them to the giant siege guns, and if all was well, to walk around amongst the soldiers to get both sides used to each other. It was only then that they learned the secret of elephant training – elephants have to copy a leader. Watched by the other elephants, Maureen was led forward and harnessed, and then led gently around the siege gun. All appeared well, and the signal was given to hitch the gun to the harness. With the gun only half-secured, Maureen decided that enough was enough. She had spent the last two days cooped up in a giant transporter, and suddenly here was grass, blue skies and space.

With the cannon bouncing along behind her, she headed for a small strip of woodland running alongside the Berlin Wall. Luckily, the other five elephants were still shackled, but even so, made strenuous efforts to follow their leader. Maureen was chased by an enraged Bobby Roberts and a horrified Major Groves. The cannon smashed to pieces against a tree, and relieved of the encumbrance she raced towards the guard tower. The commanding officer was just wondering how to explain this border incursion, when luckily she was cornered against the wall, and shamefully turned around to face her master.

In between smacks on the trunk, Bobby delivered a telling off which made even the hardened Poachers cringe. Eventually a crestfallen Maureen – eyes down and ears drooped, her every move by this time being followed and no doubt reported by the guard tower – was led back to the hockey pitch, and started again. From then on she never put a foot wrong.

Most of the Poachers serving at the time would have taken away fond memories of this event and of the final performances, except perhaps Lieutenant Jim Badger who, as he was in charge of the 'enemy' Sikh contingent, had to be defeated repeatedly on the ramparts.

A famous picture of the Poachers' re-enactment of the battle of Sobraon for the Berlin Tattoo.

SPANDAU PRISON GUARD

One of the more interesting duties in Berlin in 1964 was guarding Spandau Prison. The prison at that time housed three of the original seven senior Nazis imprisoned following the Nuremberg Trials: Rudolph Hess, Hitler's deputy; Albert Speer, Minister of Armaments; and Baldur von Schirach, who set up the Hitler Youth and as Governor of Vienna was later responsible for the deportation of thousands of Jews.

Responsibility for the Spandau guard rotated monthly between the four powers and the guard comprised 38 men. On an international handover day the old and new guards paraded facing each other; when handing over, the British commander would say: 'On behalf of Her Britannic Majesty, I delegate you responsibility for the safe-keeping of Spandau Military Prison. Old Guard to the New Guard Present Arms'. This was followed by a lunch, attended by the two guard commanders and the prison directors, their deputies, wardens, administrators, doctors and interpreters of each of the four powers. At one of these Lieutenant Colin Groves tested the strength of allied relations by explaining to the French officer the significance of the Essex Eagle. The American found this hilarious until told of the Regiment's forebears' part in burning the White House. The Russian thoroughly enjoyed what he had heard and presented Colin, as an evident good friend of the Soviets, with a bottle of vodka. Guard duties, meticulously covered by international agreement, were tedious, involving such restrictions as no talking to the prisoners. The prisoners were seen regularly in the garden and on one occasion, a fight was witnessed over a wheelbarrow, which ended with Hess soaking the others with a hose. Hess also wrote rude slogans about the Regiment in the snow. Six watchtowers were manned, one of which was reputed to be haunted. The NCO for that stag often selected a nervous young soldier for this tower, who would express his terror at being locked into that watchtower. One such soldier screamed into the phone that he had heard the ghost scratching on the window, only to then hear the words: 'Got a fag, mate?' It was one of the other guards, who had scrambled along the wall from a neighbouring watchtower. In later years Hess was the only prisoner. Following his suicide in 1987 the site was bulldozed, to be replaced by a NAAFI complex that was nicknamed 'Hessco's'.

Mess and Corporals' Mess draws and the troops' Christmas Luncheon all helped to make our final Christmas in Berlin one which will be long remembered.

The Poachers' second Christmas in Berlin, in 1980, was described in *Castle*:

Christmas was celebrated with a Battalion Carol Service and carols were sung around the quarters on Christmas Eve. The officers and sergeants served the soldiers with their Christmas Dinner and once again, many thanks are due to the chefs who prepared an excellent meal. The generous hospitality of the West Berliners and our own 'pads' [slang term for married soldiers] ensured that many of our single men had Christmas 'at home'.

With the end of the Cold War leading to German reunification in 1990, the rationale for the Berlin Brigade evaporated, and it was disbanded in 1994.

GIBRALTAR

The strategically important rocky promontory of Gibraltar was captured by British forces in 1704 during the War of the Spanish Succession and has remained in British hands ever since, despite several major sieges. It is only some 2.6 square miles (6.7km²) in area but hosts a population approaching 30,000. The Regiment has had a long-standing relationship with Gibraltar, stemming from the great siege of 1779–83, when the French and Spanish tried to exploit Britain's preoccupation with the American War of Independence to take the fortress.

Modern aerial photograph showing the distinctive landscape of Gibraltar.

Royal Anglian cap badge.

Three of the Regiment's forebears were at this great siege: the 12th, 56th and 58th Regiments of Foot, which became the Suffolk, Essex and Northamptonshire Regiments, and then eventually all became Royal Anglian. The 12th, 56th and 58th Regiments served throughout the long siege and they were each awarded the battle honour 'Gibraltar'. In addition, they were also awarded the honorary distinction of the Castle and Key, which remained a symbol of the Suffolk, Essex and Northamptonshire Regiments, through their incorporation into East Anglian then Royal Anglian Regiments, and now forms the centre of today's cap badge.

From the formation of The Royal Anglian Regiment, the first unit to serve in Gibraltar was the 2nd Battalion under command of Lieutenant Colonel John Akehurst, from December 1968 to August 1969. The 4th Battalion, by this stage reduced to company strength as Tiger Company, under command of Major John Heggs, was resident in Devil's Tower Barracks from January to July of 1972. The 1st Battalion served as the resident battalion in Gibraltar from January 1987 to February 1989, initially under command of Lieutenant Colonel Mike Walker, OBE, later handing over to Lieutenant Colonel John Sutherell, MBE. Service on 'the Rock', as Gibraltar was known, consisted of a mixture of ceremonial duties including the unique Ceremony of the Keys, useful low-level training in the somewhat unusual but limited rocky setting, overseas training in Portugal and extensive adventure training and sport.

By far the most notable security incident in Gibraltar took place on 6 March 1988 when IRA terrorists Danny McCann, Sean Savage and Mairead Farrell were shot dead by the SAS. From the Regiment's point of view, it was somewhat chilling as the probability was that the Viking Mortar Platoon under Lieutenant Alan Wylie and Band and Drums may have been the

B Company of the Poachers on guard in Gibraltar in 1969 – Private Muncey, Sergeant Warrington, Private Rheumer and Private Cross.

target of the car bomb as they changed the guard at the Governor's Residence. The Vikings were not involved in the build-up to this covert operation, called Operation *Flavius*, but they were heavily involved in providing security after the event.

The Regiment has always had a close affiliation with the Royal Gibraltar Regiment, and a formal alliance was established in 1968 during the Poachers' time there. When the Vikings left the Rock in 1989, some members of the Regiment chose to transfer to the Royal Gibraltar Regiment and remain there. To this day there are members of the Gibraltar Regiment attached to 1st Battalion. By 1991, regular troops had withdrawn from Gibraltar, leaving the Royal Gibraltar Regiment as effectively the resident battalion.

Second Lieutenant David England leads 5 Platoon of the Vikings on their first Ceremony of the Keys in 1987.

THE ROYAL ANGLIAN WAY

This half-mile pathway along the edge of the natural escarpment of the Rock was originally created by the 2nd Battalion in 1969. It has a series of vantage points with spectacular views and it rises to some 200m on the western side. As it does not come under the category of a nature reserve, its maintenance is not financed. However, it is in continuous use and regularly receives maintenance attention from the Regiment. For example, Company Sergeant Major Dave 'Necky' Riley took a party of

Essex Army Cadet Force to visit the Rock in 2010. He wrote in *Castle*:

> But armed with the knowledge about their Regiment and what they fought for, the cadets took part in cleaning, weeding and restoring the path and the Royal Anglian sign. The task itself took two full days, but the hard work was definitely worth it.

Poachers working to create the path in 1969.

Company Sergeant Major Riley and the Essex Army Cadet Force at the Royal Anglian Way sign, 2010.

Private Galliano of the Royal Gibraltar Regiment serving with the 1st Battalion on Operation *Herrick 6* in Afghanistan.

CYPRUS AND BELIZE

CYPRUS

The Regiment has had a long affiliation with the sunny island of Cyprus in the eastern Mediterranean. Lying some 65km south of Turkey, the island's population has risen from around half a million in 1964 to just over a million in 2013. Approximately 80% of the population is Greek and 20% is Turkish. The ownership of the island has long been a source of dispute between Greece and Turkey; it became a British Protectorate from 1878, then a crown colony from 1925 to 1960, becoming independent within the Commonwealth afterwards. A civil war rumbled on between the Greek and Turkish factions from 1955 to 1960 and flared up occasionally thereafter, especially in 1963, which triggered the deployment of a UN peacekeeping force called UNFICYP the following year. In 1974, following a coup, Turkey invaded the northern part of the island, causing the Greek Cypriots there to flee south. The UN eventually established a peace line between the two sides but not before more than 4,500 Cypriots died.

The early UN tours were full of incidents as Greeks and Turks fired at each other and occasionally at the UN forces across the buffer zone. The British garrison is based in two separate areas called Sovereign Base areas: Western at Akrotiri and Eastern at Dhekelia. Royal Anglian battalions have been based in both of these or have undertaken UN peacekeeping tours as shown in the overleaf chart:

Corporal Graham of C Company, the Poachers on exercise in Cyprus, 1966.

BATTALION	DATE	BASE
2nd Battalion	October 1964–July 1967	Eastern
3rd Battalion	October 1969–April 1970	UNFICYP
1st Battalion	March 1972–May 1974	Western, one company to Eastern
3rd Battalion	February 1976–February 1978	Western
3rd Battalion	November 1980–May 1981	UNFICYP
2nd Battalion	December 1983–June 1984	UNFICYP
2nd Battalion	February 1998–March 2000	Eastern
2nd Battalion	August 2010–August 2012	Eastern, Theatre Reserve
3rd Battalion Company Group	March 2011–October 2011	Operation *Tosca*, UNFICYP

Sadly, three Poachers died in Cyprus in the early years. Private Kenneth Atkin was killed in a road accident in December 1964, then Corporal Herbert Jackson and Lance Corporal Malcolm Boothright were killed in an ammunition explosion, along with four policemen, in February 1965. Three Pompadours also died on duty in Cyprus on later tours: Private David Newstead on 11 February 1970, Staff Sergeant Trevor Bodenham on 28 April 1976 and Private Keith Stacey on 26 April 1977.

By the 1980s the peacekeeping efforts were proving effective and the number of incidents declined. As tourism in Cyprus increased in the 1980s and then further in the 1990s, both sides came to realise that they had more to lose by renewing the conflict, so the situation gradually became calmer. UNFICYP is still, however, deployed and the buffer zone is still in place, although it is now possible to carry out many of the policing tasks unarmed.

In March 2011 a novel deployment took place for the Regiment as the Steelbacks deployed to police the buffer zone on an operation called *Tosca*. Under command of Lieutenant Colonel Richard Lyne, the Steelbacks took over Sector 2 of the buffer zone. The mobilisation and pre-deployment training activities were complex, but eventually some

273 personnel were deployed with the group in total, mainly Steelbacks but with many attached personnel. The battalion headquarters were based in the Ledra Palace Hotel, which was also the headquarters of UNFICYP in the capital of Nicosia, through which the buffer zone runs.

Operations Company was 120 strong and under command of Major Mark Bevin, again mostly Steelbacks but with other units attached. Their mission was to prevent a recurrence of the fighting and to maintain a stable environment, which they accomplished by patrolling their 30km stretch of buffer zone on foot, and by quad bike, 4x4 vehicle and helicopter. Their area was broken down into three platoon sectors: east, centre and west. With approximately 10km of buffer zone per platoon, they were stretched thinly. The platoons worked through a rotation of day patrols, night patrols, guard and standby and other duties. They had an Argentine UN contingent on their western boundary and a composite Hungarian and Slovak contingent to their east. Liaison with other UN, Greek and Turkish units also formed an important part of this operation, as did the hosting of various visitors. The Steelbacks completed a successful tour of Operation *Tosca*, returning to Bury St Edmunds in October of that year.

Pompadour on UNFICYP duty, 1970.

Major Mark Bevin about to conduct an air reconnaissance, with an Argentine pilot.

The Chinese Deputy Chief of Staff thanks Lieutenant M. Hart of the Steelbacks for a tour of the buffer zone.

The nature of deployment to Cyprus changed again in 2010 as one of the infantry battalions based there was designated as 'Theatre Reserve Battalion' with a view to being deployed to Afghanistan as reinforcements at short notice if required. The 2nd Battalion, under command of Lieutenant Colonel Ralph Wooddisse, MBE, MC, undertook this role from August 2010

Steelbacks on their UN Medal Parade.

STEELBACK IN CYPRUS

Poachers training for IED clearance.

to August 2012 based in Dhekelia. Being theatre reserve meant that the battalion had to be fully trained and ready to deploy on operations, which also entailed a programme of in-theatre training in Afghanistan to keep them up to date. The challenge of maintaining these skills at high readiness to a high standard for a long period was considerable, but the Poachers succeeded notably, earning themselves a good reputation with commanders in Afghanistan. The Poacher sub-units were brought up and down the states of readiness several times, but in the event they did not actually deploy to Afghanistan. They later switched to a more normal Cyprus operations role, before relocating back to the UK in August 2012.

Corporal Fields of the Poachers directs casualty evacuation training.

The relatively well-appointed Holdfast Camp, 1982.

BELIZE

Belize is a small state on the east coast of Central America, bordered by Mexico to the north and Guatemala to the west and south. Originally a Mayan region, it was conquered by the Spanish in the 16th century before coming under British influence in the 19th century, becoming the crown colony of British Honduras in 1862. It received independence in 1981. The threat posed to Belize by Guatemala, which had made several claims to Belizean territory, led to the deployment of British troops there from the 1970s. Having seized power in Guatemala in June 1982, José Efraín Ríos Montt tried to take advantage of British focus on the Falklands War to mount a series of 'sabre rattling' events with highly visible troop movements, featuring old M5 Stuart light tanks, up to the Belizean border as mock thrusts. It is likely that there were also covert incursions made into the Belizean jungles by small teams of Kaibiles, the Guatemalan special forces. The British battalion based in Belize had two roles: deterring the Guatemalans by acting as a trip wire to discourage any invasion; and supporting and developing the local force, the Belize Defence Force.

The aftermath of the Falklands War threw the normal regular deployment and rotation of British forces, called the Arms-Plot, into some disorder. Consequently, the 3rd Battalion, then based in Colchester under command of Lieutenant Colonel Alan Thompson, MBE, MC, received very short notice that they were to deploy to Belize in May 1982 for seven months to take the place of the 2nd Battalion of The Parachute Regiment, who had been deployed to the Falklands. With no time for any pre-training, on arrival the battalion split into two battle groups, each of two companies with attached artillery. Battle Group South occupied Salamanca Camp with A Company inland, and Rideau Camp near Punta Gorda on the coast with D Company and Battalion Headquarters. Battle Group North, which also had attached Scorpion light tanks, occupied Holdfast Camp near the town of San Ignacio inland with C Company, and Airport Camp near Belize City on the coast with B Company. This last was

Lieutenant Colonel Alan Thompson, Pompadours (left), hands over to Lieutenant Colonel Tony Calder, Vikings in September 1982.

also the main logistics base and the location of 1417 (Tactical Ground Attack) Flight of the RAF with their six Harrier GR3 aircraft, which provided a considerable deterrent force. A handful of Army Gazelle and RAF Puma helicopters were also based there, providing

Members of C Company, the Pompadours, with their Belize Defence Force friends.

essential air mobility in a jungle-covered country with a long border covered by very few troops.

A noteworthy handover between battalions of the Regiment then took place in October 1982, as the 1st Battalion under command of Lieutenant Colonel Tony Calder arrived out from Oakington, also at short notice, to take over. The Vikings deployed in a similar way to the Pompadours for their six-month tour, but with their A Company in Holdfast, B Company in Salamanca, C Company and Battalion Headquarters in Airport and Support Company in Rideau camps.

Both battalions had a very similar experience in Belize. The normal routine was to mount a programme of patrols: some normally of a longer duration along the Guatemalan border in the deeper jungle areas, combined with shorter duration patrols in the more populated areas. Typical long-range patrols might be of 12 men for nine or more days at a time; while the shorter patrols, often of an eight-man section, typically lasted two or three days. With temperatures peaking at 30°C, and with 90% humidity, the climate presented some special challenges. The Belizean jungle provided the battalions with a very different soldiering environment and some spectacular sights, especially on the central mountain range. There were Mayan temples, a natural arch where two rivers flow from opposite directions into a sinkhole, jungle peaks, dense foliage in almost impassable ravines and lots of gigantic trees. Much of the training and patrol work was carried out jointly with the Belize Defence Force, with whom the Regiment got along well, so well in fact that a formal alliance was established with them in 1988.

In addition to patrol tasks, there were two permanent observation posts overlooking the

The Mayan temple of Xunantanich near the town of San Ignacio in Central Belize, which was occasionally used as a temporary observation post.

Sergeant Charles 'Chico' Duncan of 7 Platoon, B Company, the Vikings, by a maize store in a southern village, November 1982.

Corporal Chris 'Soapy' Soames and Lieutenant Steven Bowns of 1 Platoon, A Company, the Vikings, share a joke on the Holdfast helicopter landing site prior to a long-range patrol in 1982.

Guatemalan border, called Cayo in the north and Tree Tops in the south. These were manned permanently by a section or more, by rotation. In addition the camps themselves had to be guarded, along with a host of other duties. Many live-firing exercises were carried out on a set of ranges in the central highland area called Baldy Beacons, because they were not jungle covered.

Special equipment was issued for the tours comprising a lightweight camouflage suit of shirt and trousers, US Army jungle boots and a floppy brimmed jungle hat. Most patrols were armed with a commercial variant of the US Army 5.56mm M-16 automatic rifle called the AR-15, although most would also take at least one GPMG. Because it had automatic fire, was very reliable in mud and rain and was a much more handy patrol weapon in jungle terrain, the AR-15 was usually preferred, although the SLR was used on occasion. Most troops would

carry a Bergen backpack – the Army issued a frame Bergen at this time but many soldiers bought their own personal commercial Bergens. Other bespoke equipment included a hammock, mosquito net and a lightweight poncho that enabled soldiers to sleep above the ground. It was highly inadvisable and usually not really possible to sleep on the insect-infested ground in the jungle, although many tried it once. Another novelty was the extensive use of High Frequency (HF) radios, using the Clansmen PRC 320 radio. This was necessary due to the long distances and difficult terrain, but it came with some interesting side effects such as a communications blackout at sunset as the ionosphere polarised. Communications were often difficult, requiring the occasional use of morse code and the rigging of some novel styles of antenna, often involving wires strung from very tall trees.

There was a regular and memorable programme of rest and recuperation, which could involve short trips to the coast to visit the spectacular Cayes or the occasional weekend in San Pedro across the Mexican border. Many Pompadours and Vikings will also remember the Belikin Brewery just outside Airport Camp, which organised frequent tours for the troops, usually followed by

POMPADOUR OR VIKING IN BELIZE, 1982

Poachers in jungle equipment with SA80s on Exercise *Panther Cub* in 2002.

a few free crates of beer, except for one notable occasion when one platoon sergeant, who shall remain nameless, famously took half his platoon to the brewery for a tour on the wrong day. Some said that this finally proved what many had said before, that he could not in fact organise a booze-up in a brewery.

Although there were several minor border alarums and excursions over the year, no actual engagements took place and no fatalities were suffered. However, many medical issues arose from soldiering in a tropical jungle. In addition to the threat of a Kaibiles incursion, there were a number of other jungle wanderers including drug smugglers, and local bandits, some of whom were known as Chicleros after their habit of collecting the sap of the chico tree, which used to be an ingredient in chewing gum. Most patrol encounters, however, were with the local population, and the Regiment's usual restraint and politeness with a tough edge worked well in this role. The 1st Battalion returned to Oakington in April 1983. Throughout their tour the Commander British Forces Belize was a former commanding officer, Brigadier Tony Pollard. By 1994 the threat had subsided to such an extent that the commitment was reduced to just a training cadre to support jungle exercises. Belize is still an excellent training environment for jungle warfare and continues to be used as a location for these activities, for example in 2002, when the Poachers deployed for a six-week jungle exercise called *Panther Cub*.

MILITARY AID TO THE CIVIL AUTHORITIES

O ver 50 years the Regiment has carried out a host of tasks that come under the category of Military Aid to the Civil Authorities (MACA), which is the generic term for the different types of aid and assistance given by the military to the civil authorities.

Company Sergeant Major Bartlett and his car-cutting crew of Poachers.

MILITARY AID CATEGORIES

MACA is divided into three categories depending on the sort of assistance called for. Each has its own legal status and parameters for the employment and participation of troops.

Military Aid to the Civil Power (MACP) heads the list as aid given in the most serious situations and usually consists of helping the civil power, i.e. the government, to maintain law and order. While troops deployed are usually unarmed, for MACP they may well be armed. The Army's deployment to Northern Ireland is an extreme example, but the Vikings' involvement in the disturbances at Greenham Common described in this chapter is an example of MACP at a lower level.

Military Aid to the Civil Community (MACC) covers situations where the local community is the recipient of the aid

being given. It is usually a local authority that requests and co-ordinates the assistance. This is generally associated with natural disasters or major accidents such as snow clearance, forest fires or flood relief. The help given in the Norfolk floods described in this chapter is a classic example.

Military Aid to Government Departments (MAGD). Here the aid is being given to a government department that finds itself unable to cope with the situation confronting it. Examples include the services' involvement in the Glasgow rubbish strike of 1975, the foot-and-mouth epidemics of 1967 and 2001 and several firemen's strikes of which the story in this chapter is but one example. The use of troops during the 2012 Olympics is another example.

FLOOD RELIEF IN SOUTH NORFOLK

The Bungay–Beccles area.

This four-day task supporting the community was initiated at short notice on 17 September 1968 when Second Lieutenant John Sutherell was ordered to take his platoon of Poachers from their barracks in Felixstowe to Loddon in south Norfolk to help the local police with flood relief operations. This account is based on his article in the May 1969 *Castle*. They knew very little of the situation when they deployed, other than that as a result of heavy rain, the River Waveney had overflowed its banks and flooded the area between Bungay and Beccles on the Norfolk–Suffolk border. On arrival the platoon was briefed by the local police inspector and they settled into their new home, the Geldeston village hall, for the night.

Next morning they got on with the main task, which was helping families to clear the mud from their houses, disinfect, and dry them out. This work could only be done once the floodwaters in the area had subsided sufficiently, so they began in the village of Ditchingham to the west. With the water level falling slowly, it was two days before they could make a start in Geldeston. In addition to this main task, it became clear there was also a need for an emergency meals service as the electricity had been cut off as a safety precaution, and those families that had refused evacuation were in any case confined to the upper storeys of their homes. Norfolk County Council provided meal containers and the Poachers used an attached Royal Engineer Stalwart amphibious truck and their own 3-ton truck to take these

The flooded main road at Loddon.

meals out to the families. The Stalwart also provided a bus service along the flooded Gillingham–Beccles road for shoppers, schoolchildren and people getting to and from work. The four days went quickly and the troops got along very well with the local people. Second Lieutenant Sutherell wrote:

Nevertheless, as time passed it became apparent that our help was being sincerely appreciated. Shortly before we left, my driver Private Cross, a veteran of 'foot and mouth ops'[1], maintained that he had never seen such warm relations between soldiers and civilians.

COVERING A FIREMEN'S STRIKE

We will next look at an example of the provision of cover for the long-running firemen's strike of 2002 to 2003. The 2nd Battalion was to have a very busy two years in 2002 and 2003. Based in Chepstow at this time, the Poachers had deployed to Belfast on an operation called *NIBAT 4* from May to December 2002 in support of the Police Service of Northern Ireland (PSNI), who were having trouble maintaining order. Consequently, when the Fire Brigade Union announced that strikes would start in December, the Poachers were suitably placed to pick up the task of providing cover for fire-fighting in Northern Ireland. The whole provision of cover was named Operation *Fresco*, with the Northern Ireland component called Operation *Fresco (Zulu)*. The morality of the firemen's strike has always presented an element of irony to the troops, who have to work very hard re-training and providing cover, but whose terms of service are considerably less favourable than those of the striking firemen. Nevertheless, the Poachers approached this complex task with their customary cheerfulness. The additional difficulties of the security situation – although much calmer than earlier decades – were still an important consideration.

Poachers training with a hose on Operation *Fresco*.

The command arrangements were complex too, with each of the brigade areas allocated a Poacher company headquarters, then a joint operations control centre established with the PSNI headquarters. There were many issues in establishing the temporary service fire stations, ranging from additional force protection requirements to a 'South Armagh Problem'. This last came from the fact that it was still deemed too dangerous to operate the Yellow Goddess fire engines in South Armagh, so an airborne fire fighting and rescue service had to be established. Northern Ireland had different emergency fire engines to the mainland – Yellow Goddesses instead of Green.

The Poachers started their training in September 2002 at RAF Aldergrove where in the main they provided the force protection element to other units providing the fire and rescue services, although they also trained on the fire-fighting equipment. The unpredictability of the union's negotiations and strike-calling added difficulties, and in the end the Poachers had to deploy to cover a one-, a two- and an eight-day strike. The majority of the actual call-outs were hoaxes and lures in Belfast and Londonderry, but they dealt with a range of real incidents: house fires, road traffic accidents and industrial accidents. Just as Operation *Fresco (Zulu)* was coming to an end, the Poachers were warned off for another Operation *Fresco* deployment, this time fire-fighting in Strathclyde. Captain Chris Davies, the operations officer, described in *Castle*:

> *NIBAT 4* was unlike any other operational tour anyone had previously completed. It seemed a swirling cocktail of counter-terrorist, public order and fire fighting operations.

The Poachers handed over in Northern Ireland on 4 December and enjoyed a short but well-earned period of Christmas leave as the Fire Brigade Union announced that there would be no more strikes until the end of January. By 2 January 2003 the Poachers were assembling in Glasgow to form the Strathclyde Fire and Rescue Group. This was just as well because, against all expectation, a strike was called for 21 January. This put a great deal of pressure on the Poachers, who again rose to the considerable training challenge to ensure that they were fully prepared in time. The Strathclyde Fire and Rescue Group was some 850 personnel strong, drawn from all three services, with the Poachers providing the command and control and logistical infrastructure and some 25 Green Goddess crews, based in 18 fire stations. On their second night of cover an immense blaze in Glasgow city centre required the attendance of five

Green Goddesses, and a tanker full of aerosol propellant crashed and caught fire on the M74, which required the deployment of specialist equipment in the form of an aerial water tower. Captain Guy Foden, of D Support Company, described the city centre blaze of 30 January in *Castle*:

> There were a number of problems confronting the crews – the sheer size of the building, its proximity to a student hall of residence and its prime location which ensured considerable interest from the press and local residents. In all 300 people had to be evacuated before the real business of fire fighting began. As the fire took hold a request was made to the striking firemen for assistance as there was a real fear that the fire might spread, thereby devastating the commercial heart of the city. Unfortunately this request was turned down leaving the Poachers and their attached BART crews on their own.
>
> Water was rapidly directed onto the fire but, as the fire spread, Sergeant Clarke soon realised that the Green Goddesses' pumps were not able to reach the top floor of the building. Luckily Private Mason of the Mortar Platoon provided a solution which involved attaching the hoses to the roof of the vehicles. By quick thinking and the reactions of the crews the extra range was achieved, thereby preventing the fire from spreading. Admittedly his solution was not pretty, the hoses being directed by a whack from a pick helve, but it worked.

Just as their month in Glasgow was coming to an end, the Poachers were warned off for a third task under Operation *Fresco*, providing Breathing Apparatus and Rescue Teams (BART), which would require yet more specialist training. The Poachers' BART training took place at the MOD Central Fire Service training establishment at RAF Manston in Kent and it lasted for about five weeks for each individual, starting in February 2003. B Company, under

Poachers undertaking BART training.

command of Major John Wright had been scheduled to carry out Exercise *Mayan Warrior* in Belize at this time but this had to be cancelled because of the BART task. The BART training was based on individuals going through a progressive course, and then forming into teams. The training was intense, carried out in shifts over 24 hours for six days a week on a two-shift day and night system, with a staggered start to optimise the use of the facilities. A whole host of fire-fighting skills were imparted and tested on exercises and specific tests, as Lieutenant Simon Poulter recalled in *Castle*:

> There were several milestones on the course, a good one was the 'live carry down'. This involved carrying another person down a ladder from a second storey window. On paper this seems like a straightforward enough exercise but negotiating a window sill with a person on your back is definitely hard work

Other exercises involved mock road traffic accidents, dealing with a range of different types of fires using the Green Goddesses, and working with a host of other equipment. Once their training was complete, the Poacher BART teams were deployed all over, some to Northern Ireland (D Support Company), others to South Yorkshire and Humberside (C Company), Wales (HQ Company) and the West Midlands, Shropshire, Staffordshire, Hereford and Worcester and Hertfordshire (B Company). In total some 272 Poachers were BART trained.

Negotiations to end the strike started in March 2003, and by 12 June an agreement was reached and the dispute came to an end. Thereafter the Poachers were gradually stood down from their BART tasks and returned to Chepstow, just in time to start training for their next tasks. A Company under command of Major Simon Etherington had already deployed to Kabul in February 2003 on Operation *Fingal*. The Poachers, along with most of the rest of the British Army, were exceptionally busy at this time. Drummer Stephens, writing in *Castle* described this time as:

> Busy – that's what it's been for the last six months! One minute we were recruiting around Dunstable, Cambridge and Luton areas – which was very successful – the next we were off to Northern Ireland for the fire strikes.

The Poachers emerged from this busy period with their reputation for cheerfulness in adversity considerably enhanced and having demonstrated flexibility and professionalism in taking on and succeeding at so many disparate and complex tasks, in a blizzard of activity.

VIKINGS AT UPPER HEYFORD AND GREENHAM COMMON, 1983

The last example of military aid was a more controversial deployment. In 1977 the Soviet Union deployed a highly accurate intermediate-range missile, the SS-20, against targets in Western Europe. This destabilised the nuclear balance, and in December 1979 NATO agreed to deploy Pershing II and cruise missiles in Europe to re-set the balance. The UK government agreed to base cruise missiles in the UK. It was planned for these to arrive in 1983. This decision saw an increase in support for the Campaign for Nuclear Disarmament (CND), which increased its activity targeted at US nuclear weapons based on British soil. The main focus of the protest was the proposed base for the cruise missiles, at Greenham Common in Berkshire, around which the protestors established several improvised camps. However they also demonstrated at RAF Upper Heyford where the United States Air Force

(USAF) based their F-111 bombers which constituted NATO's primary nuclear response until the Pershing II and cruise missiles were established.

The USAF guards for the F-111s and their nuclear weapons were equipped with live rounds and would open fire in accordance with their strict rules of engagement if required, as indeed the British troops providing nuclear site guards would have done in Germany. Guarding NATO nuclear weapons was a serious matter and testing this guard to distraction was clearly of interest to the Soviet Union at this time. Knowing this, the CND protestors sought to get themselves into a situation that would severely test the US guards' response; almost seeming to want to force the US guards to shoot some of them. The connections between the CND movement and far-left-wing groups, some of which were linked to the Soviet Union, added complexity to an increasingly dangerous political situation.

The difficult situation was in the hands of the local police, but as time wore on they struggled to halt every attempt to breach the perimeter fence and protesters found their way onto the airfield on several occasions. The solution was clever: unarmed British troops were deployed to form an inner cordon around the USAF nuclear guards while an outer cordon, also of unarmed troops, patrolled just inside the perimeter fence. Any protesters getting through the police would be intercepted first by the outer cordon, and any who managed to break through that were caught by the inner cordon, removing the danger of protesters getting close enough to the nuclear weapons to force the US guards to open fire.

The 1st Battalion, under command of Lieutenant Colonel Tony Calder, deployed from their home at Oakington near Cambridge, first to Upper Heyford USAF base in Oxfordshire for a week in May 1983, where large numbers of CND protesters were expected to attempt to blockade the base. In the event, relatively few protesters appeared and, after a wet and muddy weekend, the protest was not sustained. The Vikings returned to Oakington after a week in rudimentary accommodation, very well looked after by the USAF, but otherwise not overly taxed.

In the following months, however, as the planned arrival of the cruise missiles approached, trouble at the main protester site at Greenham Common increased. The Vikings were one of four battalions deployed to assist in the perimeter defence of the Greenham Common airfield to ensure the cruise missiles were flown in without interruption. Arriving on 6 November 1983 for a two-week spell, the whole 1st Battalion were again deployed. Once the missiles had arrived safely, the other units were thinned out, leaving the Vikings with the responsibility for the whole perimeter. There were several unsavoury incidents with the protestors. One memorable event involved a typical 'little old lady' character who wandered around the perimeter chatting to the troops for several days, befriending them and posing as a grandmother-type character, handing out the odd sweet and playing on the troops' natural sympathy. However, she carried a large handbag in which was concealed a tape recorder and microphone, and she recorded many of her conversations with the Vikings without their knowledge. Cleverly edited, these 'highlights' were then broadcast on the local radio station causing some minor public relations embarrassment. The Vikings' response was to ban all talking on the perimeter – a considerably difficult order to enforce as the boredom of manning observation posts and pacing up and down the perimeter fence for long hours was increased significantly by not even being able to have a chat. However, enforced it was, and the Vikings did not talk again on the perimeter fence. Within A Company, Sergeant Glyn Brooks bore the brunt of having to enforce such a difficult and unpopular order, but his effectiveness ensured that there were no further public relations incidents of this type. Company seniors and Battalion Headquarters staff walked the perimeter regularly to talk to those on watch to help relieve the boredom, but also to explain 'the reasons why'. Notwithstanding the circumstances there was an understanding that the

Battalion was, in an indirect way, defending the rights of those who wished to protest and protecting them from the worst consequences of their actions.

This benign approach was not always reciprocated; another disagreeable incident arose during one attempted breech in the perimeter fence. A group of protestors gathered and stated shaking the fence, prompting a response from 3 Platoon. Alerted by the radio, the platoon commander, Lieutenant Simon Rees, arrived promptly on the scene with reinforcements and started explaining the situation to the women, pointing out that even if they broke through the fence, they would just be arrested. However, the incident was a set-up, and the protesters hurled several plastic bags at the fence. The bags, which were full of urine, burst on the fence and showered Lieutenant Rees and those standing near him. Some saw the funny side of this incident, but being treated like this by 'peace protesters' was very galling at the time. Thermal imagers were deployed for the first time by the Vikings in the form of two Chatelaine devices on tripods. Although these were first generation, so somewhat primitive by modern standards, they were an effective addition to the surveillance capability, particularly as some early morning mist tended to obscure the view of the IWS image intensifiers that were then in use.

By the end of their deployment in the last week of November, the Vikings had provided an extremely effective outer cordon, preventing all the attempted penetrations of the perimeter fence in their sector. After the Vikings had departed, there was a large break-in during December when several thousand protesters cut sections of the fence and hundreds of arrests were made, but no protester ever got close to the USAF nuclear guards.

NOTES

1. 2nd Battalion was heavily involved with the 1967 foot-and-mouth epidemic.

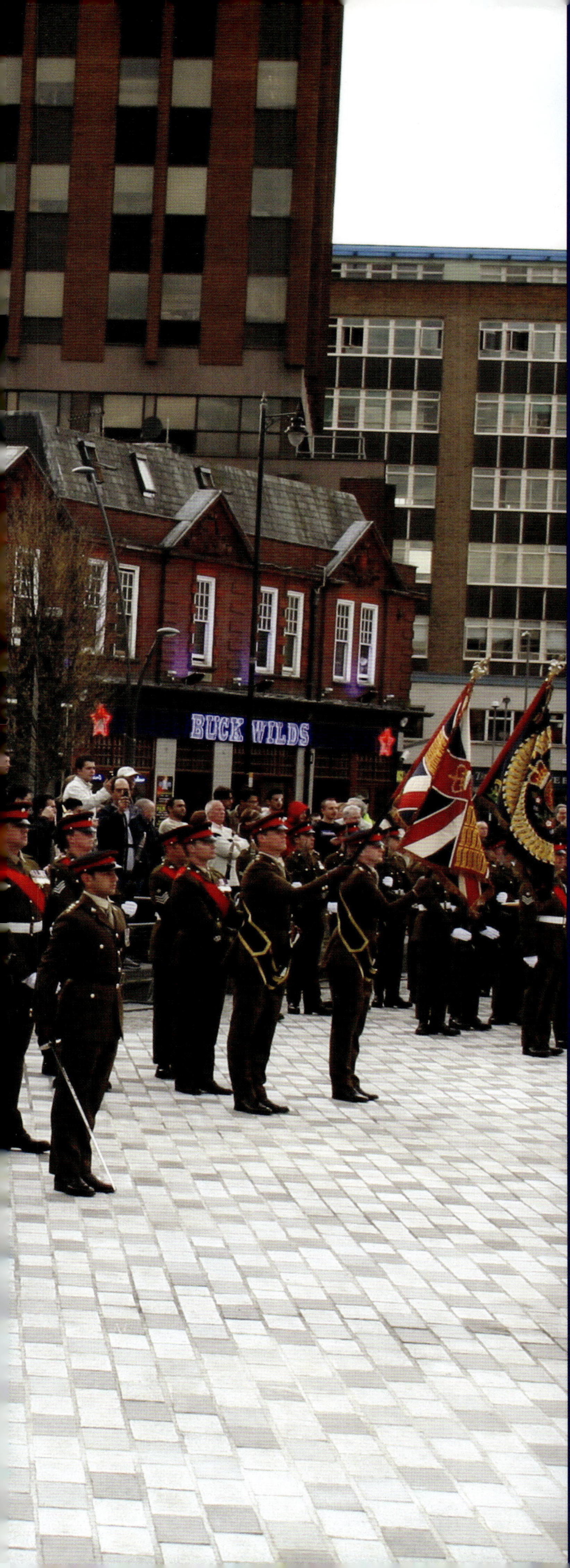

THE REGIMENT'S FAMILIES

Poachers on parade in Luton.

THE REGIMENT'S FAMILIES

Life in the infantry is demanding, not only on those who serve but also on their families. In this section we will examine some of those aspects of life that impact upon the families of the Regiment, who often bear a great but possibly under-publicised burden. The families are also a huge source of support, which is known and appreciated within the Regiment but not always grasped outside it. Family life has of course changed a great deal over the last five decades so some of these changes will also be examined.

FAMILIES ABROAD

Today, accompanied family postings abroad are almost a thing of the past. Only Cyprus and Germany remain and by 2020 there will only be Cyprus. In the early years families abroad lived in 'Little Englands', experiencing very little contact with the local community. They were subject to military law and had little independence from the Army. This was a less liberated age. On all forms women were referred to as 'Wife of…'. They lived in flats or houses supplied by the Army; they gave birth in military hospitals; their children were christened in garrison churches and went to military schools; they shopped in a British shop – the NAAFI (and in Berlin in the 1960s paid with Army money) and watched English-language films at a military cinema. Either because of the language barrier or the frequency of postings, job opportunities were few and far between. Not having their own home often resulted in long stays with parents or temporary accommodation in military hostels. A host of facilities and activities was developed to cater for the fact that families were far from home. Although living in such close-knit communities resulted in strong and long-lasting friendships, living in such proximity also had its disadvantages.

For all battalions a large percentage of the 50 years has been spent in Germany, much of it during the 30 or so years of the Northern Ireland campaign, meaning that the men were frequently away for four months at a time leaving young wives caring for small children in blocks of flats in isolated places. In the 1960s and 1970s very few had cars. Instead of family round the corner to turn to, there was a hard-pressed Families Officer – now known as the Welfare Officer – and a small staff. He was supported by officers' wives, who by tradition were expected to care for the welfare of the families of their husband's

The Colonel of the Regiment with Mrs Jones, Major General Porter, Regimental Sergeant Major 1st Battalion, Commanding Officer 1st Battalion, and Mrs Guy at the Drumhead Service at the Regimental Gathering at Duxford on 1 September 2013.

soldiers. However, as the social changes of the 1960s and 1970s took hold, many senior non-commissioned officers' wives started to play a more and more important part in providing this vital support, especially as they provided continuity. There was often a hierarchy of wives' clubs overseen by the commanding officer's wife supported by the wives of the company commanders and senior non-commissioned officers.

Penny Dixon arrived in the battalion in early 1982, and remembers her experience as the wife of a Pompadour company commander:

> Shortly afterwards, as a result of the Falklands conflict, the men left with no notice for Belize. Having trained as a nurse and midwife I felt reasonably confident in taking on the welfare role of the Company Commander's wife. I was soon taken under the wing of the Sergeant Major's wife who told me what to do.
>
> I visited all my wives at the beginning of the tour asking them to coffee at our quarter and then to regular coffee mornings at a centre on the camp. With only a few wives it was amazing how many problems I encountered; the raiding of the electric meter due to lack of money, the taking in of a different partner to the consternation of the overseas husband, the possible annexation of a quarter by the in-laws, to name a few. On visiting the Families Officer with one problem I was told it was an old trick to try to get a husband home – I felt very naive.
>
> The men, having returned from Belize, then went on exercise in USA after 2–3 months. I rode on my bike round all the wives once again but several could not even come to the door. They looked very sheepish a few months later when we met at the same antenatal clinic.

She also remembers the impact of Army life on her small son:

> One problem I had was with my 3-year-old who watched all the men leaving for the Falklands and then returning on *John Craven's Newsround*. Over a few weeks he got quieter and quieter until I eventually found out that he was convinced his daddy had died as he thought his daddy, having left at the same time, should have come back at the same time. It is easy to forget the effect Army life has on children.

FAMILIES OFFICER, 1970s

Captain Tony Downes was the Pompadours' Families Officer for their 1972 Belfast Tour:

You very quickly learn that dealing with families requires a good deal of flexibility and amenability and sometimes the need to throw oil on troubled waters. As always we never have enough staff to deal with everything when the battalion is deployed, but with the collaboration of company commanders' wives and the more senior wives of the Sergeants' Mess most personal problems could be solved. I must say that having served in other units, the family spirit of the infantry battalion is much to be thankful for. The ability to deal with day-to-day problems is a 'must' as it gives peace of mind not only to individual soldiers but also to their commanders who have their minds on operational commitments.

Deployed or not, the routine of the job does not change. Handover/takeovers of married quarters, reception and departures of families, 'get-you-in packs', have they been adequately housed? The list goes on. Including the families of attached personnel at one time we had over two hundred families to administer. All of that makes boring reading I know, but there was a lighter and more enjoyable side to the job. I have forgotten the number of younger children who referred to me as 'Uncle Tony' and the production of chicken and chips and sausages and chips washed down by gallons of ice-cream at least once a month became routine while 'Dad' was away. I was eternally grateful to the Messing Officer and the catering staff. It made a welcome break for unaccompanied 'mums' and the children thought it was great and it proved once more that teamwork always pays dividends.

The ladies of the Battalion have a lot to contend with and in the majority of cases they deal with all the turbulence of being married to a soldier admirably. That was certainly my experience. The lads go off and 'do their thing' operationally and get medals for what they do and quite right too. However, I have always thought that if anyone deserved a 'gong', the ladies do for their patience and management skills dealing with life on the 'Home Front'.

MARRIED LIFE

Married life in the Army in general has always been very different from the normal experience of the institution. There are some unusual challenges and rewards, and we will use an example to highlight of some of these aspects. Many people in the wider regimental family will know Jenny Bullock and her husband Stan, a true regimental character who served in all ranks from private to major and in just about every battalion in the Regiment, both regular and territorial. As Stan had in effect two careers, and spent nearly twice as long in the army as most, their experience is not entirely typical.

Jenny and Stan were teenage sweethearts and the story of Jenny's married life starts before formation day when, at the age of 20, she married Stan, who was then a sergeant. He was posted to the territorial D (Cambridgeshire) Company of the Suffolk Regiment in 1958, based at Coldham's Lane in Cambridge. She clearly remembered that in those days, everything you needed was included in the married quarter – furniture, crockery, pots and pans, bed linen – there was no need to buy anything. When she moved in, everything was immaculately laid out and spotlessly clean; the previous occupiers had even whitewashed the coal shed. Jenny remembers that this handover set a high standard that started her off well, and she tried to live up to it for the rest of her married life in the Regiment. It was always more stressful to handover a quarter on leaving than to takeover on arrival. Jenny recalls that the actual handover process was just something that had to be adapted to – go along with it and try to enjoy it – otherwise you would just make yourself miserable. Later she learned to leave handovers to Stan, partly out of preference but also out of necessity as she had to look after the children. Their posting to Londonderry in Northern Ireland with the 1st Battalion in July 1970 was especially difficult because Ebrington Barracks and the married quarters had

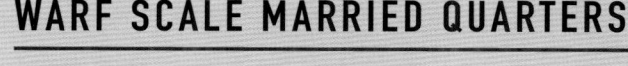

WARF SCALE MARRIED QUARTERS

In those early days army married couples did not really need many possessions as almost everything was provided by the Army. This was called 'Warf Scale' at the time; it included all the furniture, bedding, crockery, cutlery and cooking utensils, everything a family needed. By the 1980s, however, this Warf Scale was scaled back so that married quarters only came with the furniture.

Kitchen of a married quarter in Tidworth, 1966.

previously belonged to the Royal Navy, and many of the quarters were in appalling condition. In the house they took over in Campsie, a small village east of Londonderry, her cooker was in such a terrible state that Stan had to start the clean-up process with a big, wire, engine-cleaning brush.

An early posting was to Iserlohn in Germany, just after the merging of the Royal Norfolk and Suffolk Regiments as Stan was posted back to the battalion. There was a lack of married quarters, and along with several other families from the battalion, they spent the first three months in the Bahnhof Hotel in Iserlohn. This was quite a difficult time because their daughter Tina was only 15 months old and German hotels of the era were not renowned for their child-friendliness. They were then posted to Berlin when the 1st East Anglian Regiment (now 1st Battalion) moved there in January and February 1960, and the family moved into a married quarter in the Charlottenburg district of Berlin. A run-down area far away from the barracks, it was not a great place for a young mum with a toddler, indeed the area was still nicknamed 'Grotty Charlotty' by the troops many years later. Eventually, Jenny was able to move to a better quarter in the Kladow district, which was much nearer to Montgomery Barracks. This proximity was important because much of their social life revolved around the Sergeants' Mess, which was always inside the barracks.

At the end of the tour in Berlin, Jenny remembers that a whole trainload of 1st Battalion wives and children had to assemble at the railway station at 06.00. They got off the train at the Hook of Holland 16 hours later. Jenny had Tina and five-week-old baby Glenn with her while one lady had five children with her. Entertaining and caring for children on a train for so long without the help of their husbands was not easy, but the wives helped each other and made the best of it. These arrangements might seem odd looking back, but it was just the way the Army did things at that time.

On arrival in Harwich in 1962, there were again insufficient married quarters. With the battalion soon to be posted to British Guiana (now Guyana) for an eight-month unaccompanied tour, Jenny moved in with her parents for a year.

The kids were four and two when the family flew out to Aden in early 1964. Jenny remembers that there were a few security problems, but the insurgents posed no direct threat to the families. The tour was not without its moments, though. The men were paid weekly, but were deployed into the Radfan for two or three months at a time, so a minibus parked on a back road of Ma'alla Straight each week to hand out the housekeeping money. The

BRITISH MILITARY TRAIN

Land transport to and from Berlin was carefully monitored through 'the corridor', a narrow rail and road link that crossed East Germany. The rail link was used by the British Military Train, operated by the then Royal Corps of Transport, which came with its own set of rules and regulations. Families also used this train.

Private Richard Aves, 3rd Battalion, during his tour of duty on The Berliner, the regular troop train carrying British personnel from West Berlin, through East Germany to the West.

housewives queued up, with locals wandering about everywhere. Jenny never really felt threatened or frightened and the children seemed to enjoy the exotic environment.

After some nine months in Aden the Bullocks were posted to the then 4th Royal Norfolk Territorial Army at King's Lynn. Jenny remembers enjoying this posting; their quarter was next door to the drill hall and although Stan was very busy, especially at the weekends, the family had a settled and happy two-and-a-half years. The family had moved house some nine times in seven years of marriage. This almost nomadic lifestyle was one of the costs of being promoted, as it meant that in addition to moving frequently with the battalion, the family moved for individual postings. Nine months in Celle, north Germany was followed by a return to Catterick before moving to the sunshine of Cyprus with the 1st Battalion in March 1972. The family was not long in Cyprus, however, as Stan was promoted to Regimental Sergeant Major and posted to the 3rd Battalion by special request of the commanding officer, Lieutenant Colonel Hall-Tipping, who wanted Stan as his RSM for the 1973 Creggan tour.

They were made very welcome by the 3rd Battalion. Jenny was very busy because, as the RSM's wife, she was effectively a social worker for the battalion, keeping an eye on the wives and making sure the wives' clubs and their activities were well organised and ran smoothly. She and Stan were already friends with Captain Tony Downes, the 3rd Battalion Families' Officer, which was a great help. Jenny relished this role, made lots of friends, many of them lifelong, and thoroughly enjoyed this time.

Stan was next commissioned, promoted to Captain then posted to the 2nd Battalion in Münster in Germany; a year later the family returned to Gillingham in the UK. During this posting Tina started work, married Tom Wesley of the Poachers and moved out. With Glenn staying in Gillingham to complete his schooling, Stan and Jenny left Gillingham alone – they bought a labrador. After time in Leicester, Colchester and Minden, the couple were back in Northern Ireland, posted to the 5th Battalion of the Ulster Defence Regiment (5 UDR). The house in Ballykelly, near Campsie, was larger, but they did not now need all the bedrooms. It was a strange time for Jenny as she did not know any of the UDR wives, and being in Ballykelly on her own without the children was not the happiest time. The situation improved greatly when Tina's husband Tom was posted to 5 UDR, and she was on the next patch. Their last postings were to Zimbabwe and then to Grantham with a quarter in Bassingbourn, before Stan retired from the Army.

The Bullock family in 2007.

Looking back over some 34 years of married life in the Army, overall Jenny has fond memories. It is the children, the friendships and sense of community that sustain, but all Army wives go through some tough times of loneliness when their men are away. Jenny and Stan moved house some 19 times in their married life in the Army. Jenny and Stan Bullock now live in blissful retirement in an idyllic setting in a small village in Suffolk. This author thinks they thoroughly deserve it.

Tina Bullock while at school.

SCHOOLING

A major disadvantage of service life used to be the schooling of the Regiment's children. It was not unusual for children to change schools every 18 months to two years. However good the school – and service schools had and still have a very high reputation – this inevitably had an effect on the child's education.

Jenny and Stan Bullock's children, Tina and Glenn, each went to some eight schools, and both got seven O Levels. They spent time in local schools, and also Service Children's Education schools in Germany. It wasn't always easy for them: when the family moved to Münster, Glenn was 15 and he did not really want to go to the new school – his sixth – because it had a poor sporting record. He stopped trying for a while, but soon got on with it. When the family moved next, to Gillingham, they had no say in which school Glenn went to; instead the local authority allocated him a place. Glenn was not too pleased to be allocated to an all-boys' school, but again he adapted quickly and settled down. He was happy there and got seven O Levels. Jenny recalls that despite the risks of moving schools so often, both Tina and Glenn have turned out as well-rounded people. Tina always says that what she lost on the swings she gained on the roundabouts – meaning that while there were

Kate Woodrow aged 11.

disadvantages, there could also be benefits to moving so regularly, such as increased self-reliance and confidence, but it very much depends on the child.

Although local schooling was available to all service children, the disruption caused by frequent school changes caused many parents to make the agonising decision to send their children away to school, sometimes when they were as young as seven. Today with almost no overseas postings and longer stays in one place, the problem is not as great as it was, but it still exists. Kate Robinson (née Woodrow) and her brother Patrick grew up in the Pompadours. This was a painful and difficult story to tell for Kate, so it is told entirely in her own words:

I was nine when I made my first unaccompanied flight and seventeen when I made my last. I don't like remembering those early journeys. The first, to and from Berlin were the worst. Matron asked me if I was ready to go and had packed my things, but I hadn't because I didn't know what to pack, overwhelmed by the task. I cried because I didn't know what to do while she put my teddy and pyjamas in the little white case. I didn't know there were loos on the 'plane and I held on for the whole flight. I remember that more than arriving at the airport and seeing my parents waiting. And I remember arriving at our new house for the first time, only it wasn't new for the others because they had already been living there a while and that felt strange.

On arriving back in London I will never forget the overwhelming sense of loneliness when that little white case appeared on the belt, open, with my things spilling out. I vaguely remember the ground crew lady in charge making light of it but I vividly remember how much it mattered to me.

To start with I was on my own, but when he was old enough, I was joined by my brother, but even then we did not always travel on the same flight and it was so much worse when I had to go first. It was always the same. Two or three days before the end of the holiday a solid dread would appear in my stomach. Then there was the ritual of packing the suitcase with school uniform and whatever else was allowed while my mother sewed name tapes on new stuff. The drive to the airport, whether Dusseldorf, Hannover or Wildenrath, always seemed to take forever. We were always quiet while my father tried to be cheerful and failed spectacularly. After check-in I never knew whether it was best to get it over with and say 'goodbye' as quickly as possible or hang on till the last minute. Although I was usually in tears I hated seeing my parents shed the occasional tear too. It was not much better at 'the other end' – usually Luton – where I would be met either by grandparents or an aunt and driven to school. Again, I was usually quiet while Granny or Auntie Patricia tried unsuccessfully to cheer me up.

As I got older it did get easier, even fun, especially if there were other children on the flight. Sometimes there were hoards of us and most of the other children seemed to enjoy the adventure. There was always much bravado and confidence and I remember the older children buying duty free cigarettes to sell at school and bolster their pocket money.

All that was thirty-odd years ago. If I think about those flights now, they still seem like yesterday and I found it difficult to write this. I always vowed I would never marry anyone in the Army and my children would never go to boarding school. But I did, and they do. As an adult, putting our elder daughter, aged 10, on a 'plane and driving home in an empty car to a quieter house while that great metal machine took her away was one of the hardest things I have ever had to do. But when you are very young you don't question whether you like what is happening, you live in the moment, accept it and get on with it. I hope she doesn't remember her first journeys too painfully when she is my age and I vehemently hope if I have grandchildren they don't have to fly the nest so young.

THE 'LOLLIPOP SPECIAL'

Patrick Woodrow aged 12.

The Lollipop Special was a nickname given to flights from Germany to the UK just before the start of school term as they were sometimes almost entirely full of schoolchildren. The departure lounges were full of upset children, reluctantly leaving their parents behind to go to boarding schools in the UK. There were tears and worse as the children had to say goodbye, occasionally approaching almost a collective hysteria. Some children, however, seemed to enjoy the flights. Patrick Woodrow, now in his 40s, remembers:

> Flying to Luton from RAF Wildenrath was more like catching a bus than a plane.

There were no queues at check-in, your parents could wave you off from the gate, and being in the middle of an RAF base, there was virtually no security. If my bag was x-rayed I don't remember it. I used to collect empty GPMG cases from ranges and take them back to school but I am not sure I would get far with a handful of those in my luggage today. Flying in and out at the beginning and end of term gave you some small but unequivocally valuable degree of status at boarding school. Luton wasn't quite as prestigious as Heathrow and Wildenrath didn't have quite the same ring to it as Hong Kong, Lima or Nairobi – where the kids from the Diplomatic Corps lived – but the extra day of holiday that you occasionally got as a result of the charter schedule was nonetheless envied by the remaining 99% of my peers who travelled home along the M4.

You wouldn't get me near some of those old DC-10s now. Old and rickety, they made Aeroflot's fleet look like top of the range private jets. On one occasion as we arrived at Luton a section of the wing fell off and went bouncing down the runway behind us. As we disembarked, I enquired of the stewardess if we had landed or been shot down by the Russians. I was ten years old. She was not amused.

Since those days there have been major changes in society, changes that have been mirrored in the Army. Today, rather than follow the drum, many wives live in their own homes which is convenient for work and means their children enjoy the stability of staying in one home and one school; most families have a car and the relationship in the hierarchy of wives has changed immeasurably. Although now stationed at home, none of this has lessened the anxieties of the families when their men are away. With the casualties from Afghanistan these are difficult and testing times for the families, perhaps even harder than before.

WELFARE OFFICER, 2014

Captain Kevin Jordan is currently Welfare Officer of the Poachers serving in Afghanistan:

The Welfare Officer's title changed from Families Officer in 2008 allowing single soldiers to have the same level of welfare support as married soldiers with a single point of contact. This change has now given the Welfare Officer a greater responsibility in the amount of individuals that they look after, increasing from 400 to around 2,500. This figure captures all soldiers, officers, dependents and extended families wherever they live in the world.

I still take on the familiar roles such as housing issues and dependents' briefings and organising family events. This sees me engaging with the local county council, schools, social services and Neighbourhood Watch. I also advise the Commanding Officer on issues that the soldiers or the dependents may have with community engagement. I work in line with the Medical Officer ensuring that the correct Care Action Plan is implemented for every individual who needs extra support with any medical issue, whether physical or mental. This is ever-more present now the Army is actively trying to combat Post Traumatic Stress Reaction. I spend a lot of time with the Casualty and Compassionate cases that arise both on and off operations.

With the battalion deployed on operations it is my responsibility to ensure that the soldiers and the dependents have the correct level of briefings prior, during and after the tour relating to the tour and the effect that it will have on the individual and the family dynamic. To further enhance the welfare provision that is provided for the families whilst their loved ones are away, I provide a 24-hour dedicated team to assist with literally everything from hospital trips to putting fences back up after strong winds. Trying to provide a link and keep the passage of communication open between the chain of command and the families that are left behind is vital and we use Facebook, e-mail, text and the good old-fashioned monthly newsletter.

Life is very busy for the Welfare Officer and the one thing that I am sure has not changed is that 'you never know what your day will bring'.

In addition to the established organisation to support the families, other informal groups have formed to provide support. A splendid example is the Viking Family Support Group, which was founded by Alison Burgess and Tracey Cadman in 2008 – when their sons were serving in the 1st Battalion. Alison and Tracey recognised that good systems were in place within the Army to support married couples and their families but there was need for help and support to members of a soldier's wider family and friends. The mothers felt that this was something that could be created by the families themselves, so they set up the Viking Family Support Group.

With the full support and backing of the Vikings' Welfare Team, Alison and Tracey launched the Viking Family Support Group (FSG) website. The website forum makes it easy to communicate with others and share information that could otherwise be hard to obtain – in fact the Welfare team has used the Viking FSG website to share information. In conjunction with Viking FSG the Welfare team held information meetings across the recruiting counties before major tours, which enabled families to meet up, receive information about the upcoming tour and meet the Welfare team.

Viking FSG also arranges social events for families and friends of soldiers. These have been particularly helpful in providing extra support for families when the soldiers have been in Afghanistan. The group has had tremendous support from the general public who recognise the sacrifices made by Army families and want to show their appreciation. Generous donations and fundraising events have enabled Viking FSG to support soldiers and their families in innovative ways, including providing casualty bags for injured soldiers, housewarming gifts to soldiers and families moving to new accommodation, and homecoming gifts to returning soldiers; supporting battalion children's events; sponsoring sporting challenges for injured soldiers; and supporting bereaved families.

BEREAVEMENT

The death of a soldier on operations is a blow to the whole Regiment, but the cost is borne most heavily by the family and those close to the person killed. The same applies to those who have been seriously injured. It is almost impossible to convey to those who have never experienced it the intensity of the sense of bereavement that comes from the sudden death of a loved one on operations. We will nevertheless try to do this important task by telling the story from the perspective of those people who have experienced such loss, using one example. We should say that they have taken part in this process willingly and have seen this text before publication, generously and courageously giving their permission for us to share this most painful of intimate experience with the reader.

Lance Corporal Alex Hawkins in his vehicle in Afghanistan.

Jan and Bob are the parents of Lance Corporal Alexander Hawkins, who was killed on 25 July 2007 by a Taliban IED, which detonated under the vehicle he was travelling in. Alex was their third child; their two daughters Terrie and Nicola were older and Nigel was his younger brother. Alex had just been home on rest and recuperation (R&R), and Jan was away, three days into running an Army Cadet camp at Wathgill, North Yorkshire when a military policeman in plain clothes gave her the terrible news. Jan remembers just wanting him to go away so she did not have to listen, she also tried to run out of the room, but had to listen. She did not want to have to believe the news. Meanwhile, back in their home in Dereham in Norfolk, Bob was collecting Alex's brother Nigel who was serving in the Blues and Royals at the time, from the station, but Nigel had to give Bob the news. This was possibly a mistake, as it may have been thought that Bob already knew, but he did not. Both parents were in shock, totally numb and not able to remember much of the next few days.

Both remember fondly the great care and compassion of Andy Garvey, Welfare Officer from the Regiment, and of Major Dean Sefanetti, who was the officer commanding the Vikings rear party, for the efficient but compassionate way that the funeral was organised. Jan remembers that they did not have to worry about organising the funeral but they were consulted every step of the way. Alex had already told his parents what he wanted, a full military funeral. Jan decided to walk out to Swanton Morley one morning to have a look at the church to see if it was big enough. Although it looked big enough initially, in the end there was extra seating outside and rows of people standing too. Bob remembers that Alex had a terrific send-off from the Regiment. The ceremony could not take any of the pain away and it was very poignant; everybody seemed to be in tears. Jan and Bob both remember the ceremony well. Jan remembers that she had promised to keep it together for the actual ceremony; it was afterwards that she went to pieces. At first it was a little easier because there was such a lot going on as they went to RAF Lyneham for the repatriation of Alex's body, then there was a weekend and a dinner with the Vikings rear party at Pirbright, so there was so much happening, this all helped a great deal. After the funeral, the box with Alex's personal effects arrived home. This was difficult, to go through Alex's things and to decide what to keep. Jan recalled:

> After the funeral it was like living in a bubble. Life goes on around you but you do not participate, you are like a spectator. Life goes on, but it goes on without you, you are not in it. His music used to get me, if I heard his favourite songs, he liked Snow Patrol's 'Chasing Cars', that used to play two or three times a week. I played it and played it to try to harden myself to it.

Jan was only 16 days into a new job, quite a technical job that required a level of concentration that she could no longer maintain, so she had to leave. Bob recalled that at first the memory of Alex was very fresh; he found himself missing him more and more as time wore on, so five years later it was, if anything, worse. He remembers:

There was the odd period when you don't remember so much, but it keeps coming back, then the pain is just as bad. You always think what might have been as well. There was talk of Alex trying for officer training at Sandhurst, but it was not to be.

At the end of *Herrick 6*, several of the people with Alex on that fateful day made contact with Jan and Bob. They both wanted to know all the details of how Alex had died, even though it was hard to hear. Their views on the military have not changed. Jan continues to do her work with the Army Cadets, is very active in fundraising for the Regiment and still recommends The Royal Anglian Regiment to anyone.

Bob commented that the whole process is a long, on-going saga; it goes on and on, there is no end to it. He said, 'The bereavement carries on, sometime just sitting down you go back, you find yourself thinking about Alex.' They both wanted to convey that there is no end point, it is not a process that comes to a logical conclusion, the sorrow is always there. It helps to talk to the serving people who knew Alex, especially those who were there at the time. Jan recalls that one of the hardest things for her was at the end of the *Herrick 6* tour when the 1st Battalion returned and carried out a freedom parade in Norwich. She recalls:

I knew they were there. I had a word with the RSM and CO, I had already spoken to them, then we walked around to the front, we could hear the band then as they came around the corner. The cheer that went up was tremendous, I just broke down. There were over 15,000 people there. I was so proud of the boys in the Battalion, but it hurt, Alex should have been there.

THE ELIZABETH CROSS

The Elizabeth Cross and Memorial Scroll are granted to the next of kin of UK Armed Forces personnel who have died on operations or as a result of an act of terrorism in national recognition of their loss and sacrifice. The Elizabeth Cross is not a posthumous medal for the fallen but an emblem demonstrating tangible national recognition for service families for their loss. The Elizabeth Cross was instituted specifically to recognise the unique challenges that service personnel face on operations and from terrorism, and the particular burden this places on service families. The award was instituted by HM The Queen on 1 July 2009 and can be granted retrospectively from the end of the Second World War.

Jennifer Burt, sister of Private Ian Burt killed in Belfast on 29 September 1972, being presented with the Elizabeth Cross on 6 January 2011 by the Lord Lieutenant of Essex.

The Elizabeth Cross, of sterling silver with the floral symbols of England, Scotland, Ireland and Wales on the arms.

We should remember these points, that Jan and Bob Hawkins are still paying the price of the Regiment's operations. They are grieving still. Nor should we forget that from Afghanistan alone there are another 14 grieving families. Fourteen more mothers or wives or next of kin, each entitled to wear the Elizabeth Cross.

THE INJURED

It is part of the Regiment's ethos that the families of the fallen are not forgotten. Nor are those of the injured. From Afghanistan alone 17 members of the Regiment have received life-changing injuries – 13 who have lost one or more limbs – and there are others from earlier conflicts. They undergo long and painful recoveries with incredible bravery, first at Selly Oak Hospital in Birmingham and then the Rehabilitation Centre at Headley Court. They remain part of the regimental family long after they have left the Regiment.

PRIVATE STEVEN GILL'S STORY

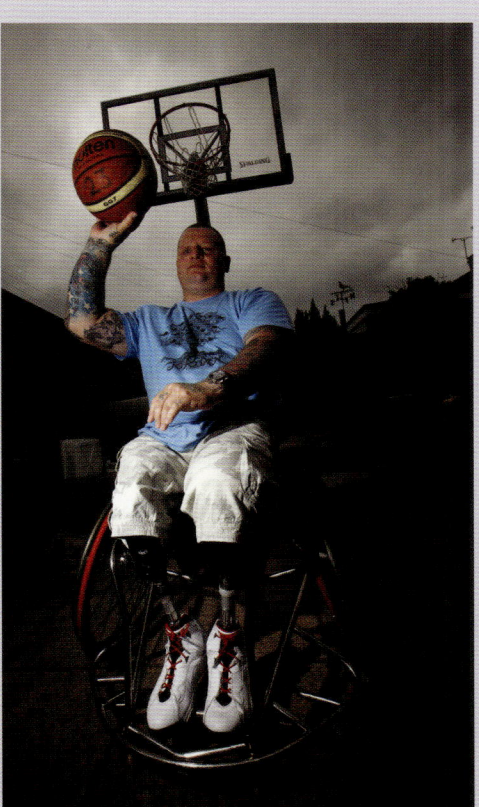

Private Steven Gill playing wheelchair basketball.

Private Steven (Fish) Gill joined B Company, the Poachers in 1986 and in May 1989 was with them in Howard Road, Belfast. He writes about his life-changing experience:

On 10 May whilst on foot patrol I was hit by an IED where I sustained the loss of my right leg above the knee and my left leg below the knee, and my right eye.

Life changed dramatically. I spent a year in Queen Elizabeth Hospital Woolwich (now closed) and had to rebuild my life. Civvy Street was very different, everything takes longer, nobody rushes. Frustration sets in and you are on your own. But BLESMA (British Limbless Ex-Service Men's Association) came calling and I started to rebuild my life through their rehab events and friendship of likeminded people. Soon it was me who was visiting newly injured soldiers and telling them my tales of adventure and fun; such things as adventure training, shooting, climbing, quad bikes, paintball fights etc.

My welfare reps Keith Meakin and then Charlie Streather, along with the wife and kids, have really pushed me along and given me the drive to be the man I am today. I have sailed the Atlantic, taken part in two Fastnet races, the Antigua 600 race and sailed across to France many times, and I have a fear of water. I have hand-cycled hundreds of miles in the UK and USA. I have played basketball for Leicester and coached for 15 years. I also appeared on *Big Brother* and that opened a lot of new doors for me, one being the setting up of my own charity Baron Motor Sports. This is the latest chapter in my life and I am as busy as ever trying to raise the profile of my charity to get disabled people to get involved in things like karting.

While doing all these things I am dad to 10 children whom I love so much. I am still campaigning for injured troops to be treated as equals when it comes to medical care and prosthetic limbs. I do a small bit of welfare work for BLESMA and my brand-new venture is to try to get to Rio 2016 as part of the GB Paralympic archery team. This is going really well and I am just about to enlist some GB coaching to help me on my way. My thanks to RHQ (regimental headquarters) for helping me with this.

SUPPORT FOR THE REGIMENT

The public support for the battalions throughout their tours in Afghanistan and Iraq, and the identification with 'their county regiment' – as demonstrated by the many thousands who turn out to welcome battalions home after an operational tour – is very important to the Regiment. The public outpouring of grief for casualties has been very genuine, as has the largely unreported support and practical help given by many of our local authorities and the social services to our injured soldiers and retired soldiers and families who need help. This is in concert with the significant, practical, charitable support from SSAFA, The Royal British Legion, the Army Benevolent Fund – The Soldiers' Charity and other service charities that provide a network of support across the Regiment's counties. This includes the Regiment's Benevolent Charity, which currently disburses some £120,000 a year to help former members of the Regiment and their families. Regimental Headquarters also plays a very significant role in all this, and provides the major link between the battalions and the counties.

In addition to the official bodies that support the Regiment, each year an increasing number of individuals and groups raise enormous amounts of money for the Regimental Benevolent Charity. Much of this fundraising is low-key but some has become high profile. The Allthe4s[1] started by Mrs Christine Bonner is an example:

In May 2007 my eldest child and only son, Corporal Darren Bonner, was killed in a landmine explosion in southern Afghanistan. My whole world fell apart and my life was changed forever. How was I ever to carry on bearing this horrific pain and heartache? But I had to keep it together for my three daughters who had also lost their big brother. Feeling I had to do something positive for Darren, I have organised walks since 2008 raising money for The Royal Anglian Regiment Benevolent Charity.

For four years from 2008, Christine undertook an annual ten-day walk of 150 miles through three of the Regiment's counties. Each year the walk became better known, and

From left to right, Jan Hawkins, Christine Bonner and Captain Ty Smith lead the walkers towards the finish.

Christine Bonner being met at the end of her 2012 walk at the Regimental Chapel at Warley by Colonel Julian Lacey and the Mayor of Brentwood.

it was not unusual for her to be met in towns and cities by the mayor, reporters and even television crews. In 2013, instead of a walk she made a sponsored parachute jump. So far she has raised nearly £200,000 – a magnificent contribution to the Regimental Benevolent Charity.

NOTES

1. Allthe4s means: 4 the boys, 4 the families, 4 the fallen, 4 ever.

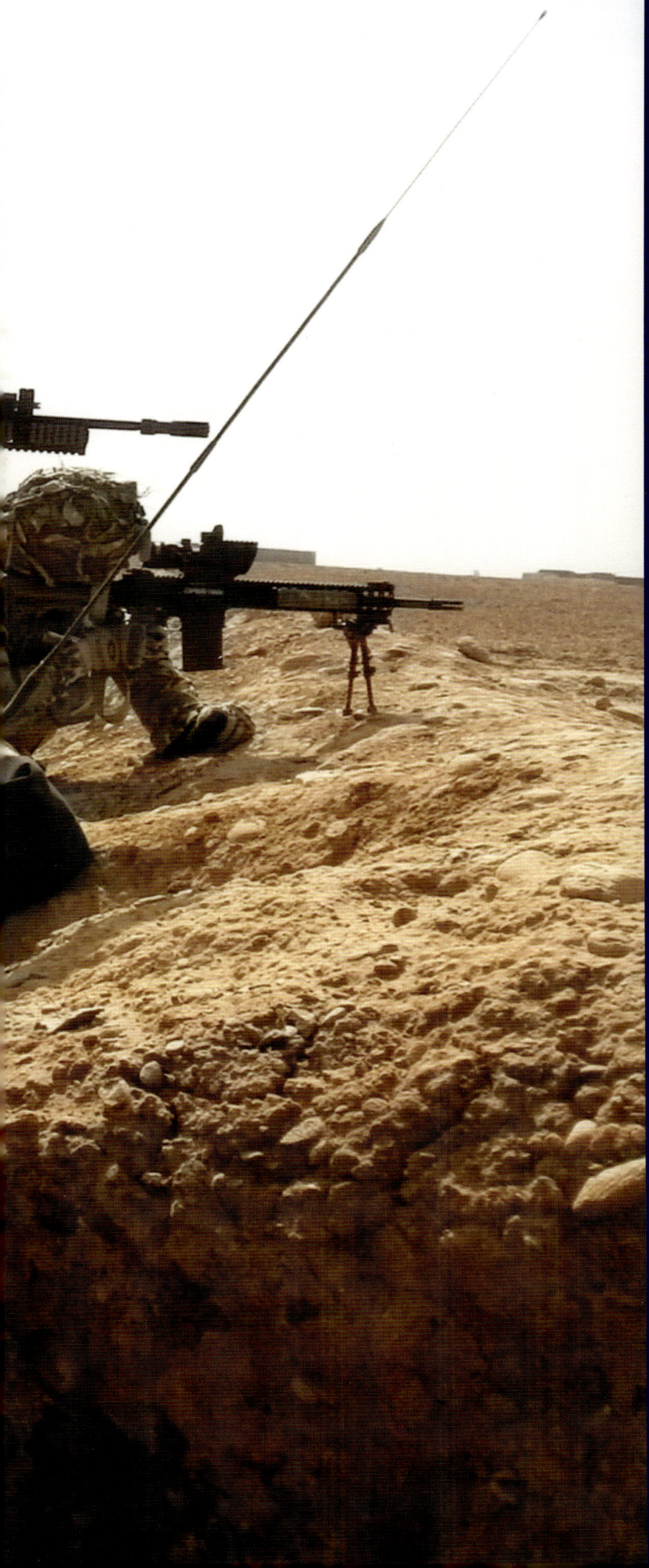

THE FUTURE OF THE REGIMENT

Major Adam Wolfe on Operation *Herrick 16*.

THE FUTURE OF THE REGIMENT

LIEUTENANT GENERAL PHIL JONES, CBE

COLONEL OF THE REGIMENT

Private Gary Lowe of 6 Platoon, the Vikings, taking up a fire position in the Nad-e-Ali area on *Herrick 11*.

This history explains the first 50 years of our regiment. We are proud that our roots go far deeper than the past five decades, and we follow in the glorious footsteps of soldiers and officers recruited from our counties over more than 33 decades. As one looks back over this span of time, it becomes clear that there have been very few constants: our regional heritage founded on local recruiting is one; reliability in battle is another. And change is another. Neither the British Army nor its component parts have ever stood still: from wars to campaigns; from peacetime eras to long periods of tension and conflict; from times of plenty to years of austerity. Since our earliest days change and reform have been ever present and part of our lives. Our ability to respond well to changes in form, function and political context has been part of our make-up, and still is. We have been buffeted by bruising change time and time again only to emerge stronger, better, more modern and more able to perform well on the battlefield.

None of us can predict the future, but we know for sure that the need for a British Army will continue beyond our lifetimes. And while the British Army exists, it will evolve to keep pace with the demands of conflict and to respond to the social, economic and political priorities of our nation. The faster conflict evolves, the faster we need to evolve to keep ahead of our foes. At the tactical level, the learning cycle is constant. Strategically, major reforms tend to happen every few years. In this sense, despite the discomfort and turbulence generated, change is more than a virtue: it is an existential necessity.

But not everything changes. The search to find technological solutions to mitigate the role of the infantry on the battlefield has so far failed. War remains, in the end, a very human struggle that more often than not requires soldiers to be present, on their feet, at the very point of conflict. Irrespective of huge advances made in land, air and sea power, in intelligence and surveillance, in our ability to wield soft and hard effects in the information domain, sooner or later someone has to pull on their body armour, fill their magazines, sharpen their bayonet, and close with the enemy. Of course, the idea that we can remove ourselves from the dirty, ugly, lethal business of the infantry fight will remain an attractive concept – and so it should. Putting the lives of our young men and women at risk must remain a last resort. But, as the 'shock and awe' concept that was used to launch the campaign in Iraq in 2003 so clearly demonstrated, we delude ourselves if we think that the infantry's days are numbered. The demand for the world's best infantry will ebb and flow from year to year. And every time a bloody conflict comes to an end people will wish away the need to do it all again in another theatre of war. Or they will hope for new methodologies and technologies that will prevent our people from coming to harm on foreign shores. But when unavoidable conflicts, despite our best efforts, require us to fight 'up close and personal' on land, infantry soldiers from our Anglian counties will be in the thick of it.

So, if we accept that the world will not stand still, and that nor will the profession of arms, what does this mean for us today?

Lance Corporal Thorpe and Private Holland in action in Afghanistan.

The Vikings on the march.

For the time being, we retain three magnificent battalions in the Army's order of battle. We are a line infantry regiment that has matured extremely well over the past five decades. In the history of the Regiment our people have never been more operationally experienced, or better trained, or highly motivated, or more committed to this noble profession of ours. Our manning remains among the best in the Army; the quality of our officer and soldier recruits is impressive; and the atmosphere of quiet, understated, professional self-confidence pervades all three battalions. Our families, our cadets, our wider regimental community of veterans, and the civic leaders in our counties form active and collaborative networks that are vibrant, healthy and incredibly supportive.

Our battalions continue to be committed to operations year in and year out. Our reputation in combat is second to none. Collectively, we continue to deliver utterly reliable, consistent and high-grade combat power to Her Majesty across all dimensions of military life. Our engine has been running hot in recent years and, despite the campaign in Afghanistan coming to a close, there are no prospects of an era of peace breaking out. Indeed, the Regiment has prospered and flourished on a 'hot' engine. Despite the danger and stress of combat, between tours our men yearn for the tempo and purpose of operations and they rail against the return to barrack life for, as they call it, 'the stuff in between'.

But this is not to say that we don't have to think deeply and carefully about our future so that we keep the Regiment right at the cutting edge of the British Army. Our regimental system has a multitude of strengths; strengths which have kept the system alive and well for hundreds of years. But in the wrong hands it can become a constraint to creative thinking and a block to positive change. Tradition, wielded incorrectly, can narrow minds and form antibodies to the future. We have to be sufficiently self-aware that we understand our modern strengths and play to them while fighting hard to retain all the goodness of our history, tradition and county character. While cherishing and nurturing our unique personality, we have to be ready to adapt and evolve internally and externally, physically and intellectually, as the Army executes strategic change programmes such as Army 2020 and the Future Army Reserve.

Already we find ourselves in a changing context. Our Regiment survived the most recent amalgamations, but the Queen's Division did not survive unscathed; our proud sister regiment, the Royal Regiment of Fusiliers lost one of her fine and well-recruited battalions. We find ourselves now in a Queen's Division in the infantry order of battle alongside a number of new 'large' regiments who are learning, as we did in the 1970s and 1980s, the virtue of size.

The Colours on parade.

In my view, the current Queen's Division structure of three distinct and unique county regiments remains a perfectly viable model for infantry force generation. All three regiments have proud histories and all three have performed magnificently on recent operations. Sufficiently different to prevent in-breeding and group-think, we are more similar than we realize in personality and character. We share the same strengths and we deploy the same quality of combat power.

To make this division fulfil its potential in the new Army 2020 construct, we all need to be part of a vibrant Queen's Division that celebrates the diversity of three regiments who see themselves as brothers in arms – three regiments which go from strength to strength, building on our shared history of the past 50 years. Regiments that are rooted deeply in the character, personality, self-belief, sense of purpose and modest pride that flows from our county heritage. Meanwhile, between us, together we prosecute the opportunities and stretch the potential that lies in the large regiment format.

Our Queen's Division battalions will be in a range of infantry roles across several all-arms formations in a number of locations. Some of our battalions will continue to arms-plot and some will not. It is up to us to seize the opportunities for career, lifestyle and family choices inherent. It is up to us to use the variety of roles to develop our brightest and best, and to maintain the breadth and depth of experience in our leaders. Together with our sister regiments, we need to wring every synergy out of the Queen's Division, playing to our collective strengths. We need to demonstrate beyond any doubt that we can continue to deliver ever-improving infantry combat power at the very edge of thinking.

This is not a defensive mind set that seeks to use tactics to defend our cap badge from future amalgamations come what may. It is a mind set that consciously and continuously seeks to adapt with the self-confidence and self-belief that comes from everything symbolised by our cap badge. It demonstrates for all to see that our regiment, alongside our sister regiments, is consistently ahead of the game (any game you like) with the character, inner strength, robustness and reliability generated by our modern take on the county regimental system. It demonstrates to friend and foe that our rock-solid core honed over the past five decades has the intellectual agility to embrace change and be always one step ahead of the enemy.

In amongst all of this, of what are we most proud? What do we feel when we think of our regiment? How do we see it in decades to come? What must we fight to preserve at all costs and what can we cast aside?

Of course we are proud of our heritage, our traditions, our Colours, our long history and our glorious and impressively long list of battle honours. This is part of who we are and, despite those who sniff at heritage and history, this aspect of our character deserves the utmost respect. And for sure, we gaze back fondly at our own personal histories, proud of our achievements and sad about comrades killed and injured. But many of us are most proud of what we have become, and what this heralds for the future.

We are proud to be part of a living regiment that we have all nurtured from its earliest days; a regiment that year on year has gained depth and substance; a regiment that has been a labour of love for us all and is a direct product of our blood, sweat and tears; a regiment that now, after five decades, has a depth of quality and a richness of character that we can taste, touch and feel. This is a regiment that always delivers, has a reputation for excellence, that refuses to suffer from arrogance or complacency, and is fun to be around. We are proud of our modesty and humility. We are proud to be our own biggest critics, and proud that we are never satisfied with our performance in battle or the scale of the hangover following a night in the mess. We are proud that we know our soldiers as we know each other, as we know ourselves. We are proud of our families – especially our families. They sacrifice so much and serve as a vital part of the Regiment with every bit as much pride, commitment and duty as those in uniform. And they too carry the scars of battle. None of our men wear an Elizabeth Cross.

We have no truck with class or elitism or nepotism; we are as close to a meritocracy as we can make ourselves. The bond between the ranks is something very special and something incredibly productive on the battlefield; something that can only evolve over decades; something that cannot be generated by artifice or design; something that is a direct product of our regional personality. We are comfortable in our skins but never content to rest on our past glories. We know we are only as good as our next fight – and we love to be judged in this manner.

And there is no dilemma between the past and the future here; this is not a binary choice that has to be made. In its very essence, our life today has the hallmarks of that of the infantryman of the past 33 decades. To do our job we summon our personal courage and we put our lives directly into danger in order to defeat our enemy in a very physical and lethal sense: we see our enemies' faces and we look into their eyes. But we are highly attuned to the context of today and tomorrow. This eternal quality of the infantry life is shaped by the world of today; we may have to sharpen a bayonet to win a fight but the way we think and behave before and after the fight can win or lose a war. To understand this, to understand these delicate nuances within modern combat is not easy. But we are good at it and long may we be good at it. We are a very human regiment and we know the value of compassion.

This is what we want to preserve into the future – a set of values and a way of conducting ourselves; an authentic representation of our home communities and the society from which we are drawn with roots that reach deep into our counties; a self-sustaining system of excellence bounded by modesty and humility; the desire to be the best we can possibly be, but the recognition that we never will reach this aim.

Royal Anglian machine gunner.

All of this is represented by our cap badge, but our cap badge is not all of this. I hope fervently that our cap badge outlasts my lifetime, but this is not a given. I have been and always will be proud to have been part of a very special community of people who have made history, a community called The Royal Anglian Regiment. No matter what happens to our name, form and function over the next five decades, we must preserve this unique Anglian way of soldiering, not for any sense of nostalgia but because it works. It worked for the past five decades (and before) and it will work for decades to come.

Lieutenant General Jones with Captain Frank Atkins in Afghanistan.

SECTION 6
REFERENCE

Vikings homecoming parade in Norwich after *Herrick 6*.

APPENDIX 1

ROLL OF HONOUR

Ramp ceremony in Afghanistan.

The Regiment remembers with gratitude and with pride those of its members who have died while on duty or as a result of terrorist action between 1 September 1964 and 31 December 2013, whose names are inscribed on the Regimental Memorial at Duxford and on the Armed Forces Memorial at Alrewas.

23700587	Private	Kenneth Atkin	24 December 1964
23882566	Private	Walter Frederick Frazer	31 December 1964
23717835	Lance Corporal	Malcolm Roy Boothright	20 February 1965
23668982	Corporal	Colin Herbert Jackson	20 February 1965
24045230	Private	Laurie Edward John Wallace	4 July 1965
24093118	Junior Drummer	Ian William Skinner	20 October 1966
23901657	Corporal	Richard Watson	24 October 1966
23545801	Corporal	Michael Graham Shirley	15 November 1966
23921722	Corporal	John Ernest Herbert	3 March 1967
23462111	Private	Colin Rodgers	4 March 1967
23896810	Private	David Newstead	11 February 1970
432785	Major	Peter Doidge Taunton	26 October 1970
24161554	Private	Brian John Sheridan	20 November 1970
23853267	Private	Roger Wilkins	11 October 1971
23999635	Lance Corporal	Ian Maynard Curtis	9 November 1971
490347	Second Lieutenant	Nicholas Edwin Hull	16 April 1972
24219619	Private	John Henry Ballard	11 May 1972
23892350	Corporal	Kenneth Charles Mogg	13 July 1972
24146534	Lance Corporal	Martin Rooney	13 July 1972
23984303	Corporal	Michael Philip Boddy	17 August 1972
24110135	Corporal	John Michael Barry	25 September 1972

24182510	Private	Ian Stuart David Burt	29 September 1972
24210289	Private	Robert Michael Mason	24 October 1972
24187221	Private	Anthony Goodfellow	27 April 1973
24210158	Private	Nigel Markwick	12 September 1973
24269460	Private	Eric William Edwards	15 September 1973
24114728	Lance Corporal	William John Murray Ainslie Owens	15 September 1973
23855732	Lance Corporal	Roy Grant	2 November 1973
24171775	Private	Parry Lloyd Hollis	13 November 1974
492713	Captain	Michael Guy André Shipley	8 March 1975
23516824	Staff Sergeant	Trevor Rex Bodenham	28 April 1976
24386014	Private	Keith Stacey	26 April 1977
24383172	Private	Stephen Foster	13 November 1978
24424749	Private	Paul Anthony Wright	8 October 1979
24455741	Private	Ashley Arthur Cooper	20 March 1980
24180604	Lance Corporal	Karl Heinz Johnson	4 July 1980
24507452	Private	Kevin Andrew Brewer	29 August 1981
24400761	Private	Tony Anderson	24 May 1982
431008	Major	Patrick Cavanagh Ford	22 December 1983
24661690	Private	Andrew Paul Linnett	29 July 1984
24692612	Private	Martin Robert Patten	22 September 1985
492940	Major	Andrew Foxcroft French, MBE	22 May 1986
24689233	Private	Mitchell Robert Bertram	9 July 1986
24527424	Private	Carl James Davies	9 July 1986
24606985	Private	David Jonathan Knight	26 July 1986
24558399	Private	Paul Alec Tee	7 October 1986
24756556	Private	Darren John Back	19 August 1987
24763628	Private	Nicholas David Peacock	1 February 1989
24651452	Lance Corporal	Stephen Langridge	27 March 1990
24554346	Corporal	Nigel William Collishaw	9 May 1990
24763644	Lance Corporal	Peter John Faulkner	9 May 1990
24912211	Private	Michael Thomas John Linney	5 April 1991
25006724	Junior Leader	James Simon Windsor	4 September 1991
24242170	Sergeant	James Bernard Devaney	23 May 1992
519749	Captain	Steven Peter Wormald	29 April 1994
25007501	Lance Corporal	Jason Glen Rout	13 February 1999
24899285	Corporal	Geoffrey Towler	15 February 2002
25096163	Lance Corporal	Darren John George	9 April 2002
25152868	Private	Joseva Lewaicei	13 May 2006
25175826	Private	Adam Peter Morris	13 May 2006
25218223	Private	Christopher Gray	13 April 2007
25145045	Lance Corporal	George Russell Davey	20 May 2007
25029000	Corporal	Darren Wayne Bonner	28 May 2007
25234459	Private	Andrew James Borkertas	15 June 2007
25164651	Lance Corporal	Alexander Hawkins	25 July 2007
25136740	Private	Tony Alan Rawson	10 August 2007
557466	Captain	David Charles Hicks, MC	11 August 2007
25220423	Private	Robert Graham Foster	23 August 2007
25218969	Private	Aaron James McClure	23 August 2007
25189115	Private	John Steven Thrumble	23 August 2007

25211552	Private	Scott James Mugridge	14 April 2008
25238217	Lance Corporal	Adam Paul Drane	7 December 2009
30062524	Private	Robert Stephen Hayes	3 January 2010
565710	Captain	Martin Oliver Driver	15 March 2010
30040130	Private	James Douglas Grigg	16 March 2010
25115713	Lance Corporal	Scott Thomas Michael Hardy	16 March 2010
25022690	Corporal	Alexander William Guy, MC	15 June 2012
30043203	Lance Corporal	Craig John Roberts	13 July 2013

The 'Remembrance' section of the Regimental Museum at Duxford includes an interactive display listing all those who have died while serving with the Regiment, whether or not they were on duty at the time, and giving where available further details.

APPENDIX 2
AWARDS FOR OPERATIONAL SERVICE

The following members of the Regiment, and attached personnel, have received significant awards for gallantry or distinguished service while involved in operations.

COMMANDER OF THE MILITARY DIVISION OF THE MOST EXCELLENT ORDER OF THE BRITISH EMPIRE (CBE)

407841	Brigadier	R. E. J. Gerrard-Wright, OBE	11 January 1977	Northern Ireland
433251	Brigadier	D. C. Thorne, OBE	18 December 1979	Northern Ireland
481887	Brigadier	M. J. D. Walker, OBE	29 June 1991	Gulf
485317	Brigadier	J. C. B. Sutherell, OBE	11 May 1993	Northern Ireland
495202	Colonel	J. C. McColl, OBE	13 May 1997	Former Yugoslavia
497573	Brigadier	R. M. Brunt, OBE	14 April 2000	Northern Ireland
511036	Major General	P. D. Jones, MBE	23 March 2012	Afghanistan

COMPANION OF THE DISTINGUISHED SERVICE ORDER (DSO)

495202	Major General	J. C. McColl, CBE	29 October 2002	Afghanistan
528569	Lieutenant Colonel S. W. Carver		7 March 2008	Afghanistan
550579	Lieutenant Colonel M. P. Aston, MC		22 March 2013	Afghanistan

OFFICER OF THE MILITARY DIVISION OF THE MOST EXCELLENT ORDER OF THE BRITISH EMPIRE (OBE)

130095	Lieutenant Colonel J. M. Petit, MBE	13 December 1966	Borneo Territories
403501	Lieutenant Colonel R. L. Jackson	3 October 1972	Northern Ireland
429944	Lieutenant Colonel M. E. Thorne	19 March 1974	Northern Ireland
448908	Lieutenant Colonel C. M. J. Barnes, MBE	13 December 1977	Northern Ireland
451227	Lieutenant Colonel W. T. Dodd, MBE	26 June 1979	Northern Ireland
451228	Lieutenant Colonel R. J. M. Drummond, MBE	15 April 1980	Northern Ireland
473975	Lieutenant Colonel R. Howe, MBE	14 December 1982	Northern Ireland
469420	Lieutenant Colonel T. B. Thomas	21 June 1983	Northern Ireland
475225	Lieutenant Colonel M. E. Romilly	11 November 1986	Northern Ireland
485774	Lieutenant Colonel T. Longland, MBE	15 May 1990	Northern Ireland
485317	Lieutenant Colonel J. C. B. Sutherell, MBE	6 November 1990	Northern Ireland
488431	Lieutenant Colonel P. W. Field	12 May 1992	Northern Ireland
486682	Lieutenant Colonel J. D. Lacey	12 May 1992	Northern Ireland
485831	Lieutenant Colonel A. D. Slater, MBE	12 May 1992	Northern Ireland
495202	Lieutenant Colonel J. C. McColl	26 April 1994	Northern Ireland

497573	Lieutenant Colonel	R. M. Brunt, MBE	9 May 1995	Northern Ireland
499715	Lieutenant Colonel	R. E. Harrold	10 May 1996	Northern Ireland
529798	Lieutenant Colonel	C. A. Cocker	8 November 1996	Former Yugoslavia
534926	Lieutenant Colonel	S. J. R. Browne, MBE	11 September 2009	Iraq

MEMBER OF THE MILITARY DIVISION OF THE MOST EXCELLENT ORDER OF THE BRITISH EMPIRE (MBE)

471719	Second Lieutenant	W. J. Hawkins	19 November 1965	Aden
477074	Captain	J. S. Cox RAMC	4 July 1967	Aden
470081	Lieutenant	B. A. R. Harrington-Spier	22 August 1967	Aden
473533	Captain	J. R. Hart	5 October 1971	Northern Ireland
471365	Captain	A. E. Thompson, MC	1 May 1973	Northern Ireland
448908	Major	C. M. J. Barnes	3 July 1973	Northern Ireland
473975	Captain	R. Howe	3 July 1973	Northern Ireland
432484	Major	G. H. Bradshaw	18 September 1973	Northern Ireland
451227	Major	W. T. Dodd	19 March 1974	Northern Ireland
451228	Major	R. J. M. Drummond	19 March 1974	Northern Ireland
470114	Captain	M. J. Menage	18 June 1974	Northern Ireland
469025	Major	J. S. Houchin	27 March 1979	Northern Ireland
492940	Captain	A. F. French	1 July 1980	Northern Ireland
485774	Major	T. Longland	12 April 1983	Northern Ireland
481846	Major	P. P. Rawlins	12 April 1983	Northern Ireland
504723	Major	D. W. Spalding	11 November 1986	Northern Ireland
523710	Lieutenant	P. L. Ludbrook	14 April 1987	Northern Ireland
24197305	Warrant Officer Class 2	T. D. Smith	14 April 1987	Northern Ireland
487574	Major	K. M. Ryan	13 October 1987	Northern Ireland
485831	Major	A. D. Slater	13 October 1987	Northern Ireland
500011	Major	H. S. Bullock	11 October 1988	Northern Ireland
497573	Major	R. M. Brunt	31 October 1989	Northern Ireland
503802	Major	R. J. Edmondson-Jones	14 May 1991	Northern Ireland
517057	Major	W. Burford	27 October 1992	Northern Ireland
498674	Major	D. J. Clements	11 May 1993	Northern Ireland
505991	Major	R. J. Kemp	26 April 1994	Northern Ireland
511036	Major	P. D. Jones	9 May 1995	Northern Ireland
514042	Major	A. J. C. Wild	9 May 1995	Former Yugoslavia
519726	Major	T. J. Smith	10 May 1996	Former Yugoslavia
523711	Major	M. M. McGowan	8 November 1996	Northern Ireland
522969	Major	R. G. Burns	5 December 1997	Former Yugoslavia
544876	Captain	D. S. J. Biddick	30 October 2001	Northern Ireland
534926	Major	S. J. R. Browne	29 April 2003	Afghanistan
24498244	Warrant Officer Class 1	R. G. Gray	30 September 2003	Northern Ireland
24626442	Colour Sergeant	M. J. Howard	31 October 2003	Iraq
24756139	Colour Sergeant	M. J. Gray	23 April 2004	Afghanistan
549630	Captain	C. W. Swallow	9 September 2005	Iraq
563506	Captain	R. J. Bredin	11 September 2009	Iraq
544305	Major	C. D. Davies	24 September 2010	Afghanistan
30085958	Private	L. J. Treloar	22 March 2013	Afghanistan
550852	Major	A. P. Wolfe	22 March 2013	Afghanistan

MILITARY CROSS (MC)

472597	Second Lieutenant	M. J. Peele	17 November 1964	Borneo Territories
480255	Captain	S. M. Brogan	27 November 1973	Oman
24756675	Corporal	A. J. Rainey	9 May 1995	Former Yugoslavia
533577	Captain	R. W. Wooddisse	29 October 1999	Kosovo
516042	Major	E. E. C. Thorne	29 October 2002	Afghanistan
524400	Major	J. M. Woodham	24 March 2006	Iraq
546171	Major	M. A. P. Nooney PWRR	15 December 2006	Iraq
25159784	Lance Corporal	L. D. Ashby	7 March 2008	Afghanistan
550579	Major	M. P. Aston	7 March 2008	Afghanistan
544876	Major	D. S. J. Biddick, MBE	7 March 2008	Afghanistan
557466	Captain	D. C. Hicks (killed in action)	7 March 2008	Afghanistan
25018926	Corporal	R. W. Moore	7 March 2008	Afghanistan
25172103	Lance Corporal	O. S. Ruecker	7 March 2008	Afghanistan
25067216	Sergeant	A. R. Hill	24 September 2010	Afghanistan
25022690	Corporal	A. W. Guy (killed in action)	22 March 2013	Afghanistan
25157427	Lance Corporal	L. M. C. Kayser	22 March 2013	Afghanistan

DISTINGUISHED CONDUCT MEDAL (DCM)

23945040	Sergeant	N. Whitfield	3 July 1973	Northern Ireland

MILITARY MEDAL (MM)

24114763	Corporal	N. Jephcote	20 February 1973	Northern Ireland
24088200	Lance Corporal	W. J. Simpson	18 December 1973	Northern Ireland
23852083	Staff Sergeant	A. J. Underwood	19 March 1974	Northern Ireland
24135346	Corporal	K. J. Mallon	22 June 1976	Northern Ireland

QUEEN'S GALLANTRY MEDAL (QGM)

24029202	Sergeant	P. M. Smith	14 December 1982	Northern Ireland
24298976	Sergeant	F. N. Rimmer	16 October 1984	Northern Ireland
24472659	Sergeant	T. H. Smith	29 June 1991	Gulf
24619885	Lance Corporal	P. A. Plant	24 December 1991	Kuwait
25083760	Lance Corporal	M. A. Wilkinson	19 July 2007	Iraq
25138951	Private	L. C. Nadriva	7 March 2008	Afghanistan

BRITISH EMPIRE MEDAL (BEM)

14747109	Sergeant	J. W. Jones	27 April 1965	Radfan
23945091	Private	J. V. Elba-Porter	17 September 1965	Aden
23921727	Private	A. D. Kent	17 September 1965	Aden
22771566	Sergeant	W. I. Allen	4 July 1967	Aden
23945669	Corporal	J. M. Valentine	22 August 1967	Aden
23898645	Staff Sergeant	M. F. Nugent	5 October 1971	Northern Ireland
23882230	Sergeant	R. W. Nicholls	18 June 1974	Northern Ireland

24128659	Staff Sergeant	R. J. Fidler RRF	15 December 1981	Northern Ireland
24099732	Warrant Officer Class 2	K. W. Taylor	12 April 1983	Northern Ireland
24026822	Colour Sergeant	T. H. Wesley	21 June 1983	Northern Ireland
24261648	Sergeant	M. J. M. Rutland	15 April 1986	Northern Ireland
24221108	Sergeant	M. P. Morton	13 October 1987	Northern Ireland

The dates given above are those on which the awards were formally made by publication in *The London Gazette*, rather than the dates of the operational service or event involved, and cover the period from 1 September 1964 to 31 December 2013.

The 'Honours' section of the Regimental Museum at Duxford includes an interactive display listing all those who have been honoured for any reason while serving with the Regiment, and giving where available further details.

APPENDIX 3

BATTALION TOURS OF DUTY
1 SEPTEMBER 1964–31 DECEMBER 2013

1ST BATTALION

September 1964–September 1965	Waterloo Lines, Aden
October 1965–February 1968	Trenchard Barracks, Celle, Germany
February 1968–June 1968	Alma and Bourlon Barracks, Catterick, Yorkshire
June 1968–July 1970	Somme Lines, Catterick, Yorkshire
July 1970–March 1972	Ebrington Barracks, Londonderry, Northern Ireland
March 1972–May 1974	Salamanca Barracks, Episkopi, Cyprus and Slim Barracks, Dhekelia, Cyprus (Support Company)
May 1974–August 1978	Assaye Barracks, Tidworth, Hampshire

Unaccompanied tour:

September 1974–December 1974	*Armagh, Northern Ireland*	*Operation* Banner

August 1978–May 1982	Trenchard Barracks, Celle, Germany

Unaccompanied tours:

May 1979–September 1979	*Belfast, Northern Ireland*	*Operation* Banner
August 1981–January 1982	*Fermanagh, Northern Ireland*	*Operation* Banner

May 1982–December 1984	Oakington Barracks, Cambridge

Unaccompanied tour:

October 1982–April 1983	*Belize*

December 1984–January 1987	Ebrington Barracks, Londonderry, Northern Ireland
January 1987–February 1989	Lathbury Barracks, Gibraltar
February 1989–July 1996	Hyderabad Barracks, Colchester, Essex

Unaccompanied tours:

August 1989–January 1990	*South Armagh, Northern Ireland*	*Operation* Banner
April 1991–November 1991	*Fermanagh, Northern Ireland*	*Operation* Banner
December 1993–June 1994	*East Tyrone, Northern Ireland*	*Operation* Banner
August 1995–October 1995	*Croatia, Former Yugoslavia*	*Operation* Grapple

July 1996–May 1999	Oakington Barracks, Cambridge

Unaccompanied tour:

November 1996–May 1997	*Belfast, Northern Ireland*	*Operation* Banner

May 1999–May 2001	Ebrington Barracks, Londonderry, Northern Ireland
May 2001–December 2011	Elizabeth Barracks, Pirbright, Surrey

Unaccompanied tours:

March 2002–June 2002	*Kabul, Afghanistan*	*Operation* Fingal
December 2002–June 2003	*East Tyrone, Northern Ireland* (4 platoons only)	*Operation* Banner
April 2005–October 2005	*Basra, Iraq*	*Operation* Telic 6

March 2007–October 2007	*Helmand Province, Afghanistan*	*Operation* Herrick 6
October 2009–April 2010	*Helmand Province, Afghanistan*	*Operation* Herrick 11
December 2011–	Picton Barracks, Bulford, Wiltshire	
Unaccompanied tour:		
March 2012–October 2012	*Helmand Province, Afghanistan*	*Operation* Herrick 16

2ND BATTALION

September 1964–October 1964	Normandy Barracks, Felixstowe, Suffolk	
October 1964–July 1967	Alexander Barracks, Dhekelia, Cyprus	
Unaccompanied tour:		
May 1966–July 1966	*RAF Khormaksar, Aden (B Company only)*	
July 1967–November 1969	Normandy Barracks, Felixstowe, Suffolk	
Unaccompanied tour:		
December 1968–August 1969	*RAF Gibraltar*	
November 1969–May 1971	Hyderabad Barracks, Colchester, Essex	
Unaccompanied tour:		
October 1970–February 1971	*Belfast, Northern Ireland*	*Operation* Banner
May 1971–June 1976	Oxford Barracks, Münster, Germany	
Unaccompanied tours:		
August 1972–December 1972	*Belfast, Northern Ireland*	*Operation* Banner
July 1973–November 1973	*Londonderry, Northern Ireland*	*Operation* Banner
August 1975–December 1975	*Belfast, Northern Ireland*	*Operation* Banner
June 1976–August 1978	Gordon Barracks, Gillingham, Kent	
Unaccompanied tours:		
August 1976	*Lathbury Barracks, Gibraltar and Buena Vista Barracks, Gibraltar (Support Company)*	
March 1977–June 1977	*Belfast, Northern Ireland*	*Operation* Banner
August 1978–January 1981	Montgomery Barracks, Berlin, Germany	
January 1981–January 1983	Ebrington Barracks, Londonderry, Northern Ireland	
January 1983–March 1987	Hyderabad Barracks, Colchester, Essex	
Unaccompanied tours:		
December 1983–June 1984	*Alexander Barracks, Dhekelia, Cyprus and St David's Camp, Nicosia, Cyprus*	
January 1986–February 1986	*Fermanagh, Tyrone, Armagh, Northern Ireland*	*Operation* Caracara
April 1986–September 1986	*South Armagh, Northern Ireland*	*Operation* Banner
March 1987–February 1996	Trenchard Barracks, Celle, Germany	
Unaccompanied tours:		
January 1989–June 1989	*Belfast, Northern Ireland*	*Operation* Banner
March 1991–July 1991	*Kuwait*	*Operation* Granby
December 1992–July 1993	*East Tyrone, Northern Ireland*	*Operation* Banner
May 1994–November 1994	*Bosnia, Former Yugoslavia*	*Operation* Grapple 4
February 1996–February 1998	Battlesbury Barracks, Warminster, Wiltshire	
February 1998–March 2000	Alexander Barracks, Dhekelia, Cyprus	

Unaccompanied tour:
March 1999–July 1999   *RAF Mount Pleasant, Falkland Islands*
                                  (B Company only)

March 2000–February 2004   Beachley Barracks, Chepstow, Monmouthshire
Unaccompanied tours:
June 2000–July 2000   *Sierra Leone (B Company only)*   *Operation* Basilica
November 2000–May 2001   *Belfast (D (Support) Company only)*   *Operation* Faction
June 2002–December 2002   *Belfast and Omagh, Northern Ireland* *Operation* Banner
March 2003–October 2003   *Kabul, Afghanistan (2 companies only) Operation* Fingal 5

February 2004–December 2005   Shackleton Barracks, Ballykelly, Northern Ireland

December 2005–August 2007   Clive Barracks, Tern Hill, Shropshire
Unaccompanied tour:
April 2006–November 2006   *Basra, Iraq*   *Operation* Telic 8

August 2007–August 2010   Trenchard Barracks, Celle, Germany
Unaccompanied tours:
May 2008–November 2008   *Basra, Iraq*   *Operation* Telic 12
May 2009–June 2009   *RAF Mount Pleasant, Falkland Islands*
                                  (D Company only)

August 2010–August 2012   Alexander Barracks, Dhekelia, Cyprus
Unaccompanied tour:
March 2012–April 2012   *RAF Mount Pleasant, Falkland Islands*
                                  (D Company only)

August 2012–   Kendrew Barracks, Cottesmore, Rutland
Unaccompanied tour:
September 2013–   *Helmand Province, Afghanistan*   *Operation* Herrick 19

3RD BATTALION

September 1964–August 1966   Wavell Barracks, Berlin, Germany

August 1966–December 1968   Assaye Barracks, Tidworth, Hampshire
Unaccompanied tour:
October 1966–May 1967   *Radfan Camp, Aden*

December 1968–December 1970   Normandy Barracks, Aldershot, Hampshire
Unaccompanied tour:
October 1969–April 1970   *Polemidia Camp, Limassol, Cyprus*

December 1970–August 1975   Alanbrooke Barracks, Paderborn, Germany
Unaccompanied tours:
April 1972–August 1972   *Belfast, Northern Ireland*   *Operation* Banner
March 1973–July 1973   *Londonderry, Northern Ireland*   *Operation* Banner
November 1974–March 1975   *Londonderry, Northern Ireland*   *Operation* Banner

August 1975–February 1976   Alma Barracks, Catterick, Yorkshire

February 1976–February 1978   Salamanca Barracks, Episkopi, Cyprus

February 1978–May 1978   Kiwi Barracks, Bulford, Wiltshire

May 1978–November 1979   Palace Barracks, Holywood, Northern Ireland

November 1979–January 1984   Meeanee Barracks, Colchester, Essex

Unaccompanied tours:

November 1980–May 1981	*Alexander Barracks, Dhekelia, Cyprus and St David's Camp, Nicosia, Cyprus*
May 1982–October 1982	*Belize*
January 1984–February 1989	Elizabeth Barracks, Minden, Germany

Unaccompanied tour:

November 1986–March 1987	*Belfast, Northern Ireland*	*Operation* Banner
February 1989–May 1991	Roman Barracks, Colchester, Essex	

Unaccompanied tour:

July 1989–November 1989	*RAF Mount Pleasant, Falkland Islands (C Company only)*
May 1991–August 1992	Ebrington Barracks, Londonderry, Northern Ireland
August 1992–October 1992	Meeanee Barracks, Colchester, Essex

4TH BATTALION

September 1964–November 1965	Doniford Camp, Watchet, Somerset

Unaccompanied tour:

February 1965–August 1965	*Radfan Camp, Aden*
November 1965–July 1968	St Patrick's Barracks, St Julian's, Malta

Unaccompanied tours:

December 1965–February 1968	*Tripoli and Benghazi, Libya (one company only)*
January 1967–March 1967	*RAF Khormaksar, Aden (C Company only)*
July 1968–December 1970	Gordon Barracks, Gillingham, Kent

Unaccompanied tour:

August 1969–May 1970	*Hamala Camp, Bahrain*
January 1971–July 1972	Mons Barracks, Aldershot, Hampshire (Tiger Company)

Unaccompanied tour:

January 1972–July 1972	*Devil's Tower Barracks, Gibraltar (Tiger Company)*
August 1972–June 1975	Howe Barracks, Canterbury, Kent (Tiger Company)

Unaccompanied tour:

March 1974–July 1974	*East Tyrone/Armagh, Northern Ireland (Tiger Company)*	*Operation* Banner

The list above shows both routine battalion postings and operational deployments of one company or more. There have been occasional operational deployments of less than one company, but these are not shown; neither are training exercises. Generally, main locations only are given and small or temporary detachments are ignored. Dates are based, wherever possible, on either the official change of operational control or the movement of the main body of troops, and disregard advance parties, rear parties, and other small elements.

Precise dates for postings have proved problematic as it is normal for military moves to have an advanced party, main body and rear party and the sources often conflict with some giving dates for advanced parties, others for main bodies and so on. Some moves take several days and on occasion these can spread over month or even year endings. We have tried where possible to use the official change of operational control or the movement of the main body as the date, tending to rely on the Regimental newsletter as the main source, but there remains some uncertainty with some of the dates quoted.

APPENDIX 4
REGIMENTAL APPOINTMENTS

COLONELS-IN-CHIEF

All members of the British Army swear allegiance to the sovereign, and up to and including the battle of Dettingen in 1743 (in which the 12th Regiment of Foot, later to become the Suffolk Regiment, played a distinguished part) the king would usually lead his troops personally. The sovereign remains the head of the Army, but from the early 20th Century it became the practice for another member of the royal family, or sometimes a member of a foreign royal family, to be appointed as the sovereign's ceremonial representative within some regiments. The office became generally known as Colonel-in-Chief. Those who have held this appointment in the Royal Anglian Regiment are as follows:

HER MAJESTY QUEEN ELIZABETH THE QUEEN MOTHER,
1 SEPTEMBER 1964–30 MARCH 2002

The Honourable Elizabeth Bowes-Lyon was born on 4 August 1900 and spent much of her childhood at the family home at St Pauls Walden Bury in Hertfordshire. On 26 April 1923 she married His Royal Highness The Duke of York, second son of King George V. The elder son succeeded his father, as King Edward VIII, but then abdicated on 11 December 1936 so that his younger brother became King George VI and his wife became Queen Elizabeth. When King George VI died on 6 February 1952, he was succeeded by the present Queen, and his widow assumed the title Queen Elizabeth The Queen Mother. She died on 30 March 2002.

The Queen Mother's first association with the Regiment was her appointment as Honorary Colonel of the 1st Battalion The Hertfordshire Regiment (TA) on 18 February 1938. She then became Colonel-in-Chief of the Bedfordshire and Hertfordshire Regiment on 9 September 1949, Colonel-in-Chief of the 3rd East Anglian Regiment on its formation on 2 June 1958, and Colonel-in-Chief of the Royal Anglian Regiment on 1 September 1964.

HER ROYAL HIGHNESS PRINCESS ALICE, DUCHESS OF GLOUCESTER,
10 APRIL 2002–29 OCTOBER 2004

Lady Alice Montagu Douglas Scott was born on 25 December 1901 and married His Royal Highness The Duke of Gloucester, third son of King George V, on 6 November 1935. In 1938 the couple purchased Barnwell Manor, Northamptonshire, as a family home. On 11 May 1937, as Her Royal Highness The Duchess of Gloucester, she was appointed Colonel-in-Chief of the Northamptonshire Regiment, then became Colonel-in-Chief of the 2nd East Anglian Regiment on its formation on 1 June 1960. On 1 September 1964 she was appointed Deputy Colonel-in-Chief of the Royal Anglian Regiment. After her husband died on 10 June 1974, she assumed the title Princess Alice, Duchess of Gloucester. She was appointed Colonel-in-Chief of the Royal Anglian Regiment on 10 April 2002, and died on 29 October 2004.

Clockwise from top left:

Her Majesty Queen Elizabeth The Queen Mother.

Her Royal Highness Princess Alice, Duchess of Gloucester.

Her Royal Highness The Princess Margaret, Countess of Snowdon.

His Royal Highness The Duke of Gloucester.

HIS ROYAL HIGHNESS THE DUKE OF GLOUCESTER, 21 APRIL 2006–

Prince Richard of Gloucester was born on 26 August 1944, second son of the Duke and Duchess of Gloucester. His elder brother having been killed in a flying accident, he succeeded his father on his death on 10 June 1974. He was appointed Colonel-in-Chief of the Royal Anglian Regiment on 21 April 2006.

DEPUTY COLONELS-IN-CHIEF

It is not usual for an infantry regiment to have a Deputy Colonel-in-Chief, but the predecessors of the Royal Anglian Regiment had three royal Colonels-in-Chief. Accordingly, when the Regiment was formed, the senior was appointed Colonel-in-Chief of the new regiment and the other two were made Deputy Colonels-in-Chief, as follows:

HER ROYAL HIGHNESS THE PRINCESS MARGARET, COUNTESS OF SNOWDON, 1 SEPTEMBER 1964–9 FEBRUARY 2002

Princess Margaret, younger daughter of King George VI and Queen Elizabeth, was born on 21 August 1930. She was appointed Colonel-in-Chief of the Suffolk Regiment on 1 June 1953, then became Colonel-in-Chief of the 1st East Anglian Regiment on its formation on 29 August 1959. On 6 October 1961, after her husband was made an earl, she assumed the additional title Countess of Snowdon. On 1 September 1964 she was appointed Deputy Colonel-in-Chief of the Royal Anglian Regiment. She died on 9 February 2002.

HER ROYAL HIGHNESS PRINCESS ALICE, DUCHESS OF GLOUCESTER, 1 SEPTEMBER 1964–9 APRIL 2002

See details above.

COLONELS OF THE REGIMENT

Since the creation of a standing army in 1685 each infantry regiment has had a colonel at its head, originally responsible for everything connected with his regiment including recruiting, rations and clothing. The duties of the Colonel of the Regiment, a senior serving or retired officer, are today more limited, but he remains the guardian of the Regiment's history, traditions and general well-being. The following have served as Colonel of The Royal Anglian Regiment:

Lieutenant General Sir Reginald Denning, KBE, CB, DL, 1 September 1964–14 January 1966
Lieutenant General Sir Richard Goodwin, KCB, CBE, DSO, 15 January 1966–30 September 1971
Lieutenant General Sir Ian Freeland, GBE, KCB, DSO, DL, 1 October 1971–30 September 1976
Major General J. B. Dye, CBE, MC, DL, 1 October 1976–5 November 1982
General Sir Timothy Creasey, KCB, OBE, 6 November 1982–5 October 1986
General Sir John Akehurst, KCB, CBE, 6 October 1986–31 October 1991
Major General P. P. D. Stone, CB, CBE, 1 November 1991–29 January 1997
General Sir Michael Walker, GCB, CMG, CBE, ADC Gen, 30 January 1997–29 June 2002
Major General J. C. B. Sutherell, CB, CBE, 30 June 2002–31 March 2007
General Sir John McColl, KCB, CBE, DSO, 1 April 2007–6 September 2012
Lieutenant General P. D. Jones, CBE, 7 September 2012–

COMMANDING OFFICERS

1ST BATTALION
Lieutenant Colonel J. B. Dye, OBE, MC, 1964–65
Lieutenant Colonel T. M. Creasey, OBE, 1965–67
Lieutenant Colonel B. H. C. Emsden, 1967–69
Lieutenant Colonel R. L. Jackson, 1969–72
Lieutenant Colonel D. C. Thorne, 1972–74
Lieutenant Colonel W. R. W. Pike, 1974–77
Lieutenant Colonel A. J. G. Pollard, 1977–79
Lieutenant Colonel J. R. Hart, MBE, 1979–82
Lieutenant Colonel A. J. K. Calder, OBE, 1982–85
Lieutenant Colonel M. J. D. Walker, OBE, 1985–87
Lieutenant Colonel J. C. B. Sutherell, MBE, 1987–90
Lieutenant Colonel D. S. B. Phipps, 1990–92
Lieutenant Colonel R. M. Chisnall, OBE, 1992–93
Lieutenant Colonel R. M. Brunt, OBE, 1993–95
Lieutenant Colonel R. E. Harrold, OBE, 1995–98
Lieutenant Colonel R. J. Kemp, MBE, 1998–2000
Lieutenant Colonel P. D. Jones, MBE, 2000–03
Lieutenant Colonel E. E. C. Thorne, MC, 2003–06
Lieutenant Colonel S. W. Carver, DSO, 2006–08
Lieutenant Colonel J. M. Woodham, MC, 2008–11
Lieutenant Colonel M. P. Aston, DSO, MC, 2011–13
Lieutenant Colonel D. S. J. Biddick, MBE, MC, 2013–

2ND BATTALION
Lieutenant Colonel W. R. Chambers, 1964–65
Lieutenant Colonel I. A. Haycraft, 1965–68
Lieutenant Colonel J. B. Akehurst, 1968–70
Lieutenant Colonel R. E. J. Gerrard-Wright, OBE, 1970–73
Lieutenant Colonel M. E. Thorne, OBE, 1973–75
Lieutenant Colonel C. M. J. Barnes, MBE, 1975–77
Lieutenant Colonel P. P. D. Stone, MBE, 1977–80
Lieutenant Colonel R. Howe, MBE, 1980–82
Lieutenant Colonel D. J. W. Browne, MBE, 1982–85
Lieutenant Colonel P. P. Rawlins, MBE, 1985–87
Lieutenant Colonel T. Longland, OBE, 1987–90
Lieutenant Colonel A. P. Deed, 1990–92
Lieutenant Colonel J. C. McColl, OBE, 1992–94
Lieutenant Colonel D. J. Clements, MBE, 1994–96
Lieutenant Colonel S. L. Porter, 1997–99
Lieutenant Colonel A. J. C. Wild, MBE, 1999–2001
Lieutenant Colonel R. J. Ladley, MBE, 2001–04
Lieutenant Colonel D. P. O'Driscoll, 2004–06
Lieutenant Colonel S. J. R. Browne, MBE, 2006–09
Lieutenant Colonel R. W. Wooddisse, MBE, MC, 2009–11
Lieutenant Colonel N. A. Johnson, 2011–

3RD BATTALION

Lieutenant Colonel C. C. Norbury, MBE, MC, 1964
Lieutenant Colonel P. J. H. Leng, MBE, MC, 1964–66
Lieutenant Colonel J. L. Dymoke, MBE, 1966–69
Lieutenant Colonel K. Burch, MBE, 1969–71
Lieutenant Colonel J. Hall-Tipping, 1971–74
Lieutenant Colonel M. A. Aris, 1974–76
Lieutenant Colonel W. T. Dodd, MBE, 1976–79
Lieutenant Colonel R. J. M. Drummond, OBE, 1979–81
Lieutenant Colonel A. E. Thompson, MBE, MC, 1981–83
Lieutenant Colonel C. Groves, 1983–86
Lieutenant Colonel A. Behagg, MBE, 1986–89
Lieutenant Colonel J. D. Lacey, 1989–91
Lieutenant Colonel R. M. Chisnall, OBE, 1991–92

4TH BATTALION

Lieutenant Colonel J. A. C. Cowan, MBE, 1964–66
Lieutenant Colonel D. R. C. Carter, 1966–68
Lieutenant Colonel T. Holloway, 1968–70

4TH BATTALION THE ROYAL NORFOLK REGIMENT (TA)

Lieutenant Colonel A. W. J. Turnbull, MC, 1964–67

THE ROYAL NORFOLK REGIMENT (TERRITORIAL)

Lieutenant Colonel C. B. Grant, MC, TD, 1967–69

4TH/6TH BATTALION THE ROYAL LINCOLNSHIRE REGIMENT (TA)

Lieutenant Colonel A. J. Bennett, MBE, TD, 1964–65
Lieutenant Colonel H. H. Moore, 1965–67

THE ROYAL LINCOLNSHIRE REGIMENT (TERRITORIAL)

Lieutenant Colonel B. S. Foster, TD, 1967–69

THE SUFFOLK AND CAMBRIDGESHIRE REGIMENT (TA)

Lieutenant Colonel C. C. Wells, TD, 1964–65
Lieutenant Colonel G. C. Howgego, 1965–67

THE SUFFOLK AND CAMBRIDGESHIRE REGIMENT (TERRITORIAL)

Lieutenant Colonel J. P. Davey, TD, 1967–69

1ST BATTALION THE BEDFORDSHIRE AND HERTFORDSHIRE REGIMENT (TA)
Lieutenant Colonel D. W. Browne, 1964–66
Lieutenant Colonel J. V. Miseroy, 1966–67

THE BEDFORDSHIRE AND HERTFORDSHIRE REGIMENT (TERRITORIAL)
Lieutenant Colonel B. J. Elliott, TD, JP, 1967–69

4TH/5TH BATTALION THE ROYAL LEICESTERSHIRE REGIMENT (TA)
Lieutenant Colonel J. P. Creagh, 1964–66
Lieutenant Colonel R. G. Wilkes, TD, 1966–67

THE LEICESTERSHIRE REGIMENT (TERRITORIAL)
Lieutenant Colonel R. G. Wilkes, TD, DL, 1967–69

4TH/5TH BATTALION THE ESSEX REGIMENT (TA)
Lieutenant Colonel R. J. Randall, 1964–65
Lieutenant Colonel J. M. Barstow, 1965–67

THE ESSEX REGIMENT (TERRITORIAL)
Lieutenant Colonel G. H. Brewer, TD, 1967–69

4TH/5TH BATTALION THE NORTHAMPTONSHIRE REGIMENT (TA)
Lieutenant Colonel F. G. Barber, OBE, TD, 1964–67

THE NORTHAMPTONSHIRE REGIMENT (TERRITORIAL)
Lieutenant Colonel R. C. Jeffery, TD, DL, 1967–69

5TH (VOLUNTEER) BATTALION
Lieutenant Colonel H. H. Moore, 1967–68
Lieutenant Colonel P. D. Blyth, 1968–71
Lieutenant Colonel J. R. Heath, 1971–73
Lieutenant Colonel P. D. L. Hopper, 1973–75
Lieutenant Colonel J. Tadman, 1975–77
Lieutenant Colonel F. A. H. Swallow, 1977–80
Lieutenant Colonel R. T. J. Wreford, TD, 1980–82
Lieutenant Colonel P. B. D. Long, 1982–85
Lieutenant Colonel R. G. Greenham, 1985–87
Lieutenant Colonel N. H. Kelsey, TD, 1987–90
Lieutenant Colonel C. G. Stallard, 1990–92
Lieutenant Colonel P. G. R. Horrell, TD, 1992–95
Lieutenant Colonel D. J. W. Baylis, 1995–96

6TH (VOLUNTEER) BATTALION

Lieutenant Colonel P. W. Raywood, TD, 1971–73
Lieutenant Colonel T. C. B. Swayne, TD, 1973–76
Lieutenant Colonel R. C. Tomkins, TD, 1976–78
Lieutenant Colonel T. D. Dean, 1978–81
Lieutenant Colonel D. W. James, 1981–83
Lieutenant Colonel A. R. A. Veitch, 1983–86
Lieutenant Colonel A. C. Taylor, 1986–88
Lieutenant Colonel P. R. C. Dixon, 1988–91
Lieutenant Colonel A. D. Chissel, TD, 1991–93
Lieutenant Colonel C. A. F. Thomas, TD, 1993–96
Lieutenant Colonel H. N. D. Gill, TD, 1996–99
Lieutenant Colonel C. A. Newell PWRR, 1999

7TH (VOLUNTEER) BATTALION

Lieutenant Colonel W. G. Wallace, OBE, TD, 1971–74
Lieutenant Colonel W. G. Dawson, TD, 1974–77
Lieutenant Colonel W. J. Gleadell, TD, 1977–79
Lieutenant Colonel D. R. Baily, MBE, 1979–82
Lieutenant Colonel H. W. Lambert, 1982–84
Lieutenant Colonel D. K. Harris, MBE, TD, 1984–87
Lieutenant Colonel G. I. G. Brett, 1987–89
Lieutenant Colonel R. E. Haes, 1989–92
Lieutenant Colonel R. M. L. Colville, 1992–94
Lieutenant Colonel J. C. B. Prescott, 1994–97
Lieutenant Colonel P. M. Holme, 1997–99

EAST OF ENGLAND REGIMENT (TA)

Lieutenant Colonel C. A. Newell PWRR, 1999–2001
Lieutenant Colonel N. A. ffitch, TD, 2001–04
Lieutenant Colonel R. C. J. Goodin, MBE, 2004–06

3RD BATTALION (TA/ARMY RESERVE)

Lieutenant Colonel R. C. J. Goodin, MBE, 2006
Lieutenant Colonel M. Googe, TD, 2006–08
Lieutenant Colonel D. G. Vincent, MBE, 2008–10
Lieutenant Colonel R. F. L. Lyne, 2010–13
Lieutenant Colonel T. P. B. Morris, 2013–

REGIMENTAL SERGEANT MAJORS

1ST BATTALION

Warrant Officer Class 1 E. J. Hazelwood, 1964–65
Warrant Officer Class 1 M. S. Fowler, 1965–67

Warrant Officer Class 1 B. B. Day, 1968–69
Warrant Officer Class 1 R. E. Sharpe, 1969
Warrant Officer Class 1 J. M. Nichols, 1969–72
Warrant Officer Class 1 J. J. P. Buffine, BEM RRF, 1972–74
Warrant Officer Class 1 F. J. Perry, 1974–76
Warrant Officer Class 1 J. S. J. Rourke, 1976–79
Warrant Officer Class 1 F. C. L. Slinn, 1979–80
Warrant Officer Class 1 J. G. G. Ross, 1980–82
Warrant Officer Class 1 A. Powell, 1982–84
Warrant Officer Class 1 P. L. Ludbrook, 1984–86
Warrant Officer Class 1 P. A. Cookson, 1986–88
Warrant Officer Class 1 A. Jones, 1988–90
Warrant Officer Class 1 R. J. Allen, 1990–92
Warrant Officer Class 1 R. P. Grenfell, 1992–94
Warrant Officer Class 1 C. D. Hoyles, 1994–96
Warrant Officer Class 1 G. J. Webb, 1996–98
Warrant Officer Class 1 D. J. Stefanetti, 1998–99
Warrant Officer Class 1 S. P. Prime, 1999–2000
Warrant Officer Class 1 D. Mackness, 2000–01
Warrant Officer Class 1 S. D. Robinson, 2001–02
Warrant Officer Class 1 P. N. Blanchfield, 2002–03
Warrant Officer Class 1 C. J. Tate, 2003–05
Warrant Officer Class 1 A. L. Buff, 2005–06
Warrant Officer Class 1 I. J. Robinson, 2006–08
Warrant Officer Class 1 T. R. Newton, 2008–11
Warrant Officer Class 1 J. E. Self, 2011–12
Warrant Officer Class 1 A. R. C. Faupel, MBE, 2012–

2ND BATTALION

Warrant Officer Class 1 M. D. Franks, 1964–66
Warrant Officer Class 1 L. J. de-Bretton Gordon, 1966–69
Warrant Officer Class 1 I. J. Marjoram, 1969–70
Warrant Officer Class 1 A. D. Bird, 1970–72
Warrant Officer Class 1 R. E. Sharpe, 1972–74
Warrant Officer Class 1 D. H. Greenfield, 1974–76
Warrant Officer Class 1 P. Keal, 1976–78
Warrant Officer Class 1 A. R. Ainsworth, 1978–80
Warrant Officer Class 1 A. J. Underwood, MM, 1980–82
Warrant Officer Class 1 D. Whitehead, 1982–85
Warrant Officer Class 1 D. R. Dunthorne, 1985–86
Warrant Officer Class 1 W. O'Driscoll, 1986–88
Warrant Officer Class 1 R. J. Brown, 1988–90
Warrant Officer Class 1 D. G. Goude, MBE, 1990–92
Warrant Officer Class 1 A. E. Todd, 1992–93
Warrant Officer Class 1 G. L. Cutter, 1993–95
Warrant Officer Class 1 S. N. Pallant, 1995–97
Warrant Officer Class 1 F. A. Ralph, 1997–99
Warrant Officer Class 1 T. P. Beighton, 1999–2000

Warrant Officer Class 1 P. G. Martin, 2000–01
Warrant Officer Class 1 D. M. Hazlewood, 2001–03
Warrant Officer Class 1 R. J. Bredin, 2003–05
Warrant Officer Class 1 A. J. Rainey, MC, 2005–07
Warrant Officer Class 1 A. J. Bartlett, 2007–09
Warrant Officer Class 1 L. A. Waghorn, 2009–10
Warrant Officer Class 1 B. P. Lewis, 2010–12
Warrant Officer Class 1 M. J. David, 2012–

3RD BATTALION

Warrant Officer Class 1 R. Jenns, 1964–66
Warrant Officer Class 1 R. A. Blood, 1966
Warrant Officer Class 1 T. H. Bullock, 1966–70
Warrant Officer Class 1 R. G. Ford QUEENS, 1970–72
Warrant Officer Class 1 J. M. Jephcott QUEENS, 1972
Warrant Officer Class 1 H. S. Bullock, 1972–75
Warrant Officer Class 1 J. D. Fletcher, 1975–77
Warrant Officer Class 1 B. McDonnell, 1977–80
Warrant Officer Class 1 C. J. C. Kett, 1980–81
Warrant Officer Class 1 W. Burford, 1981–83
Warrant Officer Class 1 R. E. Eke, 1983–84
Warrant Officer Class 1 J. P. Sweeney, 1984–86
Warrant Officer Class 1 P. D. Thurston, 1986–88
Warrant Officer Class 1 R. W. Potter, 1988–89
Warrant Officer Class 1 M. V. Beaumont, 1989–91
Warrant Officer Class 1 A. F. Twell, 1991–92

4TH BATTALION

Warrant Officer Class 1 H. D. Benham, 1964–65
Warrant Officer Class 1 N. H. P. Jenks, MM, 1965–67
Warrant Officer Class 1 R. E. Sprason, 1967–68
Warrant Officer Class 1 P. F. Garman, 1968–70

4TH BATTALION THE ROYAL NORFOLK REGIMENT (TA)

Warrant Officer Class 1 M. S. Fowler, 1964–65
Warrant Officer Class 1 G. E. Veitch, 1965–67

4TH/6TH BATTALION THE ROYAL LINCOLNSHIRE REGIMENT (TA)

Warrant Officer Class 1 R. A. Blood, 1964–66
Warrant Officer Class 1 R. Jenns, 1966
Warrant Officer Class 1 A. M. McCarthy, 1966–67

THE SUFFOLK AND CAMBRIDGESHIRE REGIMENT (TA)
Warrant Officer Class 1 J. F. Parrott, 1964–65
Warrant Officer Class 1 L. G. Drew, 1965–67

1ST BATTALION THE BEDFORDSHIRE AND HERTFORDSHIRE REGIMENT (TA)
Warrant Officer Class 1 A. F. Charlesworth, 1964–67

4TH/5TH BATTALION THE ROYAL LEICESTERSHIRE REGIMENT (TA)
Warrant Officer Class 1 L. E. Loader, 1964–65
Warrant Officer Class 1 H. D. Benham, 1965–67

4TH/5TH BATTALION THE ESSEX REGIMENT (TA)
Warrant Officer Class 1 L. F. Cotter, 1964–65
Warrant Officer Class 1 A. R. Smith, 1965–67

4TH/5TH BATTALION THE NORTHAMPTONSHIRE REGIMENT (TA)
Warrant Officer Class 1 R. J. Pond, 1964–66
Warrant Officer Class 1 H. J. George, 1966–67

5TH (VOLUNTEER) BATTALION
Warrant Officer Class 1 R. A. Blood, 1967–69
Warrant Officer Class 1 J. K. Duke, 1969–71
Warrant Officer Class 1 D. B. Harris, 1971–74
Warrant Officer Class 1 A. J. Prudence QUEENS, 1974–76
Warrant Officer Class 1 J. C. Beckett, 1976–78
Warrant Officer Class 1 M. N. J. Dawe, 1978–79
Warrant Officer Class 1 D. S. Donaldson, 1979–81
Warrant Officer Class 1 L. B. Keogh, 1981–83
Warrant Officer Class 1 C. R. Hill, 1983–85
Warrant Officer Class 1 H. D. Smith, 1985–88
Warrant Officer Class 1 P. L. Smith, BEM, 1988–90
Warrant Officer Class 1 A. E. Todd, 1990–92
Warrant Officer Class 1 B. G. Hillier, 1992–95
Warrant Officer Class 1 P. D. Woodcock, 1995–96

6TH (VOLUNTEER) BATTALION
Warrant Officer Class 1 R. E. Sharpe, 1971–72
Warrant Officer Class 1 D. F. Knight, 1972–75
Warrant Officer Class 1 D. W. Spalding, 1975–77
Warrant Officer Class 1 M. B. Dear, 1977–80
Warrant Officer Class 1 R. A. Carpenter, 1980–82
Warrant Officer Class 1 R. E. Eke, 1982–83
Warrant Officer Class 1 I. R. Bowden, 1983–84

Warrant Officer Class 1 M. K. Flynn, 1984–87
Warrant Officer Class 1 M. J. Abbott, 1987–89
Warrant Officer Class 1 D. L. Powley, 1989–91
Warrant Officer Class 1 W. H. Eke, 1991–92
Warrant Officer Class 1 K. P. Brett, 1992–94
Warrant Officer Class 1 C. R. G. Duncan, 1994–97
Warrant Officer Class 1 G. J. Keeble, 1997–99
Warrant Officer Class 1 P. J. Thomas, 1999

7TH (VOLUNTEER) BATTALION
Warrant Officer Class 1 B. L. Callow RRF, 1971–72
Warrant Officer Class 1 C. C. McColgan, 1972–74
Warrant Officer Class 1 G. H. Price RRF, 1974–76
Warrant Officer Class 1 T. S. Fisher QUEENS, 1976–78
Warrant Officer Class 1 R. E. Jones, 1978–80
Warrant Officer Class 1 D. N. Pryce, 1980–81
Warrant Officer Class 1 M. N. J. Dawe, 1981–83
Warrant Officer Class 1 G. N. Taylor, 1983–85
Warrant Officer Class 1 G. P. Halewood, 1985–87
Warrant Officer Class 1 D. G. Wilson, 1987–89
Warrant Officer Class 1 J. J. Wilcox, 1989–91
Warrant Officer Class 1 C. Norman, 1991–92
Warrant Officer Class 1 P. J. Pacey, 1992–94
Warrant Officer Class 1 F. B. O. Kelly PWRR, 1994–95
Warrant Officer Class 1 S. West, 1995–97
Warrant Officer Class 1 P. J. Thomas, 1997–99

EAST OF ENGLAND REGIMENT (TA)
Warrant Officer Class 1 P. J. Thomas, 1999–2000
Warrant Officer Class 1 M. J. Abbs, 2000–02
Warrant Officer Class 1 G. J. Spencer WFR, 2002–04
Warrant Officer Class 1 N. H. Breen WFR, 2004–06
Warrant Officer Class 1 D. M. Caesar, 2006

3RD BATTALION (TA/ARMY RESERVE)
Warrant Officer Class 1 D. M. Caesar, 2006–07
Warrant Officer Class 1 A. J. Penn, 2007–08
Warrant Officer Class 1 D. R. Curtis, 2008
Warrant Officer Class 1 A. J. Penn, 2008–09
Warrant Officer Class 1 D. T. Granfield, 2008–09
Warrant Officer Class 1 K. Main, 2010–12
Warrant Officer Class 1 C. Hopkin, 2012–

The appointments given above are correct (as far as can be ascertained) up to 31 December 2013. Ranks and honours are those held at the conclusion of the appointment concerned.

APPENDIX 5
FREEDOMS AND ALLIANCES

FREEDOMS

The practice of granting freedom of entry into a town (usually just referred to as 'The Freedom of ...') began in the Middle Ages. At that time most towns were fortified and the inhabitants were naturally suspicious of armed troops. Once mutual confidence had been established, the town authorities would allow local troops to enter freely.

As government became more centralised, it began to take full control over all armed forces raised in the country and the practice died out. It was revived later as a formal, ceremonial honour.

This honour is not often granted. When it is, it means a great deal to both the local community granting it and to the regiment receiving it. The town usually creates an elaborate decorated scroll to record the grant of freedom, and the regiment exercises its right to march through the town with 'drums beating, bands playing, bayonets fixed and Colours flying'.

Subsequently, freedom parades are held from time to time. These often mark specific events such as a battalion returning home from a tour of duty overseas or some significant regimental or civic anniversary.

As at 31 December 2013, The Royal Anglian Regiment has been granted, or has inherited from its predecessors, the Freedom (or equivalent) of 48 cities, boroughs or towns, as follows:

Barking and Dagenham	9 December 2009
Basildon	14 April 2011
Bedford	18 September 1946
Boston	29 May 1981
Brentwood	26 May 1993
Bury St Edmunds	1 August 1944
Cambridge	29 September 1946
Celle	15 July 2010
Charnwood	4 September 2006
Chelmsford	27 May 1946
Cleethorpes	19 September 1946
Colchester	3 April 1946
Corby	3 May 2012
Diss	16 November 2011
Dunstable	20 June 1964
Ely	22 November 1976
Grantham	21 September 1946
Great Yarmouth	30 April 1963
Grimsby	27 January 1958
Harborough	24 February 2011
Harlow	27 September 2012
Harpenden	12 September 2013

Havering (formerly Romford)	21 May 1947
Hertford	7 April 1954
Hinckley & Bosworth	20 May 1978
Huntingdon	21 January 2010
Ipswich	24 March 1948
Kettering	14 December 2011
King's Lynn	10 March 1983
Leicester	27 June 1944
Lincoln	8 June 1946
Lowestoft	2 June 1960
Luton	8 October 1996
Newham (formerly East Ham)	20 August 1946
Northampton	8 June 1946
Norwich	6 March 1945
Oadby and Wigston	20 July 2011
Peterborough	6 June 1953
Redbridge (formerly Ilford)	20 May 1947
St Neots	12 September 2013
Southend-on-Sea	19 February 1946
Stamford (honorary status)	29 April 2008
Stevenage	23 May 2012
Sudbury	10 February 1953
Thurrock	18 July 1990
Watford	4 July 1959
Wellingborough	27 April 1985
Wisbech	24 March 1949

The dates given above are those on which the formal council resolution granting the freedom was passed. Often the scroll recording the grant of freedom was presented at a later date.

The 'Honours' section of the Regimental Museum at Duxford includes an interactive display giving full details of all civic honours granted to or inherited by the Regiment.

ALLIANCES

Formal alliances with various regiments of the Commonwealth have been established over the years, with both partners taking pride in a common *esprit de corps*:

AUSTRALIA – THE ROYAL TASMANIA REGIMENT

In 1931 the Suffolk Regiment, formerly the 12th Foot, and the 12th Infantry Battalion (The Launceston Regiment) of the Australian Army formed an alliance based on the shared number 12. The latter was renamed The Royal Tasmania Regiment and is now part of the Australian Army Reserve.

BARBADOS – THE BARBADOS REGIMENT

This alliance was originally established by the Royal Leicestershire Regiment in 1949, reflecting not only service by the Regiment in Barbados in the late 19th Century but also service by a number of Barbadians in the Regiment in the 1940s.

BELIZE – THE BELIZE DEFENCE FORCE

The Royal Anglian Regiment established a formal alliance with the recently formed Belize Defence Force in 1988, reflecting the close cooperation that had grown up between the two regiments.

BERMUDA – THE BERMUDA REGIMENT

Shortly after the First World War an alliance was established between the Lincolnshire Regiment and the Bermuda Rifles, reflecting the fact that 126 volunteers from Bermuda had served with the Lincolnshires during the war. The Second World War saw a similar influx of volunteers, and a close relationship has been maintained between the two regiments ever since.

CANADA – THE ESSEX AND KENT SCOTTISH REGIMENT

This alliance, originally between the Essex Regiment and the Essex Scottish Regiment of Canada, dates from 1926 and was based on their common county names. Following later reorganisation, the Essex and Kent Scottish Regiment is now part of the Canadian Army Reserve.

CANADA – THE LAKE SUPERIOR SCOTTISH REGIMENT

In 1933 the Northamptonshire Regiment, wanting to extend its links to the Dominions, established an alliance with the Lake Superior Regiment. Subsequently retitled, the Lake Superior Scottish Regiment is now part of the Canadian Army Reserve.

CANADA – THE LINCOLN AND WELLAND REGIMENT

The 19th Lincoln Militia Battalion of Canada established an alliance with the Lincolnshire Regiment in 1912, based on the commonality of name. Subsequently becoming the Lincoln and Welland Regiment, it is now part of the Canadian Army Reserve.

CANADA – THE SHERBROOKE HUSSARS

In 1934 the Leicestershire Regiment, wishing to promote friendship and goodwill within the armed forces of the Commonwealth, established an alliance with the Sherbrooke Regiment. The latter subsequently became the Sherbrooke Hussars, and is now part of the Canadian Army Reserve.

GIBRALTAR – THE ROYAL GIBRALTAR REGIMENT

The alliance between The Royal Anglian Regiment and the Gibraltar Regiment, now the Royal Gibraltar Regiment, was established in 1968, reflecting not only the major part played by former regiments in the siege of Gibraltar from 1779 to 1783 but also the cooperation that had grown up between the regiments in the 1960s.

MALAYSIA – 1ST BATTALION THE ROYAL MALAY REGIMENT

Officers of the Lincolnshire Regiment helped set up the Malay Regiment in the late 1930s, and a formal alliance between the Royal Lincolnshire Regiment and the 1st Battalion The Malay Regiment was established in 1954. The 1st Battalion The Royal Malay Regiment is now the senior regular battalion in the Malaysian Army.

NEW ZEALAND – 3/6 ROYAL NEW ZEALAND INFANTRY REGIMENT

In 1913 various alliances were set up between units of the British Army and units of the New Zealand Army, including the Suffolk Regiment with the Auckland Regiment and the Northamptonshire Regiment with North Auckland (Northland) Regiment. These affiliations reflected the service of the two British regiments in New Zealand in the 19th Century. The two New Zealand regiments subsequently underwent a series of amalgamations, today forming part of the New Zealand Reserve Army.

PAKISTAN – 5TH BATTALION THE FRONTIER FORCE REGIMENT

Although the alliance between The Royal Anglian Regiment and the 5th Battalion The Frontier Force Regiment was only established in 1964, it reflected the lengthy service together, in the First World War, of their predecessors the Leicestershire Regiment and the 53rd Sikh Regiment. The 5th Battalion The Frontier Force Regiment is a regular unit of the Pakistan Army.

SOUTH AFRICA – THE FIRST CITY REGIMENT

In 1928 an alliance was formed between the Bedfordshire and Hertfordshire Regiment and the 4th Infantry (First City) Regiment of South Africa. Today the First City Regiment is a reserve regiment of the South African National Defence Force.

SOUTH AFRICA – THE REGIMENT DE LA REY

De La Rey was a Boer commander who fought with distinction against the Northamptonshire Regiment in the South African War. A regiment of the South African forces having been named after him, a formal alliance was established with the Northamptonshire Regiment in 1937. The Regiment De La Rey is now a reserve regiment of the South African National Defence Force.

APPENDIX 6

THE COLOURS AND BATTLE HONOURS

THE COLOURS

For centuries flags and standards of various types were carried in battle so that the soldiers involved could quickly identify a rallying point in a confused situation. By the middle of the 18th Century the government was exercising more centralised control over the armed forces, and this included standardised Colours in infantry regiments: the 'King's (or Queen's) Colour' was to be based on the Union Flag while the 'Regimental Colour' was to be of specific regimental design.

As the conditions of warfare changed, Colours were no longer carried into battle. Instead they became, and remain, formal and much respected symbols of the regiment.

At the time of writing, the 1st and 2nd Battalions of The Royal Anglian Regiment carry identical Colours (apart from the number of the battalion), which were presented by Her Royal Highness The Princess Margaret at Duxford on 29 April 1995. The 3rd Battalion carries a similar set of Colours originally presented to the former 6th Battalion by Princess Margaret at Bury St Edmunds on 24 June 1979, and in addition has custody of a set of Colours presented to the former 7th Battalion by Her Royal Highness Princess Alice, Duchess of Gloucester, at Leicester on 20 April 1980.

New Colours are to be presented to all three battalions by His Royal Highness The Duke of Gloucester at Duxford on 31 August 2014. Subsequently, all four sets of old Colours will be formally laid up in suitable locations.

BATTLE HONOURS

In the late 18th Century regiments began to receive official approval to display the names of important battles in which they had taken part on their Colours, drums and uniforms. These came to be called 'battle honours'. Permission to display them remains strictly controlled.

The Royal Anglian Regiment itself has not yet been awarded any battle honours, but is the proud custodian of those won by its predecessors. The total number of such honours is 344 (75 for battles before 1914, 124 for the First World War, 143 for the Second World War, and two for the Korean War). For reasons of space only a limited number, chosen by the Regiment as being those of greatest regimental significance, are emblazoned on the Colours. They are listed here:

THE QUEEN'S COLOUR (41 HONOURS FROM THE TWO WORLD WARS)

Mons	Loos
Le Cateau	Somme, 1916, '18
Marne, 1914	Arras, 1917, '18
Aisne, 1914, '18	Cambrai, 1917, '18
Ypres, 1914, '15, '17, '18	France and Flanders, 1914–18
Neuve Chapelle	Macedonia, 1915–18

Gallipoli, 1915–16
Gaza
Palestine, 1917–18
Shaiba
Mesopotamia, 1914–18
St. Omer-La Bassée
Dunkirk, 1940
Normandy Landing
Brieux Bridgehead
Venraij
North-West Europe, 1940, '44–45
Tobruk, 1941
Defence of Alamein Line
North Africa, 1940–43
Villa Grande

Salerno
Anzio
Cassino I–II
Gothic Line
Italy, 1943–45
Crete
Singapore Island
Malaya, 1941–42
Yu
Ngakyedauk Pass
Imphal
Kohima
Chindits, 1944
Burma, 1943–45

THE REGIMENTAL COLOUR (45 HONOURS FROM OTHER CONFLICTS)

Namur, 1695
Blenheim
Ramillies
Oudenarde
Malplaquet
Dettingen
Louisburg
Minden
Quebec, 1759
Martinique, 1762, '94
Havannah
Seringapatam
Corunna
Talavera
Albuhera
Badajoz
Salamanca
Vittoria
Peninsula
Bladensburg
Waterloo
Ava
Ghuznee, 1839

Khelat
Cabool, 1842, '79
Moodkee
Ferozeshah
Sobraon
New Zealand
Goojerat
Punjaub
South Africa, 1851–53, '79
Inkerman
Sevastopol
Lucknow
Taku Forts
Afghanistan, 1878–80
Nile, 1884–85
Tirah
Atbara
Khartoum
Defence of Ladysmith
Paardeberg
South Africa, 1899–1902
Korea, 1951–52

It should be noted that some of the above are actually 'combined' battle honours, for example 'South Africa, 1851–53, '79' is a combination of 'South Africa, 1851–2–3' awarded to the Suffolk Regiment (but not until 1882) and 'South Africa, 1879' awarded to the 58th (Rutlandshire) Regiment (in 1881). Likewise 'Cabool, 1842, '79' represents 'Cabool, 1842' awarded to the 9th (East Norfolk) Regiment (in 1844) and 'Kabul, 1879' awarded to the same regiment (in 1881). Commas which are properly included in battle honours, as in the list above, are usually left out on emblazoning, for reasons of space.

The 'Honours' section of the Regimental Museum at Duxford includes an interactive display giving full details of all battle honours inherited by the Regiment.

Until about 1980 it was customary for the Army List to show, at the start of the list of First World War battle honours for each regiment, the number of battalions of that regiment which took part in that war. As this history is being published in the year which marks the 100th anniversary of the start of the First World War as well as the 50th anniversary of the formation of The Royal Anglian Regiment, it is worth noting that its regular and territorial predecessors provided no fewer than 150 battalions for service between 1914 and 1918, a very significant contribution.

The new Colours of the 1st Battalion, to be presented on 31 August 2014.

APPENDIX 7

SIGNIFICANT REGIMENTAL DATES

SOBRAON DAY, 10 FEBRUARY (1846)

In the early 19th Century the Punjab, in northern India, was a separate Sikh kingdom. From 1839 there was considerable internal disorder, and relations with the British, who controlled most of the rest of India, steadily worsened. Late in 1845 Sikh forces moved into disputed territory, and the First Sikh War began.

After some small initial battles the British army under Sir Hugh Gough attacked the main Sikh bridgehead over the River Sutlej, at Sobraon, on 10 February 1846. The position was strongly fortified and the Sikh forces outnumbered the British. Following an intense artillery bombardment the infantry assaulted. After very fierce fighting a break-in was achieved, and, their pontoon bridge across the river having broken, the Sikh army was completely defeated. Sobraon was the decisive battle of the First Sikh War, and Gough's forces subsequently occupied the Punjab.

The 10th (North Lincolnshire) Regiment of Foot played a prominent part in the attack, their brigade commander later commenting: 'The gallantry of Her Majesty's 10th will never be effaced from my memory. The 10th were the cornerstone of the victory ... I never saw anything to equal their cool and resolute courage on that day.' The 9th (East Norfolk) Regiment of Foot was also involved in the action, though not as heavily as the 10th, and both regiments were awarded the battle honour 'Sobraon'.

Sobraon Day was the main regimental day of the Royal Lincolnshire Regiment and is today marked by the 2nd Battalion. In addition, it is traditional for the 2nd Battalion to exchange greetings with 'our cousins', 2nd Battalion The Mercian Regiment, successors to the 29th (Worcestershire) Regiment of Foot; this commemorates the linking up of the 10th and the 29th, who had attacked from different directions, on the ramparts of Sobraon.

ALMANZA DAY, 25 APRIL (1707)

The War of the Spanish Succession, which lasted from 1701 to 1714, was brought about by disagreement between the European nations over who should succeed King Charles II of Spain, who had died in 1700 with no clear heir. Had the French candidate been accepted, the thrones, and empires, of France and Spain would have been united, tilting the balance of power in Europe and abroad. To prevent this, England formed an alliance with the Dutch Republic, Portugal and others to promote the rival Austrian candidate.

In 1707 an allied force under the Earl of Galway was in south-east Spain aiming to march on Madrid. It encountered a far superior French and Spanish force at Almanza, which Galway decided to attack on the morning of 25 April. At first things went well as the assault developed on the allied left and in the centre. Portuguese troops on the right, however, failed to follow up, and were subsequently driven off by the French cavalry. This left the flank of the advance exposed and the bulk of the allied force was soon overrun. It was only by some gallant rearguard action that part of the force, hardly more than a quarter of those originally committed to the battle, was able to withdraw.

Steuart's Regiment of Foot, later to become the 9th (East Norfolk) Regiment of Foot, performed with conspicuous gallantry in this rearguard action and took heavy casualties. As Almanza was a significant defeat, no battle honour was awarded. However, it is believed that as a result of its conduct there Queen Anne granted the Regiment the right to wear the badge of Britannia. The badge was certainly in use by the Regiment later in the 18th Century, although the first official record that can be traced is a letter of 30 July 1799 'confirming' the Regiment's right to it, and it is on the Regimental Colour to this day. Blood's Regiment of Foot, later to become the 17th (Leicestershire) Regiment of Foot, also took part in the battle of Almanza, with almost the entire regiment being killed or captured.

Almanza Day used to be celebrated by the Royal Norfolk Regiment, but on the formation of the 1st East Anglian Regiment in 1959 the custom rather fell into disuse. It is, however, still marked by the 1st Battalion.

ROYAL TIGERS' DAY, 25 JUNE (1825)

The regimental day of the Royal Leicestershire Regiment was, unusually, not connected with a battle but with the grant of an honorary distinction on 25 June 1825 when His Majesty King George IV was pleased to approve the 17th (Leicestershire) Regiment of Foot 'bearing on its Colours and appointments the figure of the "Royal Tiger", with the word "Hindoostan" superscribed, as a lasting testimony of the exemplary conduct of the corps during the period of its service in India, from the year 1804 to 1823.'

This long period had involved a great deal of active service as British rule in India was consolidated and various lawless factions were brought under control, and the Regiment had been given much praise for its efficiency and discipline.

The grant of this distinction is commemorated today by its presence on the Regimental Colour and on the buttons worn by all ranks of the Regiment in formal dress. Although the day is not specifically marked by the 2nd Battalion, there is an annual reunion at Leicester in the form of Royal Tigers' Weekend.

SALAMANCA DAY, 22 JULY (1812)

Following the French Revolution in 1789, Great Britain was at war with France for most of the period 1793–1815 as Napoleon Bonaparte, seizing power in 1799, attempted to dominate the whole of Europe. Much of the action was at sea, but the Peninsular War, from 1808 to 1814, was the setting for the Army's major contribution to Napoleon's eventual defeat. For most of the time the British forces in the Peninsula were under the command of General Sir Arthur Wellesley, later to become the Duke of Wellington, and fought alongside Portuguese and Spanish allies.

On 22 July 1812 at Salamanca, north-west of Madrid, Wellington's army, from a strong and well-concealed defensive position, was able to launch a surprise attack on the flanks of the French forces. After repeated assaults the whole French army was driven back in confusion, and the way was open for Wellington to advance to Madrid.

The 2nd Battalion of the 44th (East Essex) Regiment of Foot, which had been raised in 1803, played a significant part in the battle, and Lieutenant William Pearce captured the Eagle Standard of the French 62nd Regiment of the Line. The 1st Battalion of the 9th (East Norfolk) Regiment of Foot, the 1st Battalion of the 48th (Northamptonshire) Regiment of Foot, and the 2nd Battalion of the 58th (Rutlandshire) Regiment of Foot were also involved in the action and, like the 2/44th, were granted the battle honour 'Salamanca'.

Subsequently, the 44th Foot, as the 1st Battalion of the Essex Regiment, adopted an eagle as their badge. The tradition was continued during further reorganisations so that today the Regimental Colour includes an eagle and all ranks of the Regiment wear an eagle badge on the upper left arm in formal dress. Salamanca Day itself is marked by the 1st Battalion and a Salamanca Day Reunion is held annually at Area Headquarters in Warley. The Salamanca Eagle is displayed in the Essex Regiment Museum in Chelmsford, and from time to time is taken out to appear on formal parades with the 1st Battalion.

TALAVERA DAY, 27 JULY (1809)

Like Salamanca, above, Talavera was a battle of the Peninsular War. Wellington had advanced into Spain with the intention of bringing to battle a large French army. On 27 July 1809 his forces occupied high ground at Talavera, south-west of Madrid, alongside a large Spanish force. Late in the evening the French attacked, before the left of the British line was properly in position, and occupied an important hill. A swift counter-attack, in which the 1st Battalion of the 48th (Northamptonshire) Regiment of Foot played a prominent part, drove the French off the hill, and other troops, including the 2nd Battalion of the 48th, came up to help secure the position. A large-scale French assault the following morning was repulsed, but later in the day when the French attacked the centre of the British line a dangerous gap was opened up. Wellington summoned the 1/48th to plug that gap, which they did with great dash and bravery. In his subsequent dispatch Wellington wrote, 'The battle was certainly saved by the advance, position, and steady conduct of the 48th Regiment.' Later, the 48th was granted the battle honour 'Talavera'.

Talavera Day was celebrated within the Northamptonshire Regiment and the 2nd East Anglian Regiment, and is today the main regimental day of the 2nd Battalion.

MINDEN DAY, 1 AUGUST (1759)

The Seven Years' War began in 1754 (although hostilities in Europe did not commence until 1756) and lasted until 1763. It was a result of tensions overseas between Britain and France, as each sought to extend their influence worldwide, and concerns regarding British interests in Hanover (the British Royal Family were at that time also rulers of Hanover). Prussia allied herself with Great Britain, Austria with France.

France invaded Hanover in 1757 and made significant advances. Prince Ferdinand of Brunswick initially had some success in driving the French back, but by July 1759 they had advanced again to a very strong defensive position around Minden (north-western Germany). Ferdinand, his Hanoverians reinforced by a large British contingent, deceived the French as to his intentions and they moved forward in the early hours of 1 August, only to find themselves exposed to the entire allied army. Although it was the result of an incorrect order, six battalions of British infantry and two Hanoverian battalions advanced against the entire French cavalry, and by their steadiness, discipline and marksmanship survived six charges, then the onslaught of an infantry force, wreaking such havoc that the enemy fled in panic and confusion. Counter-attacks were given the same treatment, and by the end of the day the French were in full retreat. The allied force had achieved a great victory.

As the British battalions passed through gardens on the morning of the battle, the soldiers picked roses and wore them in their caps. The senior of those battalions, in the forefront of the action, was the 12th Regiment of Foot, later to become the Suffolk Regiment. The 12th was awarded the battle honour 'Minden', as were the other British battalions. The custom grew up of wearing red and yellow roses in headdress on Minden Day each year, and of placing rose wreaths on the Colours and drums if they are on parade.

Minden Day was always strongly commemorated by the Suffolk Regiment, and this tradition was handed down to the 1st East Anglian Regiment then to the 1st Battalion of The Royal Anglian Regiment who today ensure that, wherever they are, it is a day of great celebration. In addition, there is an annual Minden Day Reunion at Regimental Headquarters, Bury St Edmunds.

BLENHEIM DAY, 13 AUGUST (1704)

Like Almanza (see page 363), Blenheim was a battle of the War of the Spanish Succession. In 1702 the Duke of Marlborough was appointed to command a combined English, Dutch and Prussian force, which campaigned with some success against the French in the Low Countries (Belgium and the Netherlands). By 1704 Vienna was threatened, so Marlborough took his English and Prussian troops down the valley of the Danube to Munich. Deciding that it was too strongly defended to capture, he pulled back and sought to engage a strong French force in a well-defended position around the village of Blenheim.

Early in the morning of 13 August Marlborough began manoeuvring for his assault, taking the French by surprise. First attacking the flanks, the village itself being on the British left, he was able to get the French to send in reinforcements, thus weakening their centre. He then launched his main assault, and after a long and very hard battle achieved a breakthrough, subsequently rolling up the flanks in turn. The French were completely routed, losing over 30,000 troops. It was a very significant victory, and many historians consider that it was pivotal to the subsequent history of Europe.

Stanley's Regiment, afterwards the 16th (Bedfordshire) Regiment of Foot, played a significant part in the assaults on the left flank, and was subsequently granted the battle honour of 'Blenheim'. In the adjacent brigade on the left flank was North's Regiment, later to become the 10th (North Lincolnshire) Regiment of Foot, and it too received the battle honour.

Ops Company, Minden Day, FOB Pimon.

Blenheim Day subsequently became the main regimental day of the Bedfordshire Regiment, and is still marked by the 2nd Battalion.

IMAGE ACKNOWLEDGEMENTS

Artwork on pages 60, 63, 81, 102, 125, 139, 174, 196, 197, 205, 206, 215, 225, 235, 250, 267, 273, 293, 299 © 2014 Clive Farmer.

Photographs are used courtesy of
Andy Callan/Alamy, page 286 (top); Crown copyright, Corporal John Bevan, Royal Logistics Corps, page 32; Crown copyright, Mike Weston ABIPP, page 41 (bottom); Hulton-Deutsch Collection/CORBIS, page 227; Imagery © 2014 DigitalGlobe, Map data © 2014 Google, pages 78 (bottom), 134 (top), 233, 245 (bottom); Imperial War Museums, pages 11 (NA 24308), 12 (H11931), 13 (B 15048), 160 (middle, FIR 10769), 320 (right, OMD 6855); iStock, page 30; © Royal Armouries, pages 62 (PR.13074), 80 (top left, PR.6943; and top right, PR.8324), 86 (PR.9090), 130 (top, PR.5383), 160 (top); Tony Margiocchi, page 311; US Marine Corps, page 67 (bottom); the MOD website, page 138 (bottom); National Museums Northern Ireland, page 168; The Tank Museum, Bovington, page 283 (8840-031); Brian Willoughby, page 243 (left); Imagery © 2014 Infoterra Ltd & Bluesky, Getmapping plc, Data SIO, NOAA, US Navy, NGA, GEBCO, Map data © 2014 Google, page 302 (top).

Foreword and Introduction: *Castle.*

Heritage and Ethos: *Castle*; Cambridgeshire Regiment Association collection; Author's collection.

Afghanistan: *Castle*; Regimental Museum collection; 1st Battalion Tour Booklets, *Herrick 6, 11* and *16*; Lieutenant Colonel Biddick personal collection; Captain Newton personal collection; Lieutenant Colonel Biddick Battle Orders; Reconnaissance Platoon collection, 1st Battalion; 6 Platoon collection, 1st Battalion; Lieutenant Colonel Davies personal collection; Corporal Warren personal collection; Captain Benstead personal collection; Major Smith personal collection; Major Wolfe personal collection; Major Allen personal collection.

Iraq: *Castle*; Regimental Museum collection; 1st Battalion Tour booklet, Op *Telic 6*; 2nd Battalion Tour Booklet, Op *Telic 8*; Author's collection; Colonel Browne personal collection; Colonel O'Driscoll personal collection; Captain Rainey personal collection; Ministry of Defence website.

Northern Ireland: *Castle*; Regimental Museum collection; Regimental Headquarters files; 1st Battalion Tour booklet, Londonderry 1984–86; *Pompadour*, *Belfast Telegraph*, microfiche collection; Saville Enquiry online; Author's collection; Lieutenant Colonel Brunt personal collection; Lieutenant Colonel Davenport personal collection; Colonel Jackson personal collection; Colonel Hall Tipping personal collection; Warrant Officer Class 2 Orton personal collection; Major Price personal collection; Lieutenant Colonel Veitch personal collection; Colonel Woodrow personal collection.

Bosnia: *Castle*; Regimental Museum collection; Author's collection; Captain Rainey personal collection.

Aden: *Castle*; Regimental Museum collection; Author's collection; Major General Stone personal collection; Major Williamson personal collection; Colonel Woodrow personal collection; Major Harrington-Spier personal collection; Colonel Jackson personal collection.

Other Operations: *Castle*; Regimental Museum collection.

Deployments and the Cold War, and The Regiment's Families: *Castle*; Regimental Museum collection; Author's collection; Lieutenant Colonel Dixon personal collection; Captain Spinks personal collection; Colonel, Kate and Patrick Woodrow personal collection; Jan and Bob Hawkins personal collection; Jenny Bullock personal collection.

Regiment of the Future: *Castle*; Regimental Museum collection.

Cartography is used courtesy of
Base maps used in maps on pages 173, 186, 194: This Intellectual Property is based upon Crown Copyright and is reproduced with the permission of Land & Property Services under Delegated Authority from the Controller of Her Majesty's Stationery Office, © Crown Copyright and database right (2014).

Maps on pages 158 (by Peter Bull 2011), 221 (by The Map Studio 2003), 281 (by The Map Studio, Romsey, UK 2008): © Osprey Publishing.

Maps on pages 33, 38, 47 (bottom), 52 (top), 68, 77, 82 (top), 90, 98 (top and bottom), 104, 116, 121 include intellectual property based upon: UK MOD Crown Copyright, 2014, Canadian Aerial Survey Mission (CASM), Applanix imagery. Produced by the Mapping and Charting Establishment, Department of National Defence, Canada, © 2009. Her Majesty the Queen in Right of Canada, © 2008 Applanix imagery. National Geospatial-Intelligence Agency, no copyright claimed under Title 17 USC, © Royal Netherlands Army Geographic Agency (RNLAGA), 2013, © Her Majesty the Queen in Right of Canada, 2013.

Maps and diagrams on pages 6, 38, 47 (bottom), 52 (top), 67 (top), 68, 76, 77, 82 (top), 90, 98 (bottom), 104, 116, 121, 133, 143, 173 (top), 186, 210, 228, 230, 239, 263, 290, 296 : © The Royal Anglian Regiment, created by Bounford.com

INDEX